FROM THESE BEGINNINGS . . .

Volume I

From These
Beginnings...

A Biographical
Approach
to American History
SECOND EDITION

Roderick Nash

University of California, Santa Barbara

HARPER & ROW, PUBLISHERS
New York   Hagerstown   San Francisco   London

We gratefully acknowledge the use of photographs from the following sources:

Facing page 1: The Columbus Gallery, Ponce de Leon y Laguardia, N.Y. 1893. Page 8: *top*, Map Division, The New York Public Library, Astor, Lenox and Tilden Foundations; *center*, from the Page-Holgate facsimiles of the original John White paintings in the North Carolina Collection of the L. R. Wilson Memorial Library of the University of North Carolina at Chapel Hill, with the permission of The University of North Carolina Press; *bottom*, reprinted with permission of The Macmillan Company from *Columbus* by Landstrom. Copyright 1966 Björn Landström. Copyright 1967 by Bokforlaget Forum AB. Page 9: *top*, Columbus Memorial Library, Pan American Union; *bottom*, *Narrative and Critical History of America*, Winsor, Houghton, Mifflin, N.Y., 1886. Page 24: New York Public Library Picture Collection. Page 40: John Carter Brown Library, Brown University. Page 41: *top*, U.S. Department of the Interior; *center*, *The River Towns in Connecticut*, Andrews, Johns Hopkins University, 1863; *bottom*, Massachusetts Historical Society. Page 60: New York Public Library Picture Collection. Page 70: Harry T. Peters Collection, Museum of the City of New York. Page 71: *top*, Henry E. Huntington Library; *bottom*, Library of Congress. Page 89: *top*, Underwood and Underwood; *bottom*, Benjamin Franklin Collection, Yale University. Page 102: Frick Art Reference Library, Collection of Charles F. Adams. Page 114: *top*, Library of Congress; *bottom*, John Trumbull, *The Declaration of Independence*, Yale University Art Gallery. Page 115: *top*, New York Historical Society; *bottom*, Thomas Jefferson Memorial Foundation. Page 150: The Granger Collection. Page 172: *top*, The Granger Collection; *bottom*, New York Historical Society. Page 173: *top*, Fort Malden National Historic Park; *bottom*, Museum of the American Indian, Heye Foundation. Page 188: Denver Public Library, Western History Department. Page 196: *top*, Maryland Historical Society; *bottom*, Walters Art Gallery. Page 197: *top*, Henry E. Huntington Library; *bottom*, Denver Public Library, Western History Department. Page 215: *top*, Utah State Historical Society; *bottom*, Union Pacific Railroad. Page 226: The Granger Collection. Page 232: *top*, Library of Congress; *bottom*, The New York Historical Society, Bella C. Landauer Collection. Page 233: *bottom*, Chicago Historical Society. Page 248: Library of Congress. Page 249: *top*, Library of Congress. Page 268: Mark Twain Birthplace Memorial Shrine. Page 278: Harpers Monthly. Page 292: *top*, Harpers New Monthly Magazine; *bottom*, H. M. de Young Memorial Museum, SF. Page 293: *top*, Mackay School of Mines, University of Nevada; *bottom*, Library of Congress.

Special Projects Editor: Mary Lou Mosher
Project Editor: Henry Krawitz
Designer: T. R. Funderburk
Production Supervisor: Marion A. Palen
Photo Researcher: Myra Schachne
Compositor: Maryland Linotype Composition Co., Inc.
Printer and Binder: The Murray Printing Company
Art Studio: Graphic 70

FROM THESE BEGINNINGS . . .
A BIOGRAPHICAL APPROACH TO AMERICAN HISTORY, VOLUME 1
Second Edition

Library of Congress Cataloging in Publication Data

Nash, Roderick.
  From these beginnings . .

  Includes bibliographies and indexes.
    1. United States—History. 2. United States—
Biography. I. Title.
E178.N18   1978   973'.0992   77-17091
ISBN 0-06-044717-6 (v. 1)
ISBN 0-06-044718-4 (v. 2)

For Laura and Jennifer

Contents

Preface   *viii*

1   Christopher Columbus   *1*
2   John Winthrop   *25*
3   Benjamin Franklin   *61*
4   Thomas Jefferson   *103*
5   Tecumseh   *151*
6   Jim Bridger   *189*
7   Frederick Douglass   *227*
8   Mark Twain   *269*

Index   *320*

Preface

The need for a revised edition of *From These Beginnings: A Biographical Approach to American History* provides added evidence for the old adage that the proper study of mankind is man. Certainly the proper study of the historian is man—not laws, treaties, elections, or eras but people who loved, hated, achieved, failed, and shared with all humanity, including us, a fascinating complexity of thought and feeling. Like its predecessor, this revised edition is dedicated to the proposition that teaching and learning about history loses significance and fun when it is divorced from human beings. The past dies because we fail to see it as a collection of individuals.

The biographical approach is one way to enliven the study of history. The logic behind this choice is obvious: people are interested in people. History concerns, or should concern, people. Historical writing can be made as exciting as life itself if we think of it as a series of biographies. These assumptions underlie the novel structure of this book.

This is hardly a radical approach. Much of our best historical writing is in the form of biography or family history. Consider the light Alex Haley's *Roots* shed on the Afro-American experience. Consider, also, the inherent excitement of Haley's approach, the compelling drama that made *Roots* the most popular production in the history of American television. Millions of viewers "studied" American history for the first time during the January 1977 telecasts, even though they did not realize it at the time. Haley created a painless approach to an often boring subject. His success challenged professional historians. Why should history be "dry as dust"? Why shouldn't history have all the drama of life itself, which, after all, is what it is? Yet, surprisingly, no textbook used a biographical form of organization prior to the first edition of *From These Beginnings*.

I credit my students at Dartmouth College and the University of California, Santa Barbara, with the inspiration for the biographical approach that follows. Facing large classes comprised of upperclassmen who, as college freshmen and sophomores, had "taken" American history at least three times since elementary school, I determined to try something new. I inserted several biographical lectures into the standard syllabus. Their popularity encouraged me to organize an entire survey course on a biographical basis. The best lectures, expanded into chapters, from the core of this book.

The standard textbook method of dividing the past into periods, eras, or ages has been discarded. Fourteen often overlapping lives provide the organizational framework. The larger story of the American experience is woven around these lives. In this way, broad concepts are tied to specific examples. The frontier, slavery, and industrialization, for instance, acquire a sharper focus when viewed from the perspective of a pioneer, a slave, and an industrialist. Conversely, the narrative of national events deepens one's understanding of the fourteen individuals.

One problem in using a biographical approach is finding a happy compromise between "straight" biography and "straight" American history. This is not difficult, of course, when an individual life impinges directly on the course of national events. Thomas Jefferson writing the Declaration of Independence, Henry Ford revolutionizing transportation, and Martin Luther King, Jr., leading the civil rights movement are good examples. But frequently even a famous person sinks back into the general citizenry; his life becomes typical rather than unusual. On such occasions I have employed a life-and-times approach consisting of a description of the historical context surrounding the individual. The technique is justifiable, I believe, on the grounds that any life is in large part shaped by the stream of events in which it floats.

Another problem arose in choosing the fourteen lives through which I would recount the history of the United States. Actually, this proved to be one of the more enjoyable tasks associated with the writing of the present book. For many months I besieged my classes, my colleagues, my publisher, my family, and anyone else who would listen with the question of a suitable cast of characters. The final slate is the result of considerable experimentation, several false starts, much wall staring, and occasional midnight fits of inspiration. The chapter on Tecumseh represents a new addition to this revised edition, as does the chapter on Richard Nixon, which was substituted for that on Neil Armstrong. Both Tecumseh and Nixon illustrate painful yet revealing truths about the American past. Despite the care taken in their selection, these fourteen people are not completely satisfactory choices. There is some comfort, however, in the realization that the choice of individuals is not all-important. A surprising amount of information about the course of national events can be tied to *any* American life. Try it, for example, with your own. *From These Beginnings* could feature any of the approximately half-billion people who have called themselves Americans. As Americans they all affect, and are affected by, American history.

Roderick Nash

Christopher Columbus

With a rising moon and a strong east wind behind them, the three
ships sailed headlong into history. It was shortly before 2 A.M. on
October 12, 1492, but most hands were on deck. The usual signs of a
landfall—a green branch, a carved stick, many birds—had made
them eager, desperate, for their first sight of land in thirty-three
days. The tall, gray-haired captain braced himself on the sterncastle
of the Santa Maria. *His face showed the strain of a twenty-year*
dream on the brink of realization. Suddenly, a muffled shot from the

lead ship, Pinta, *broke the rhythmic hiss of the waves. It was the signal for land ahead, and the* Pinta *fell off the wind waiting for the flagship. As she approached, her captain too could see the pale gleam of limestone cliffs. Christopher Columbus had reached a new world.*

The son and grandson of humble weavers in the Republic of Genoa, north and west of Rome, Columbus, one might imagine, had little reason to anticipate a life of discovery and exploration. But the Europe into which he was born in 1451 simmered with the forces that eventually propelled him across the Atlantic. Some were already centuries old. Beginning in 1095, the several crusades to free Jerusalem from Turkish control had opened European eyes. Nobles and fighting men who had journeyed to the Holy Land had encountered a whole new standard of living at this crossroads where East met West. For the first time, the crusaders saw luxurious silk cloth, which contrasted sharply with their rough woolen garments such as those Columbus's family wove. And there were heavy, colorful tapestries that made ideal wall hangings for dark, drafty European castles and Oriental spices to preserve as well as flavor food.

The Europeans also saw fabulous quantities of gold and gems. They heard about still more, especially in the late thirteenth century when Marco Polo reported his overland journey to China, Japan, and the Spice Islands. Columbus's copy of Marco Polo's book was underlined where the author mentioned "pearls, precious stones, brocades, ivory, or pepper, nuts, nutmeg, cloves and an abundance of other spices." He also noted the reference to the palace of the king of Japan "which is entirely roofed with fine gold, just as our churches are roofed with lead." This knowledge of Asia whetted the appetite of Columbus's generation and lifted its eyes to far horizons.

European desire for the treasures of the East could be satisfied by traders. After goods from Asia arrived at eastern Mediterranean ports such as Constantinople and Alexandria, merchants from Genoa, along with those from Venice, Florence, and Pisa, distributed them throughout Europe. Prices, however, were exceedingly high. In addition, Europe soon faced an unfavorable balance of trade: money flowed east

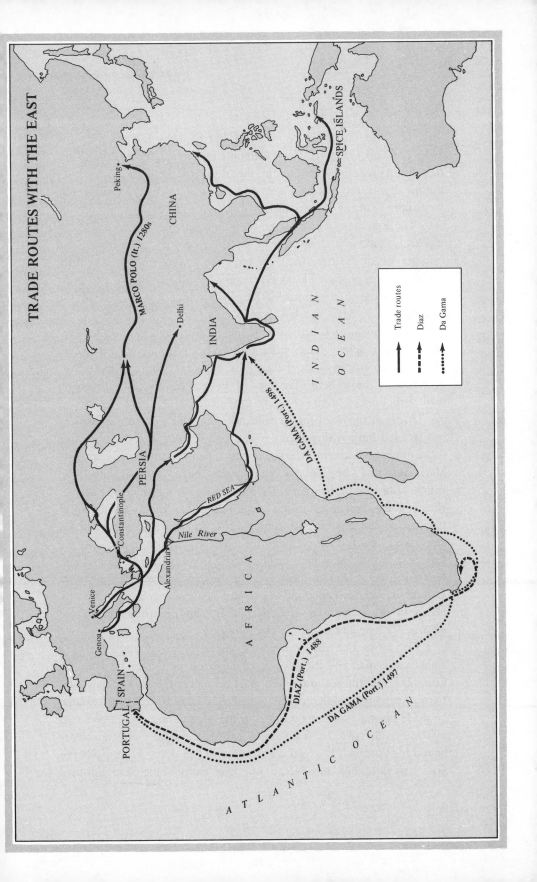

TRADE ROUTES WITH THE EAST

SPICE ISLANDS

Peking

CHINA

MARCO POLO (It.) 1280s

Delhi

INDIA

INDIAN OCEAN

PERSIA

DA GAMA (Port.) 1498

Constantinople

RED SEA

Alexandria

Nile River

Venice

Genoa

PORTUGAL

SPAIN

AFRICA

DIAZ (Port.) 1488

DA GAMA (Port.) 1497

ATLANTIC OCEAN

Trade routes

Diaz

Da Gama

and goods west. Asia had no use for Europe's bulky agricultural products. The economic situation was bad, but to make matters worse, in
1453 the Turks captured Constantinople and thus closed to the Christian Europeans the key link in the route to the East. Columbus's
Europe desperately needed cheap and direct access to the Orient. The
vast highway of the sea promised both.

The Renaissance also played an important role in readying Christopher Columbus and his society for the discovery, exploration, and
colonization of the Americas. The term *renaissance* suggests a rebirth.
To be sure, the so-called Dark Ages were not all that dismal except by
contrast to the accomplishments of Greece and Rome. Around the
twelfth century Arab and Jewish scholars alerted their European counterparts to the cultural brilliance of the classical civilizations. A shiver
of excitement spread north from Italy. A society long accustomed to
the Christian emphasis on the afterlife, the next world, glimpsed the
potential of the present. The idea of improving man's condition on
earth—the idea of progress—gained momentum.

A major theme of the Renaissance was pride in man. Christianity
had stressed human unworthiness and helplessness, but the heroes of
the Rennaissance were Alexander the Great, Aristotle, Caesar, and
Mark Anthony. They had not been helpless, but rather had shaped the
course of history in their time. Their triumphs were secular, not sacred;
their rewards, very much in this world rather than in a heavenly world
to come. Could not fifteenth-century men do likewise? A passion for
fame, for glory, for achievement, for mastery gained a foothold in the
European mind. Individualism flourished. It spread from the arts and
letters to politics and business, and fed the development of capitalism.
Columbus and his contemporaries were restless, increasingly unsatisfied with the status quo. Understandably, this dissatisfaction created
an urge for new lands and new beginnings.

Columbus had the restlessness, confidence, and ambition of a
Renaissance man and the sea offered a perfect outlet for his energies.
Columbus met the sea in the harbor of his native Genoa and may well
have transported woolen cloth along the Italian coast. In his twenties
he made his first extensive voyages in the Mediterranean as a common
seaman. In the year 1476 Columbus sailed in a large Genoese convoy
bound for Portugal, England, and the North Sea ports. Just outside the
Straits of Gibraltar, however, a war fleet from France and Portugal

descended on the convoy. In the furious battle that followed, Columbus was wounded and his ship sunk. Grasping an oar for support, he struggled six miles to the southern coast of Portugal. As he crawled onto the beach of an unknown country, his chances of ever commanding an expedition to the New World seemed remote. But Columbus was an unusual man with a knack for persevering in the face of adversity.

The country Columbus reached in such unpromising circumstances was then the European leader in maritime discovery. Much of the credit for Portugal's eminence goes to Dom Henrique, better known as Prince Henry the Navigator. This talented prince, who died in 1460, personified the spirit of the age of European expansion. From his headquarters on the Atlantic Ocean he sent expeditions into the unknown. Some went north, and developed a brisk trade with England and Iceland. Others pushed west, a thousand miles into the open ocean, to find the Azores. But Prince Henry reserved his keenest enthusiasm for those who sailed south to coast along the dark continent of Africa. Here was a way to circumvent the Italian monopoly on trans-Mediterranean trade with Asia and India. Access to Africa also gave Portugal an opportunity to cash in on the lucrative slave trade. Driven by a desire for trade and wealth, Prince Henry's captains had, at the time of his death, reached within ten degrees of the equator.

The Portuguese also achieved preeminence in developing the sciences of sailing and navigation. Not only exploration, but the entire colonization movement depended on establishing safe and reliable sea transport. Prince Henry created a fifteenth-century equivalent of Cape Kennedy, gathering around him the best navigational minds in the Western world. The charts, tables, and astronomical observations they compiled made possible long expeditions on the open ocean without the need to stay close to shore. The refinement of the astrolabe, for example, permitted a captain to determine his latitude on the basis of star sightings with considerable accuracy. Equally important were the institutions of early capitalism, the banks and joint-stock companies that enabled Portugal to finance far-flung exploration. A shipwreck, ironically, had left Columbus in the best place to pursue the life of an explorer.

Within six months of dragging himself onto the Portuguese beach, Columbus recovered his health and once again put to sea. This time Iceland was the goal and trading the purpose. During the next few years he mastered Latin and Spanish, married into a prominent Portuguese family, and gained respect both as a gentleman and a seaman. He lived on one of the Madeira Islands west of Gibraltar for a year or more and, in the early 1480s, made at least one voyage around the hump of West Africa to Guinea and the Gold Coast. The African experience added greatly to his skill as a sea captain. It also produced an unexpected dividend. Columbus noticed that south of the Canary Islands the prevailing winds always blew from the east. Further north, off England and Portugal, they came out of the west. Gradually it dawned on him that to sail west into the North Atlantic winds was foolish. A far better course would be to sail south to the trade winds and then west on their wings. To return, one had simply to set a northerly course, catch the west wind, and ride it back to Europe.

Driftwood that storms frequently cast on European shores provided exciting evidence that Columbus was right in his theory that land lay to the west. When he lived on Madeira he could scarcely avoid noticing the huge tropical canes, seed pods, and tree trunks that we now know came from Central and South America. Even carved wood had been found, and on one occasion, two flat-faced human bodies, of an appearance strange to Europeans, washed onto the beach. The significance of all this was not lost on Columbus.

Returning from Africa with knowledge about wind patterns, Columbus gave increasing attention to the possibility of sailing west to reach the Far East. The roots of this idea lay in his understanding that the world was round. Educated Europeans had taken a spherical earth for granted for two thousand years; Columbus simply attempted a feat discussed for centuries. The size of the earth, however, and the distribution of its land masses were still hotly debated among the foremost scholars of Columbus's time. "Knowledge" tended to be a blend of fact, myth, and wishful thinking.

In constructing his conception of world geography, Columbus drew on a variety of ancient and contemporary sources. He owned an early fifteenth-century translation of the work of the Greek mathematician Ptolemy, whose calculations fell short of the earth's actual size. He also owned the standard geography of the Late Middle Ages, Pierre d'Ailly's *Imago Mundi*, which was written in 1410 but not printed until 1480. Columbus pored over his copy, making marginal notations on almost every page. "The earth is round and spherical," he jotted at one point, ". . . between the end of Spain and the beginning of India lies a narrow sea that can be sailed in a few days." Further confirmation of this error came from the renowned Florentine physician and geographer Paul Toscanelli, to whom Columbus wrote for information sometime in 1481. Toscanelli stated confidently that the voyage Columbus proposed "is not only possible to make, but sure and certain, and will bring inestimable gain and utmost recognition." He also sent a map that Columbus used to calculate the distance from Portugal to Marco Polo's gold-roofed Japan as 3000 miles. This was only 9200 miles short!

Toscanelli's correspondence with Columbus perpetuated another geographical mistake. According to the Florentine, only open ocean lay to the west between Portugal and Japan. Most fifteenth-century Europeans agreed that at least an island or island group lay between these limits of geographical knowledge. No one, however, had conceived of a continent dividing the sea into the Atlantic and Pacific Oceans. Even if Columbus and his contemporaries knew of the Irish and Viking contacts with North America dating possibly from the sixth century and certainly from the eleventh, they did not realize it was a continent. Yet ignorance, in this case, proved advantageous. Rightly informed, Columbus would more than likely never have ventured west.

Myth also played an important role in his motivation. In company with Europeans since the Greeks, Columbus believed in an earthly paradise. Life was good in paradise, really good. Ripe fruit hung heavy on every bough. The climate was delightful, flowers perfumed the air. Precious stones and quantities of gold could be picked up at will. In some paradise traditions, these sensual joys were subordinated to spiritual ones. Paradise became a place where sin was unknown and men lived in accord with God's commandments. Those lucky enough to enter paradise, it was thought, left behind all worry, fear, and discomfort—even death was unknown.

According to the Christian tradition, man once occupied paradise, but somewhere along the way he had become separated from it. Adam and Eve, for instance, were driven from the Garden of Eden by an angry God. Later generations, however, remembered—or at least

Many Europeans of Columbus's time believed that along with the economic, political, and scientific opportunities inherent in discovering new lands went a religious responsibility. Christianity had to be extended to the heathen. In this sketch from a 1500 map of the world, Columbus is shown wading ashore in the New World with an infant Christ on his shoulders. Appropriately, Columbus's first name was Christopher—literally, "Christ bearer."

Only the blind or the extremely biased could have regarded the North American Indians encountered by the first Europeans as wild animals. Many did so, however, in spite of the sophistication of villages such as this one in North Carolina.

The whole age of discovery and exploration depended upon a device as relatively simple as a compass. This reconstruction of a late fifteenth-century model, similar to the one Columbus used, consists of a wooden bowl, an iron needle, and a thin directional "rose" made from wood or paper. The rose could be turned to compensate for magnetic variation.

Lisbon, Portugal was one of the most exciting places in fifteenth-century Europe. It was a jumping-off place—a Cape Kennedy of its time. This 1590 engraving shows Columbus's fleet returning from his first voyage to the New World. The ships are caravels, about 75 feet long.

Columbus received this map from the geographer Paul Toscanelli and used it as evidence of the feasibility of sailing west to reach the Far East. The map accurately portrayed this possibility, but it contained two glaring errors. Using the grid-shaped pattern for measurement, "Zipangu" (Japan), the other Spice Islands, and the Asian mainland were located over 9000 miles closer to Europe than in actuality. The second error was the complete omission of North and South America. The large island in the center of the map existed only in European legend.

they dreamed. Almost every culture in Western history has subscribed to the idea that paradise still existed: somewhere there was an island or a mountain or an enchanted valley. . . . If men could only find it, the good life could be regained. The thought was irresistible, particularly so when parts of the earth were yet unknown. It was tempting and easy to believe that paradise lay around the next bend, over the known horizon.

The idea of going *west* to find the lost paradise had existed for centuries before Columbus's venture. The Jews, wandering in the desert after fleeing Egypt, traveled back in that direction to find Canaan—their promised land of milk and honey. The Greeks, Romans, and Phoenicians had similar traditions of an earthly paradise to the west. These mythical places even appeared on maps, set in the middle of the Atlantic under the names of Antilla, Atlantis, the Islands of the Blest, Elysium, and the Isle of Fair Women. In the sixth century an Irish monk named St. Brendan supposedly sailed west in an attempt to reach the paradisiacal Fortunate Isles. According to the legend that grew up around this voyage, Brendan crossed the North Atlantic to Newfoundland, struck south to Bermuda, and then west to Florida. When he arrived, he found a settlement of Irish monks already enjoying the luxuriance of the tropics. True or not—and there is some evidence that Europeans of this time really did reach North America, if not paradise—the prospect of finding it continually fired imaginations. In Columbus's time serious discussions of the location and characteristics of paradise were common in every European port. *Imago Mundi*, for example, declares that "the Earthly Paradise is an Elysian spot . . . far distant from our inhabited world both by land and sea." To be the discoverer of this place was reason enough to motivate a man like Columbus.

To implement his plans for a westward voyage to the East and perhaps to paradise, Columbus needed financial backing. He turned first to King John II of Portugal. Late in 1484 Columbus enthusiastically unfolded his plan to the king's advisory committee. This distinguished group of mathematicians and astronomers was not impressed. In particular, they doubted Columbus's calculation of the distance to Japan and China, contending, correctly, that it was closer to 10,000 than to 3,000 miles. The commission favored a course around Africa.

Portuguese mariners were continuing the explorations to the south begun under Prince Henry, and it seemed only a matter of time before they would round Africa and open a sea route to India. Columbus watched in frustration and envy when in 1488 Bartholomeu Díaz sailed triumphantly into Lisbon after performing this feat. Now Portugal had no further use for Christopher Columbus.

At this low point in his career, Columbus became the beneficiary of Europe's changing political structure. Before the fifteenth century an endless series of nobles, barons, earls, and dukes vied for dominance within particular regions. The abundance of leaders scattered wealth and power into small and relatively weak units. From this feudal chaos, however, kings and nations began slowly to emerge. By the late fifteenth century a few families had proved superior in the political struggle for existence. Forcing subservience on what became the lesser nobility, they created a series of hereditary monarchies. Extremely competitive and ambitious, these emerging national rulers aspired to the Roman example of world domination. Discovery and expansion appealed to them as avenues to glory. The nation that could find an easy route to Asia and establish lucrative trading colonies would have an immense advantage over its rivals.

Columbus saw the personal advantages in this political situation. Portugal's good fortune in its African venture in 1488, he thought, might increase the appeal of his scheme elsewhere. So Columbus dispatched his brother to the courts of Henry VII in England and Charles VIII in France. He himself went to Spain, where Ferdinand and Isabella were ending a successful struggle for control of a kingdom.

At first, Columbus made little headway. Ambitious and conceited, he insisted, as a prerequisite for any voyage, on a guarantee of three fully equipped ships, one-tenth of all the treasures he might find, an appointment as governor and viceroy of the lands discovered, and a place in the Spanish nobility with the title Admiral of the Ocean Sea. Detractors raised the old question of distance; Columbus was again accused of unwarranted optimism. But other voices in the Spanish court, impressed with his brash confidence and aware of the need to compete with Portugal, were reluctant to dismiss him. Skepticism vied with desire. Now Columbus probably played his trump—the pattern of the winds. He explained *how* to reach Asia by following the northeast winds in the South Atlantic. Even if the trip proved longer than anticipated, it would be easy to turn north and ride the west winds home.

The king's treasurer, Luis de Santángel, thought it was worth the risk. He pointed out that the surrender of Granada, the last stronghold of African Moors in Spain, on January 2, 1492, had freed the nation's resources for discovery. The voyage just might prove a bonanza. Moreover, Columbus could be Spain's vehicle for spreading Christianity to heathen peoples. Considerations of gold, God, and glory, Santángel concluded, lent Columbus's proposal irresistible appeal.

The monarchs agreed. Queen Isabella even offered to pledge her jewels. Columbus, already on his way to France, was recalled by royal messenger. Ferdinand and Isabella accepted his terms in a formal agreement of April 17, 1492; and with ample money and connections, his pent-up energy exploded into action. Less than three months after arriving in the port of Palos, Columbus was ready to begin his quest.

Two of the three ships in his expedition, the *Pinta* and *Niña*, were caravels. Light and narrow, these vessels of approximately seventy-five feet had been designed for extended voyages. They were swift and could sail almost directly into the wind. Columbus's flagship, the *Santa Maria*, was longer, bulkier, and slower. The shipowners of Palos apparently were unwilling to risk a third caravel on so dubious a venture. Still, ninety men volunteered for the crew. On August 3, 1492, they left Palos bound for the unknown.

Just as he had proposed, Columbus led his expedition on a southwest slant to the Canary Islands, then due west along the 28th parallel of latitude. The winds proved favorable, as predicted, and the ships made good time. Of course, there were misgivings. Columbus had continually to restrain the crew from altering course to search for islands that seemed just out of sight. As the days stretched into weeks and no land appeared, whispers and then open complaints spread among the men. The sailors did not fear a sudden drop off a flat earth or sea monsters; they were simply a long way from home across an open ocean.

Responding to these challenges, Columbus offered reminders of the riches that lay ahead in Asia. He also deliberately falsified his log to make the distance back to Spain seem shorter. But ultimately it was a question of will. Columbus was committed. Only death or mutiny

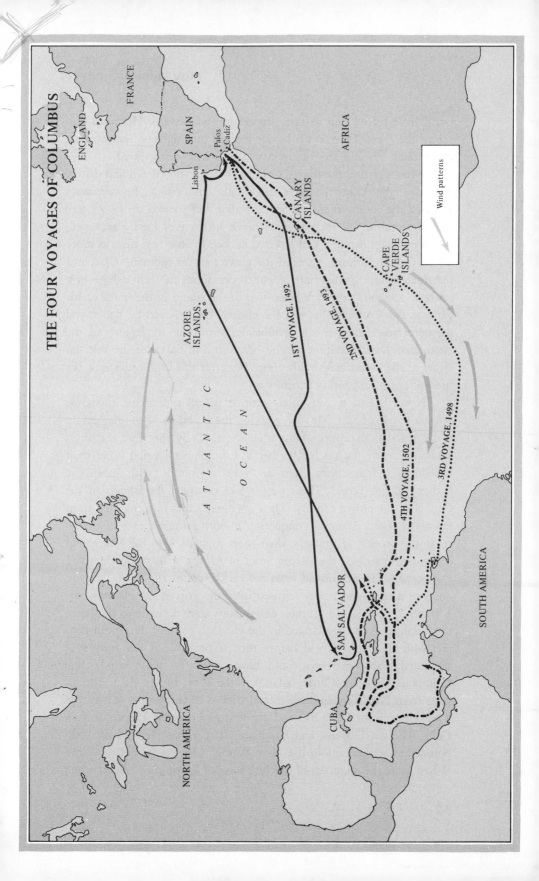

THE FOUR VOYAGES OF COLUMBUS

ENGLAND

FRANCE

SPAIN

Palos
Cadiz
Lisbon

AFRICA

CANARY ISLANDS

CAPE VERDE ISLANDS

AZORE ISLANDS.

ATLANTIC OCEAN

NORTH AMERICA

CUBA

SAN SALVADOR

SOUTH AMERICA

1ST VOYAGE, 1492

2ND VOYAGE, 1493

4TH VOYAGE, 1502

3RD VOYAGE, 1498

Wind patterns

could have forced him to turn around in mid-passage. His spirit sustained the crew. Then San Salvador loomed into sight on the morning of October 12, and the misgivings temporarily disappeared.

After sighting the island, Columbus wisely furled sail and drifted until daylight. With the reefs and shoals now visible, he cautiously rounded the southern end of San Salvador and coasted up its western side in search of an anchorage. A break in the reef finally appeared; the ships sailed through and lowered anchor for the first time in more than a month. Columbus sensed the gravity of the moment. Clad in a red doublet brought specially for such occasions, he went ashore in a rowboat and solemnly took possession of the island in the name of his patrons. For Columbus, it was the climax. He believed he had found the outermost island in an archipelago stretching to Japan and the Asian mainland. Standing on the beach at San Salvador, he felt the riches of the Orient within his grasp. But after this bright morning, his life was one of increasing frustration.

Nevertheless, it was surely one of history's dramatic moments when a native of San Salvador, walking the beach at dawn, glanced up to see three ships approaching from the east. By the time the ships anchored, many natives had gathered. Columbus's journal notes their nakedness and describes them as "very well built, with handsome bodies and fine faces." These people had occupied the islands of the Caribbean for only a century. Their ancestors came into the area from mainland South America, conquering a more primitive race of islanders in the process. Ultimately, their roots went back to the Mongoloid hunters who crossed the Bering Strait to Alaska at least ten thousand and perhaps forty thousand years before Columbus appeared. Fanning out over a continent newly released from the grip of the glaciers (see Chapter 5, pp. 152–154), their descendants were on hand to challenge the Vikings when they landed in the eleventh century. European contact with the New World before then is probable if not fully substantiated. Early mariners could have sailed the trade winds, like Columbus, from the Canary Islands to the West Indies. Rock inscriptions from New England and inland sites as distant as the Mississippi Valley date from 1000 B.C. and are written in scripts known only to Celts, Basques, Libyans, and Egyptians. If these peoples did establish permanent settlements in the New World, what happened to them? Where were the members of this first wave of European pioneers when

Columbus touched on San Salvador? The answer of scholars who hold to the early-contact theory is they were still present—absorbed into the tribes of the still earlier migrants from Asia.

When Columbus termed the San Salvador people "Indians," he was, unknowingly, partly right. Their most distant ancestors *had* come from India (a term loosely applied in the fifteenth century to Asia generally). But Columbus's conscious use of the term was strictly a product of wishful thinking and erroneous geography. As a twentieth-century Sioux, commenting on the history of the subjugation of the native American, put it, "Even the name Indian is not ours. It was given to us by some dumb honky who got lost and thought he'd landed in India."

European arrogance toward the so-called Indians began with Columbus. From the start he regarded them as inferior even as he noted their good looks and idyllic environment. Nonchalantly he took possession of a land they had occupied for thousands of years. And while gathering specimen flowers, fruit, and birds to take back to Europe, he also collected seven natives. In his mind they were just another type of animal, and his journal contains frank speculations on the ease with which they could be enslaved. "These people," he noted on October 14, "are very unskilled in arms, . . . with fifty men they could all be subjected and made to do all that one wished." The statement proved a grim prophecy.

The first island disappointed Columbus. There were no treasures of the Orient. But he saw what he wished to see, what *must*, he felt, be there. The Indians wore small gold ornaments. By signs, they gave the strangers to believe that much more could be found elsewhere. Columbus assumed that Japan was close at hand. On the afternoon of October 14 he left San Salvador intending to island hop to Asia. The Spaniards cruised among several smaller islands and then, following natives' directions, pushed on to Cuba. When its high blue mountains appeared to the south, their goal once more seemed on the brink of realization. But again disappointment followed exaggerated expectation. No Grand Khan, wallowing in gold, could be located. Parties sent on inland explorations of Cuba returned with the same depressing story of poor natives and forbidding jungle.

The island of Hispaniola to which the explorers sailed next proved more promising. The Indians had considerable gold and told

Columbus of rich mines in the interior. But just when success seemed imminent, the *Santa Maria* ran aground on a reef and was abandoned on Christmas Day in 1492. Columbus made a quick decision. He would plant a colony, called Navidad, and leave forty men on Hispaniola to find the gold and ascertain the location of Asia. On January 16, 1493, the *Pinta* and the *Niña* began the voyage home.

Columbus's arrival in Lisbon on March 4 triggered a surge of excitement. People debated whether he had found the outskirts of Asia or islands midway between Europe and Asia or a whole new continent, but few remained indifferent. Hunger for the Oriental trade combined with Renaissance curiosity and political ambition to create a climate in which Columbus's reports ignited imaginations. Europe was ripe for the news he brought. This had not been true at the time of the earlier discoveries of the New World. When the Vikings, for example, made contact in the eleventh century, Europeans were not straining impatiently at their physical and intellectual bounds. Asia and its riches were unknown. The Crusades had not begun. Neither capitalism nor nationalism had appeared. Open-ocean navigation was a risky, hit-or-miss operation. Consequently, the Viking feat had little impact on history. Christopher Columbus, on the contrary, had the good fortune to sail at a time when Europe was ready. His "discovery" began the continuous European expansion that led directly to the formation of the United States. Not literally, then, but significantly, Columbus discovered America.

After completing his first round trip to the Caribbean, Columbus could have retired with his laurels, but for a man of his temperament, the first voyage could only be prelude. Ferdinand and Isabella were similarly inclined. Their Admiral of the Ocean Sea had come to Barcelona and astounded them with his collection of strange fish, wood, and fruit. Columbus spread gold before the monarchs, assuring them that it was but a token of what existed. The Indians Columbus displayed to the court provided additional incentive. On command, they recited the *Ave Maria* and crossed themselves. In the eyes of fervent Catholics like Ferdinand and Isabella, this was reason enough to continue the western exploration. A whole civilization of heathen seemed to be waiting for conversion to Christianity. And by a Papal Bull of May 4, 1493, which set a Line of Demarcation one hundred leagues west of the Azores, Spain was given exclusive right to exploit and colonize the new lands.

With the stakes so high, Columbus found little difficulty in assembling the men and means to support his return to the Caribbean. On September 25, 1493, seventeen ships and between 1200 and 1500 men left the Spanish port of Cadiz. Once again the ocean crossing caused no problem, but the expedition failed to fulfill expectations. Neither the Asian mainland nor Japan materialized, although the search was much more extensive. The amount of gold was far smaller than Columbus expected. The Indians, moreover, proved as poor subjects for missionary work as the Spaniards proved missionaries. Columbus fought the cannibals of the Leeward Islands, and made them slaves and concubines. The Indians, however, turned the tables at Hispaniola. When Columbus returned to his Navidad colony, he found nothing but bones and charred timbers. Every Spaniard had been killed or carried off into the jungle.

Columbus's fortunes went from bad to worse. He attempted to start another colony, called Isabella, on Hispaniola, but his men suffered from sickness, dissension, and apathy. When they realized that gold could not be picked up on the beaches, they quickly became disenchanted with the New World. Actually, their situation was a symptom of the more general failure of the trading-post colony in the Americas. In wealthy and sophisticated societies like those of India and coastal Africa, Europeans simply set up shop and traded for valuable goods. Amid the comparatively poorer and more primitive peoples of the Caribbean and North America, however, there was little for which to trade. Men would have to *work* for wealth in these places; they would have to invest time, effort, and money before they could expect returns. Columbus unconsciously realized this in one of his official reports. Hispaniola, he declared, "is a wonder, with its hills and mountains, plains and meadows, and a land so rich and fertile for planting and sowing, for raising livestock of all sorts, for building towns and villages." But for over a century neither he nor his followers proved capable of translating this vision into reality. The lure of quick, easy wealth blinded them to the real abundance of the new land.

Troubled by discontent among his men, Columbus had to face

the additional problem of full-scale war with the Indians. The missionary ideal broke down completely. Headstrong men, thousands of miles from home, did not respect Ferdinand and Isabella's directive that their new subjects be treated gently. Between 1494 and 1496, about a third of the 300,000 natives of Hispaniola were slaughtered, and the remainder enslaved in the gold mines. Fifty years later, only 500 Indians remained. Shortly thereafter, they were exterminated and replaced as a labor force by enslaved blacks from Africa.

As a colonial governor Columbus proved an almost total failure. Yet for a time he retained the confidence of Ferdinand and Isabella. In 1498 and 1502 the Admiral led new expeditions west, but he no longer pioneered. He had shown the way, and now others followed. His authority continued to dwindle, and at one point he was actually arrested and sent back to Spain in chains. Eventually he lost his position as governor.

Even Columbus's own assurance that he had found the edge of Asia began to waver. On his third voyage in 1498 he made the first recorded sighting of the South American continent. At first he supposed it another island, but there was disconcerting evidence to the contrary. Far from the coast, Columbus was amazed to find the sea fresh and suitable for drinking. He concluded, correctly, that the flow of a river had temporarily overcome the salinity of the ocean. But what a river! Columbus knew that only large land masses could produce rivers of this size. The experience forced him to admit that this land might be a continent, "another world," as his journal expressed it. But the old dream died hard. Perhaps, Columbus desperately reasoned, he had found a magic island not far from Asia that was none other than the earthly paradise.

Apart from such thoughts, there was little to cheer his declining years. Queen Isabella, whose faith in Columbus had been instrumental in making his first voyage possible, died late in 1504, and the Spanish court became increasingly deaf to the Admiral's pleas for restoration of his former incomes and positions. And then his health failed. Embittered and disappointed, yet still proud, Columbus gave up the struggle on May 20, 1506, in Valladolid, Spain. But the cruelest slight came a few years later. Martin Waldseemüller, a renowned German geographer, drew a map and wrote a book in which he mistakenly attributed the discovery of South America to Amerigo Vespucci, a vain and deceitful man who actually followed in Columbus's footsteps. By the time Waldseemüller realized his error, it was too late. Europeans were using "America," not "Columbia," to refer to the entire New World.

Columbus opened the door for further European discovery and exploration of the Americas. The little-known John Cabot, probably a Genoese like Columbus, carried England's flag along the northern route of the Vikings to Newfoundland in 1497. He sailed along the coast and may have reached Maine before returning. A year later Cabot was back, searching for Japan and the Spice Islands, but finding Delaware and the Chesapeake Bay instead. Although he died before completing his second voyage, Cabot laid the basis for England's claim to North America north of Florida. English colonization, however, did not start for almost a century. When it did, in the 1580s, Sir Walter Raleigh learned that the New World could deal lethal doses of the unexpected. His settlement on Roanoke Island off the North Carolina coast met the same fate as Columbus's Navidad. And only relief expeditions and radical reassessment of its purpose saved Jamestown, Virginia, from similar extinction during its "starving time" from 1607 to 1609. Europeans needed time to learn how to pioneer in a wilderness.

French contact with the New World began with fishing expeditions to Newfoundland's Grand Banks as early as 1504, but a formal effort at discovery awaited the appointment by Francis I of Giovanni Verrazano, another Genoese mariner, as national explorer. In 1524 Verrazano became the first to sail the whole coast of North America from Florida to Newfoundland, but he found no northwest passage to Asia. Jacques Cartier tried again in the 1530s, sailing as far as the first rapids on the St. Lawrence River and solidifying the French claim to Canada. As in the Caribbean, the northland spawned rumors of fabulous golden kingdoms that vanished like mist as the explorers penetrated the wilderness. In the end France had to be satisfied with fish and fur.

For the Portuguese, the urge to explore the New World lessened considerably when in 1498 Vasco da Gama actually reached India after rounding Africa. But the Spanish successors to Columbus continued to search for the elusive passage *through* the Americas. The pace of this quest increased after 1513 when Vasco Nuñez de Balboa

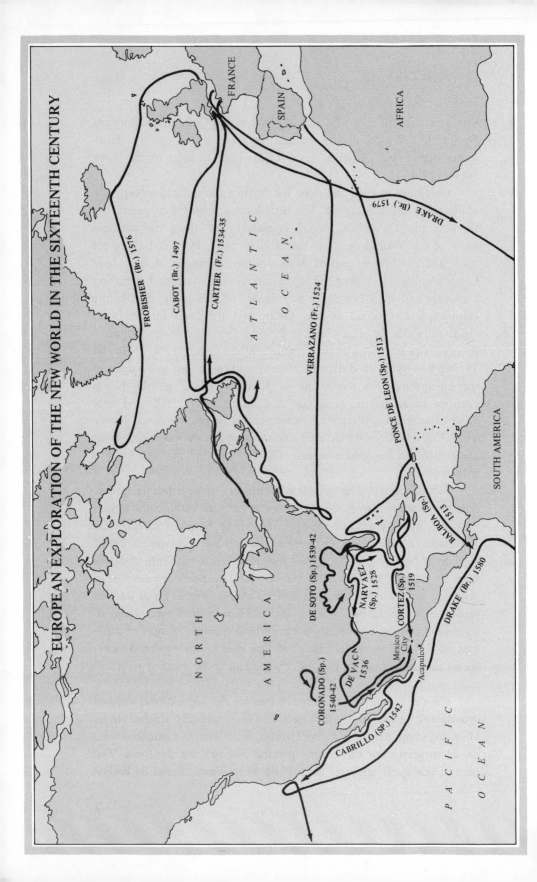

EUROPEAN EXPLORATION OF THE NEW WORLD IN THE SIXTEENTH CENTURY

FRANCE
SPAIN
AFRICA

FROBISHER (Br.) 1576
CABOT (Br.) 1497
CARTIER (Fr.) 1534-35

ATLANTIC OCEAN

VERRAZANO (Fr.) 1524

DRAKE (Br.) 1579

PONCE DE LEON (Sp.) 1513

SOUTH AMERICA

NORTH AMERICA

DE SOTO (Sp.) 1539-42

BALBOA (Sp.) 1513

NARVAEZ (Sp.) 1528

CORTEZ (Sp.) 1519

DRAKE (Br.) 1580

CORONADO (Sp.) 1540-42

DE VACA 1536

Mexico City

Acapulco

CABRILLO (Sp.) 1542

PACIFIC OCEAN

struggled across the narrow isthmus of Panama and became the first European to see the Pacific Ocean from the west. The unlucky Columbus had spent the entire winter of 1502–1503 sailing up and down the Panamanian coast, unaware that he was only forty miles away from a clear passage to India.

Despite the failure to find India, Spain lost no time in improving on the opportunities Columbus had created in the Caribbean and the adjacent mainlands. Juan Ponce de León, a member of Columbus's second expedition, found little except mangrove swamps in Florida in 1513, but Hernán Cortés in Mexico (1519) and Francisco Pizarro in Peru (1531) struck it rich. The gold they stole from the Aztecs and Incas, respectively, made Spain the foremost power in Europe. It also sustained the New World treasure hunt through a succession of wild goose chases. In 1527–1528, for example, Pánfilo de Narváez led four hundred men through present-day Florida and Georgia and along the Gulf Coast to Texas. Disaster piled upon disaster until only two men remained. They staggered into Mexico City in 1536, after having traveled great distances with Indian tribes. One of these survivors, Cabeza de Vaca, returned with an incredible pack of lies about the Seven Cities of Cibola, where kings bathed in gold dust. The governor of Cuba, Hernando de Soto, could not resist. In 1539 he landed on the Florida coast with six hundred men. In the next four years de Soto marched north to the Appalachian Mountains, then west through the Mississippi Valley and finally as far as Oklahoma. At the same time, Francisco Vásquez de Coronado sought the mythical Seven Cities from the west. He traveled north from Mexico City into Arizona, discovered the Grand Canyon, and pushed east into Kansas only to return empty-handed in 1542. The accompanying sea voyage by Hernando de Alarcón up the Gulf of California and into the Colorado River was similarly unrewarding. Undaunted, the viceroy of New Spain immediately sent Juan Rodríquez Cabrillo sailing up the California coast past San Francisco Bay. Again there was no gold, but much frustration.

The false expectations of Columbus lived on in men like de Soto, Coronado, and Cabrillo. In spite of their courage and persistence, they failed to see the real potential of the New World. They set their sights fixedly on gold. They did not understand that in their disappointment they walked over and sailed along some of the most fertile land in the world—land capable of sustaining a great civilization. The problem, of course, was that, beginning with Columbus, the Spaniards were *conquistadores*, not farmers and settlers. Their purpose was the collection of treasure, not the extension of civilization. Even when souls, not gold, were the objective and priests rather than soldier-adventurers the agents, the Spanish proved inept colonizers. Their idea of a settlement was a virtual prison that forced both labor and religion down the throats of bewildered Indians. The primary concern of Spain in the Americas was, like France in its preoccupation with furs, a triumphant return to the Old World, not a permanent place in the New. The ultimate cost of such conduct was the loss of North America to the English latecomers who, after a few false starts, learned to accept the land for what it was. Christopher Columbus and his Spanish successors never even tried. Their dreams stood in the way.

SELECTED READINGS

The Person

JANE, LIONEL CECIL (ed.): *Select Documents Illustrating the Four Voyages of Columbus* (2 vols., 1930–1933). A comprehensive collection of letters, dispatches, log books and journals. A shorter collection is *John M. Cohen (ed.): *The Four Voyages of Christopher Columbus* (1969).

LANDSTRÖM, BJÖRN: *Columbus* (1966). A biography embellished with dozens of magnificent, full-color drawings and maps.

MORISON, SAMUEL ELIOT: *Admiral of the Ocean Sea: A Life of Christopher Columbus* (2 vols., 1942). The best biography and one of the most impressive examples of biographical writing we have. Abridged as *Christopher Columbus, Mariner* (1955).

SMITH, BRADLEY: *Columbus in the New World* (1962). A spectacular photographic record of the lands and seas Columbus saw.

The Period

*BAKELESS, JOHN: *The Eyes of Discovery: America as Seen by the First Explorers* (1950). A unique description of the environment the first Europeans encountered in the New World.

* Available in paperback.

BREBNER, JOHN B.: *The Explorers of North America, 1492–1800* (1933). The best general account.

*CRONE, G. R.: *The Discovery of America* (1969). The best short account of the background and aftermath of Columbus's feat.

FELL, BARRY: *America B.C.* (1976). A fascinating, if still tentative, hypothesis that Europeans settled the eastern coast of North America before the birth of Christ.

HOLAND, H. R.: *Explorations in America before Columbus* (1956). A review of the numerous claims of North American contact by Europeans before 1492.

*JONES, HOWARD MUMFORD: *O Strange New World* (1964). The impact of North America on the European imagination.

*PARRY, J. H.: *The Age of Reconnaissance* (1963). A survey of European culture at the beginning of the age of discovery and exploration.

*PENROSE, BOIES: *Travel and Discovery in the Renaissance, 1420–1620* (1952). A competent survey that puts Columbus's voyages in the perspective of an expanding Europe.

QUINN, DAVID BEERS: *England and the Discovery of America 1481–1620* (1974). The latest book by the leading contemporary student of North American discovery and exploration.

* Available in paperback.

John Winthrop

It was a Sunday morning in the spring of 1630, and the faithful gathered for worship. Being in the middle of the North·Atlantic on the Arbella made little difference to Puritans. Religion came first, always. The preacher was a layman, but governor of the migrating band, and they quieted as he mounted the forecastle. Pausing, John Winthrop looked out at the expectant faces and beyond to the open ocean. These people had cast their lots with the New World. Unlike the Spanish gold seekers, they came as

*settlers, hoping to find freedom to live according to their ideals.
These involved nothing less than the continuation of the
Protestant Reformation and the creation of a godly society.
Winthrop fully appreciated the obstacles in their way, and as he
began to speak his tone was grave. He tried to show his followers
how the very freedom that made the North American wilderness
attractive could also prove a liability. It would be easy to forget high
purposes. Discipline and unity were consequently cardinal virtues.
If the colonists weakened, he warned, God's special protection would
be replaced by the full measure of His special wrath. Near the
end of the shipboard sermon, Winthrop created a striking metaphor
that has reverberated through American history. "For we must
consider," he shouted against the sound of waves and wind,
"that we shall be as a city upon a hill, the eyes of all people are
upon us." Here was recognition of the unprecedented opportunity
as well as the awesome responsibility that went with a fresh start
in a new world. While he lived, the force of John Winthrop's
conviction and character played a major role in sustaining the
Puritans in this self-conceived mission. Inevitably, that zeal waned
and with it the tight social control Winthrop prized, but not before
Puritanism made a deep impression on the American character.*

The year of John Winthrop's birth, 1588, proved exceptionally exciting for his native England. Queen Elizabeth had occupied the throne for three decades, and under her guidance the nation had become the most powerful in Europe. English "sea dogs," notably John Hawkins and Francis Drake, brazenly pirated Spanish galleons in Caribbean and South American waters. In 1580 Drake returned with a cargo of Spanish gold after circumnavigating the globe. A proud Elizabeth promptly knighted him. Spain, however, was furious and in 1588 sent a mighty fleet against the upstart English. But the quick British warships, with help from the weather, demolished the Spanish Armada. Now England ruled the seas, and, armed with a different philosophy of colonization, prepared to replace Spain as the dominant power in North America.

At home, England's economy was flourishing under the influence of a burgeoning capitalism. The effects were at once invigorating and dislocating. Prices and profits soared during the sixteenth century. With the woolen industry leading the way, manufacturing became a large-scale enterprise. To supply the mills with raw material, fields once used for crops were fenced (the sixteenth-century term was *enclosed*) for sheep pastures. Some farmers suffered, but for others change created opportunity. John Winthrop's grandfather Adam, for example, quit farming early in the sixteenth century to try his luck in commerce. He did well. Entering the clothworkers' guild, or union, as an apprentice, he subsequently became a journeyman and then a master clothier. He also became rich enough to purchase the manor of Groton in Suffolk, acquire a coat of arms, and join the landed gentry.

John Winthrop grew up in the comfortable, rustic setting of Groton. As his parents' only son and heir, John seemed destined for a life devoted to the gentlemanly art of estate management. At fifteen he journeyed to Cambridge for the traditional two years of polishing in that university's Trinity College. In 1605, at the age of seventeen, Winthrop married Mary Forth, a bride carefully selected by his father for her economic assets and social connections. Ten months later there was a baby, and John Winthrop appeared ready to settle down in Suffolk. At this point, North America seemed totally irrelevant to his life, but he was soon to encounter an influence that ultimately transformed the country gentleman into a wilderness colonizer. The new force was the Protestant Reformation, and it led John Winthrop to the New World, just as the Renaissance spirit of discovery and glory had led Christopher Columbus.

The Reformation began in Germany in 1519 with the work of Martin Luther. Fed as well by the ideas of the French theologian John Calvin, it spread rapidly throughout Northern Europe. Numerous variations in doctrine existed, but in general, Protestants favored reducing the elaborate organization Catholicism placed between the individual believer and God. Their goal was recovery of the simplicity and sincerity of the original Christian faith.

In England, the Reformation quickly acquired political as well as theological importance. Henry VIII, king since 1509, had little sympathy for Protestant ideas, but he coveted power and property. The

Catholic Church in England had both in plenty. And Henry harbored personal grounds for resentment: the Pope refused to grant him a divorce. Finally, in the 1530s, Henry made his move. Defying Rome, he appointed himself head of the Church in England, granted himself a divorce, and confiscated all the property of the Catholic Church, which amounted to about a quarter of the entire kingdom. One beneficiary of the confiscation was John Winthrop's grandfather, who bought the old monastic estate of Groton from Henry in 1544.

It remained for Henry's daughter Elizabeth to pursue the Reformation in England. In 1559, at the beginning of her reign, Elizabeth established Anglicanism (the Church of England) as the nation's official religion and proceeded to define what and how Englishmen could worship. The penalty for disobedience was fine and imprisonment. For most Protestants this arrangement proved satisfactory, since the Church of England did eliminate some of the hierarchy and ritual of Roman Catholicism. But the more radical regarded Anglicanism as little better than what it replaced. Many of these dissenters joined hands after 1560 under the banner of Puritanism with the intent of purifying Christianity. In terms of doctrine, this meant accepting the Bible as the sole source of authority and eliminating the hierarchy of church officials in favor of government by local congregations. Since under Anglicanism the king headed the church, Puritans tended to oppose monarchical authority. Here lay the seeds of strife—and also the beginnings of New England.

Puritanism touched the life of John Winthrop in 1606, when he was eighteen and just settling down as squire of Groton. His diary gives the details. On February 2, "a seacret desire after pleasures & itchinge after libertie & unlawfull delightes" on Winthrop's part coincided with his wife's illness. The latter, he assumed, must be a warning to him from the Lord. But his "sinnes" continued, and he himself fell ill. Finally, on April 20 John Winthrop made an agreement (Puritans called it a *covenant*) with God. Winthrop would undertake to purge himself of "pride, covetousnesse, love of this worlde, vanitie of minde, unthankfulnesse [and] slouth . . . both in His service & in my callinge." The Lord's contribution, Winthrop continued, was the provision of "a new heart," strength to resist the temptations of the "Divell," and forgiveness in case Satan temporarily triumphed. "God give me grace to performe my promise," the entry for April 20 concluded, "& I doubt not but he will performe His. God make it fruitfull. Amen."

Winthrop's personal covenant, painstakingly set down as a constant reminder, reflected the core of the Puritan mind. Following Calvin, he assumed that original sin damned all men and destined them to hell's fiery pit. All, that is, but an undeserving few whom God regenerated and granted salvation. These heaven-bound "elect" or "saints," as Winthrop frequently called them, did not in any sense earn their pardon. The best any man could do was to make his covenant, have faith, and seek in the course of his life some sign of the Lord's predetermined decision respecting his fate. Good deeds, a godly life, and success in one's career were such signs—the evidence, not the cause, of salvation. As a saying popular in Winthrop's time went, "a good man does good works, but good works do not make a good man." Living with this paradox was part of being a Puritan.

Once planted in Winthrop, Puritanism took root rapidly. Even as he became absorbed in a career of law and the management of Groton, his concern for religion increased. His central problem was how to live in the real world without loving worldly pleasures too much. This is not to say that Puritans like Winthrop had to be the solemn, gloomy, self-righteous killjoys of the stereotype. The important thing was to love God above all. If a man could enjoy a tankard of ale, a good dinner, a pipe, and his wife without lessening his enjoyment of God, fine. The danger lay in forgetting one's first duty. John Winthrop, who was by his own admission strongly drawn to the lusts of the flesh, teetered between secular and spiritual delights for most of his early life. The pattern was cyclical: after a bout of sensuality, Winthrop's conscience drove him to a period of monastic abstinence. But his resolve always weakened, and the cycle continued. After thirty years of struggle with himself, Winthrop concluded that the key virtue was discipline. Since sinful man could not be continually good, he had to learn to deal with his lower desires and channel their energies upward whenever possible.

While the individual soul dominated the attention of English Puritans, the condition of society also concerned them deeply. Winthrop and his fellows believed it their duty to make the world as godly as possible. The welfare of a nation depended on a social or group covenant between God and its people. Just as in the case of the individual covenant, God was thought to protect and sustain an entire people who endeavored to live according to His laws. Conversely, if society broke those laws, a wrathful God was expected to dispense lethal punishment. Government, then, was crucial as a way of ensuring godliness.

With the stakes so high, Puritans like Winthrop looked with growing uneasiness at the course of English political history in the early seventeenth century. In 1603 James I succeeded Queen Elizabeth, and religious dissenters hoped the change meant greater sympathy for their cause. But in January 1604, at Hampton Court, James made his position clear: "I shall make them conform themselves," he declared in reference to the Puritans, "or I will harry them out of this land, or else do worse." Winthrop was only sixteen at the time, but as a member of a Puritan family, news of James's pronouncement must have sent cold chills along his spine. As his involvement with Puritanism grew, he knew he was inviting royal displeasure or, as James had said, "worse." The cells in the Tower of London and the executioner's block provided vivid illustrations of the king's meaning. Yet Winthrop could not think of abandoning his covenant with God. Almost as distasteful was the prospect of watching his country forget the Reformation and perhaps slip back to Roman Catholicism. What could be done?

The alternatives, at least, were not hard to discover, and Winthrop surely weighed them on the long, solitary rides from Groton to his law duties in the Court of Wards in London. One possibility was revolt. In the seventeenth century, however, kings cast awesome shadows. One did not dismiss their authority lightly. Even when Charles I, James's successor, married a Catholic and in 1629 dissolved Parliament, Winthrop could not entertain revolutionary thoughts. A decade later bolder and more desperate English Puritans would overthrow the throne, but by this time Winthrop had found a different solution.

Another alternative Winthrop considered was separating from England and leaving that unhappy country to the bitter fruits of its own ungodliness. Many precedents existed in the Christian past for this kind of response to evil. Hermits and monks had repeatedly fled to lonely retreats to make their separate peace with God. Occasionally an entire group of people, following the example of the Israelites, escaped from persecution. After James's ominous pronouncement at Hampton Court, some radical Puritans from the village of Scrooby in Nottinghamshire organized under the leadership of William Brewster, William Bradford, and John Robinson. Extremely dissatisfied with the incomplete purification of the Anglican Church, they determined to reject it entirely.

Although these Separatists desired only to be left alone, the Anglicans harassed them unmercifully. In the winter of 1608–1609 they left England for the more permissive climate of Holland. But their troubles continued. The materialistic Dutch culture offered many temptations, and Catholic Spain threatened to conquer the country and crush all forms of Protestantism. The Separatists finally decided that their best hope for freedom was a complete break with Europe. They would seek the wilderness of the New World. Securing a grant of land from the settler-hungry Virginia Company, thirty-five Separatists and sixty-seven other colonists (we have come to call them all Pilgrims) sailed for New England in the fall of 1620 on the *Mayflower*.

The Pilgrims proved the feasibility of separation, but John Winthrop remained unconvinced. He could not escape a sense of responsibility to his fellow-man. No matter how ungodly society had become, the true Christian, as Winthrop defined him, could not turn his back. The goal, after all, was the reformation of Christendom. The purification of a tiny part of it had no meaning. On a more fundamental level, Winthrop perceived that all men were united by original sin. Man could not escape from evil in the world any more than he could flee from evil in himself. Both had to be confronted. Winthrop knew that in this respect the Separatists on the *Mayflower* had failed. They had simply deserted England. In quest of the perfection of their little group, they had forgotten the meaning of the Reformation.

Yet Winthrop could not but envy the Pilgrims their opportunity to build a society according to their understanding of God's wishes. Musing on this apparent dilemma in the 1620s, he gradually formulated a solution. Suppose he left England in order to create a model Christian community that by its very godliness would command the attention and admiration of the rest of the world? Eventually, Winthrop reasoned, other societies would follow the New England example in their own homelands. Surely this would be a contribution to the Reformation. Leaving in order to lead and ultimately to save all mankind—here was an alternative he could support.

Although Winthrop had found good grounds to justify migration, he remained uncommitted at the beginning of 1629. The events of the next ten months, however, forced a decision. During this time the New World became an increasingly familiar subject of conversation around the Winthrop table. A group of Puritan merchants known to the Winthrop family had formed the New England Company and were already involved in colonization. John Winthrop, Jr., even toyed with the idea of joining the company outpost at Salem, Massachusetts. Eventually he declined, but not before his father had reviewed the enterprise favorably. The elder Winthrop also thought a stint in the wilderness would serve to cool the blood of another son, Henry. But in the spring of 1629 Winthrop could think of himself only as squire of Groton and attorney to the court of Charles I.

After two earlier marriages left him a widower, he had finally found in Margaret Tyndal a woman who not only survived, but understood Winthrop's determination to enjoy worldly pleasures without being absorbed by them. As a consequence, he was only mildly interested when on March 4 the New England Company secured a new royal charter confirming its grant and renamed itself the Massachusetts Bay Company. Six days later, however, Charles I dissolved Parliament. Now there was nothing to stand between the Puritans and the hostility of the king. Suddenly New England acquired much greater appeal for John Winthrop.

As the English political climate chilled for men of his persuasion, Winthrop resigned his position as a royal attorney (or perhaps he was fired). Returning to Groton, he contemplated an uncertain future. His friends in the Massachusetts Bay Company, however, knew exactly what Winthrop should do. A man of his substance and experience, they pointed out, was needed in the colonial enterprise. He might well become its leader. And thousands of miles from Charles I and the Anglican Church, such a leader could use his own ideals to shape society. The prospect appealed to Winthrop, as did the argument that his participation was crucial to the success of the entire effort. He was told, probably with some truth, that many Puritans were reserving judgment about America until after John Winthrop decided. For someone with his sense of social responsibility, this situation generated considerable pressure.

But for Winthrop, the central question was how the Massachusetts Bay Company would be governed. He knew what had happened in the case of the Virginia Company's colony on Chesapeake Bay. In 1624, after seventeen years of existence, James I simply voided its charter, disbanded its representative assembly (the House of Burgesses), and placed a royal governor in control. If this could happen to Massachusetts Bay, Winthrop reasoned, then there was no point in proceeding further with plans for a Puritan community. It would be crushed by the Crown. He was right, of course, but in July of 1629 those interested in securing his support made a telling bid. A careful reading of the March 4 charter, they explained, revealed no provision regarding the location of the company's government. Normally, the directors were Englishmen who remained at home under the watchful eye of the king. Yet it appeared that the Massachusetts Bay Company had the option of directing itsélf from a New World location far removed from royal scrutiny. Winthrop relished this prospect. Here was assurance of the independence he considered essential for the success of a spiritual experiment. In August 1629 Winthrop cast his lot with the New World and began preparations for departure.

It was difficult enough to conclude his personal affairs, but on October 20 the General Court (assembly of members) of the Massachusetts Bay Company elected him governor. "So it is," he wrote to Margaret, "that [it] hath pleased the Lorde to call me to a further trust in this business of the plantation, than either I expected or finde my selfe fitt for."

Despite this initial lack of confidence, Winthrop proved an extremely able governor in the busy months before the Puritan exodus. He understood his first task was recruiting colonists for the holy experiment. Turning to the pen, Winthrop wrote down the reasons for migrating. Widely circulated among Puritans, these "Conclusions," combined with Winthrop's prestige, proved highly persuasive. He began by pointing out that the New World offered few temptations to the younger generation, whereas England was full of "evill examples." Indeed, the corruption of church and society in Europe invited an unfavorable judgment from the Lord. Perhaps the Old World was doomed. New England, Winthrop argued, might be the refuge God provided for those "he means to save out of the generall callamity." Elsewhere in his "Conclusions" he relied on the rivalry between religions in the seventeenth century to drive home the point that if Protestants did not colonize the New World, Catholics would.

Worldly considerations also figured in Winthrop's inducements. He emphasized the depressed English economy and how a man could scarcely earn a living even with hard work. Better to seek new fields where success—that sign of God's pleasure—might crown one's efforts. Moreover, in the New World land was abundant and free. For those who argued that the land belonged to Indians, Winthrop replied according to Scripture. He interpreted Genesis 1:28, the first commandment of God to man, to give Christians the right to conquer and subdue those parts of the world that "lie waste without any improvement." The North American wilderness, in Winthrop's mind, was intended by God to be colonized, civilized, and made fruitful by people like himself. The heathen Indians did not count—except as subjects for conversion. Finally, Winthrop answered the charge that he was deserting Europe with the assertion that the Puritans were actually spearheading the Reformation.

In addition to recruiting colonists, he was responsible for provisioning and partly financing the expedition. Like Noah and the Ark, he had to think of everything necessary to begin civilization anew. Seeds, livestock, tools, books, even limes to ward off scurvy went onto his careful lists and into the holds of the ships. Also needed were representatives of the various crafts and professions, and Winthrop chose his colleagues with this in mind. As a result, the thousand Englishmen who gathered in April of 1630 at Cowes to board the eleven ships of the Massachusetts Bay Company were a society in miniature.

Thus far John Winthrop's energy and idealism had been equal to the task of leaving England. But when the Puritan fleet left Cowes on April 8, his challenge had only begun. In quiet moments, gazing over the ocean, thinking of Groton and of Margaret, who remained behind temporarily, misgivings crowded in upon him. He knew the difficulties encountered in previous efforts at colonizing North America. The complete disappearance of Sir Walter Raleigh's 1585 settlement on Roanoke Island was an extreme example, but subsequent English outposts in the New World had fared only slightly better.

The Virginia Company's colony at Jamestown was started in May 1607, when 105 survivors of a voyage that claimed 39 lives landed on the north bank of the James River a few miles upstream from Chesapeake Bay. Their troubles began at once. The site chosen for the colony was a tidal marsh characterized by foul water and malaria-bearing mosquitoes. Tied as they were to ships, the colonists hesitated to move inland to better locations. But attitude as well as environment produced the nightmare of the next several years. Self-styled gentlemen and adventurers in the *conquistador* mold, the first Virginians balked at performing tasks such as farming that were essential for survival. Their supplies dwindled. Disease swept the colony. By January of 1608, only 38 of the original contingent remained. At this point, realistic, hard-boiled John Smith engineered a temporary improvement with his insistence that Jamestown make crops and livestock, rather than gold, its principal concern. But in 1609 Smith was ousted and sent back to England. Now exposed to the full force of their ignorance, the settlers entered upon a "starving time." The winter of 1609–1610 reduced them to a diet of rats, snakes, horsehide, and even human flesh. Of approximately 500 colonists, only 60 survived, and they were en route back to England when they met a relief expedition entering the mouth of the James. Conditions improved slowly, but only because the London Company pumped a stream of new men into Virginia to replace the discouraged and the dead. By the 1620s people no longer starved and tobacco production flourished, but the settlement still clung tenuously to the edge of the wilderness.

As he sailed for America, John Winthrop was keenly aware of the difficulties in Virginia. Indeed, one of the "Objections" in his 1629 argument for migrating had been that "the ill success of other Plantations may tell us what will become of this." But his "Answer" pointed out that most of Virginia's problems "happened through . . . slouth and security." The Puritans, never forgetful of their duty to God and the rest of mankind, would, Winthrop hoped, avoid these perils. Yet only a fool would make light of the immense obstacles associated with

New World colonization. A wilderness environment demanded radically different skills and temperaments than rural England. English country squires did not immediately become American frontiersmen. Acknowledging this in his "Conclusions," Winthrop faced the fact that the Puritan endeavor "is attended with many and great difficulties." But his answer to this objection went right to the point: "soe is every good action." This frame of mind gave promise of the physical and mental toughness necessary for survival.

The record of earlier settlement north of Virginia likewise offered little cheer. They knew that in 1607 English merchants had sent colonists to Maine, only to see them straggle back after a few miserable months. The story of the Pilgrims in 1620 was almost as discouraging. The *Mayflower* transported William Bradford's little group to New England at the worst possible time of the year—November. With snow already on the ground and a slate-gray sky promising more, Bradford described the New World as "a hideous and desolate wilderness." Half the Pilgrims died that first winter. Summer brought crops and the assistance of Indians such as Squanto, but the precariousness of their hold on the land gave the celebration of the first Thanksgiving in 1621 a hollow ring. From such experiences, Winthrop learned the full price of religious freedom.

After the frantic months of preparation, the slow Atlantic crossing afforded him an opportunity to meditate on the problems ahead. But Winthrop would not have been on the *Arbella* without a sense of the bright promise of new beginnings. The concept of mission, so central to Puritan thought, captured both these moods. In Winthrop's mind mission resulted from a covenant with God. It meant the responsibility of performing special work for Him and the opportunity of receiving His special protection. Winthrop and the migrating Puritans believed they were a chosen people. God, they thought, had singled them out to lead mankind. And He had given them an almost incredible opportunity. The New World was a vacuum, a clean slate on which man could write a fresh and, perhaps, a better record. None of the mistakes of the past need be made again. For John Winthrop in the seventeenth century, the New World was like another habitable planet for us. But in Winthrop's mind the most logical analogy to the New World was the Garden of Eden. And he was a latter-day Adam. The New World gave him and all mankind another chance.

Winthrop expounded the theme of mission and some of its consequences in a mid-Atlantic sermon, "A Modell of Christian Charity," on board the *Arbella*. He began by enumerating the purposes of the migration: to serve the Lord, to preserve themselves from "the common corruptions of this evil world," and to "work out our salvation." The core of the sermon was the covenant struck between the America-bound Puritans and God. If God brought them safely across the Atlantic, then they had the obligation to keep the faith. For Puritans this was no casual agreement, but a solemn promise that touched every aspect of their lives. "Thus stands the cause between God and us," thundered Winthrop. "We are entered into covenant with Him for this work; we have taken out a commission." Every aspect of Puritan policy was directed to this end. Again and again Winthrop stressed the importance of discipline and unity if the mission was to be accomplished. "We must be knit together in this work as one," he insisted. "We must delight in each other, make others' conditions our own, rejoice together, mourn together, labor and suffer together; always having before our eyes our commission." Of paramount importance, Governor Winthrop continued, was the need for the people to obey their governors and for the governors to obey God. If they did, God would adopt and protect the wilderness colony as He had the ancient Jews. The result would be a model society, "a city upon a hill."

No one knew better than John Winthrop that the extraordinary opportunity of the New England Puritans also meant extraordinary responsibility. Because of this chance to build a godly society, failure would be especially loathsome in the eyes of the Lord. Winthrop felt certain that breaking the covenant and ignoring the mission would bring divine wrath crashing down on their colony. If we "embrace this present world," he warned, "and prosecute our carnal intentions," an angry God will "be revenged of such a perjured people" by stranding them without protection in a wilderness.

As the *Arbella* drew near New England, such considerations became increasingly real. On June 6, 1630, Winthrop's shipmates enjoyed their first sight of land in almost two months. They struck the coast well north of their destination and for the next several days sailed southwest along the coast of Maine. On June 12 the ship anchored off John Endicott's Puritan outpost at Salem, and the passengers feasted on venison and wild strawberries. In time, the other vessels straggled into port, and by the end of the summer the population of New England more than doubled. The previous occupants were only a few Pilgrims under William Bradford at Plymouth, a scattering of survivors from the unsuccessful fishing and trading settlements of Sir Ferdinando Gorges's Council for New England, and gentlemen of wealth and independence like Samuel Maverick and William Blackstone. Winthrop's initial problem as governor was to keep up morale. The long ocean voyage had sapped the Puritans' physical strength and the vigor of their ideals. Face-to-face contact with the New England wilderness further eroded their resolve. Was the migration a huge mistake, the "city upon a hill" a sorry joke? When strong leadership was imperative, Winthrop took command.

His first decision was to find a better location than Salem. Exploration southward into Massachusetts Bay revealed the land around the mouth of the Charles River to be rich, flat, well-watered, and abounding with good harbors. Winthrop approved, and the Puritans quickly spread out around the bay. After a few false starts, the Governor located himself immediately south of the Charles on a narrow-necked peninsula he called Boston. Though death claimed eleven of Winthrop's servants and some two hundred other Puritans the first winter, compared to the "starving times" of earlier settlers, this survival rate was good. Not being first had some great advantages. Older New England hands, some with ten years of pioneering under their belts, helped with advice and gifts of food.

The Puritans were also relatively rich and could buy supplies from England. The arrival of a ship bearing reinforcements of goods and people in February 1631, for instance, contributed a great deal to maintaining the settlement through the first winter. Even so, by spring some of the Puritans were weary of being God's guinea pigs and booked passage back home. Winthrop stood firm. He believed that merely surviving the winter signified God's pleasure with New England. "I would not have altered my course," he wrote to his third and much loved wife, Margaret, "though I had foreseen all these Afflictions: I never fared better in my life, never slept better, never had more content of minde." Only Margaret herself was missing, and on November 4, 1631, she arrived in Boston harbor with the rest of the Winthrop family. The reunion was a joyous time of feasting for the entire colony—the Puritan equivalent of the Pilgrim thanksgiving ten years before.

Margaret Winthrop arrived in Boston as part of a growing stream of Puritans fleeing political adversity in England. Throughout the 1630s Charles I ruled without Parliament, while William Laud, Bishop of London, and after 1633 the powerful Archbishop of Canterbury, harassed Puritans continually. The combined oppression of state and church drove about 20,000 Englishmen to America before 1640. John Winthrop was glad to see them come. The newcomers not only brought sorely needed supplies and skills, they also reinforced the cherished city-upon-a-hill concept. In the 1630s, with immigrants continuously arriving, Massachusetts nearly approached Winthrop's hope for it as a refuge and an example. Yet the growth of Massachusetts Bay created problems for leaders like Winthrop. They found that ideals and realities, theory and practice, did not often correspond in the New World. European plans shattered on the rocks of American circumstances. Winthrop learned this lesson quickly in regard to government.

The charter of the Massachusetts Bay Company gave John Winthrop and a few other "freemen" full authority to legislate for the colony and to choose its governor. In theory, this oligarchic arrangement suited the purposes of the holy experiment quite well. Puritans believed that among the several covenants ordering their lives was one respecting the relationship of people and their governors. It held that God's laws could be enforced among imperfect men only if they agreed to submit to political leaders who could best interpret divine will. Governors, in Puritan thought, were like Old Testament prophets, chosen by ballot. Though they were elected by the people, their authority, drawn from God, was unquestionable.

The first years of Massachusetts Bay revealed the presence of forces working against this political arrangement. The New World situation, in the first place, gave the individual, no matter what his previous status, potential. On the clean slate of the American wilderness he had opportunities unimagined in the older, established European society. Pioneering placed a premium on performance. On the New England frontier a man believed he succeeded or not according to his ambition and ability. Under such circumstances, the successful

Any modern camper has his choice of a variety of what-to-take lists and guides designed to facilitate his stay in the wilderness. But the first settlers in the New World wilderness had none until this 1622 broadside was printed in London for the use of the Virginia Company. We can suppose that John Winthrop provided similar information to prospective colonists a decade later.

THE INCONVENIENCIES
THAT HAVE HAPPENED TO SOME PER-
SONS WHICH HAVE TRANSPORTED THEMSELVES

from *England* to *Virginia*, vvithout prouisions necessary to sustaine themselues, hath greatly hindred the Progresse of that noble Plantation: For preuention of the like disorders heereafter, that no man suffer, either through ignorance or misinformation; it is thought requisite to publish this short declaration: wherein is contained a particular of such necessaries, as either priuate families or single persons shall haue cause to furnish themselues with, for their better support at their first landing in Virginia; whereby also greater numbers may receiue in part, directions how to prouide themselues.

Apparrell.

	li.	s.	d.
One Monmouth Cap	oo	o1	10
Three falling bands		o1	o3
Three shirts		o7	o6
One waste-coate		o2	o2
One suite of Canuase		o7	o6
One suite of Frize		10	oo
One suite of Cloth		15	oo
Three paire of Irish stockins		o4	—
Foure paire of shooes		o8	o8
One paire of garters		oo	10
One doozen of points		oo	o3
One paire of Canuase sheets		o8	oo
Seuen ells of Canuase, to make a bed and boulster, to be filled in Virginia 8.s.	o8	oo
One Rug for a bed 8. s. which with the bed seruing for two men, halfe is		
Fiue ells coorse Canuase, to make a bed at Sea for two men, to be filled with straw, iiij.s.		
One coorse Rug at Sea for two men, will cost vj. s. is for one	o5	oo
	o4	oo	oo

Apparrell for one man, and so after the rate for more.

Victuall.

	li.	s.	d.
Eight bushels of Meale	o2	oo	oo
Two bushels of pease at 3.s.		o6	oo
Two bushels of Oatemeale 4.s. 6.d.		o9	oo
One gallon of Aquauitæ		o2	o6
One gallon of Oyle		o3	o6
Two gallons of Vineger 1.s.		o2	oo
	o3	o3	oo

For a whole yeere for one man, and so for more after the rate.

Armes.

	li.	s.	d.
One Armour compleat, light		17	oo
One long Peece, fiue foot or fiue and a halfe, neere Musket bore	o1	o2	—
One sword		o5	—
One belt		o1	—
One bandaleere		o1	o6
Twenty pound of powder		18	oo
Sixty pound of shot or lead, Pistoll and Goose shot		o5	oo
	o3	o9	o6

For one man, but if halfe of your men haue armour it is sufficient so that all haue Peeces and swords.

Tooles.

	li.	s.	d.
Fiue broad howes at 2.s. a piece	—	10	—
Fiue narrow howes at 16.d. a piece	—	o6	o8
Two broad Axes at 3.s. 8.d. a piece	—	o7	c4
Fiue felling Axes at 18.d. a piece	—	o7	o6
Two steele hand sawes at 16.d. a piece	—	o2	o8
Two two-hand sawes at 5. s. a piece	—	10	—
One whip-saw, set and filed with box, file, and wrest	—	10	—
Two hammers 12.d. a piece	—	o2	oo
Three shouels 18.d. a piece	—	o4	o6
Two spades at 18.d. a piece	—	o3	—
Two augers 6.d. a piece	—	o1	oo
Sixe chissels 6.d. a piece	—	o3	oo
Two percers stocked 4.d. a piece	—	oo	o8
Three gimlets 2.d. a piece	—	oo	o6
Two hatchets 21.d. a piece	—	o3	o6
Two froues to cleaue pale 18.d.	—	o3	oo
Two hand bills 20. a piece	—	o3	o4
One grindlestone 4.s.	—	o4	—
Nailes of all sorts to the value of	o2	oo	—
Two Pickaxes	—	o3	—
	o6	o2	o8

For a family of 6. persons and so after the rate for more.

Houshold Implements.

	li.	s.	d.
One Iron Pot	—	o7	—
One kettle	—	o6	—
One large frying-pan	—	o2	o6
One gridiron	—	o1	o6
Two skillets	—	o5	—
One spit	—	o2	—
Platters, dishes, spoones of wood	—	o4	—
	o1	o8	oo

For a family of 6. persons, and so for more or lesse after the rate.

For Suger, Spice, and fruit, and at Sea for 6 men — oo 12 o6

So the full charge of Apparrell, Victuall, Armes, Tooles, and houshold stuffe, and after this rate for each person, will amount vnto about the summe of — 12 10 —

The passage of each man is — o6 oo —

The fraight of these prouisions for a man, will bee about halfe a Tun, which is — o1 10 —

So the whole charge will amount to about — 20 oo oo

Nets, hookes, lines, and a tent must be added, if the number of people be greater, as also some kine.

And this is the vsuall proportion that the Virginia Company doe bestow vpon their Tenants which they send.

Whosoeuer transports himselfe or any other at his owne charge vnto *Virginia*, shall for each person so transported before Midsummer 1625. haue to him and his heires for euer fifty Acres of Land vpon a first, and fifty Acres vpon a second diuision.

The marshy flats of the lower James River just above its entrance into Chesapeake Bay were a poor place to plant a colony. But by 1620, the approximate date this modern painting depicts, the Virginia Company's settlement was beginning to show signs of permanency. Houses are spreading outside the protective confines of James Fort (left foreground, behind the stockade), and some attempt has been made at clearing fields for the tobacco plants John Rolfe introduced in 1612. But the ocean-going vessel at the main dock suggests the continued dependence of the colony on the mother country.

John Winthrop and his Massachusetts Bay contemporaries had an obsession about orderly existence. When a new town was "planted" in the wilderness, an elaborate survey preceded settlement. Each settler was assigned his designated parcel of land. Other parcels were reserved for the church, schools, and the "commons" that everyone shared. This was the plan for Wethersfield, Connecticut.

Colleges ranked high on the list of early American priorities. They were regarded as evidence that civilized standards could and would be maintained in the New World wilderness. Harvard College, founded across the Charles River from Boston in the community of Cambridge in 1636, was the showpiece of seventeenth-century Massachusetts Bay. This view of the college in 1726 reveals buildings that must have been among the most imposing in the colony. They were tangible evidence of the determination of New Englanders to succeed in their colonizing endeavor.

—and mere survivors were successful at first—gained self-respect. These individuals began to chafe under ideas and institutions that stifled initiative. The wilderness also had a way of blurring the social distinctions so carefully maintained in older civilizations. Equality meant more in the New World than it did in the Old. Men sensed the difference as soon as they landed, and the impact on politics showed almost immediately.

On October 19, 1630, Governor John Winthrop opened the first meeting of the General Court of the Massachusetts Bay Company. Seven other "assistants" attended. Under the terms of the company's charter, these few prepared to conduct the business of the colony. But other men also came. Some drew Winthrop aside and let him know their desire to have a voice in the affairs of the plantation. It was difficult to refuse. These people, after all, were Winthrop's colleagues in colonization. They had dared together. Many had come as a direct result of his encouragement. They were partners in performing God's work on earth. And, Winthrop realized, the Massachusetts Bay Company was not just a joint stock company, but in the New England context, a civil government. Still, he was no democrat. Sovereignty rested with God, not the people. Strong, theocratic leadership, based on a correct reading of God's will, must continue.

The solution, he decided, was to broaden the base of government by creating a new political category, the *freeman*. Any adult male, indentured servants excepted, who was a member of the Puritan church could apply for such status. As a consequence, the second meeting of the General Court in May 1631 included 118 freemen. They had no legislative authority, but they could elect the assistants who did. Election of the assistants also indirectly influenced the choice of governor. Thus, less than a year after its beginnings, Massachusetts government had moved in a republican direction.

The new arrangement pleased Winthrop, who remained governor, but his liberalism soon received a harder test. In 1632 various communities in Massachusetts Bay launched a protest against a tax assessed by Winthrop and his fellow assistants. According to the disgruntled colonists, taxation without some form of representation was contrary to the tradition of English liberties. Winthrop gave ground grudgingly. He finally agreed to consult with two representatives from every town before the next tax. He also consented to the direct election of the governor by the freemen instead of by the assistants.

The drift away from oligarchy continued in 1634, when Thomas Dudley, a political opponent of Winthrop, concluded that the wording of the Massachusetts Bay charter gave all freemen, not just the assistants, the power to make laws. Winthrop balked at this idea. God's will, not the public's, he believed, should determine policy. The people might select their leaders, but once selected, the leaders must answer only to God. The laws of men were not acceptable substitutes, in Winthrop's opinion, for the laws of God.

Respected as he was in Massachusetts, Winthrop could not prevent the continued erosion of his political ideas. Most of those who migrated to New England had come in search of freedom from the power of a king or an archbishop. Their deep-rooted aversion to arbitrary authority did not end with the trans-Atlantic crossing. Indeed, the lack of restraints inherent in a wilderness situation encouraged an even more passionate dedication to liberty. God's authority, of course, went unquestioned, but increasing numbers felt they too could discern His will, and demanded a role in translating it into law. This attitude, in fact, was part of the priesthood-of-all-believers concept of the Protestant Reformation, and one that especially influenced the congregational theory to which the American Puritans subscribed. Even Winthrop's repeated assurances that he and the other assistants best knew God's desires did not placate popular suspicion. There seemed to be too much arbitrary power in an arrangement under which a small group ruled at their own discretion.

In 1634 Winthrop was pressured into permitting each of the ten towns to send two deputies to the General Court. These deputies actually made laws along with the assistants in a semirepresentative assembly. The same year Thomas Dudley, the beneficiary of political criticism of John Winthrop, replaced him in the governor's chair. For the next three years, Winthrop was merely one of the assistants.

During this time the freemen took steps to base the government of Massachusetts Bay on explicit law, rather than the judgment of an oligarchy. Nathaniel Ward of Ipswich prepared the Body of Liberties, which spelled out the rights and obligations of citizenship. In the manner of the English Magna Carta (1215), it reflected the idea that a government of laws offered better protection for popular liberties than a government of men. Winthrop, who regained the governorship in 1637, fought the Body of Liberties doggedly. It was not that he quarreled with its substance, but rather that he believed such rules should result from the slow accumulation of the magistrates' interpretation of the Bible. Time and place, however, were against him. In December 1641 the General Court adopted Ward's code of laws.

Continued sparring between leaders and followers in Winthrop's New England resulted in 1644 in the division of the General Court into two houses—into a bicameral legislature. Winthrop and the other assistants in the upper chamber benefited from this arrangement because they secured a veto over laws made by the deputies in the lower house. The following year, however, the deputies struck back, and again the controversy revolved around Winthrop. The trouble began in the town of Hingham when the people refused to accept the militia officer appointed by Winthrop and the assistants. In his place they nominated another man. Feelings ran hot on both sides. One citizen of Hingham vowed to "die at the sword's point, if he might not have the choice of his own officers." Another simply rejected the idea that the Boston officials had anything to do with the affairs of Hingham. This was the beginning of frontier independence. But for Winthrop, it was a serious breach of the covenant that merited the strongest punishment. The men of Hingham responded by accusing Winthrop of overreaching the powers granted him in the Body of Liberties. Whereupon the lower house of the General Court impeached John Winthrop! A remarkable trial followed. Those who feared concentrated and continuous power hoped to clip Winthrop's wings. Others believed the kind of authority he represented was essential to the Puritan mission. The stormy trial sessions therefore went far beyond the Hingham mutiny. Finally, on July 3, 1645, the General Court was ready with its verdict: not guilty. Winthrop must have anticipated it, because he was ready with what he termed a "little speech." It was one of his greatest moments.

"I entreat you to consider," he began, "that when you choose magistrates, you take them from among yourselves, men subject to like passions as you are." Of course assistants, or "magistrates" as Winthrop called them, could make mistakes. Winthrop even implied that he regretted some of his own recent actions. But, he quickly countered, "when you see infirmities in us, you should reflect upon your own." It was the Puritan mind at its best and worst. Winthrop then advised the people that once they had selected a leader, the terms of the social covenant obliged them to "run the hazard of his skill and ability" as long as he tried to follow God's law.

The second part of Winthrop's speech took up the vexing problem of liberty. In Winthrop's view, there were two kinds. "Natural" liberty belonged to man as it did to "beasts and other creatures," and simply meant to do as one pleased. Good might result, Winthrop conceded, but more frequently evil did because no restraint stood between desire and action. Natural liberty, then, left man's imperfect nature uncontrolled and in time made men "worse than brute beasts." Such considerations were not academic in the wilds of America. The other kind of liberty, which Winthrop called "civil or federal," meant the freedom to do what is "good, just and honest." The definition of "good, just and honest" came from God through the medium of those who could best discern His purposes—magistrates like John Winthrop. In accepting this more restricted form of liberty, man showed his ability to rise above the animals, restrain evil tendencies, and fulfill the terms of the covenant with God. "So shall your liberties be preserved," Winthrop concluded, "in upholding the honor and power of authority amongst you." Thus rebuked, the Hingham radicals subsided.

European feudal and monarchical tradition figured more prominently in Winthrop's 1645 speech than did the currents of individualism and popular sovereignty already percolating through New World society. But of course, all but the children in Massachusetts Bay in 1645 *were* Europeans. Coupled with Winthrop's personal prestige and the unifying concept of mission, this fact served to delay social and political change in New England.

Elsewhere in North America, however, Old World expectations and institutions collapsed more quickly. Indeed, in the light of the experience of other plantations, Winthrop had reason to be encouraged with the Massachusetts record. The original plans of the Virginia Company, for instance, called for a military dictatorship combined with feudal landholding policies. In 1619, however, settlers demanded

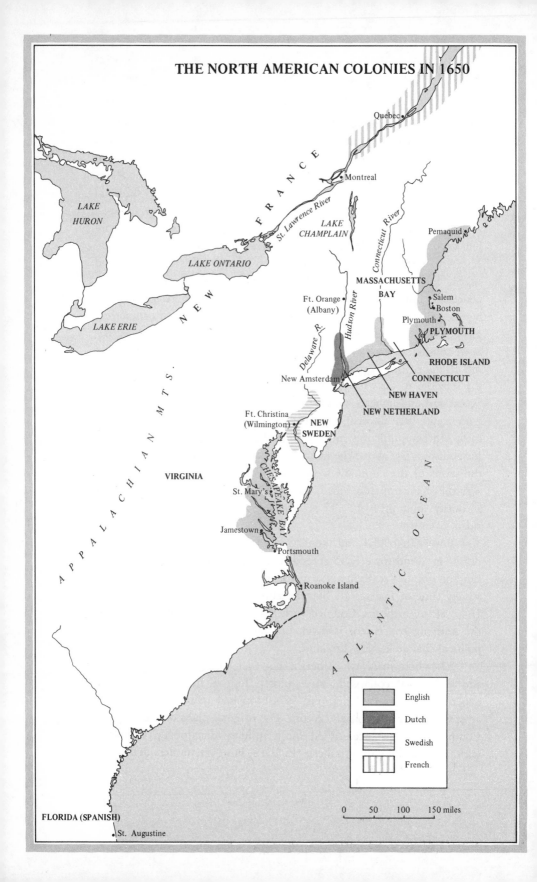

THE NORTH AMERICAN COLONIES IN 1650

Quebec

LAKE HURON

NEW

FRANCE

LAKE ONTARIO

LAKE ERIE

Montreal

St. Lawrence River

LAKE CHAMPLAIN

Connecticut River

Pemaquid

MASSACHUSETTS
BAY

Ft. Orange
(Albany)

Hudson River

Salem
Boston
Plymouth

PLYMOUTH

Delaware R.

New Amsterdam

RHODE ISLAND

CONNECTICUT

NEW HAVEN

NEW NETHERLAND

Ft. Christina
(Wilmington)

NEW
SWEDEN

APPALACHIAN MTS.

VIRGINIA

CHESAPEAKE BAY

St. Mary's

Jamestown

Portsmouth

Roanoke Island

ATLANTIC OCEAN

	English
	Dutch
	Swedish
	French

FLORIDA (SPANISH)

St. Augustine

0   50   100   150 miles

and received from the London-based directors of the company a representative assembly, the House of Burgesses. The same year, local political authority was removed from Jamestown and given to the several counties. The change indicated a trend. Virginians desired autonomy and continued to resist European directives. By 1624, a frustrated Virginia Company gave up its attempt to control the unruly Americans and turned the colony back to the king. But royal agents proved no more successful. From their wilderness environment, the Virginians derived a passion for independence and a driving ambition. From their English background as ambitious country squires they inherited a persistent localism, a casual religion—at least when compared to Winthrop's—and an emphasis on the liberties and privileges of a land-holding aristocracy. Both tendencies led them to question any authority other than their own and contributed to stamping the American character at the outset with its primary traits: making money and getting ahead.

Further north on Chesapeake Bay, Sir George Calvert, Lord Baltimore, and his son launched Maryland at the same time Winthrop founded the Puritan plantation. Their early histories differed sharply. The Calverts held complete power and intended Maryland to be a feudal estate on the European model, complete with a landed gentry, serfs, and feudal dues. The scheme existed only on paper. The proprietors and their agents were first simply ignored, then defied, and at length made to concede the rights of land ownership and meaningful political representation to most of the settlers.

Neither Maryland nor Virginia became a democracy overnight. Aspirations remained aristocratic, but they were not limited to an aristocracy. Everyone wanted to skim the cream off the top. Men had not crossed 3000 miles of ocean merely to change masters. Political authority that stood in the way of individual ambition was among the first casualties of the American experience. Winthrop would have preferred it otherwise, but he understood the mood of the people. This realism coupled with the spiritual commitment of the Puritans allowed him to retain the essence of oligarchic authority in Massachusetts long after it had faded elsewhere.

We have evidence of this in Winthrop's high-handed treatment of Robert Child. In 1645, while Winthrop was lecturing the General

Court on the meaning of liberty, Child, a physician, wrote a "Remonstrance and Humble Petition" that challenged the basis of the entire Puritan political system. It spoke for the rights of those who were not church members and therefore not voting freemen. Either suffrage or church membership ought to be expanded, Child argued. And for good measure he challenged the right of the General Court to legislate without regard to Parliament. He even threatened to return to London and tattle on the colony. Winthrop lost no time in clamping down on the upstart. Arbitrary seizures, fines, and imprisonment were the colony's answers to Child. Before being sent back to England in 1647, he was thoroughly discredited. Time and America, to be sure, were on Child's side, but in the 1640s his challenge to authority brought the conservatism latent in Puritan political theory crashing down on his defenseless head. Winthrop found the result immensely satisfying. The Lord's will was upheld, the unity of the New England way preserved.

Despite the attention paid to politics, the dominant concern of Winthrop's Massachusetts Bay was religion. Churches were the core of New England intellectual and social life and consisted of the "saints" and their ministers. Others might worship in the congregation, hoping for that searing flash of regeneration that would qualify them to sit among the elect. Yet membership in the church was restricted to those who succeeded in convincing themselves and their peers that they had been regenerated or saved. Over time, the restrictions disintegrated. More and more people joined the church under compromise arrangements such as the Half-way Covenant of 1662, whereby children of regenerate parents were automatically included in the elect. In the 1630s and 1640s, however, the lines remained firm. One consequence was an intense intolerance in the Puritan mind. They believed, quite literally, that they and they alone knew God's will. Anyone who disagreed with Puritan theology was not only wrong, but in league with evil. As Nathaniel Ward put it in 1645, "poly-piety is the greatest impiety in the world." A man who tolerated other faiths could not be sincere in his own. Toleration was thought to be particularly unbecoming in a society that regarded itself as God's chosen, a city upon a hill. This left dissenters from Puritan orthodoxy with little choice but to leave. In Massachusetts, religion was far too weighty a matter for variations to be allowed.

As governor, Winthrop carried the responsibility of preserving the plantation's piety, a task that brought some of his most trying moments. The first crisis involved a personal friend, the brilliant and charismatic Roger Williams. Only twenty-seven years old when he came to Massachusetts Bay in 1631, Williams fused the intense idealism of youth with a religious fervor exceptional even among Puritans. His conflict, in fact, resulted from his high standards. Williams began by refusing to associate with those who would not denounce and separate from the Church of England. This included Winthrop and most of the colonists in Massachusetts Bay. Displeased as they were with Anglicanism and Archbishop Laud, they took pains to make clear that in leaving for New England, they were not abandoning the church back home. They preferred to think of themselves as good examples, not deserters. Williams could not live with this compromise, and his zeal led him to other unorthodox stands. He declared that a saint must not even pray in the company of unregenerate people and thus challenged the structure of all New England churches. Scrupulous in every ethical matter, Williams even went so far as to question the legitimacy of taking land from the Indians. Perhaps the whole political edifice of the New World colonies rested on the sands of injustice. Before leaving England, Winthrop had attempted to bury such doubts. Roger Williams had a disconcerting knack for unearthing them.

On several occasions in the early 1630s Winthrop attempted to moderate his idealistic young friend. Experience had taught the governor that a man must live with and try to correct the evil he finds in the world and in himself. Removal to America in search of a clean slate was all right, but ultimately a man had to take a stand. The holier-than-thou attitude of Williams, Winthrop argued, might result in personal salvation, but the proper concern of the godly man should be world reformation. Williams in turn advised Winthrop to "abstract yourselfe with a holy violence from the Dung heape of this Earth." Winthrop balked. His style was to clean dung heaps, not flee them.

Williams first tried Boston, but found that settlement cool to his ideas. Next he moved to Plymouth, where the Pilgrims had at least fully separated from the Church of England. But in time, predictably, Williams found imperfections there too. He moved on to Salem, and here he made his strongest impression. Captivated by the charm and sincerity of the young zealot, the citizens of Salem chose him as their minister. Winthrop's eyebrows must have risen at the news. One dissenter was bad enough, but now Williams threatened to convert an entire congregation. In 1635, Winthrop and the General Court ordered Salem to dismiss Williams. The town exploded. In its eyes, this was not only an intrusion of the state into church affairs, but a violation of the principle of congregational autonomy. Salem prepared to elicit sympathy for its cause in other communities, and the fate of Massachusetts Bay hung in the balance. In fact, Williams explicitly called for those who agreed with him to withdraw from Massachusetts Bay into a purer, independent organization. The self-styled leaders of the Reformation were themselves to be reformed. For most Puritans, this was too much. Williams lost support even in Salem.

At this juncture the General Court chose to have it out with Roger Williams. No one, especially not Winthrop, wanted to punish this sweet-tempered visionary. If only he would retract his extreme statements and work for the colony. But Williams was unyielding: Massachusetts, he insisted, should work with *him*. This left the General Court with no choice. In October 1635 Roger Williams was banished and given six weeks to leave the colony.

The Williams decision pained John Winthrop. He knew at firsthand the passion that impelled the man. He too had been young and idealistic—sufficiently so to migrate 3000 miles to the New World. He too dreamed of a city upon a hill. In Winthrop's eyes, Williams was not a sinner; his error was an excess of virtue. So while Winthrop the magistrate sternly banished the young upstart, Winthrop the man privately suggested where he might go to find a sanctuary: Narragansett Bay, now Rhode Island. Winthrop, moreover, may have been instrumental in blocking a move on the part of his more conservative colleagues in the General Court to send Williams back to England. Part of Winthrop wanted to see Williams succeed—as long as he left Massachusetts. Besides, in the 1630s there was sufficient wilderness in North America for a variety of Zions. So it happened that in January of 1636 Roger Williams and four followers trudged through the snow toward Narragansett Bay in pursuit of perfection. They bought, rather than took, land from the Indians and founded a town, Providence, that attracted a steady flow of refugees from the northern colonies. Even

Winthrop, whom Williams still greatly admired, was invited to join. He refused, of course, but with a certain wistfulness.

Winthrop followed the history of Providence with considerable interest. For a time, Williams spiraled into ever narrower circles of perfectionism and intolerance; at one point he found himself conscience-bound to worship with no one except his wife. But time taught him that absolute purity was, after all, unattainable, and tolerance accompanied this realization. In the end, the toleration of Williams far surpassed that of the Puritans.

Even as Winthrop was breathing a sigh of relief over the departure of Roger Williams, another religious tempest loomed on the horizon. William and Anne Hutchinson arrived in Boston on September 18, 1634. The man was totally undistinguished, but his wife proved one of the most remarkable women in American history. Even Winthrop, who came to loathe her, conceded that she possessed "a ready wit and bold spirit." Anne Hutchinson also had an abundance of charm and, in common with Roger Williams, a natural talent for leadership.

The doctrine she advocated was known to the seventeenth century as *antinomianism*. According to the antinomians, salvation was entirely a product of God's mysterious grace. A man could not earn entrance into Heaven. This was orthodox Puritanism, but antinomians like Anne went further. The behavior of a man on earth, they alleged, bore no relation whatsoever to his ultimate fate at God's hands. Orthodox Puritans vigorously protested this conclusion. In the first place, it seemed to divest the individual of all moral responsibility. If conduct was meaningless even as a sign of salvation, then why worry about being good at all? The prospect horrified John Winthrop, who envisioned wholesale anarchy and immorality. Moreover, antinomianism undermined the whole structure of Puritan civil and church government, which was based on the idea of leadership by God's elect. Anne Hutchinson said in effect that the most flagrant sinner might be the very person that God in his mysterious wisdom would choose to save. And John Winthrop might not. Indeed, Anne implied, most of the ministers and magistrates in Massachusetts were only self-styled saints. At any rate, no one could know for sure.

Obviously, these ideas did not endear Anne to the Puritan leaders. Neither did her claim of the power to receive private revelations directly from God. But this persuasive woman attracted a growing following in the church at Boston. At first she merely interpreted the sermons of its minister and her hero, John Cotton, but gradually her weekly discussions acquired a bolder and more original quality. By the autumn of 1636 the majority of the members of the Boston church accepted her interpretations. Had Anne Hutchinson been a man, she would probably have been chosen minister at Boston, but instead her brother-in-law, John Wheelwright, was proposed for the position. Now Winthrop made his move. It seemed to him that the colony stood on the verge of a fatal split.

Throwing the full weight of his reputation against Wheelwright, Winthrop succeeded in blocking his election. The resulting bitterness divided Massachusetts Bay into hostile factions. In May 1637 Winthrop regained the governorship in a tense election. Patiently, even in the face of personal insult, he set about undermining the antinomians. A colony-wide convention of clergy met in August and supported his stand. Encouraged, Winthrop convinced the General Court that Wheelwright should be banished. But the root problem remained, and in November 1637 Anne Hutchinson was summoned to a showdown before the court. The confrontation was packed with drama. Repeatedly, the nimble-minded woman parried the charges of the magistrates or trapped them in their own logic. But as the relentless questioning continued, Anne lost her poise. In a hysterical flood of words, she defiantly told the court that God spoke to her directly and that He would "ruine you and your posterity, and this whole State." That was enough for Winthrop, and he called the court into private session. Its verdict: banishment. But the court at least postponed the sentence to allow Mrs. Hutchinson to deliver the baby she carried.

Winthrop's victory over Anne Hutchinson was hardly one of the mind. The real reason she could not remain in Massachusetts was the threat she posed to order, unity, and authority—and ultimately to covenant and mission. The threat disappeared when in March 1638 the Hutchinsons and a few disciples left for Rhode Island, which was fast becoming a refuge for Puritan castoffs. Winthrop rejoiced greatly in his triumph. He had brought the colony through its most serious spiritual crisis. But Anne Hutchinson's troubles continued. After a series of controversies in Rhode Island, she moved in 1642 to Dutch-controlled New York, where the following year she fell victim to an Indian massacre. Winthrop reacted to the news with the smugness so characteristic of the Puritan mind. The judgment of Massachusetts, he reasoned, must have been confirmed by the Lord.

A different kind of threat to John Winthrop's conception of a covenant community came from Robert Keayne. A genuinely self-made man, Keayne overcame his beginnings as a poor London butcher's helper to become one of the wealthiest men in New England. His trade was the importing business. The colonists were desperate for manufactured goods such as cloth, pots, glass, guns, and saws. Keayne had these items in stock, and he knew the laws of the marketplace. He charged high prices and made high profits. It was good business, but unfortunately for Keayne, Massachusetts Bay was not a business venture. It was not that Puritans opposed material success; rather, they insisted that all such worldly accomplishments must be subordinated to spiritual ones.

In regard to business, John Calvin and other leaders of the Reformation in Europe had carefully instructed the faithful with a doctrine later labeled the "Protestant ethic." Keayne, Winthrop, and their colleagues believed that worldly success was related to virtue, diligence, and the blessing of the Lord. They also knew that a man might strive to succeed in his calling provided he did so for the glory of God and not his personal gain. The Protestant ethic also required that a businessman observe fair "rules for trading," as Winthrop called them. The first was restraint: one must not press an economic advantage to the utmost, but should rest content with a "just" price and profit.

The Keayne case first came to John Winthrop's attention in 1639, just as the colony was relaxing from the tension of the Hutchinson controversy. Various reports reached the governor that the merchant was reaping too large a profit. Word had it that he went so far as to double his own cost in pricing an item. One Boston widow accused Keayne of seizing her prize pig when she could not meet his exorbitant charges. Winthrop responded by calling Keayne before the General Court and conducting a full inquiry into his business practices. At its conclusion, according to Winthrop, the merchant "did, with tears, acknowledge and bewail his covetous and corrupt heart." He was, nonetheless, severely reprimanded and fined.

In Winthrop's eyes, Robert Keayne was a frightening example of how the New World's economic opportunities could lure even a member of a holy experiment away from godliness. Keayne put personal considerations ahead of those of the commonwealth. He was so severely rebuked, one suspects, because Winthrop wanted to make him an example to those who might be tempted to imitate his enterprising practices. Still, the economic individualism Keayne represented was not easily put down. New England merchants proved increasingly unmanageable, and invariably took a stand against the Puritan oligarchy and the repressive authoritarianism it represented. All but the most devout had taken the side of Anne Hutchinson in 1637 because they thought her doctrine promised less centralized control of economic life. And in the late 1680s, when the structure of New England government underwent reorganization, the merchants even sided with English royal authority in preference to that of the American Puritans. By that time, of course, it was becoming clearer that for better or for worse the Robert Keaynes of the New World would prevail over the John Winthrops.

Different as they were, Winthrop's experiences with Roger Williams, Anne Hutchinson, and Robert Keayne taught a common lesson: individualism, "separatism" in seventeenth-century terms, posed the greatest threat to New England's covenanted purposes. Winthrop had anticipated this on board the *Arbella* when he underscored the need for keeping "knit together" in Massachusetts. But at that time he could not have anticipated the full force of the frontier against his ideal of unity and godliness. In a wilderness, he quickly discovered, there was no order except that which the newcomers established. And the structure was always tenuous. It was so easy for someone to spin off the approved track. Total freedom, unprecedented in the Old World, lay only a few miles away in the forest. Consequently, the American Puritans worked at maintaining standards with an urgency born of desperation.

One result of this mentality was the rigid supervision Winthrop and the General Court gave the process of westward expansion. Town "planting" involved a series of careful steps. First, the area to be settled was selected and the boundaries of fields laid out. Sites for homes and, most important, a church were designated, and some construction begun. Then an entire community moved into the wilderness.

In numbers, Puritans thought, lay the strength to resist barbarism. Nonetheless, the pioneers were carefully instructed "to carry and behave yourselves as good and sober men" and reminded that "you are in this voyage concerned not only for a worldly interest but . . . for the translating of Christ's ordinances and worship into that country." Here was an extension of the mission idea that applied originally to the planters of the seaboard towns. Puritan pioneering was a controlled, group effort. The Daniel Boone type of frontiersman, whom later generations of Americans celebrated, was definitely not heroic to John Winthrop and his contemporaries. On the contrary, such men appeared to have forgotten the holy mission, followed their own conception of liberty, and become, in Winthrop's words, "worse than brute beasts."

After 1640 when the Puritan Revolution in England caused Massachusetts to lose its appeal as the cutting edge of world Protestantism, orderly settlement of the frontier became even more important. The transformation of wilderness into civilization became the core of a concept of a new mission. And such a restatement was sorely needed. Winthrop himself felt the pangs of uncertainty. In the 1630s the most important English Puritans, including Oliver Cromwell, had at least contemplated moving to New England. But in the next decade the action shifted to England, and it was Winthrop who contemplated a move. That he remained in the New World was due in part to his ability to redefine the Massachusetts mission in terms of westward expansion. Replaced as a city upon a hill by events in England, Americans could still take satisfaction from expanding the boundaries of Christendom.

Frontiersmen were especially suspect, but the American Puritans also considered it essential to discipline individuals in the older towns. Winthrop's journal history of Massachusetts Bay is full of entries describing the General Court's efforts to stamp out sin. Its tool was a body of regulations on personal conduct known retrospectively as "blue laws." Perhaps the most interesting of them stipulated that every person in the colony had to be a member of a family. It was illegal to live alone. If a person lacked a spouse or relatives with whom he could live, he was obliged to join a family as a serving man or maid. The theory behind the law was that the family would provide an excellent means of social control. There were other laws regulating sexual prac-tices, the use of alcohol, and recreation on the Sabbath. It is, however, a mistake to regard Winthrop and his group as sour-faced enemies of fun. They simply felt that their situation and purpose made it impera-tive not to relax one's guard. Against the dark background of the wilderness, the flame of civilization seemed tiny and fragile. Unpoliced frivolity could lead to abandonment of standards, and individuals could not be entirely trusted with their own policing. The blue laws provided an incentive to preserve order in a potentially chaotic envi-ronment.

The struggle against barbarism also entailed reconstructing the full range of civilizing and humanizing institutions known in Europe. Simple survival, even prosperity, was not enough. A city upon a hill required more. As a 1643 tract explained, "after God had carried us safe to *New England*, and wee had builded houses, provided neces-sarries for our livelihood, rear'd convenient places for Gods worship, and setled the Civill Government: One of the next things we longed for, and looked after was to advance *Learning* and perpetuate it to Posterity." One of the first results of this determination was the found-ing of Harvard College in 1636. Retrospectively, it is astonishing that only six years after Winthrop and the bulk of New England's settlers came to the wilderness, they created a college. No better indication exists of the Puritan temperament. Virginia, in contrast, did not found a college (William and Mary) until 1693. Massachusetts' first press was operating in 1639; Virginia's, in 1729. The Puritans also prized elementary and secondary education. A grammar school began in Bos-ton in 1636, and eleven years later a Winthrop-led General Court required every town of one hundred families to establish a school. With such institutional support, lofty purposes and the discipline es-sential for their achievement could be maintained.

John Winthrop's beloved Margaret died in 1647, after three dec-ades of married life that in its joyous warmth belies much of the Puritan stereotype. A year after her death the lonely governor married for the fourth time and, at the age of sixty, fathered his sixteenth child. But the driving energy that had carried Winthrop so far was running low. A six-week bout with fever preceded his death on March 26, 1649. It was a timely end. The great age of Puritan mission was gradually fading. Puritanism, as Winthrop conceived it, was a failure in the New World. As a social and intellectual system, it never held the support of the majority of his contemporaries. Puritanism, after all, was an extreme form of Protestantism that few shared on either side of the Atlantic. Also esoteric and reactionary, in terms of seventeenth-century English culture, was the idea of a corporate state. Furthermore, second-generation New Englanders born in America could not know the strength of the vision that carried their fathers to the wilderness. Other-worldly ideals gave way before considerations of the present. John Winthrop, Jr., for instance, allowed both science and industry to rival religion as the dominant concern of his life. But the temperament if not the creed of his father proved difficult to dislodge from the American character. Commitment, discipline, and self-righteousness, along with a contradictory sense of guilt and inadequacy, all topped with an obsession for perfection, were a lasting legacy.

SELECTED READINGS

The Person

*DUNN, RICHARD S.: *Puritans and Yankees: The Winthrop Dynasty of New England, 1630–1717* (1962).

*MORGAN, EDMUND S.: *The Puritan Dilemma: The Story of John Winthrop* (1958). The most satisfying (and succinct) biographical study.

*MORISON, SAMUEL ELIOT: *Builders of the Bay Colony* (rev. ed., 1946). Contains chapters on Winthrop, on John Winthrop, Jr., and on other leaders of early Massachusetts.

RUTMAN, DARRETT: *Winthrop's Boston* (1965). An excellent life and times.

The Winthrop Papers (5 vols., 1929–1947, published by the Massachusetts Historical Society). The most authoritative edition of John Winthrop's journal, which records the main events of New England's early history.

The Period

*BAILYN, BERNARD: *The New England Merchants in the Seventeenth Century* (1955). Documents the tension between secular and spiritual success in early New England society.

BATTIS, EMORY: *Saints and Sectaries: Anne Hutchinson and the Antinomian Controversy in the Massachusetts Bay Colony* (1962). A Freudian interpretation of the most remarkable woman in seventeenth-century America.

*BOORSTIN, DANIEL: *The Americans: The Colonial Experience* (1964). An interpretive study of American history in the seventeenth century.

*McGIFFERT, MICHAEL (ed.): *Puritanism and the American Experience* (1969). An excellent recent collection of primary and secondary writings.

* Available in paperback.

*MILLER, PERRY: *Errand into the Wilderness* (1956). The essence of the ideas of this foremost scholar of Puritan thought in the New World. See especially Chapter One, "Errand into the Wilderness," and Chapter Three, "The Marrow of Puritan Divinity."

*NASH, RODERICK: *Wilderness and the American Mind* (1967). Attitudes toward the New World environment at the time of colonization.

*POWELL, SUMNER CHILTON: *Puritan Village: The Formation of a New England Town* (1963). A study of everyday Puritan life.

ROWSE, ALFRED L.: *The Expansion of Elizabethan England* (1955). The background of English expansion to New England.

* Available in paperback.

BENJAMIN FRANKLIN, L.L.D. F.R.S.

CHAPTER THREE

Benjamin Franklin

*Busying himself in the rear of his brother's printing shop, the
sixteen-year-old apprentice kept an ear cocked on the conversation
in the front of the store. Some literary gentlemen were excitedly
bending over a lengthy letter he had secretly slipped under the door
the previous night as a contribution to the* New England
Courant. *The letter purported to be the work of a Mrs. Silence
Dogood, but in the early eighteenth century every satirist used a
pseudonym. Guesses as to the identity of the author ranged over the*

*most talented writers in Boston, and with each name mentioned,
the apprentice's amusement and pride increased. Yet his
understanding of human nature kept him silent. On April 2, 1722,
"Mrs. Dogood's" first letter appeared in the* Courant. *The practical
apprentice was on his way to becoming Benjamin Franklin.*

In origin, station, and ambition, the Franklin family typified much
of American society at the beginning of the eighteenth century. Their
nationality was English; Franklins have been traced back to the 1550s
in the parish records of Northamptonshire. Their religion was Protestant, but stopped short of the purifying zeal of people such as John
Winthrop. The Franklins had accepted Anglicanism and remained in
England while the first waves of settlers began New England's history.
The decision to stay did not involve much strain of conscience, for the
Franklins as a rule were more concerned with being artisans and
farmers than theologians. But near the end of the long reign (1660–
1685) of Charles II, Josiah Franklin, Benjamin's father, experienced
religious conversion and began to attend illegal meetings of dissenters
from the Anglican Church. In 1683 he opted for America, and moved
his family to Boston in pursuit of the goals of religious freedom and
economic opportunity. He found a measure of both, establishing a
soap and candle shop on Boston's Milk Street and, in 1694, gaining
admission to the Old South Church.

Although Benjamin Franklin later wrote in the manner of the
English demographer Thomas Robert Malthus about the danger of a
population explosion, the circumstances of early eighteenth-century
America encouraged large families. There was, after all, a continent to
fill, and work for many hands. Josiah had seven children by his first
wife and ten by his second. Benjamin, born in 1706, was the youngest
son of the second union.

Franklin later recalled that his father intended him to be "the
tithe of his sons to the service of the church," a kind of human
offering. So while the other Franklin boys were apprenticed to various
tradesmen in Boston, Benjamin received instruction in reading at
home. "I do not remember," he declared in later life, "when I could
not read." At a time when literacy was a luxury, this ability was a

great advantage. In his eighth year Franklin attended the Boston Grammar School, an institution founded in the 1630s in informal association with Harvard College and concerned chiefly with the intricacies of Latin. The year at Boston Grammar proved profitable. Franklin notes, characteristically, how he had "risen gradually from the middle of the class . . . to be at the head." But lack of money obliged Josiah to end Benjamin's formal schooling almost before it had begun. At the age of ten, he entered the family business. A refined hatred of the mindless work with wax and tallow was the immediate result. At twelve, seeking an avenue of rebellion, Benjamin threatened to go to sea. Josiah reacted intelligently. His son's apprenticeship was transferred to the printing business of an older brother, James.

It was a brilliant solution. A self-styled "bookish lad," Benjamin thrived in an environment of words. As part of a campaign of self-education, he read voraciously—often, with the aid of his father's candles, far into the night. Franklin also tried his hand at writing. Obtaining a copy of Joseph Addison's and Richard Steele's satiric London periodical, *The Spectator*, he tried to imitate its pithy style. Taking notes on the essays, he reconstructed them in his own words and then compared his efforts with the originals. After some weeks of practice, Franklin could report that he "sometimes had the pleasure of fancying that in certain particulars of small import I had been lucky enough to improve the method or the language." The deceptively unassuming language hid pride and ambition of colossal proportions. Coupled with enormous energy and considerable talent, these traits led both to his success and, in certain quarters, to his unpopularity. The same might be said, parenthetically, about his nation.

Occupied by his apprenticeship, Franklin had to steal the time for self-improvement. The principal victims were his sleep and his religion. Although raised by strict Puritan principles, he found it tempting to cut corners. On Sundays, while his family worshipped at the Old South Church, Franklin read and wrote in the quiet of the closed printing shop. It was not that he denied or despised religion; simply that new gods and new goals arose to challenge the old ones. In Franklin's words, "I still thought [public worship] a duty, though I could not . . . afford the time to practice it."

As horrifying as this attitude would have been to John Winthrop's generation, Benjamin Franklin spoke for growing numbers of his contemporaries. The ninety years that separated Winthrop's Boston from Franklin's witnessed a gradual erosion of spiritual energies. The initial New England ideal of a closely knit, covenanted community proved difficult to maintain in the face of economic growth. The Puritan old guard, fearful of worldliness, tried to bridge the gap between the sacred and the secular with the Protestant ethic and the idea of a Christian calling. But glorifying God with worldly success did not provide a clear means for choosing *between* God and success. Franklin's experience comes immediately to mind. If one could get ahead by skipping church, why not? Was this kind of diligence in one's work evil?

The tendency to answer in the negative was apparent even in Winthrop's time, when New England merchants reacted with amazement and resentment to charges that they were making too much money. The business community also resented the way the church controlled the politics of Massachusetts Bay. At every opportunity, the merchants sided with those who favored greater toleration rather than with the defenders of rigid Puritan orthodoxy. In the 1630s, this had meant supporting Anne Hutchinson; forty years later, it meant defending Charles II's Lords of Trade and that body's colonial agent, Edward Randolph, against the Puritan Establishment. When the Massachusetts charter, which John Winthrop had defended so vigorously, was finally revoked in 1684, the reaction in the colony was mixed. Though they were unhappy to lose a measure of their independence to England, many merchants welcomed anything that promised relief from the strait jacket of Puritanism. In the long run, economic freedom proved more potent in Massachusetts Bay than either spiritual purity or political autonomy.

As shipowners and shopkeepers, both sides of Benjamin Franklin's family experienced the tension between the sacred and the secular. Benjamin's maternal grandfather, Peter Folger, even wrote caustic verses attacking the magistrates of Massachusetts for their intolerance. The Franklins and Folgers, then, were not unhappy at the prospect of colonial reorganization in the late 1680s. The Dominion of New England, as the revised plan came to be called, placed all colonies north of New Jersey under a royal governor. Representative assemblies were eliminated, but the prospect of escaping the Puritan oligarchy sweetened even this pill enough for merchant tastes. They could not, however, stomach Sir Edmund Andros, the Dominion's tactless governor. Miraculously, he managed to alienate all factions. In 1688 Bostonians responded to news of the revolution in England against James II by imprisoning Edmund Andros. Three years later, Massachusetts Bay received a new charter that amounted to a compromise between the Puritan system of government and the Dominion. For people like the Franklins, the new arrangement was a signal improvement; property rather than godliness became the criterion for suffrage.

With the yoke of Puritanism partially lifted, Franklin's Boston surged ahead in pursuit of the main chance. By 1720 the population numbered more than 10,000 persons, and in terms of shipping the city was one of the busiest ports in the British Empire. Secular concerns seemed to carry all before them, but Puritanism had been too strong for too long to vanish overnight. James Franklin and his apprentice were made aware of this late in the spring of 1722, when the *New England Courant* drew the fire of the conservative Boston clergy and the General Court. The leading spokesman of Puritan orthodoxy, Cotton Mather, cited the appearance of disrespectful articles, some of the most subversive of which appeared under the name of Mrs. Silence Dogood. For example, the disguised Benjamin Franklin had written: "It has been for some time a question with me whether a commonwealth suffers more by hypocritical pretenders to religion or by the openly profane. But some late thoughts of this nature have inclined me to think that the hypocrite is the more dangerous person of the two, especially if he sustains a post in the government."

Of course, the *Courant* took pains to accompany such statements with a defense of freedom of thought and speech. Nevertheless, James Franklin was arrested and imprisoned after his June 11 issue appeared on the streets. For a month he languished in jail while Benjamin carried on the paper. Unrepentant after his release, James continued his jibes at the Establishment. Finally, in January 1723 an order from the General Court prohibited him from printing in the city of Boston. Not so easily defeated, the Franklins quickly arranged for Benjamin to assume ownership of the business. The subterfuge saved the *Courant* but fed the apprentice's already burgeoning ego to such an extent that coexistence with James was no longer possible. After repeated quarrels and some blows, Benjamin determined to find another master. The printers guild, however, closed ranks; when Benjamin applied for work, no Boston printer needed help.

At this low ebb in Franklin's life, the repulsive soap and candle business loomed ominously in the future. But Benjamin was nothing if not self-confident. A plan took shape in his mind. He would sell some of his precious books to raise a little money and, with nothing more than a rumor of a printing job in New York as encouragement, leave his native city for the first time. In the fall of 1723 he slipped quietly out of Boston to take on the world. Three days on a fast sloop brought him to New York. The city and colony had been in British hands since the ouster of the Dutch in 1664, but the pattern of large semifeudal landholding that persisted discouraged settlers. New York supported only a few printers, and Franklin found no openings. Undaunted, he pushed on to Philadelphia.

As a foil to his later achievements, Franklin's *Autobiography* takes pains to detail the lowly circumstances of his arrival in the Pennsylvania capital in October 1723. Dirty, disheveled, and dog-tired, the runaway apprentice, all of seventeen years old, staggered up Market Street. With the last of his money he bought three large rolls. Franklin's appearance as he wandered aimlessly through the streets munching his rolls amused an attractive girl standing at the doorway of her father's house. Later she would become Mrs. Franklin, but for the moment he was too tired to care. As he went along, a crowd appeared in the streets. Franklin followed it to the large Quaker meeting house. The service began with a period of quiet meditation that was too great a temptation for the exhausted apprentice. Sprawling out on an empty bench, he fell sound asleep.

The Philadelphia into which Franklin straggled so inauspiciously was the leading city of a colony that had made a comparatively late entry into North America. Yet Pennsylvania was already among its most vigorous settlements. The keys to success in this case were a favorable location and the genius of William Penn. The son of an admiral in the British Navy and a member of a radical Protestant sect called the Quakers, Penn wanted to found a colony based on the principles of religious freedom and popular sovereignty. In 1681 Charles II granted him a charter to a huge tract of exceptionally fertile land west of the Delaware River. It came to be known as "Penn's woods," or "Pennsylvania." The colony's liberal and tolerant policies, so markedly different from those of early Massachusetts, attracted large numbers of immigrants. Speaking a dozen languages and worshipping in different ways, they spread into the hinterland and used some of the richest soil on the continent to raise wheat, corn, hemp, and flax, as well as livestock. Others were city-oriented people who built a vigorous tradition of trade and craftsmanship in Philadelphia.

Two decades before Franklin arrived, Penn had taken the unusual step of responding to criticism by permitting his colonists to draft their own plan of government. They responded, as expected, with a proposal that elevated the representative assembly at the expense of the power of the governor and proprietor. Nonetheless, Penn approved this plan of government in 1701, and his colony prospered. Penn's administrative wisdom extended even to land policy: He stipulated that for every 5 acres of forest cleared, 1 acre be left with trees. In such concern for conservation, Penn was at least two centuries ahead of his contemporaries.

In 1723, then, Benjamin Franklin entered a permissive, rapidly expanding, highly mobile, and commercially oriented society that perfectly suited his ambitions and abilities. He lost no time in capitalizing on his good fortune. Upon awakening from his nap in the Quaker meeting house, Franklin proceeded to the printing shop of Samuel Keimer and immediately found employment. Quick, hard-working, and affable, Franklin made friends easily and moved ahead at a phenomenal pace. He became the New World's typical rags-to-riches success story, the creator of a legend that has shaped the aspirations of Americans ever since.

Arriving literally in rags at the age of seventeen, Franklin at twenty-four owned his own printing business and newspaper. At twenty-seven his name was known throughout the colonies as the creator of Poor Richard, of almanac fame. Three years later Franklin obtained the clerkship of the Pennsylvania Assembly, a post that proved a stepping stone to elected membership. By the age of forty-two he had accumulated sufficient wealth to reach his goal of the "free and easy life." Turning the printing business over to a manager, Franklin began new careers as scientist, inventor, statesman, and diplomat.

Benjamin Franklin succeeded not only because he lived in a favorable time and place, but also because of his character and guiding principles. As early as 1726, three years after his arrival in Philadelphia, Franklin referred in his journal to the necessity of fixing "a regular design in life . . . that, henceforth, I may live in all respects like a rational creature." In language as well as concept such a statement places Franklin squarely in the Enlightenment. This movement in the history of ideas took recognizable shape in the 1690s with the work of Isaac Newton in the physical sciences and John Locke in the social sciences. Enlightenment thought rested on the assumption that all phenomena operated according to permanent designs or laws. Rational man could discern these regularities and understand the cause and effect relationships that followed from them. According to the Enlightenment credo, everything had an explanation. All problems could be solved. Reason and the scientific method were the keys to knowledge.

Benjamin Franklin made a science of the conduct of his life. He began by fixing an ultimate goal—happiness. For Franklin, the chief components of the happy life were health, wealth, wisdom, and usefulness. He also included the principle of utility in his method for achieving the desired end. If a belief or course of action proved useful in securing happiness, it was good in Franklin's eyes; if not, it was bad. In this system of ethics there were no other criteria. Vice and virtue, Franklin believed, had little meaning if divorced from the particular time, place, circumstance, and desired result. This was the essence of relativism. Franklin made his judgments according to how something worked, and in this emphasis on results, he anticipated the philosophy of pragmatism. More exactly, the growing American tendency that Franklin personified—to judge by performance—was later given formal expression by the pragmatic philosophers. Franklin even extended this attitude toward individuals: "do not inquire concerning a Stranger," Franklin wrote in his *Autobiography*, "what *is* he? but, what can he *do?*" Imperfectly executed as this dictate was and is, it nonetheless constitutes one of America's most praiseworthy ideals.

Franklin's *Autobiography* records that about 1728 he conceived the "bold and arduous project of arriving at moral perfection." The brash confidence of the Enlightenment permeated the plan. Franklin really wished "to live without committing any fault at any time." To carry out the idea, he systematized his beliefs into thirteen "virtues": temperance, silence, order, resolution, frugality, industry, sincerity,

68

justice, moderation, cleanliness, tranquillity, chastity, and humility. These were essential, he believed, for attaining happiness, and for the purpose of measuring his progress in this direction he devised a weekly chart on which he recorded his performance. He devoted a week to each of the thirteen virtues and repeated the course four times a year. The whole undertaking simply extended the campaign for self-improvement Franklin had launched as a teenager in the Boston printing shop.

At first glance, it appears that no two Americans could be more dissimilar than John Winthrop and Benjamin Franklin. The printer's goals and conduct seem to represent the final collapse of the Puritan life style. To some extent, of course, this is true. Success in this world, not salvation in the next, anchored Franklin's philosophy of life. And in sharp contrast to the Puritans, he believed that a man could improve himself, even approach perfection, by his own efforts. For Franklin, God's saving grace was the relic of an unenlightened age. Predestination made no sense to a self-made man. Franklin also rejected the idea of divinely inspired Scripture as part of his rejection of all systems of fixed moral precepts. "Revelation," he declared, "had . . . no weight with me as such." So much for the Puritans' sacred Bible.

A closer examination of Franklin's philosophy, however, reveals some close parallels to Puritanism. Many of the virtues Franklin adopted on the basis of utility proved to be precisely those prescribed by Revelation and stated in Scripture. Franklin saw that the Puritan virtues had utilitarian value, that they were often the means to ends he desired. The *Autobiography* presents Franklin's reasoning succinctly: "vicious actions are not hurtful because they are forbidden, but forbidden because they are hurtful, the nature of man alone considered [and] . . . it was therefore in everyone's interest to be virtuous who wished to be happy even in this world." Starting from a secular perspective, Franklin arrived at a position much like that reached by Winthrop. Their missions differed, but they pursued them with common means and a common zeal.

Another trait that links Franklin to the Puritans and partially redeems him from a degree of self-esteem that borders on the insufferable is his willingness in the long run to admit failure. After years of effort, Franklin abandoned his campaign for moral perfection. Charac-

As a printer as well as a self-made man, Franklin must have been pleased with this handsome lithograph. In elevating money-making to the status of an art, it substituted a whole new set of values for those of Winthrop's generation. From such publications stem the popular image of Franklin as a man obsessed with material concerns and, too, the American reputation for materialism.

In the autobiography he wrote as an old man, Franklin included this breakdown of his typical day. The legend of Franklin as a person of superhuman discipline and organization has arisen from such evidence. Note this very secular man's way of referring to God and also the moralism of his morning and evening questions. Although worlds apart in the matter of ends or goals, Franklin and John Winthrop had much in common in regard to means.

From Massachusetts to the Carolinas the American colonists rebelled against the Stamp Act of 1765 as a classic instance of taxation without representation. In this scene sheaves of stamps, or possibly documents bearing them, are being burned on the cobblestones of a town square. The sticks and axes and pitchforks in the background suggest that the mob was bent on more violent expression of its displeasure, probably directed against the person and property of the local stamp agent.

teristically, he made his point with an anecdote: A man with a rusty ax, Franklin began, desired to have the whole head as bright as the cutting edge. He took it to a blacksmith who agreed to polish the steel, provided the owner turned the grindstone. The process went on and on, but specks of rust persisted. At last the owner became exhausted and declared that he would take the ax in an unfinished condition. " 'No,' says the smith, 'turn on, turn on; we shall have it bright by and by; as yet 'tis only speckled.' 'Yes,' says the man, *but I think I like a speckled ax best.*' " So with Franklin, who gave up his idea of perfection and concluded he really liked himself best with a few bad habits. Rationalizing his decision on the familiar grounds of usefulness, Franklin pointed out that "a perfect character might be attended with the inconvenience of being envied and hated; and that a benevolent man should allow a few faults in himself, to keep his friends in countenance." While hardly an admission of original sin, Franklin's statement showed he had nonetheless come to terms with human frailty just as had John Winthrop.

As for his formal religion, Franklin began to question many of the assumptions of traditional Christianity while still a Boston apprentice. He turned initially to deism, whose followers believed that the natural world was God's creation and that its design and function was all the evidence one needed of God's wisdom and power. Indeed, deists rejected all forms of revelation, along with creeds, mysteries, myths, and rituals, as unreasonable and unscientific. The organized church, as the embodiment of arbitrary authority, also suffered eclipse. Deists preferred their truth to be self-evident. They acknowledged a God, but He was a Creator or First Cause—a master mechanic who set the universe in motion and then withdrew to watch it work according to natural laws. Deism, in sum, was a scientific religion for rational men. It suited a young Benjamin Franklin perfectly.

With maturity, however, Franklin's dissatisfaction with deism increased. Observing the conduct of professed deists, he noticed a tendency to make virtue and vice "empty distinctions." The absence of an immediate God dispensing reward and punishment encouraged moral anarchy. "I began to suspect," Franklin commented, "that this doctrine, tho' it might be true, was not very useful." Again considerations of utility shaped Franklin's opinions.

What, then, was a useful religion in Franklin's terms? After considerable reflection, he decided it had to be based on the assumption that a deity or, as Franklin put it, "SOMETHING" existed, that it governed the world, and that "all crime will be punished and virtue rewarded either here or hereafter." The last point ensured socially acceptable behavior. Perhaps some individuals could sustain their morality without a God, but Franklin believed most people needed Him. "If men are so wicked *with religion*," he observed, "what would they be if *without it*?" On another occasion, Franklin wrote to the atheist Thomas Paine that "talking against religion is unchaining the tiger. . . . the beast let loose may worry his liberator." Whether real or not, God was useful. Franklin felt the same way about Jesus. Near the end of his life he remarked that regardless of the truth, he saw no harm in believing Christ to be the Son of God, since it had the "good Consequence . . . of making His Doctrines more respected and better observed." As an afterthought, he added that at the age of eighty-four he was not overly concerned about Jesus and life after death, for "I expect soon an Opportunity of knowing the Truth with less Trouble." The comment struck to the core of Franklin's practical attitude toward religion.

As might be expected, Franklin had little interest in the colony-wide religious upsurge of the 1730s and 1740s known as the Great Awakening. The emotionalism of the revivals offended Franklin's reason, and the emphasis revivalists like Jonathan Edwards placed on human helplessness ran counter to his creed of self-help. Franklin did, however, admire and become lifelong friends with the Reverend George Whitefield. Yet what attracted him was not Whitefield's theology, but his prowess as a public speaker. As for doctrine, Franklin much preferred the position of the liberal opponents of the Awakening, who held that God was forgiving and predestination absurd.

Franklin adroitly shaped his faith to support his style of life. In 1728 he resolved "to be virtuous that I may be happy, that I may please Him, who is delighted to see me happy." The ultimate purpose of religion thus became not the worship of God or even the salvation of man, but man's well-being on earth. Like a warm coat, religion was useful in the here and now. Unwilling to renounce faith, Franklin tailored it to suit his purposes. He stands as a transitional figure between men for whom religion was an obsession and those for whom it was a bore.

During his Philadelphia years, which lasted into the 1750s, Franklin's philosophy was compressed into his most famous publication: *Poor Richard's Almanac.* First published in 1733, the annual quickly developed a colony-wide and even an international reputation. In a real sense, Franklin's almanacs were the first distinctively American literary productions and certainly the best-known American books of their time. "As Poor Richard says" became a preface for maxims throughout the Western world.

To call Richard Saunders "poor" as Franklin did was to camouflage the fact that from the perspective of success he actually dispensed advice on how to get rich. In 1757 Franklin collected the best of *Poor Richard* under the title "The Way to Wealth." This how-to-do-it essay became a bible for the ambitious. It preached the gospel of getting ahead. "The sleeping Fox catches no Poultry," Franklin admonishes, adding "there will be sleeping enough in the Grave." Much of *Poor Richard* is based on the idea that "there are no Gains without Pains." But the almanacs also imply that unless the effort is guided by intelligence, it will come to nothing. Franklin therefore urges his readers to live simply and frugally: "a fat Kitchen makes a lean will." He also provides advice on the management of money, marriage, and friendship to the end that one's pains may indeed produce gains.

On the basis of the almanacs, it is easy to brand Benjamin Franklin hopelessly materialistic. After all, "nothing but money is sweeter than honey," as Poor Richard says. Yet there is more to Franklin than mere acquisitiveness. He is not entirely the "snuff-coloured little trap" that his critics (in this case, D. H. Lawrence in 1923) have alleged. Money for Franklin was important—but as a means, a tool for other tasks. Reflecting the old Protestant ethic, and revealing in the process another tie with Puritanism, Franklin believed that by being successful and socially useful a man pleased his Maker.

In this sense the most immediate influence on Franklin's thought was the Reverend Cotton Mather. A pillar of the Puritan Establishment in the late seventeenth and early eighteenth centuries, Mather in 1710 published a tract entitled *Essays to Do Good.* It elaborated upon the idea that the Christian "may glorify God by doing of *Good* for *others,* and of *Good* for *himself.*" Franklin encountered Mather's work as a Boston apprentice and took it to heart. His earliest religious creed declares that "the most acceptable service of God was doing good to man." Years later Franklin again acknowledged his intellectual debt to Mather in a letter to Mather's son in which he said that the *Essays to Do Good* "gave me such a turn of thinking, as to have an influence on my conduct through life; for I have always set a greater value on the character of a *doer of good,* than on any other kind of reputation; and if I have been . . . a useful citizen, the public owes the advantage of it to that book." As he would judge all things by their usefulness, so Franklin would have himself judged. As preparation, he launched a multifaceted campaign of public service. It became his major altruistic outlet and a primary ingredient in his growing reputation.

Franklin began his career as a "doer of good" in 1727 when he organized a "club for mutual improvement" called the Junto among Philadelphia's younger artisans and intellectuals. This harbinger of the Junior Chamber of Commerce had as one of its "standing queries," which Franklin wrote, the problem: "do you think of any thing at present, in which the Junto may be serviceable to *mankind*?" The initial project the Junto undertook was Franklin's plan for a circulating subscription library, the first of its kind in American history.

Thereafter, the club became a seedbed for most of Franklin's community improvement efforts. They included a fire-fighting organization, a night watch, and a street-lighting company. Not the least of his contributions was the spearheading of a movement to pave Philadelphia's dusty streets. In 1749 Franklin took the lead in drafting plans for the Pennsylvania Academy, which was opened two years later. Its course of study reflected some of Franklin's practicality and utilitarianism, although less than he would have preferred. In time, the academy evolved into the University of Pennsylvania. A city hospital and improved medical treatment occupied Franklin's abundant energy in the early 1750s. In every case, he contributed his money and his talent for raising money along with his ideas. "Avarice and happiness never saw each other," said Poor Richard, and Franklin did not forget his own maxim. After all, the three-part goal for which one went "early to bed and early to rise"—health, wealth, and wisdom—was only one-third material. And the almanacs just pointed the way to wealth; once arrived, Franklin expected, people should know how to apply their means to worthwhile ends.

The money-making talent that freed Franklin to serve his society also gave him the leisure to pursue scientific investigations. American interest in science, or "natural philosophy" as it was more commonly called, received its initial impetus from the newness of the New World. In an unknown land, mere observation was discovery. Botany and zoology, as a consequence, became the mainstays of early American science. Astronomy also ranked high, since the different perspective of North American observers resulted in data of great comparative interest to their English and Continental counterparts. The Puritans proved eager and talented natural philosophers. John Winthrop, Jr., who corresponded frequently with Sir Isaac Newton himself, became a charter member of his world's leading scientific organization, the Royal Society, in 1663.

Puritans like the younger Winthrop had no difficulty squaring their science with their religion. Nature was God's handiwork; its processes showed the effect of His guidance. Consequently, to study natural phenomena was to observe the wisdom, power, and glory of God. Science for the Puritan mind was an act of worship. But so, in theory, was making money, and just as the Protestant ethic gave way to outright materialism, the reconciliation of naturalism and supernaturalism proved equally temporary. Earthquakes and comets, for example, were either sent as portents by an angry God or solely the products of natural processes. If investigation supported the latter explanation, why involve God at all? In the seventeenth and eighteenth centuries most Americans did not pursue such questions, but rested content with a reconciliation of religion and science.

Benjamin Franklin's career as a scientist began with youthful curiosity. He wanted to know not only how things worked, but how such knowledge could be put to use. Young Franklin, for example, was an excellent swimmer, but unlike the other boys who used the ponds around Boston, he studied the mechanics of propulsion in water. As a result of these observations, Franklin constructed "oval palettes" for his palms and "a kind of sandals" for his feet—the ancestors of swim fins. He also discovered that a flying kite would draw its holder across a body of water "in a very agreeable manner."

In 1724 Franklin made an economically disappointing trip to London. From the standpoint of his interest in science, however, the experience proved immensely stimulating. London in the 1720s rode the crest of the Enlightenment. Newton was the most celebrated figure of an age in which every thinking man knew and respected the scientific method. Franklin's hopes for meeting Newton personally did not materialize, but he did make contact with other members of the Royal Society. When he returned to Philadelphia in 1726, he brought with him the habits of careful observation and logical analysis. He began in fact to apply them, as his journal shows, on the return voyage.

Back in Philadelphia, Franklin used the Junto as a forum for discussing scientific problems ranging from the nature of sound to the causes of earthquakes. Many of his experiments had practical consequences. His investigations of the circulation of air and the transference of heat led to his invention of the Franklin or Pennsylvania stove in the winter of 1739–1740. By 1743 Franklin thought it time that American scientists establish their identity and a means of communication. So he drafted "A Proposal for Promoting Useful Knowledge among the British Plantations in America." Franklin prefaced the document with the accurate observation that "the first drudgery of settling new colonies, which confines the attention of people to mere necessaries, is now pretty well over." It was also apparent that "there are many in every province in circumstances that set them at ease, and afford leisure to cultivate the finer arts and improve the common stock of knowledge."

The American Philosophical Society, which emerged in 1744 from Franklin's "Proposal," was designed to bring these unoccupied, curious, and intelligent minds together through the medium of the mails. Franklin's utilitarianism was evident in the suggested list of subjects for discussion and correspondence. As deserving of particular attention, he mentioned the production of ciders and wines, assaying of ores, draining of meadows, and clearing of land. More abstract questions had their place too, particularly in the thought of such members as the botanist John Bartram and the mathematician Thomas Godfrey, but for the most part the group directed itself to practical questions and applied science—"useful knowledge," in Franklin's terms.

In one notable instance, however, Franklin pursued the truth first; practical applications came later as a byproduct. His fascination with electricity began in 1743, when he witnessed some demonstrations by a touring Scottish lecturer. The man could perform remarkable feats with his primitive generator, but he had no idea how it worked. Franklin determined to find out. He bought the Scot's appa-

77

ratus and devoted his spare time to investigation. After his retirement from the printing business in 1748, he became a full-time scientist. The next four years were filled with electrical experiments. The field was new, and Franklin quickly moved beyond existing knowledge. Rejecting the prevailing notion of two kinds of electricity, he proposed the idea of a single fluid with two forms, and he coined the words *positive* and *negative* to describe them. To illustrate his points, he performed the first analysis of the principle of the Leyden jar, an electrical generator and condenser.

Communicated to the European scientific community in 1751 by Peter Collinson of the Royal Society, Franklin's discoveries attracted immediate and widespread acclaim. Indeed, the slender volume Collinson had published for Franklin was the most widely hailed American book of the eighteenth century—next to *Poor Richard's Almanac*. Yet on both the intellectual and the popular level, Franklin's reputation as a scientist rested chiefly on his investigation of lightning. As his knowledge of electrical phenomena grew, Franklin began to suspect that lightning was actually electricity. In 1751 he suggested a way of testing the hypothesis by erecting an iron rod on the steeple of a high building. A team of French investigators performed the "Philadelphia experiment" successfully in May 1752. Franklin did not know this, however, when on a sultry evening in June he went into the fields near Philadelphia with his famous kite and key. As a thunderhead approached, Franklin flew the kite, but the first clouds passed overhead with no apparent effect. The second did the job. An electrical charge surged down the string and leaped from the key into Franklin's hand. After rain had wet the string, electricity flowed abundantly into the collecting device. Franklin succeeded on two counts: The hypothesis was confirmed, and the investigator escaped the electrocution that later killed a Swedish scientist engaged in an identical experiment.

Only after several years of work with the theory of electricity did Franklin draw the practical application in the form of the lightning rod. Yet so widely known is this invention that it is commonly believed Franklin was a tinkerer who experimented in order to produce lightning rods—for sale, of course. Nothing could be more unjust. Franklin was a "pure" scientist and a good one; he was also a practical man. When the time came, he made the transition from theory to practice, and as in the case of his almanacs, his lightning rods soon appeared in almost every home. Franklin's own version was equipped with bells that clanged when electrically charged, much to the distress of his wife.

The honors Franklin gleaned from his scientific avocation were legion. Harvard, which he had spurned as a critical apprentice, awarded him an honorary degree, as did Yale and the College of William and Mary. Oxford and St. Andrews topped these with advanced degrees, and Franklin quickly added "Doctor" to his name. The Royal Society conferred a medal and a membership. Yet probably his most cherished honor was his contemporary reputation as "the Newton of electricity." But success did not satiate Benjamin Franklin. In later years, when time permitted, he investigated theoretical problems in astronomy, geology, and botany. He also kept the practical side of his nature alive; he invented a glass harmonica, bifocal eyeglasses, and a "long arm" for grasping books on high shelves.

Franklin's decade of concentration on science, 1743 to 1753, brought many satisfactions, not the least of which was a buoyant feeling of contributing to human progress. Writing to fellow scientist Joseph Priestly, he regretted that he had been born so soon. "It is impossible to imagine," Franklin continued, "the height to which may be carried, in a thousand years, the power of man over matter." Musing on the theme, he forecast the airplane: "we may perhaps learn to deprive large masses of their gravity, and give them absolute levity, for the sake of easy transport." And there were other wonders: "agriculture may diminish its labour and double its produce; all disease may . . . be prevented and cured . . . and our lives lengthened at pleasure even beyond the antediluvian standard."

The optimism of the Enlightenment bubbles over in such statements. But Franklin was too wise in the ways of men to pretend that science held all the answers. "O that moral science were in a fair way of improvement," he continued to Priestly, "that men would cease to be wolves to one another, and that human beings would at length learn what they now improperly call humanity." With the hope, we may believe, of lessening the wolfish tendency in men and in nations, Franklin turned the energies of his later years more and more to public affairs. Undoubtedly he also foresaw in statesmanship new levels of success for Benjamin Franklin.

In 1751 the voters of Philadelphia elected the best-known mem-

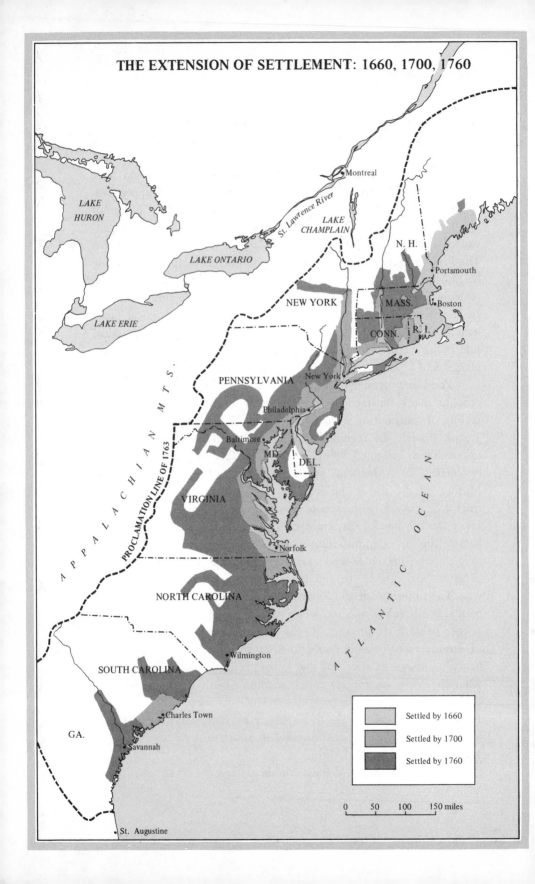

THE EXTENSION OF SETTLEMENT: 1660, 1700, 1760

LAKE HURON

LAKE ONTARIO

LAKE ERIE

St. Lawrence River

Montreal

LAKE CHAMPLAIN

N. H.

Portsmouth

NEW YORK

MASS.

Boston

CONN.

R. I.

APPALACHIAN MTS.

PENNSYLVANIA

New York

PROCLAMATION LINE OF 1763

Philadelphia

Baltimore

MD.

DEL.

VIRGINIA

Norfolk

NORTH CAROLINA

Wilmington

SOUTH CAROLINA

Charles Town

GA.

Savannah

St. Augustine

ATLANTIC OCEAN

Settled by 1660

Settled by 1700

Settled by 1760

0   50   100   150 miles

ber of their community to the Pennsylvania Assembly. For Franklin, it marked a major triumph. At a time when gentlemen-aristocrats dominated politics, he had climbed the ladder from an apprenticeship. More exactly, Franklin became a one-generation aristocrat, proving in the process the exceptional fluidity of the American social structure. His first important assignment in government came in 1754, when the Assembly chose him to be its representative at the Albany Congress. The background of this strange gathering in the wilds of northern New York lay in the tangled world of international relations 3000 miles away. Ever since the 1690s, France and England had been engaged in a series of wars and hostilities. At stake was the so-called European balance of power. Neither nation wanted the other to gain dominance. North America figured only marginally in the conflict as far as Europeans were concerned, but for the American colonists, the struggle became vital because both sides endeavored to enlist the assistance of the Indians. For communities on the outskirts of civilization, this meant the prospect of Indians swooping out of the forest for a massacre. Indians, indeed, held the key to power on the North American frontier during the period of European rivalry.

The immediate roots of the Albany Congress lay in France's determination to enhance her position with respect to England after the unsatisfactory Peace of Aix-la-Chapelle ended the War of the Austrian Succession. North America seemed a promising starting place for France in her renewed quest for power. With the aid of Indian allies, perhaps England could even be forced out of the New World entirely. In the early 1750s, therefore, the French began pushing south from their Canadian stronghold into western New York and along the Appalachian Mountains, building forts and making Indian friends. The prospect of a French-Indian alliance on their unprotected western flank terrorized the English colonists. In a powder-keg atmosphere of rumor and fear, England called the Albany Congress in 1754 to counter the threat. Iroquois chiefs from the Six-Nation Confederacy attended, along with representatives from most of the colonies. The point was to prevent collaboration between the Indians and the French.

For Benjamin Franklin, the Albany Congress provided an opportunity to broach a plan for intercolonial organization. As early as 1751 he had suggested such a union to deal with questions of defense. His appointment two years later to the office of joint deputy post-master-general of North America increased his awareness of the need for and possibility of mutual cooperation. So did his involvement in intercolonial scientific enterprises. As he rode to Albany in June of 1754, then, Franklin's mind dwelled on the problem of unification. By the time he reached his destination, he had an ambitious idea. His Albany Plan of Union called for the establishment of an intercolonial council with authority over defense, western expansion, and Indian relations. Representing the assemblies of the various colonies and headed by the king's representative, the council would maintain an army and navy, build frontier fortifications, execute Indian treaties, and buy western lands. Funds for these purposes would come from a tax levied by the colonists' representatives. Anticipating later developments in English-American relations, Franklin summarily rejected the idea of taxation without representation as inconsistent with the tradition of English liberty.

The gravity of the crisis in 1754 prompted the Albany delegates to adopt Franklin's plan. But when they carried it back to their respective assemblies, the reception was cool. An American national consciousness was in its infancy. The various colonies still eyed each other suspiciously, particularly with respect to western land claims. In reality, of course, the issue of intercolonial union was academic. Even had the assemblies cooperated, England would certainly have vetoed the proposed organization. It held forth the prospect of too much colonial power and, although few admitted it at the time, of independence. Franklin took the rebuff philosophically. The assemblies, he pointed out, "all thought there was too much *prerogative* in it, and in England it was judged to have too much of the *democratic.*"

In Pennsylvania the Indian problem of the 1750s sharpened the chronic tension between governor and assembly. William Penn's successors as proprietor lacked his facility for dealing with popular demands. In a squabble over the tax exemption of the proprietor's huge landholdings, the governor refused to pass bills funding frontier defense. With the French and Indians at the colony's western doorstep, this was a serious matter. Unable to resolve the differences in America, the Pennsylvania Assembly instructed Benjamin Franklin to go to England and plead its case directly with Parliament.

When Franklin sailed for England in 1757 to present the Pennsylvania Assembly's grievance against its governor, he became involved in long-standing problems in the English-colonial relationship. The difficulties centered on the gap between the theory and the practice of colonialism. Theoretically, colonies were supposed to be the obedient and grateful servants of their mother country. The idea received economic expression in the theory of mercantilism, according to which colonies were supposed to assist in the maintenance of the favorable balance of trade—a surplus of income over expenses—on which national power was thought to depend. The colonies would supply raw materials to the mother country and consume its manufactured goods. They would neither compete with the industries of the home country nor turn to other nations for supplies and markets. The outposts were to be subservient satellites.

Franklin was well aware of the history of mercantilism in British North America. As early as the 1620s Parliament passed laws limiting Virginia's lucrative tobacco trade to England and stipulating that it be carried only on English ships. Beginning with the passage of the first laws in 1651, a body of legislation known collectively as the Navigation Acts spelled out the economic basis of the colonial relationship. Product after product was "enumerated"—its sale or purchase restricted. To some extent this policy proved advantageous to the American settlements. They enjoyed, after all, a guaranteed market and membership in the Western world's foremost commercial empire. Yet in the minds of the colonists it was security of the feudal variety—purchased at the expense of freedom—and they openly flaunted the economic regulations.

England occasionally, as in the Dominion scheme for New England, attempted to strengthen enforcement, but bribes and smuggling permitted the colonists to do much as they pleased. In practice, 3000 miles from home, mercantilism failed. Virginia, for example, sent its tobacco where it could get the highest price, frequently the Netherlands. And the New England merchants who were engaged in a triangular trade involving rum, slaves, and West Indian molasses customarily obtained the latter from the French West Indies in preference to the British islands. The 1733 Molasses Act, designed to curtail this practice, failed completely. Even with the expense of bribing customs agents added to its cost, French molasses was still cheaper than British. England fumed but, before 1761, took little positive action. For the most part, the colonies went their own way, and when

Franklin arrived in England in 1757 he became the target for British indignation at the uncooperative colonial members of the empire.

A gap between theory and practice also existed in the matter of Franklin's immediate area of concern as Pennsylvania's agent: government. Theoretically a colony existed under a governor who either represented Parliament and the Crown directly (the royal governor) or, in the case of chartered or proprietary colonies, ruled at Parliament's pleasure. The governor was in control. He might appoint a few local leaders to a council, and most charters provided for an assembly representing the propertied citizens. Still, in theory, these groups had only advisory roles. They were regarded by the British as liberal concessions. Authority resided in England.

Franklin had observed colonial politics long enough to know that this theoretical political structure in reality quickly dissolved into more democratic forms. The colonists, in fact, regarded the assembly as their *right*—as a regularly constituted institution with the job of tempering the governor's will. This it did with a vengeance, using its power to introduce legislation, tax, and appropriate money to counter the governor's veto. As a result of this continual skirmishing with the assembly, the position of governor lost power steadily in the eighteenth century. Occasionally an exceptionally strong figure like Franklin's friend Thomas Hutchinson of Massachusetts would halt the trend temporarily, but the erosion of absolute authority in the colonies was irreversible.

Resistance to monarchical authority was not, of course, restricted to the American colonies. In his efforts to curb the power of the Pennsylvania proprietors, Franklin had the support of a tradition of English constitutionalism dating back to the thirteenth century. It received a major boost in 1688 when the English Whigs, or liberals, deposed King James II on the grounds that he had disregarded man's natural rights of life, liberty, and the possession of property. Immediately following the revolution, John Locke gave the natural-rights theory classic articulation in his famous *Treatises*. In the eighteenth century English journalists such as John Trenchard and Thomas Gordon publicized a variety of Lockean liberalism.

By 1760, when Franklin's case finally came to a head at Court, a sizable number of Englishmen were jealously guarding their constitutional liberties and closely scrutinizing the conduct of the king. Franklin sensed the mood and took pains to phrase Pennsylvania's case against the Penns in terms of "essential liberty" set against the vestiges of feudalism. After months of hearings and haggling, he succeeded in winning his point: the proprietor's lands would be subject to taxation like those of any man. Franklin's broader objective of eliminating the proprietary authority altogether proved premature. Still, he could declare the British Empire to be founded on "the greatest political structure human wisdom ever yet erected." Time would alter this opinion, but in 1760 Franklin was proud to be a subject of the king.

In 1762 Franklin returned to an America significantly changed from the one he had left five years before. The French and Indian War, which had begun inauspiciously for the English, was nearly over. At the very time Franklin was in Albany at the Congress, a young colonel of the Virginia militia named George Washington surrendered ignominiously to a French force in western Pennsylvania. General Edward Braddock repeated this act in 1755. With the advent of the William Pitt ministry three years later, however, England's fortunes took a turn for the better. In 1758 James Wolfe and Jeffrey Amherst captured the French fortress of Louisbourg, and the following year Wolfe took Quebec. Montreal fell September 8, 1760, and with it the entire French empire in North America.

It was a great victory for an imperial-minded England, but there were unexpected consequences that boded ill for the future of British colonialism. In the first place, the war was expensive, and England was determined to make the Americans, who benefited directly from the victory, pay a substantial part of its costs. As a means of raising money, England decided to dust off and strictly enforce the old Navigation Acts. Especially after a century of indifference, the tough new policy harbored the seeds of conflict.

The second unpleasant result of England's victory became apparent after the Treaty of Paris (1763) eliminated French power from North America. With the enemy gone, the colonists were less dependent on the protection of England. They could afford to treat English authority less seriously. Instead of their savior from Frenchmen and Indians, England seemed more and more an expensive encumbrance. Finally, the French and Indian War created a basis for American unity and American pride. The colonists worked together and played a major role in the victory. Moreover, they saw the British redcoats utterly frustrated by backwoods warfare. If the occasion ever demanded, perhaps even England could be defeated. In 1754 Franklin failed to arouse a sense of American identity. Eight years later, he sensed the beginnings of a more receptive climate of opinion.

The combination of England's need for revenue and the growth of colonial impatience with Parliamentary control led to trouble even before Franklin's 1762 return. Beginning in 1759, England actively attempted to control colonial elections and courts. On top of this, English customs agents, using "writs of assistance" to search homes and warehouses, cracked down on suspected smugglers. A colonial merchant accused of violating the Navigation Acts faced the prospect of being tried in the vice-admiralty court, without a jury, and in far-away Halifax, Nova Scotia. This was tantamount to conviction. Doubtless there were abuses on both sides. Merchants accustomed to being left alone bitterly resented the tightened regulations and redoubled their efforts to avoid them. England's officers retaliated with spies, frame-ups, and tight harbor patrols.

Emotions ran especially high over the Sugar Act of 1764, a revenue measure with which Treasury Minister George Grenville hoped to defray the cost of maintaining a standing army in the colonies. Americans liked neither the means nor the end involved. Another sore point of the early 1760s was the campaign of the Church of England to extend its influence in the colonies. With the exception of the first generation of Puritans, Americans distrusted state religions, and the prospect of enforced Anglicanism united all dissenters in opposition. The issue of westward expansion also contributed to the growth of animosity. England hoped to delay settlement of the trans-Appalachian region until such time as the Indians could be pacified and orderly procedures established. To this end, the Proclamation of 1763 forbade occupation of the West, and American frontiersmen boiled in anger.

Meanwhile, Pennsylvania experienced its own version of discontent in another dispute with its proprietors. Hoping to have the Penns' original charter revoked, the assembly once again dispatched Franklin to London. He arrived in the closing weeks of 1764 and was immediately caught up in the controversy swirling around Grenville's newest proposal, a stamp tax. Planned for institution in the fall of 1765, it required the purchase of a stamp for every kind of legal document, newspapers, pamphlets, even almanacs. At first Franklin accepted the idea calmly, advising a friend that "we might as well have hindered the setting sun." He even recommended an acquaintance as Philadelphia's stamp agent, and bought a supply of stamps for his own printing business. But for once Franklin was out of touch with the American temper. His countrymen regarded the Stamp Act as an outrage. They took it to be a form of "internal" taxation as opposed to the "external" variety regulating trade. The latter had at least some justification under mercantilism, but the stamp tax seemed a blatant revenue measure. Moreover, it appeared to the colonists to violate a basic tenet of English constitutionalism and natural rights theory: the sanctity of property. Since Americans were not represented, it was argued, Parliament had no right to take their property through taxation. Again and again the colonists insisted that if only they could levy their own taxes in their own representative assemblies, they would be willing to go a long way toward meeting England's fiscal demands. Otherwise, it was "no taxation without representation." Americans had found a principle on which to stand.

As the date for instituting the stamp tax approached, some Americans organized boycotts of the offending articles. Others supported an intercolonial Stamp Act Congress which, after pledging "all due submission" to Parliament, resolved that this did not include acceptance of internal taxes or of juryless admiralty courts. The mood at the gathering was one of firm, united resolve. American nationalism had made considerable gains since Franklin's abortive efforts in Albany eleven years earlier. Still other colonists resorted to violence in that tense autumn of 1765. In Boston a mob destroyed the home of the local stamp agent and threatened his life. He resigned the following day. Observing such developments from England, Franklin also got the message. Repenting of his earlier support of the tax, he prepared to lobby for its repeal. An opportunity arose in February 1766. The House of Commons was holding hearings on the controversial tax, and Franklin appeared to testify. Questioned by several members of Parliament, Franklin made plain that his countrymen would not pay the tax unless compelled by armed force. He also used the occasion to review the events of the past decade. Before 1763, Franklin declared, the colonists thought their government "the best in the world." They submitted willingly to Parliamentary authority and were governed easily "at the expense only of a little pen, ink and paper." Not only "respect," but "affection" existed for the mother country. Then came the end of the French and Indian War, the need for revenue, new taxes, and strict enforcement procedures. As a result, Franklin continued, the American attitude was "very much altered." Parliament had betrayed their trust. Franklin concluded his testimony with his conviction that all the colonists desired were their rights as Englishmen, specifically the right of representation in taxing bodies.

At the February hearings many members of Parliament assured Franklin that there was no difference between tax laws and other kinds of legislation. If the colonists accepted the regulation of trade, for instance, they should not resent the Stamp Act. These Englishmen also made it clear to Franklin that although Americans might not have "actual" representation in Parliament, as members of the empire, they were "virtually" represented. The colonists' situation, they insisted, was analogous to that of people in England who had lost their personal representative to Parliament as the result of boundary changes, but could still count on Parliament as a whole to defend their interests.

Franklin could not accept such reasoning. In his eyes and those of his countrymen, Americans were second-class citizens. They did not enjoy, Franklin insisted, "all the privileges and liberties of Englishmen," and they would rebel before conceding the point. First, however, they would refuse to purchase England's manufactured goods, and by means of this economic boycott put the power of the purse behind their cause. Franklin made the point neatly in examination form: "Q. What used to be the pride of Americans? A. To indulge in the fashions and manufactures of Great Britain. Q. What is now their pride? A. To wear their old cloaths over again, till they can make new ones."

In retrospect, Franklin thought his testimony in Parliament on the Stamp Act "contributed much to its repeal." Actually, the replacement of Grenville by the Marquis of Rockingham, a man who opposed the stamp idea from the beginning, combined with widespread realization that the act did not work, sealed its fate. In March 1766 the Stamp Act was repealed to the cheers of grateful Americans. But Franklin knew that the good feeling was premature. Parliament was not about to concede its principle. At the same time it withdrew the

The newly-independent American colonies could not have chosen a better representative to send to France in 1776 than Benjamin Franklin. French society was dazzled by the unassuming wit and wisdom of the man from the "wilds" of America. At elegant receptions such as the one depicted here, Franklin gave his nation's appeal for support in its revolution a mighty assist.

Franklin the scientist and inventor applied his talent to the problem of efficient home heating. Fireplaces were very inefficient, because only one of the sides opened on a room. Franklin's alternative was this stove, which stood in the center of a room and radiated heat from all its surfaces.

stamps, Parliament passed the Declaratory Act, which stated England's power to legislate for the colonies in "all cases whatsoever." "In my Opinion," Franklin wrote, "it will meet with the same Opposition, and be attended with the same Mischiefs that would have attended [the Stamp Act]." Again he misjudged public opinion. The Declaratory Act was pure principle; unlike the Stamp Act, it did not touch American pocketbooks. It engendered much less opposition in the colonies, a circumstance that suggests an intimate relationship between economic self-interest and constitutional principle in motivating American resistance to English government.

The situation changed radically, however, in 1767, when England's continuing search for revenue led its new treasurer, Charles Townshend, to secure the passage of duties on lead, paint, paper, glass, and tea imported by the colonists. Townshend also took steps to enforce the unpopular Quartering Act of 1765, under which American families were required to feed and board English soldiers. Finally, he expanded the customs service and the hated admiralty courts with the object of putting teeth in the new duties.

Again the colonies exploded. American merchants and consumers devised nonimportation agreements designed to choke off trade with England. The plan proved highly effective. England not only failed to collect the anticipated duties, but lost thousands of pounds worth of colonial business. On March 5, 1770, the first blood of the independence movement was drawn when a group of Boston citizens, spurred by the inflammatory rhetoric of Samuel Adams, clashed with British soldiers. Only five Americans died in the so-called Boston Massacre, but the term reflects the depth of colonial bitterness.

For Franklin, who remained in London as agent for several colonies, the clash was deplorable. As a man who made a religion of reason and order, he preferred peace at any price. Yet it was becoming clear to him that "no middle ground can be well maintained. . . . [either] Parliament has a power to make *all laws* for us, or . . . it has a power to make no laws for us." And, he added, "I think the arguments for the latter are more numerous and weighty, than those for the former." This conclusion, of course, supported independence, but in company with most of his countrymen in the early 1770s, Franklin did not as yet regard the prospect seriously. Surely men of good will on both sides would smooth out their differences. After all, the colonists were Englishmen. They wanted to remain loyal subjects of King George III, whom Franklin as late as 1768 termed "the best King . . . any nation was ever blessed with." If only George would protect their rights from an indifferent Parliament and a rapacious bureaucracy, the empire could enter a golden age.

As the 1770s progressed, however, such hopes became unrealistic. True, the Townshend taxes, except for that on tea, were repealed as the decade began. Yet the English government and society Franklin observed from his London vantage point seemed incapable of effective colonial administration. Bloated from a century of profit-making and empire-building, most Englishmen paid little attention to American grievances. Fewer still brought any consideration except profit to the colonial relationship. Again and again Franklin saw the protests and petitions of his countrymen brushed away like so many mosquitoes. Rare indeed were men like Edmund Burke and William Pitt, who with their keen sense of colonial realities could accept some limitation on British authority as the price for retaining any authority at all. As for George III, his empire was simply too large for more than cursory royal attention to American affairs. Franklin probably helped spread the story that the king persistently confused the Himalayas with the Appalachians and the Ganges with the Mississippi.

In the face of such ineptitude, Franklin lost patience and lashed out at what appeared to him to be England's mismanagement of her North American empire. The Tea Act of May 1773 was a particular sore point. The measure permitted the giant East India Company to sell tea directly to Americans at an extremely low price. Even with customs duty, the East India Company tea was cheaper than the untaxed product of non-British nations. As Franklin and his contemporaries saw it, the Tea Act was a deliberate attempt on the part of Parliament to make Americans buy taxed tea and thereby implicitly accept the principle of Parliament's taxing authority. Furious, Franklin wrote some tracts designed, in his words, to provide "a Looking-Glass in which some Ministers may see their ugly Faces, and the Nation its Injustice." The first essay was "Rules by Which a Great Empire May be Reduced to a Small One." The second, "An Edict by the King of Prussia," used a transparent disguise to jab at England's edicts. It concluded with an expression of incredulity that a nation "so wise and liberal in its sentiments, so just and equitable towards its neighbors, should, from mean and injudicious views of petty immediate profit, treat its own children in a manner so arbitrary and tyrannical!"

Words came easily to Benjamin Franklin, but his countrymen frequently turned to deeds to express their opposition to British policy. The taxed tea met with a hostile reception as it arrived in America. In some ports citizen groups forced the ships to return to England without unloading their cargoes. Other communities locked the crates of tea in storehouses and defied anyone to remove them for distribution and sale. In Boston, where Samuel Adams and his Committees of Correspondence kept alive a tradition of radicalism, there were more serious consequences. On December 16, 1773, a band of enraged colonists disguised as Indians boarded the tea ship, hacked open the boxes, and dumped them into Boston harbor.

The "tea party" elicited a mixed reaction. To radical colonial eyes it was a stroke of genius, a way of putting teeth in the American grievances. But for many Americans, and almost all Englishmen, the destruction of the tea was an outright crime. Franklin personally sided with the shocked moderates, branded the tea party "an act of violent injustice" perpetrated on the owners of the tea, and demanded "speedy reparation." In Franklin's opinion, the events of December 16 cost the American cause considerable sympathy throughout Europe. From oppressed disciples of natural rights, they had descended to behaving like anarchists and thieves.

England's response to the tea party, however, made Franklin change his mind. In quick succession early in 1774 Parliament closed the port of Boston, revised the Massachusetts constitution to reduce popular sovereignty, curbed the authority of local juries, and appointed General Thomas Gage, the commander of British troops in North America, as governor of Massachusetts Bay. The colonists labeled these measures the Intolerable Acts, and Franklin agreed that their severity shifted the burden of reconciliation from New World to Old. The Quebec Act added further fuel to the fire. Also passed in 1774, it finally settled the matter of governing the territory won from the French a decade earlier. The act made the governorship a permanent position, abolished representative assemblies of any kind, and encouraged the Roman Catholic Church. Although they were not directly affected, most Americans regarded the Quebec Act as a bad omen, particularly since it applied to all the land west of the Appalachians and north of the Ohio.

Massachusetts' misfortunes generated a wave of sympathy throughout the colonies. The Intolerable Acts created an atmosphere in which the kind of unified action Franklin dreamed about at Albany twenty years before became feasible, and the First Continental Congress assembled at Philadelphia in September of 1774. Many viewpoints were represented, but the delegates shared a sense of fear, anger, and determination to prevent further loss of their rights as Englishmen and as men. Among its first actions was institution of a tight boycott on all trade with England. The delegates also voted to support Boston in resisting the Intolerable Acts. Turning to long-range solutions, Joseph Galloway, an old political ally of Franklin's, tried to secure support for an intercolonial assembly to act in conjunction with Parliament as a kind of lower house. If adopted on both sides of the ocean, Galloway's plan might well have averted the impending revolution. American radicals, however, resented its concessions to Parliamentary authority, and the idea failed by a single vote. Franklin was just as glad. He wrote to Galloway early in 1775: "when I consider the extream corruption prevalent among all orders of men in this old rotten state, and the glorious public virtue so predominant in our rising country, I cannot but apprehend more mischief than benefit from a closer union."

But independence for Franklin did not necessarily entail war. He consistently hoped that an adjustment of America's political status could be negotiated in the conference room by diplomats rather than contested on the battlefield by soldiers. Divorce, not murder, was the sensible alternative in his opinion, and during his final months in England he poured all his skill into this approach. The current, however, ran the other way. Sentiment on both sides was hardening rapidly. Moreover, Franklin operated in 1775 under a cloud of suspicion cast by his recent involvement in the publication of some purloined letters of former Massachusetts governor Thomas Hutchinson. Sensing the futility of his compromise efforts and fearing imprisonment or worse if he remained in London, Franklin sailed for Philadelphia on March 20. While he was in mid-ocean, full-scale war began in Massachusetts between Gage's troops and amateur colonial soldiers massed, thanks in part to Paul Revere's ride, at Lexington, Concord, and along the road to Boston.

Franklin landed in Philadelphia on May 5, 1775, and before he had unpacked he was elected a delegate to the Second Continental Congress. This body found itself in charge of governing a nation at war. Its first order of business was providing for the common defense. Franklin and his colleagues organized the Massachusetts militia into the Continental Army, appointed George Washington commander-in-chief, and issued paper money to finance the fighting.

Before Washington could take charge, however, Gage's force at Boston engaged the colonists in the Battle of Bunker (actually, Breed's) Hill on June 17. The Americans retreated, but not before offering fierce resistance. Following reports of the action closely, Franklin concluded that the British must be "convinc'd by this time, that they have Men to deal with, tho' unexperienced, and not yet well arm'd." The Battle of Bunker Hill also pushed Franklin further toward a commitment to independence. Contemplating the ravages of the British in Charlestown, Massachusetts, following the colonial retreat, he remarked to a countryman in July 1775, "I think I am not half so reconcileable now, as I was a Month ago." To an English correspondent, however, Franklin revealed a rare streak of emotional anger: "you have begun to burn our Towns, and murder our People. —Look upon your Hands! They are stained with the Blood of your Relations!" Yet Franklin and the Second Continental Congress only slowly abandoned the hope of reconciliation. In July the congress addressed a petition to George III acknowledging its loyalty and begging for a restriction of Parliament's power over Americans to matters of trade only. If this were to happen, the petition made clear, Americans would gladly remain English.

Franklin supported the July petition and regarded it as a "Golden Opportunity" for England. Yet he was realistic. He knew the climate of opinion in that nation, and in his judgment, "she has neither Temper nor Wisdom enough to seize" the possibility of reunion. He was right. George III and his ministers were determined to put the unruly and ungrateful colonists in their place and insisted on Parliament's full power to make laws and assess taxes. England replied to the petition by adding 25,000 troops to her North American force.

By 1776 Franklin, with most American colonists, was convinced that independence offered the only long-term solution to their problems with England. But untying the knot promised to be painful. Revolution was a serious matter in the late eighteenth century. The idea of the divine right of kings, of their absolute sovereignty, lingered on in the popular mind as a legacy from the Middle Ages. One did not defy a monarch casually. Moreover, the cultural background of most Americans was English. Mental as well as physical preparation for separation had to be made. Thomas Paine's *Common Sense*, published in January 1776, helped in this respect. Franklin contributed directly to the appearance of the tract, since his letters of introduction had smoothed Paine's move to the colonies from England two years earlier. Franklin also provided Paine with notes and documents for writing a summary of the Anglo-American relationship. Indeed, when *Common Sense* appeared anonymously, many supposed Franklin the author. But the emotional tone of the piece should have dissuaded readers. Paine lambasted kings as the oppressive relics of an unenlightened age. Monarchy, he insisted, was inconsistent with liberty. Americans should pursue the republican way as more in keeping with their respect for the individual.

June of 1776 found Franklin enmeshed in the affairs of the Continental Congress. His tasks included membership on a committee charged with the preparation of a declaration of independence. Thomas Jefferson drafted a document that incorporated many of Franklin's suggestions. The most important involved an opening statement of principles with which the rebels hoped to justify their course of action to the rest of the world and to themselves.

Jefferson wrote: "we hold these truths to be sacred and undeniable, that all men are created equal, that they are endowed by their Creator with certain unalienable Rights, that among these, are Life, Liberty, and the pursuit of Happiness." Franklin argued successfully for substituting "self-evident" for "sacred and undeniable." It was a significant and fortuitous change. Jefferson's wording implied a divine origin for men's rights. Franklin used a term from science and based the rights on reason. All men, he implied, could investigate and prove the proposition. Franklin made natural rights sacred because they were true, while in Jefferson's version they were true because they were sacred. It was a change consistent with both the character of Franklin and the experience of his countrymen.

On July 2, 1776, the Continental Congress adopted Richard Henry Lee's motion for independence. Two days later it approved the Declaration. At the signing ceremony John Hancock supposedly warned, "we must be unanimous. . . . we must all hang together." "Yes," Franklin replied, "we must, indeed, all hang together, or most assuredly we shall all hang separately." With the deed now done, the rebels set about the enormous task of justifying their action with success. Among the most pressing needs was a military and financial alliance with a foreign power. France, the chronic opponent of England in the eighteenth century, offered the best prospects, and late in 1776 Benjamin Franklin once again received his country's call for help. Would he, nearly seventy years old, join a delegation to Paris? "I am but a fag end," Franklin replied with characteristic understatement, but "you may have me for what you please." Franklin's record in France showed that he retained considerable vitality. Arriving in December of 1776, he was immediately swept up in a wave of popular adulation. The French, who knew Franklin from his almanac and his electrical papers, regarded him as a homespun disciple of the Enlightenment, a kind of noble savage, an American Socrates. The envious John Adams, who joined the American delegation when Franklin's popularity had peaked, observed: "his reputation was more universal than that of Leibnitz or Newton, Frederick or Voltaire. . . . his name was familiar . . . to such a degree that there was scarcely a peasant chambermaid or scullion in a kitchen who was not familiar with it, and who did not consider him as a friend to human kind. . . . they seemed to think he was to restore the Golden Age." Hardly one to let such a chance slip by unused, Franklin wore a little fur cap and played the role of backwoods sage to the hilt. He reaped dividends both romantic and diplomatic. The latter climaxed in a treaty of alliance with the French government, signed February 6, 1778, four months after the key American victory in the Battle of Saratoga.

French aid sealed England's fate in the American war. A series of campaigns in the central and southern colonies led Charles Cornwallis's British force to a dead end on the Yorktown Peninsula in Virginia with George Washington in pursuit and a French fleet offshore. Surrender came October 19, 1781.

With the fighting finally over, Franklin turned to the more congenial task of peacemaking. His frame of mind is revealed in a letter to

an old English friend: "let us now forgive and forget." Both countries, he believed, could help each other move on to great if separate
futures. As one of the official negotiators of the peace, Franklin was
instrumental in bringing about the agreement of September 3, 1783. It
recognized the United States as a sovereign nation with a northern
boundary along the Great Lakes–St. Lawrence waterway and a western one at the Mississippi River. Spain remained on the south and
west, and England retained Canada, but the first nation independent of
a European power was carved from the New World. Franklin, for one,
looked forward to a brilliant future. Three years before his death he
participated in the Constitutional Convention of 1787, which restruc-
tured the federal government of the United States.[1] According to
Thomas Jefferson, Franklin took a moment of the closing session to
call the assembly's attention to the painting of a sun on the back of
President George Washington's chair. "I have often and often," he
declared, ". . . looked at [it] . . . without being able to tell whether it
was rising or setting. But now, at last, I know that it is a rising . . .
sun."

America changed greatly during Benjamin Franklin's lifetime. He
was born in 1706 into a society that still defined its purpose largely in
spiritual terms, but the old Puritanism was losing its hold. Yet Americans were loathe to lose the messianic role assumed by the Puritans; a
mission lent dignity and significance to their endeavor in the wilderness. As a people on the outskirts of civilization, they both wanted and
needed the buoyant feeling of being singled out to lead mankind to a
better world. As a result, Americans groped throughout the eighteenth
century for a new mission. They found it in the Enlightenment concept
of natural rights. Liberty rather than salvation became the new goal.
Success rather than salvation motivated Franklin's society. He died in
1790 in a society which had turned from building a holy community to
building a free and prosperous one. The good life replaced the godly
one.

Nobody reflected this redefinition more clearly nor promoted it
more vigorously than Benjamin Franklin. When he wrote at the
height of the Revolution that "our Cause is the Cause of all Mankind,

---

[1] For a discussion of the Constitution of 1787 and of the Articles of Confederation government which preceded it, see pages 122–129.

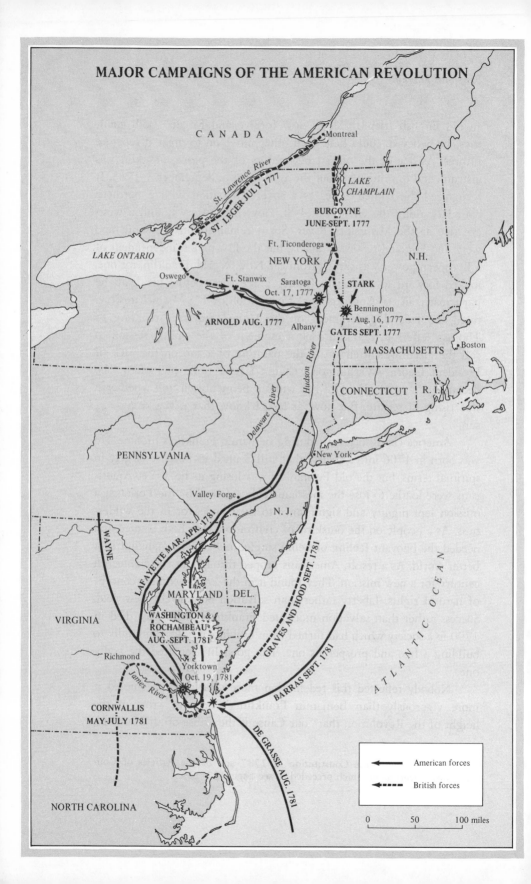

MAJOR CAMPAIGNS OF THE AMERICAN REVOLUTION

CANADA

Montreal

St. Lawrence River

ST. LEGER JULY 1777

LAKE CHAMPLAIN

LAKE ONTARIO

BURGOYNE JUNE-SEPT. 1777

Ft. Ticonderoga

NEW YORK

N.H.

Oswego

Ft. Stanwix

Saratoga Oct. 17, 1777

STARK

ARNOLD AUG. 1777

Albany

Bennington Aug. 16, 1777

GATES SEPT. 1777

MASSACHUSETTS

Boston

Hudson River

Delaware River

CONNECTICUT

R.I.

PENNSYLVANIA

New York

Valley Forge

N. J.

WAYNE

LAFAYETTE MAR.-APR. 1781

MARYLAND

DEL.

GRAVES AND HOOD SEPT. 1781

VIRGINIA

WASHINGTON & ROCHAMBEAU AUG.-SEPT. 1781

Richmond

James River

Yorktown Oct. 19, 1781

BARRAS SEPT. 1781

ATLANTIC OCEAN

CORNWALLIS MAY-JULY 1781

DE GRASSE AUG. 1781

NORTH CAROLINA

American forces

British forces

0   50   100 miles

and we are fighting for their Liberty in defending our own. Tis a glorious task assign'd us by Providence," he echoed John Winthrop. America was still a city upon a hill, but with a new message for the world.

SELECTED READINGS

The Person

*CRANE, VERNER W.: *Benjamin Franklin and a Rising People* (1954). A short interpretive biography.

JACOBS, WILBUR (ed.): *Benjamin Franklin: Statesman, Philosopher or Materialist* (1972). A recent collection of analytical essays.

LABAREE, L. W., W. J. BELL, JR., and W. B. WILLCOX (eds.): *The Papers of Benjamin Franklin* (1959–   ). The most complete and authoritative multivolume collection of Franklin's writing.

*LEMISCH, L. JESSE (ed.): *Benjamin Franklin: The Autobiography and Other Writings* (1961). A useful edition of Franklin's famous self-portrait, along with selections from his scientific, religious, and political thought.

*VAN DOREN, CARL: *Benjamin Franklin* (1938). The most detailed biography.

WRIGHT, ESMOND: *Benjamin Franklin and American Independence* (1966). Franklin's contributions to the revolutionary process.

The Period

*BAILYN, BERNARD: *Ideological Origins of the American Revolution* (1966). Traces the intellectual roots of independence.

*BRIDENBAUGH, CARL, and JESSICA BRIDENBAUGH: *Rebels and Gentlemen: Philadelphia in the Age of Franklin* (1942). Social history that emphasizes the development of the American city.

GIPSON, LAWRENCE H.: *The British Empire before the American Revolution* (15 vols., 1939–1970). The standard source for colonial political history.

GREENE, JACK P. (ed.): *The Reinterpretation of the American Revolution, 1763–1789* (1968). A collection of the most significant recent assessments.

* Available in paperback.

*HINDLE, BROOKE. *The Pursuit of Science in Revolutionary America* (1956). A thorough examination of eighteenth-century American science.

*MILLER, JOHN C.: *Origins of the American Revolution* (1957). A reliable general survey of the road to independence.

*MORGAN, EDMUND S.: *The Birth of the Republic* (1956). A clear and readable interpretation of the American Revolution.

* Available in paperback.

Thomas Jefferson

The crowd that had gathered for breakfast at Conrad and McMun's boardinghouse rose with one accord as the lanky, broad-shouldered Virginian descended the stairs. Nervously the hostess gestured to a chair left vacant at the head of the table. Thomas Jefferson dismissed the offer, and chose instead a seat along the side with the other diners. After the meal he strolled outside, squinting into the March sunlight at the collection of half-finished buildings, swamp, and forest that for less than a year had served as the capital

*of the United States. Elaborately uniformed grenadiers paraded
in the muddy streets, doing their best to dignify the occasion.
George Washington and John Adams, the two previous Presidents,
coveted such trappings, with their connotation of Old World
aristocracy. Four years earlier Adams rode to his inauguration in a
luxurious coach drawn by six horses. But the election of 1800
defeated the Federalists and brought a different temper to American
life. Jefferson reflected it as he left Conrad and McMun's for the
day's business. Spurning the suggestion of a coach and ignoring
the grenadiers, the President-elect walked to his inauguration.*

On a clear day you can see a long way from Thomas Jefferson's beloved hilltop home, Monticello. Immediately below, the town of Charlottesville, Virginia, nestles in the soft-forested folds of the Southwest Mountains. To the west, dominating the horizon, lies the Blue Ridge, backbone of the southern Appalachians. When Jefferson was a boy in the 1740s, those hazy mountains marked the edge of settlement. Few even knew what lay beyond: A few decades earlier Virginia's Governor Alexander Spotswood and his expedition had topped the Blue Ridge in full expectation of seeing the Pacific Ocean. The creeks and streams south and east of Monticello joined to form the James River, then flowed onward to the Atlantic. A seedbed of American settlement, the James was also a key artery for subsequent development. Great planters like William Byrd and Robert Carter, whose holdings included hundreds of thousands of acres of rich bottomland, located their mansions on its shores. Ocean-going ships served these plantations, carrying hogsheads of tobacco to eager Old World markets. Tidewater and navigation ended where the James plunged over the edge of the Piedmont Plateau in a series of waterfalls and rapids. Richmond, located at this transition point, became the nerve center for the tidal lowlands and the interior.

With visions of tobacco profits luring them on, planters pushed up the James so quickly that by the 1730s, when Thomas Jefferson's father, Peter, sought land, he had to journey some 100 river miles above Richmond to a tributary called the Rivanna. Peter Jefferson exemplified the one-generation aristocrat so often encountered early in the history of a developing nation. Starting as a surveyor, Peter acquired land, cleared it, built houses, bought slaves, and eventually gained political and military office and the status of squire. The country was new, and he grew up with it almost exactly as did another surveyor-soldier-squire in the adjacent Shenandoah Valley named George Washington.

A man of prodigious physical strength, Peter Jefferson could simultaneously push two thousand-pound hogsheads of tobacco from a prone to an upright position. On the frontier, where performance determined reputation, news of such feats spread rapidly. But Peter also used marriage as an avenue of advancement. Jane Randolph, who became his wife in 1739, belonged to the upper crust of eighteenth-century southern society—the First Families of Virginia. The Randolph pedigree extended far back in Great Britain as well as Virginia —"to which," Thomas Jefferson later advised, "let everyone ascribe the faith and merit he chooses." His own preference inclined him toward the self-made man, a natural aristocrat in his father's mold. But later kinship ties such as that between the Jefferson and Randolph families did provide the basis for Virginia's domination of the political life of the new nation, as well as the structure of Southern elitism.

Peter and Jane Randolph Jefferson celebrated the birth of their first son, Thomas, on April 13, 1743, at Shadwell, the estate they had carved from the wilderness of the upper James River. The boy grew up with all the advantages of a gentleman at Shadwell and at Tuckahoe, the sprawling Randolph holding downstream. Private tutoring began at the age of five, intensive instruction in Greek and Latin when he was nine. A smattering of French, some contact with the English classics, and the customary heavy dose of religion completed Jefferson's early formal education.

But he had other teachers. His father, whom he revered, was a living example of the rewards of resolution, diligence, and organization in the manner of Benjamin Franklin. And there were the red-earth hills of Albemarle County and the Blue Ridge country of Virginia. Because Jefferson's perspective on this environment was that of the gentleman rather than the frontiersman, he found delight, not challenge, in nature. Living comfortably amid cleared fields in the aftermath of the first wave of settlement, he could love the frontier in a way quite foreign to the man who did the clearing. The freedom and simplicity of the American wilderness permeated Jefferson's life style, while its mysteries sparked a lifelong interest in science and exploration, and its beauty inspired an intense patriotism.

In 1760, at the age of seventeen, Thomas Jefferson left the quiet foothills of the Blue Ridge for two years of instruction at the College of William and Mary in Williamsburg. Founded in 1693, William and Mary was the pride of the South and, next to Harvard, the oldest collegiate institution in North America. Jefferson made the perfect student. Intensely serious and capable of sustained study, he became enthralled with the world of scholarship and refinement. To be sure, there were parties, girls, and drinking, but hangovers only seemed to drive a contrite Jefferson to greater concentration on his courses. His intelligence impressed all his associates, in particular George Wythe, a professor of law.

Wythe also enjoyed good living and high thinking, and he introduced his students to the circle that gathered from time to time at the home of Francis Fauquier, Royal Governor of Virginia. In these occasions, brilliant by eighteenth-century provincial standards, Jefferson took special delight. He contributed to the musical entertainment, partook of the fine food, and participated enthusiastically in the spirited discussions. Jefferson's life and the history of his country were caught for a moment in a quiet eddy. As the music and laughter drifted from the governor's palace into the velvet of a Chesapeake evening, Concord and Lexington seemed inconceivable. And George Wythe could hardly have imagined that in a dozen years he would sign a declaration of independence from England written by his red-haired student from the backwoods academies of Albemarle County.

Jefferson's college idyll ended in 1762, but he continued to study, reading law with George Wythe. Two years later he assumed title under the terms of his father's will to an estate of several thousand acres and several hundred slaves—and became one of the colony's most eligible bachelors. But even this windfall did not bring Jefferson luck in love. After months of agony his passion for sixteen-year-old Rebecca Burwell produced, he ruefully admitted, only "a few broken sentences, uttered in great disorder" as the couple danced at a Williamsburg ball. Reconciled to being single, Jefferson continued his legal studies with even fiercer determination. When he finally took the bar examination in 1767, he probably knew more than his examiners.

The ineptness Jefferson demonstrated in the presence of Miss Burwell undoubtedly led him to admire masters of the spoken word. One of the best in Jefferson's time was another back-country boy named Patrick Henry. Jefferson first encountered this firebrand, seven years his senior, at a Christmas party in the late 1750s. He at first felt Henry to be somewhat coarse and crude, especially when he passed his bar examination after only five weeks of study. But in 1763 Henry impressed Jefferson, Virginia, and the colonies with a brilliant performance in a case known as the Parsons' Cause. The parsons were the Anglican clergymen in Virginia; their cause was to secure a higher salary from hostile local taxpayers. Americans distrusted any hint of an established religion and readily associated the Anglican Church with English government. At the climax of the dispute Patrick Henry addressed a jury sitting to decide the amount of back pay to award a disgruntled parson. In an emotional flood of eloquence, Henry accused King George III of having "degenerated into a tyrant" by overruling a Virginia law respecting the pay of clergy. The jury responded by awarding the beleaguered clergyman the grand total of one penny. Americans chortled gleefully, and Henry became a hero overnight.

He did not rest on his laurels for long. In 1765 the House of Burgesses in Virginia took up the question of Parliament's right to impose a stamp tax on the unrepresented colonists, and Henry assumed leadership of the radicals. On May 30 Jefferson was standing in the doorway of the Burgesses' chamber as a spectator when Henry arose to defend a set of seven resolutions repudiating the Stamp Act. "Caesar had his Brutus," he allegedly thundered, "Charles the First his Cromwell, and George the Third. . . ." Jefferson was aghast, and cries of "Treason!" rang through the assembly, but Henry continued: ". . . and George the Third may profit by their example." Then, turning to his hecklers, Henry shouted, "If this be treason, make the most of it." After more heated exchanges the sharply divided Burgesses passed four of Henry's resolutions and thereby helped define the ideological grounds on which the American Revolution was subsequently fought. Jefferson was moved. Henry, he confessed, "appeared to me to speak as Homer wrote." And soon after hearing Henry's tirade before the Burgesses, Jefferson adopted as his personal motto: "Rebellion to tyrants is obedience to God."

The friction between Patrick Henry and the more conservative Virginia politicians that surfaced during the debate on the Stamp Act Resolutions was part of a pattern in many colonies in the decade before independence. As historian Carl Becker has put it, men were concerned at this time not only with the question of "home rule," but also with "who should rule at home." In other words, there was an internal or domestic aspect to the Revolution paralleling the external conflict with Great Britain. At stake at home was political leadership and the power, privilege, and prestige that accompanied it. Prior to 1760 the keys to such power were held by royal officers, sometimes in collaboration with important colonists. In many colonies a single man or family controlled the political machine. Jefferson's Virginia, for instance, was run by John Robinson, treasurer and speaker of the House of Burgesses. Few went far in Virginia politics without his blessing. Although younger, ambitious men were frustrated, the Robinson-led gentry held tight rein.

About 1763, however, the issue that was to upset the traditional power structure—American independence—appeared. The young insurgents recognized its potential as an avenue for political advancement: if they could associate the colonial establishment with England, patriotism could be used to engineer its downfall. Natural rights might cut a wide swath and level the colonial oligarchy as well as Parliament and George III. Indeed, some old-line American leaders came to regret their championing of John Locke and the entire independence movement. Better to suffer English rule, they concluded, than to risk losing their favored position in a reshuffling of the American deck.

Before the Revolution Patrick Henry led the forces of internal insurgency in Virginia. It is significant that he came from the western upcountry and had the backing of small farmers and traders. The tension between this geographic and economic group and the tidewater aristocracy of great planters had long been a fact of political life in Virginia and other southern colonies. A century before Henry, for instance, Nathaniel Bacon led frontier forces in an abortive revolt against the coastal elite that was no minor squabble. In the aftermath of Bacon's Rebellion, twenty-three men were executed.

The "young hotheads," as Governor Fauquier termed them, did not precipitate such a direct confrontation in the 1760s and 1770s, but Virginians looked worriedly at neighboring North Carolina, where an association of western farmers known as the Regulators fought a pitched battle with tidewater planters. Patrick Henry, however, preferred more subtle means. Associating the oligarchy with British authority, he succeeded in swinging the balance of power in the House of Burgesses to the "hotheads." The Stamp Act debates of 1765 proved that John Robinson's system of government was on the wane. The next year the old elite received a further jolt when an examination of Robinson's accounts revealed considerable corruption. The tidewater gentry never fully recovered. By the mid-1770s, when vital questions about the English relationship had to be decided, the House of Burgesses was in the hands of radical newcomers—Patrick Henry, Richard Henry Lee, Francis L. Lee, George Mason, George Washington, and Thomas Jefferson. Without the loosening effect of the American Revolution on the internal power structure of the colonies, it is possible that none of the these men would have achieved political leadership.

Thomas Jefferson first assumed political office in 1769, when Albemarle County elected him a member of the House of Burgesses. Only twenty-six at the time, he won the approval of both gentry and plain people. Such double backing was common in the eighteenth-century South and proved effective in identifying political talent. The necessity of pleasing both camps discouraged the haughty aristocrat and also the popular rabble rouser. The final products of the system were leaders who, like Jefferson, combined the best of democracy and aristocracy and in so doing defined an American political ideal.

As Jefferson gained experience and confidence as a Burgess, he lent more and more weight to the protest against England. In 1773 he joined Patrick Henry and Richard Henry Lee in calling for a Committee of Correspondence to solidify the colonial cause. Samuel Adams had begun this practice in Massachusetts the previous year, but confined the communications to towns within the colony. The Virginians had an intercolonial organization in mind, and Jefferson personally helped get it under way with his facile pen. In the process he began to acquire a reputation outside Virginia.

The first months of 1774 brought the disquieting news of the Boston Tea Party and Parliament's punitive response. Jefferson was among those who strongly sympathized with the people of Massachusetts, and he represented their plight as an American problem rather than a local one. He also sponsored a measure in the House of Burgesses calling for twenty-four hours of fasting in Virginia on June 1, 1774, the day the Boston Port Act went into effect. An enraged Governor John Dunmore dissolved the Assembly, but its members defied him and regrouped in the Raleigh Tavern next door. There they proposed an intercolonial congress and resolved that "an attack on any one colony should be considered as an attack on the whole." Although few realized its implications, this breakdown of the royal governor's authority was Virginia's revolution.

Later in the summer of 1774, representatives of the various Virginia counties convened in Williamsburg to choose delegates to the Continental Congress. In preparation for the meeting, Jefferson wrote *A Summary View of the Rights of British America.* The tract was intended as a handbook for Virginia's members at the congress, but in pamphlet form it quickly reached a much wider audience on both sides of the Atlantic. In *A Summary View* Jefferson stood squarely on natural-rights philosophy as he had learned it from John Locke and other English constitutional theorists. He began by pointing out that the English settlers who emigrated to the New World had not thereby relinquished their liberties as Englishmen and as men. Specifically, they had not agreed to be governed by an assembly—Parliament—in which they were not represented. As for George III, Jefferson made it clear that in his view "kings are the servants not the proprietors of the people." Submission to monarchs was voluntary and could be voluntarily abandoned if the relationship threatened natural rights. Clinching his argument, Jefferson asked: "can his majesty . . . put down all law under his feet? Can he erect a power superior to that which erected himself? He has done it indeed by force, but let him remember that force cannot give right."

These were strong words, but Jefferson stopped short of actually proposing revolution. He referred to the colonies as "British America," and called for the end of Parliament's power to tax and regulate trade rather than for outright independence. Yet even this seemed too much to the majority of the Williamsburg gathering, which adopted resolutions that in Jefferson's opinion were mild as a "sucking dove." In a candid moment, however, Jefferson admitted that the leap he proposed in *A Summary View* was "too long as yet for the mass of our citizens." In 1774 all but a radical fringe of colonists regarded themselves as loyal British subjects and stood by the distinction conceding Parliament the right to impose "external" taxes concerning trade, but not those affecting only the "internal" life of the colonies. A conception of American nationality was, however, growing steadily. Thomas Paine expressed it in *Common Sense.* "In no instance," he wrote, "hath nature made the satellite larger than its primary planet; and as England and America, with respect to each other, reverse the common order of nature, it is evident that they belong in different systems. England to Europe: America to itself."

Jefferson soon had an opportunity to take the leading role in implementing this idea of independence. He arrived in Philadelphia in June 1775 to sit as one of Virginia's delegates to the Second Continental Congress. Although he was the second youngest member of the assembly, necks craned as Jefferson entered the hall. His reputation for logical thought and, in John Adams's words, a "masterly pen," had preceded him. Shortly thereafter Congress entrusted Jefferson with the drafting of several important papers, including the rejection of a proposal of conciliation from England's Prime Minister, Lord Frederick North.

On June 7, 1776, the congress passed Richard Henry Lee's motion that "these United Colonies are and of right ought to be free and independent states." A five-man committee, including Jefferson, John Adams, and Benjamin Franklin, was instructed to draft a formal declaration of the Congress's intent. Franklin, whom Jefferson revered, might well have done the writing, but he was ill at the time. Jefferson then proposed that Adams undertake the task, after which, according to Adams's recollection, the following dialog ensued:

ADAMS: Oh! no.

JEFFERSON: Why will you not? You ought to do it.

ADAMS: I will not.

JEFFERSON: Why?

ADAMS: Reasons enough.

JEFFERSON: What can be your reasons?

ADAMS: Reason first—You are a Virginian, and a Virginian ought to appear at the head of this business. Reason second—I am obnoxious, suspected, and unpopular. You are very much otherwise. Reason third—You can write ten times better than I can.

JEFFERSON: Well, if you are decided I will do as well as I can.

So it was that on June 11 the thirty-three-year-old Thomas Jefferson retired to the tiny parlor of his lodgings at Seventh and Market and began to write his way to immortality.

For over two weeks Jefferson's quill pen scratched out draft after draft of a declaration. Eighteen hundred highly polished words finally emerged. Franklin, now in good health, Adams, and the rest of the committee looked at them and made several suggestions. On June 28 the Congress scrutinized Jefferson's work. He must have cringed inwardly as his painstaking efforts were criticized, revised, and abridged. Yet the version signed on July 4, 1776 was a monument to one man.

Jefferson, to be sure, was modest. He never pretended that the Declaration of Independence was anything but a compilation of the ideas of others, a summary of the spirit of the time and place. Years afterward he wrote of the Declaration: "neither aiming at originality of principle or sentiment, nor yet copied from any particular and previous writing, it was intended to be an expression of the American mind." Jefferson's most obvious intellectual debt was to John Locke and the other Enlightenment philosophers of natural rights. But the Virginian did alter the usual trio of life, liberty, and property to read "life, liberty, and the pursuit of Happiness." George Mason had made the same substitution in his Virginia Bill of Rights of June 12, 1776, and Jefferson clearly used his friend's manifesto as inspiration and guide. Still, the flowing, compelling style of the Declaration of Independence was Jefferson's alone. Although the word was yet to be coined, he had produced a masterpiece of *propaganda*—a justification as well as a declaration.

That Jefferson was well aware of his function as a propagandist is evident in his opening lines. "A decent respect to the opinions of mankind" is stated as the reason for the Declaration. Jefferson knew that "a candid world" as well as reluctant revolutionaries at home would look at the document as an explanation of the legitimacy of the revolution.

Indeed, many colonists were frankly pro-British and loyal to George III. These Tories had no desire for independence and actively discouraged the movement. Their opposition made it imperative that the revolt be made respectable, a matter of duty rather than choice. The action of the colonies had therefore to be defended on the highest grounds of universal principle. British taxation, for example, was disliked because it flattened the colonists' purses, but economic self-interest was an unacceptable reason for a revolution. Good revolutionary technique required the expression of grievances in terms of violations of "the laws of nature and of nature's God." Using Lockean theory, Jefferson sublimated self-interest (taxes, loss of property) to principle (the natural right of the sanctity of property, liberty). Using Enlightenment ideas, he made George III appear to be not merely an inconvenience in certain ways, but a threat to a widely held ideal of human freedom. Indeed, George emerged from Jefferson's scathing pen a tyrannical ogre. Much could have been said for the English side, of course, but in writing the Declaration Jefferson's purpose was persuasion, not scholarship.

With independence declared, Jefferson, like other newly minted Americans, faced the sobering task of justifying the revolution with success. Not only did the proclaimed state of independence have to be confirmed on the battlefield, but the new nation suddenly had a host of awesome responsibilities thrust upon it. These ranged from creating a viable economy to establishing a workable system of government based on republican principles. Thomas Paine had written ecstatically in *Common Sense* about the glorious opportunity an independent America had to "begin the world over again." Doing it, however, was another matter. From our present status as a superpower we can hardly imagine the anxiety existing among Jefferson's contemporaries in the decade after independence. It may help to compare the fledgling nation with a teen-aged couple just starting married life after a bitter family war and a hurried elopement. It was thrilling in prospect and at the dramatic moment of separation, but now, alone in the quiet of a cheap apartment, the full impact strikes home. Food, clothing, order, and security no longer appear automatically from father and mother. Bills must be paid and relations with society established. To make matters worse, all the relatives and neighbors express open doubts about the eventual success of the new union and volunteer numerous predictions of its early demise.

For another perspective on the challenge of separate existence, consider that England, with its long experience in government and its immense resources, had been unable to solve many of the problems inherent in the American situation. Mercantilism had proved unworkable; the economy was in chaos, with thirteen separate and self-seek-

This is a portion of Jefferson's original four-page draft of the Declaration of Independence, which he began composing June 11, 1776 in Philadelphia.

John Trumbull's painting Declaration of Independence *was executed in the 1780s, partly while Trumbull was in Paris as a guest of Thomas Jefferson. A perfectionist, Trumbull painted thirty-six of the figures from life. Facing John Hancock (standing, right) are, from the left, John Adams, Roger Sherman, Robert Livingston, Thomas Jefferson, and Benjamin Franklin.*

As the high point of their efforts in the War of 1812 the British captured Washington, D.C. (August 24, 1814) and burned the public buildings as shown here. President James Madison and other officials fled in disgrace. But three weeks later Americans regained some measure of pride when they successfully defended the city of Baltimore against a British attack. At the conclusion of the battle Francis Scott Key observed the American flag still flying over Baltimore's Fort McHenry and composed the words for The Star Spangled Banner. Set to the tune of an old drinking song, it became the national anthem.

Among the many skills the versatile Jefferson perfected were architecture and horticulture. His own home, Monticello, overlooking Charlottesville in Western Virginia, is a monument to its owner's sense of grace and proportion. The house, which has become a Jefferson museum, is shown as it looks today.

ing entities each going its own way. The same internal discord had doomed any permanent effort at unified government of all the American colonies. England, moreover, had failed to discover ways of raising revenue for defense and administration. And there was the western land issue, which had simply been swept under the rug with the Proclamation of 1763. Inexperienced Americans were now confronted with all these same problems. Moreover, the wealth and leadership ability of 80,000 Tories, or Loyalists, who fled the country during and after the Revolution were no longer available to help build a nation.

Amid the doubt and uncertainty Jefferson's America could count a few assets in facing the formidable task of creating a nation. One was determination to establish the legitimacy of the revolution, to prove the scoffers and the critics wrong, to erase self-doubts. In addition, Jefferson and his contemporaries clung to the old idea that they were God's chosen people, destined to lead mankind in the paths of righteousness. From this perspective, the entire world had a stake in what happened on the edge of the North American wilderness. "The cause of America," as Paine put it, "is in great measure the cause of all mankind." And Philip Freneau, whose newspaper Jefferson later sponsored, solemnly proclaimed American independence an event commensurate in importance to the birth of Christ. True or not, the belief of many Americans in this rejuvenated conception of mission was one of their chief advantages in meeting the responsibilities of nationhood.

Despite all the talk about America, the united colonies, and the Continental Congress, when Thomas Jefferson thought of his country in the late 1770s, he had Virginia in mind. Most of his contemporaries shared this geopolitical orientation. Their loyalty to their respective colonies was, after all, of much longer standing than that to the larger, united body. Indeed, there were serious doubts about whether there would be unification after the fighting ended. Perhaps the various colonies would go their separate ways in the manner of the smaller European nations. Understandably, then, Jefferson's thoughts turned to Virginia immediately after publication of the Declaration of Independence. In his view, the reshaping of Virginia's laws and polity "is the whole object of the present controversy; for should a bad government be instituted for us . . . it had been as well to have accepted . . . the bad one offered to us from beyond the water." Jefferson also knew that the end of British rule meant a rare opportunity to translate political and social ideals into reality. He grew restless in Philadelphia throughout the spring and summer of 1776. Even as he wrote the Declaration of Independence he yearned to be in Williamsburg, and at the first convenient moment after its adoption, he resigned his seat in Congress.

Happily returned to Virginia, Jefferson at once launched a comprehensive effort to bring the new state's laws and institutions into conformity with republican principles and natural rights. His first target was the Virginia aristocracy. Although part of it himself, Jefferson realized that true liberty could not exist in a society dominated by an entrenched oligarchy. It was not the concept of an elite to which Jefferson objected, but rather the fact that the elite was established and perpetuated by artificial means. Instead of earning a silver spoon, its members were born with one in their mouths. What Jefferson hoped to do was "to annul this privilege, and instead of an aristocracy of wealth . . . to make an opening for the aristocracy of virtue and talent." The result should be a "natural aristocrat"—a happy blend of Jefferson's contact with both Enlightenment philosophy and the American frontier.

The foundation of Virginia's pre-Revolutionary aristocracy was land—huge holdings that passed from generation to generation according to the rules of entail and primogeniture. In this arrangement, which dated from feudal times, estates passed intact from the owner to his first-born son. They could not be subdivided nor sold outside the family.

In Jefferson's words, primogeniture and entail operated to create "a distinct set of families who, being privileged by law in the perpetuation of their wealth, were thus formed into a Patrician order, distinguished by the splendor and luxury of their establishments." Such a situation not being consistent with the right of every man to life, liberty, and the pursuit of happiness, Jefferson proposed the abolition of both entail and primogeniture. The oligarchy, of course, was suspicious; only his popularity and political tact, eventually pushed the bills through.

Religion also attracted Jefferson's reforming energies. For more than a century the Church of England had enjoyed a favored position in Virginia. Anglicanism was, in fact, the established religion, virtually a branch of the government. Jefferson deplored this situation. A disciple of the Enlightenment doctrine of freedom of thought, he believed that truth needed no enforcement other than its own inherent logic and reasonableness: "it is error alone which needs the support of government. Truth can stand by itself." This was the sense of the words "self-evident" that Jefferson, at Franklin's suggestion, used in the Declaration of Independence.

Jefferson was therefore bitterly opposed to any government effort to enforce or even assist a particular creed not only as a violation of individual liberties, but also as a poor way of making converts. Illustrating his point from the history of science, Jefferson pointed out that "the Newtonian principle of gravitation is now more firmly established on the basis of reason than it would be were the government to step in and to make it an article of necessary faith." Throughout history, Jefferson concluded, force in matters of belief only made "one half the world fools, and the other half hypocrites. . . . Reason and free inquiry are the only effectual agents against error." He held that a man's religion did not fall under the jurisdiction of civil authority. "The legitimate powers of government," he explained, "extend to such acts only as are injurious to others. But it does me no injury for my neighbor to say there are twenty gods, or no God. It neither picks my pocket nor breaks my leg."

To implement his ideas, Jefferson drafted a bill for establishing religious freedom in Virginia. After a ringing preamble, it declared in part that "all men shall be free to profess, and by argument to maintain, their opinions in matters of religion." Here was a guarantee of freedom of conscience for every citizen, be he Hindu, Christian, or atheist. Even more, Jefferson's arguments and his sweeping definition of free thought supported the principle that the opinions of men on *any* subject were not the concern of civil government.

When Jefferson's bill finally became law in 1786, it was a major milestone. The young nation had lived up to the promises of Roger Williams and William Penn. To the delight of Jefferson and his countrymen, the Virginia Statute for Religious Freedom was translated into several languages and circulated widely in Europe. Several publishers reprinted the document as an expression of Enlightenment philosophy. Jefferson believed this particular law put Americans a thousand years ahead of Europeans in respect to human freedom. "It

118

is comfortable," he wrote to James Madison in 1786, "to see the standard of reason at length erected, after so many ages, during which the human mind has been held in vassalage by kings, priests, and nobles." And with an eye to the American obsession with justifying the revolution with success, he added: "it is honorable for us to have produced the first legislature who had the courage to declare that the reason of man may be trusted with the formation of his own opinions."

Jefferson regarded education as another key to the transition from a monarchic to a democratic society. He was convinced that a people could not be both ignorant and free. Indeed, he wrote to Wythe, the most important part of the whole revision of Virginia's code of laws concerned "the diffusion of knowledge among the people." There was much to support his view. Democracy meant popular sovereignty—government by the people. Yet if the people were uninformed and incapable of making judgments about their own lives, unscrupulous opportunists could lead them into tyranny. History, he knew, offered many examples of the enslavement of an uneducated citizenry. And Virginia society, like the rest of the new states, was composed of a few islands of refinement in an ocean of ignorance. Such gross inequality created ripe soil for oppression.

As a remedy Jefferson proposed three years of free education for every white child in the state. The basic skills of reading, writing, and arithmetic would be emphasized, but so would the study of the past, for Jefferson believed that "history, by apprizing [children] of the past, will enable them to judge of the future . . . it will qualify them as judges of the actions and designs of men; it will enable them to know ambition under every guise it may assume; and knowing it, to defeat its views." Though only three years of free elementary schooling were provided, the educational ladder would have more steps. Jefferson felt students on the intermediate level would come from families "in easy circumstances" who could afford to pay tuition and board, but he stipulated that up to seventy of the best poor students in Virginia be given full scholarships. After a year the state-supported scholars would be pared to the twenty "best geniuses." They would study for five more years. Finally, a select group of ten scholarship students would receive a free education at the College of William and Mary.

It was a brilliant and farsighted plan, "adapted," as Jefferson declared, "to the capacity, and the condition of every one and directed to their freedom and happiness." Unfortunately, Virginia adopted only portions and those only gradually. Not until 1825 did an aging Jefferson have the satisfaction of seeing the University of Virginia, an institution he created almost single-handedly, open in Charlottesville as the capstone of the state's educational pyramid.

In 1779 the Virginia legislature called Thomas Jefferson to succeed Patrick Henry as governor. He assumed the office in an atmosphere of fear and gloom. The war with England was not going well. Supplies and money had run short. Even General George Washington's repeated and personal pleas for aid found Governor Jefferson helpless. His own plantations were stripped on behalf of the Revolution, and he had many companions in poverty. Less than half of Virginia's counties paid taxes in 1780. The state militia could be equipped with only one rifle for each five men. On top of this, the British decided to shift the focus of their military efforts to the south. Charleston, South Carolina, fell on May 12, 1780, to a naval strike under Generals Henry Clinton and Charles Cornwallis. On December 30 a fleet of twenty-seven British ships appeared at the mouth of Chesapeake Bay. Virginia could offer no resistance, and the force, under the American deserter Benedict Arnold, sailed up the James toward the capital city of Richmond. Jefferson supervised the removal of the state papers, transferred his family to a safe location upriver, and then returned to watch despondently from across the James as Arnold's men burned the city.

In the dark months of early 1781 it must have seemed to the harassed Jefferson that America's hopes for winning its independence were also going up in smoke. No sooner did he move the seat of government to Charlottesville than Cornwallis was at its door. On June 4 Jefferson slipped away from Monticello only minutes before a British force arrived to capture him. Seven legislators were taken. But even as the remainder fled across the Blue Ridge, the tide was turning in the southern theater of war. Tough American mountaineers under Generals Nathaniel Green and Daniel Morgan had already decisively defeated British regulars at King's Mountain, Cowpens, and Guilford Courthouse in the Carolina back country. The Charlottesville raid, in fact, was the last offensive move Cornwallis made. Less than four months later he stood defeated at Yorktown while the military bands played "The World Turned Upside Down."

With the fighting and his term as governor both at an end, Jefferson retired to Monticello, his family (he had married a young widow in 1772), his library, his horses, his music, and his science. Never again, he vowed, would he leave his hilltop oasis for the hurly-burly of public service. With enthusiasm he turned to writing *Notes on the State of Virginia*, a proud answer to a European's inquiry about the ideals and circumstances of the new society. The book was printed privately in Paris in 1785. He entertained another European, the traveling Chevalier de Chastellux, at Monticello. After four days of companionship the visitor wrote: "let me describe to you a man, not yet forty, tall, and with a mild and pleasing countenance . . . an American, who without ever having quitted his own country, is at once a musician, skilled in drawing, a geometrician, an astronomer, a natural philosopher, legislator, and statesman . . . in voluntary retirement from the world."

A classic portrait, but Jefferson was unable to play this idyllic role for long. The first crack came late in 1782 when his fragile and lovely wife succumbed to a long illness. Not long afterward, another opportunity for public service, this time in the national arena as a congressman, came Jefferson's way. At first he refused, claiming both personal grief and pique over criticism of his governorship as reasons for aloofness. But interesting developments were taking place on the federal level, and just as in the case of Virginia's government, he realized that the success of the whole revolutionary effort hinged on whether satisfactory political forms could be devised. Here was a challenge calculated to stir Jefferson to action. He knew that republics were rare in the history of civilization. Men had always relied more on authority from above (monarchy, oligarchy, theocracy) for government. In fact, the Greek city-states were the only examples of true republics in history, and these had been small units of several thousand citizens in which popular sovereignty had had great meaning. America, however, proposed to govern 3 million people in a republican framework. There were no precedents for such an undertaking, and many felt a republic on this scale would degenerate inevitably into either anarchy or tyranny.

The Continental Congress began to experiment in national

government immediately after proclaiming independence. John Dickinson of Pennsylvania proposed a strong central government in which the states had little power. Some of his colleagues, however, thought such an arrangement too similar to the one they had just overthrown. They countered with the Articles of Confederation, which deliberately created a weak national government. Under the Articles, the government had no courts, no executive leadership, no power to regulate trade and commerce, and no independent source of revenue apart from requisitions from the states. Moreover, on most important issues the approval of *all* the member states was required. This plan for a spineless central government was submitted to the states in November 1777 and, with unanimous approval finally obtained, instituted on March 1, 1781. For Americans like John Dickinson, who thought in terms of the nation rather than the states, it was not a cause for celebration. In their estimation Americans had overreacted, had rushed headlong from one undesirable extremity of the political spectrum to the other.

Thomas Jefferson reentered the national political arena in December 1783, when he rode to Annapolis, Maryland, to take his seat in Congress as a delegate from Virginia. Widely respected throughout the country, he immediately assumed a major role. One of his first assignments was to arrange for the visit of General George Washington. Already a demigod in American eyes, Washington came to Annapolis to relinquish his sword to Congress. The ceremony of December 23 was charged with emotion. Many men wept openly in gratitude. To Jefferson, however, Washington's appearance had a deeper significance. By turning over his sword, the general in effect rejected the idea that he become a military dictator. In the 1780s, with an insecure nation yearning for leadership, this was not far-fetched. In the winter of 1782–1783 a group of army officers, joined by proponents of strong central government, had approached Washington with the idea of seizing power. The general had made his disapproval very clear. Now at Annapolis the one American who had the popularity to undermine republicanism formally and publicly made his commitment to a republic. Like Jefferson, Washington had rebelled in the name of republican principles, and he meant to give them a fair trial. Had he been otherwise inclined, American history could well have been totally different.

While adamantly opposed to monarchical substitutes, Jefferson remained critical of the central government established under the Articles. As a congressman he had ample opportunity to study its weaknesses. Some problems, he believed, were related to the time and circumstance. Congress, for instance, had no money, but only because the war-ravaged state economies were temporarily in disorder. The financial position of the central government would improve with that of the country in general. A more serious difficulty was the contemptuous attitude of many of the states. Some did not even bother to send representatives to Congress. Jefferson, however, was present and determined to make the best of the Articles. His service to the new government was, typically, brilliant. One of his reports made order out of the chaotic coinage system of the time by proposing the adoption of the "dollar," divided into tenths and hundredths, as the basic unit.

Of still greater consequence was Jefferson's influence on western land policy. Congress inherited this thorny problem from Great Britain when several states, led by New York and Virginia, ceded their western land claims to the central government. The cession itself was a triumph for federalism, but it obliged America to become an imperial power with all the attendant responsibilities. The western territories, in other words, bore the same relation to the United States as the thirteen colonies once had to Great Britain. There was the same perplexing question of management, the same danger of rebellion should Congress become as unsatisfactory as Parliament.

The colonial policy that emerged owed a great deal to Thomas Jefferson. On March 22, 1784, he submitted a plan of government for the territories. Its genius was embodied in the provision that the western lands would be organized into states which, when they had a sufficient number of settlers, would be welcomed into the union *on an equal basis* with the original thirteen. No virtual representation, no taxation without representation, no second-class citizenship, but rather an invitation to join the empire. Had England granted as much in the early 1770s, the professed need for the American Revolution would have been eliminated and war, in all probability, averted. Jefferson's plan had the further advantage of encouraging settlement of the West by assuring those who migrated that they would suffer no loss of rights or liberties. It even guaranteed manhood suffrage in the territories—a step toward democracy that none of the original states had yet taken. Himself a slaveowner, he proposed that slavery be prohibited in the western territories after 1800. Finally, Jefferson, a disciple of order, suggested a rectangular survey system for the unsettled land.

The essentials of Jefferson's western plan were incorporated in the Land Ordinance of 1785 and the Northwest Ordinance of 1787. These great laws, the high point of government under the Articles of Confederation, made possible one of the most successful colonizing

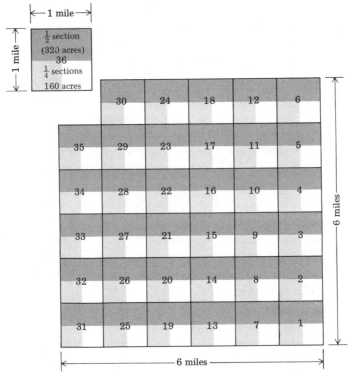

The influence on Thomas Jefferson of the Enlightenment and science generally is evident in his plan for surveying the unoccupied territory of the West. Adopted by Congress as the Land Ordinance of 1785, its geometric regularity shaped the landscape of an expanding nation. The entire six-mile square was called a "township" and consisted of thirty-six "sections," each one mile square. These in turn could be divided according to the detail in Section 36. One disadvantage of Jefferson's system was that its rigid structure did not take the natural features of the environment into account. The lines ran straight regardless of rivers, mountains, or lakes.

efforts in history. The United States expanded from the Appalachians to the Pacific without losing a single acre to an independence movement. Every territory ultimately entered the union in preference to forming a separate nation. As students of Great Britain's imperial misadventures, Jefferson and his colleagues learned their lessons well.

Valuable as Jefferson was at home, Congress needed able representatives abroad, and on July 5, 1784, he sailed for France. After assisting John Adams and Benjamin Franklin for a year negotiating commercial treaties, Jefferson took Franklin's place as American ambassador to France. It was a happy choice. Although lacking Franklin's enormous popularity, Jefferson's reputation as an architect of American independence endeared him to French liberals. As the French Revolution gathered momentum, Jefferson's counsel was increasingly sought. He personally believed that "the American war seems first to have awakened the thinking part of the nation . . . from the sleep of despotism in which they were sunk." Young French officers, Jefferson explained, had returned from service in the New World enthusiastic about the republican regime they saw in operation. When they joined other republicans in launching a revolt against *their* king, Jefferson was understandably delighted. Even as the course of the French Revolution turned toward the guillotine, he never lost faith that its basic energies sprang from the same concepts of human dignity and freedom that had motivated Americans.

Jefferson remained abroad five years. His characteristic response to what he termed "the vaunted scene of Europe" was awe. Patriotic as he tried to be, he could not help but be reminded of his provincialism by the brilliance of European cultural and intellectual life. "Were I . . . to tell you how much I enjoy their architecture, sculpture, painting, music," Jefferson wrote in 1785, "I should want words." He also coveted European books, and returned from Paris with enough to fill 250 feet of shelves at Monticello. And there were the charms of sophisticated European women, notably Maria Cosway, the wife of an English painter, with whom Jefferson traveled through France in the summer of 1786.

But at the same time Jefferson almost desperately resisted European attempts to turn his attention from his own country. Groping for ways to maintain pride in America, he pointed out that his countrymen enjoyed greater civil and economic equality than in the Old

World, where everyone "must be either the hammer or the anvil." Americans were also more moral, Jefferson generalized, and in their natural environment they possessed a resource of matchless beauty. If not culture, then nature would distinguish the young nation on the edge of the wilderness. Still "the vaunted scene" was compelling to the self-styled "savage of the mountains of America." Not for many decades would Americans acquire the cultural confidence to trust their own judgment and taste.

Returning to the United States in 1789, Jefferson enjoyed a brief rest at Monticello before resuming his career in the national government. Much had happened during his absence. Dissatisfaction with the weak central government under the Articles of Confederation grew through the decade. No matter how well it functioned, Congress simply did not possess the power to coordinate state economic policies or protect the nation's commercial interests abroad. Moreover, the mob rule that critics of democracy constantly predicted seemed on the verge of breaking out. In Massachusetts the winter of 1786–1787 brought a pitched battle between impoverished western farmers, organized under Daniel Shays, and the state militia.

Actually, Shays's Rebellion was simply a continuation of the internal contest over who should rule at home that had accompanied the larger struggle with Great Britain. Both the Shaysites and the Boston establishment understood their cause to be sanctified by natural rights and thus in keeping with the principles of the American Revolution. The problem was that this doctrine made no distinction between human rights and property rights. Both were sacred, and if the two came into conflict (as they did, for example, in debtor-creditor relationships), there was no easy solution. Those responsible for the Declaration of Independence and the Articles of Confederation assumed that men of good will could work together in interpreting and institutionalizing natural rights. But Shays's Rebellion, and the prospect of similar mass uprisings elsewhere, suggested that the spirit of 1776 had not erased old social and economic tensions.

The fundamental tension juxtaposed those traditional antagonists, the haves and the have-nots. Shays, representing the latter, preferred a weak central government with its assurance of a maximum of local control by the people. He had the support of men like Jefferson who leaned toward a human rights interpretation of Locke and who trusted democracy. Commenting on Shays's Rebellion while in Paris, Jefferson even went so far as to declare that "the spirit of resistance to government is so valuable on certain occasions, that I wish it to be always kept alive. It will often be exercised when wrong, but better so than not . . . at all. I like a little rebellion now and then. It is like a storm in the Atmosphere."

John Adams, on the other hand, spoke for the forces of law, order, and property rights. Even after independence, he remained highly suspicious of popular sovereignty. For Adams, the Shaysites were "ignorant, restless desperadoes, without conscience or principles, . . . mobish insurgents [who] are for sapping the foundation and destroying the whole fabrick at once." Americans of Adams's persuasion were not opponents of democracy, but they did insist that the voice of the people be diluted—sifted, so to speak, through the medium of a strong central government. Washington spoke for this viewpoint when he observed: "we have errors to correct; we have probably too good an opinion of human nature in forming our Confederation."

If the critics of the Articles of Confederation had a low opinion of human nature, they had a high one of human reason. With it, they believed, man could build a system of government capable of curbing his passion, greed, and selfishness. Armed with this conviction, twenty-nine men (later joined by twenty-six others) gathered in Philadelphia in May 1787 to reconstruct the government of the United States. Fortunately for the outcome of their efforts, they were agreed in certain crucial areas. All were advocates of a strong central government. Most also agreed that the Articles were so deficient in this respect as to be totally useless. It was better to start from scratch than to revise and repair. In this reconstruction, the members of the convention believed, two principles must be incorporated: First, the new constitution must be the supreme law of the land, its power unquestionably greater than that of the various states. Second, the constitution must be a combination of monarchy, aristocracy, and democracy so arranged as to prevent the dominance of any one of these political options.

Nobody in Philadelphia seriously doubted that the people should be the basis of sovereignty in the new government. The question was how to check and balance popular opinion in the interest of the nation's well-being. Here was where reason came into play. Rather than trust men to know and work for the good, the founding fathers assumed with Lord Acton that "power corrupts." They also took pains to remove direct elective power from the people—three stages in the case of the President, four in the case of judges. Like engineers, the Constitution makers of 1787 built a series of automatic cutoffs into their power system. The result, approved September 17, was a masterpiece. In a single summer and without precedents or guides, the Constitutional Convention created a framework of government that has lasted, with only minor amendment, for almost two centuries.

Jefferson, following the Constitutional Convention from Paris, had mixed reactions. He liked the tripartite division of power between the executive, legislative, and judicial branches. He approved of giving the new legislature the power to levy taxes, and he was "captivated" by the compromise that established a bicameral legislature with the states represented on the basis of population in one house and equally in the other. But other aspects of the Philadelphia convention disturbed him deeply. In the first place, he did not agree with most of the delegates that the country teetered on the brink of anarchy in 1787. The Articles of Confederation, in Jefferson's opinion, had not been all that bad. "I would rather be exposed to the inconveniences attending too much liberty," he tartly observed, "than those attending too small a degree of it."

He felt the convention would have done better to have patched up the Articles of Confederation. As for the new system, Jefferson disliked the executive position created in Philadelphia. "Their President," he wrote to John Adams in November, "seems a bad edition of a Polish king." One man might be elected to the office every four years for life. Jefferson's major complaint, however, was the failure to specify the rights and liberties retained by individuals. "A bill of rights," he told James Madison, one of the prime movers at Philadelphia, "is what the people are entitled to against every government on earth . . . and what no just government should refuse, or rest on inferences." Civil liberties, after all, were the reason for the American Revolution for Thomas Jefferson. If a strong central government destroyed them, there was no point to independence.

Jefferson therefore followed the controversy over ratification of the Constitution closely and anxiously. He noted with approval that in

Virginia patriots like Richard Henry Lee and Patrick Henry spoke emotionally against ratification. Lee referred to the proponents of the Constitution as "a coalition of monarchy men, military men, aristocrats and drones whose noise, impudence and zeal exceeds all belief." This was extreme. Of all the so-called Federalists, probably only Alexander Hamilton considered monarchy a serious possibility. But, as historian Charles A. Beard pointed out in 1913, most of those who designed and favored the Constitution were men of means who stood to benefit economically from the stability and protection of a strong central government. Some even held for speculation Congress's paper money, the value of which was directly proportional to the vigor and power of the United States. This is not to say that economics alone explains the new Constitution, but rather that economic self-interest was evident along with idealistic principle in the summer of 1787. No contemporary of Jefferson would have found this point far-fetched; only those who insist on sanctifying America's beginnings with totally idealistic explanations profess shock at an economic interpretation of the Constitution.

Those who took Jefferson's position ultimately lost the struggle over ratification. Although its margin was narrow (89–79 in the Virginia ratifying convention, 187–168 in Massachusetts), the new government went into operation in 1789 without a bill of rights. But shortly thereafter, James Madison, who had opposed a listing of individual rights as unnecessary, noted the widespread national displeasure at its omission and decided to correct the matter himself. He wrote a declaration of rights and sent a copy to Paris for Jefferson's comments. The reply, full of praise, contained a few suggestions for improvement. Madison took them and in June 1789 introduced the Bill of Rights in Congress. Two years later, after approval by the states, it became the first ten amendments to the Constitution.

Positive action on the Bill of Rights greatly encouraged Jefferson, and the selection of George Washington as the first President in 1789 further reduced his anxieties about the new government. Washington, he felt confident, had no ambition to become a king. Indeed, the more Jefferson thought about how the Constitution of 1787 smoothed out the institutional wrinkles in America's republican experiment, the more enthusiastic he became. The Constitution, he declared, was "unquestionably the wisest ever yet presented to men." How it would work in practice, of course, no one yet knew.

George Washington was determined that Jefferson should take a leading role in establishing the new central government. He invited Jefferson to become secretary of state on his return from France. Given his interest in the success of the American experiment, Jefferson could not resist. After a brief stay at Monticello he made his way north to New York, then the federal capital. There was a dramatic meeting en route at Philadelphia between Jefferson and an aged Benjamin Franklin. The two friends talked largely of mutual acquaintances and politics in France. Franklin was particularly excited about the burgeoning French Revolution. "They served their apprenticeship in America," he observed, "and now they mean to set up for themselves."

Pushing on through a snowstorm, Jefferson arrived in New York in March 1790 to take charge of a State Department consisting of five clerks. The government was already well underway. In Jefferson's opinion, however, it manifested some disturbing tendencies. Most of them stemmed from the activities of Alexander Hamilton, Washington's wartime assistant and now his secretary of the treasury. Jefferson hardly knew the ambitious and talented Hamilton when he joined the administration, but soon the two of them were "daily pitted in the cabinet like two cocks." The conflict was predictable. In direct contrast to Jefferson, Hamilton made no secret of the fact that he despised the mass of common men, distrusted democracy, and preferred an aristocratic or, better yet, a monarchical regime. Saddled with the Constitution, Hamilton determined to make the most of an imperfect situation. This meant maximizing the strength of the central government and encouraging the development of a wealthy elite.

To these ends, Hamilton pushed through Congress a program for funding the debt of the United States at its full face value. He also successfully advocated federal assumption of all state debts incurred in the war for independence and the creation of a government-dominated national bank. Expensive as these measures were, they established the national credit, asserted federal superiority over the states, and brought men of wealth, chiefly northern businessmen, to support the United States. In 1791 Hamilton's Report on Manufactures proposed a protective tariff and a system of bounties, both to encourage domestic manufacturing. Jefferson was able to help block this plan, but he could not prevent Hamilton from obtaining in the same year a 25 percent excise tax on the domestic production of whiskey. This levy struck particularly hard at small farmers, who were accustomed to converting their grain into alcohol. When a group of several hundred farmers in western Pennsylvania came to Hamilton's attention for tax evasion, he personally led a force of 13,000 militiamen to crush the Whisky Rebellion.

Jefferson looked askance at these developments. From his perspective it appeared Hamilton was creating a far stronger central government than necessary—one, in fact, that posed a threat to individual liberties and republican principles. Hamilton's advocacy of manufacturing, cities, and high finance, moreover, ran directly counter to the Virginia planter's precept that "those who labor in the earth are the chosen people of God." Agriculture, Jefferson insisted, had to be the backbone of any happy society. "Let our workshops," he declared, "remain in Europe." America could trade for needed manufactured goods. For Hamilton himself, Jefferson grew to have a well-honed contempt. In as strong language as he ever used, Jefferson labeled the secretary of the treasury "not only a monarchist, but for a monarchy bottomed on corruption." With far more regret Jefferson said almost as much of his old Revolutionary colleague John Adams, whose doubts about democracy had increased substantially. Even Washington's head seemed to have been turned by a vision of grandiose living in the ceremonial manner of Old World courts.

With the tide thus running against republicanism, Jefferson struggled desperately. He had a few allies. Friends of his ideals in the Senate who refused to be pressured by a President eager for certain decisions established a precedent for legislative autonomy. These senators also resisted attempts to make Washington's official title "His Elective Majesty" or "His Most Gracious Highness," in the manner of European kings. The designation "highness," one skeptical legislator dryly remarked, should be reserved for the tallest man in a company. This viewpoint ultimately prevailed, and the accepted form of addressing the President became, to Jefferson's delight, simply "Mr. President."

After 1791 Jefferson also had the support of Philip Freneau and his newspaper, the *National Gazette.* In fact, Jefferson gave Freneau a position in the State Department and helped him start the paper as a challenge to John Fenno's *Gazette of the United States,* which Hamilton patronized. In the hallowed tradition of eighteenth-century journalism, the papers abused each other unmercifully and in vituperative language. Washington, for one, was shocked and disappointed. He had expected, somewhat naively, that political parties would not develop in the United States. Yet by 1792 it was clear that the Federalists, grouped around Hamilton and Adams, and the Jefferson-led Republicans (sometimes called Democratic Republicans) were determining the course of national politics. This realization led a reluctant Washington to agree to a second term as President. He knew he was the only American capable of holding back the partisan deluge.

Questions of foreign policy added fuel to the political fires of the 1790s. Once again, Hamilton and Jefferson squared off. The secretary of the treasury tended to admire and favor England both as a commercial power and as a monarchy. Jefferson, on the other hand, supported France and its revolution on both philosophical and personal grounds. Even after the execution of Louis XVI in 1793 and the massacres by the Jacobins, Jefferson's loyalty held firm. But in Federalist circles around the capital and among the upper classes generally, Jefferson was a marked man. People crossed streets to avoid encountering the "Jacobin," and Hamilton exploited his advantage to the hilt. As a result, when war broke out between France and England, Jefferson was at a severe disadvantage. He attempted to obtain sympathy for France by reminding Washington of the 1778 treaty of alliance that had been so helpful to the American revolutionary cause. Hamilton countered with the argument that the old treaty had been made with the now-dethroned French monarchy and was, consequently, void. When Washington supported this interpretation, Jefferson had little choice but to resign as secretary of state, a step he took at the end of 1793. By this time the brazen behavior of the French emissary, Citizen Edmond Genêt, in commissioning American privateers to prey on English shipping had alienated even Jefferson.

In 1794 a pro-British foreign policy seemed likely, but England did little to cultivate American support. In fact, she harassed the United States both on the high seas, where American ships were seized, and on the northwest frontier, where Indians were encouraged to take the warpath. War with England seemed imminent in 1794, but

John Jay warded off hostilities by negotiating a controversial treaty. It succeeded in removing the British from frontier forts in the Ohio Valley, establishing formal commercial relations, and settling boundary and war debt questions remaining from the Revolution. On the burning issue of maritime rights, however, the Jay Treaty said nothing. It also ignored the fact that Canadian fur traders had unrestricted access to American soil and freely sold arms and ammunition to the Indians.

Leading the Republican opposition, Jefferson branded the Jay Treaty neocolonial. The Senate barely approved the agreement in June 1795. Washington, too, was torn, but finally yielded to Hamilton's arguments and signed the document in the face of widespread national criticism. His decision almost certainly postponed a second war with Great Britain, the major objective of Federalist foreign policy. When the second war finally came, in 1812, the young nation was strong enough to hold its own. Washingtonian diplomacy was further distinguished in the 1790s by the favorable Treaty of San Lorenzo (the Pinckney Treaty) of 1796. According to its terms the United States received important concessions from Spain regarding rights and boundaries in the West. The final movement in the diplomatic minuet of the 1790s involved the United States in an undeclared war with France. An insult to America's foreign ministers by Talleyrand (the XYZ affair) led to a state of open maritime conflict for several years.

John Adams and the Federalists won the Presidential election of 1796, but under the awkward electoral college system Thomas Jefferson, the Republican nominee for President, became Adam's Vice-President. From this vantage point of honored obscurity, Jefferson had ample opportunity to observe federalism play itself out.

Using the threat of war with France as an excuse, the Federalists in the summer of 1798 pushed through the Alien and Sedition Acts. The former were designed to weaken the political influence of immigrants, who generally were Republicans, by giving the President the power to imprison and deport dangerous noncitizens. The Alien Acts also lengthened the residence requirement for citizenship from five to fourteen years. Far more sinister, in Jefferson's eyes, was the Sedition Act, for under its terms the federal government could suppress American citizens. The Sedition Act provided for fines and imprisonment for persons composing, printing, or uttering "any false, scandalous, and malicious writing or writings against the government of the United States, or the President . . . with intent to defame . . . or bring them . . . into contempt or disrepute." The law, in other words, sought to end criticism of the government.

Jefferson was enraged, the more so when Matthew Lyon, a Republican congressman from Vermont, was actually jailed for verbal attacks on his Federalist opponent. In Jefferson's eyes the Alien and Sedition Acts made a mockery of those cherished principles of the American Revolution embodied in the Bill of Rights. Freedom of speech, press, and even thought were denied for purely partisan purposes. In November 1798 Jefferson channeled his wrath into the Kentucky Resolutions. Taking the position that the federal government had assumed undelegated powers in passing the acts, he set forth the doctrine of nullification. The illegal measures, Jefferson wrote, are "altogether void and of no effect," at least as far as Kentucky was concerned. Writing for Virginia, James Madison promulgated a similar doctrine. The other states did not follow suit in 1798, but the controversy raised questions about the nature and purposes of the union that would not be settled conclusively until the Civil War.

The Alien and Sedition Acts prompted some Republicans, chiefly in the South, to give serious consideration to leaving the union. Jefferson, however, believed the Federalists had dug their own grave. The great majority of Americans, he felt, would not accept such curtailment of their hard-won liberties. "A little patience," he advised his more radical colleagues, "and we shall see the reign of the witches . . . pass over and the people . . . restoring the government to its true principles." Events proved him correct, for during the closing years of the 1790s the Federalists committed one political blunder after another. They levied heavy taxes on personal property, then used the revenue to support a large standing army. In 1799 that army marched against a group of protesting Pennsylvanians under John Fries, and cries of tyranny rose on all sides.

Federalism also suffered from divisions in its own camp. After a brief trial, President Adams found he could not stand Alexander Hamilton. Adams also wanted to extricate his administration from the undeclared war with France. The "High Federalists" resisted the idea, but Adams finally repudiated his advisors and concluded a satisfactory peace. The Republicans meanwhile prepared for the election of 1800 by developing an effective party organization. There were local and statewide committees, some of them holdovers from the Democratic Clubs that had appeared earlier in the decade in support of Jefferson, republicanism, and the French Revolution. Several influential Republican newspapers sprang to life and, in defiance of the Sedition Act, attacked the Adams Administration for monarchical ambitions. The Federalists replied in kind and organized their own party. The stage was set for a showdown political battle.

The election of 1800 was unprecedented in several respects. It was the first to take place outside the shadow cast by George Washington, for with him in December 1799 died the last gentlemanly reservations about the propriety of partisan politics. Previously neither Republicans nor Federalists had quite dared bring their animosities into the open. Now it was bare knuckles. In addition, 1800 was the first election in which the contesting parties took their campaigns to the people. It was to be more of a national election and less an agreement among political insiders. With Adams put forward for re-election by the Federalists and Jefferson the natural choice of the Republicans, the start of the new century promised to be exciting.

The Federalists understandably chose to base their campaign on their opponents' shortcomings rather than on their own record. The charges against Jefferson were predictable. For one, he had spent too much time in close association with the radical democracy of France. If Jefferson were elected, charged the Federalists, guillotines would appear in the squares of the major cities, and the privileged classes could expect the worst. Another favorite Federalist smear involved Jefferson's alleged atheism. Actually he was a deist who demanded that his religion, like his other beliefs, be supportable by reason and evidence. In Federalist eyes, however, it was a question of "God—and a religious president; or . . . Jefferson—and no God!!!" One hysterical Adams partisan went further, forecasting that if Jefferson were elected, "murder, robbery, rape, adultery, and incest will all be openly taught and practiced, the air will be rent with the cries of distress, and the soil will be soaked with blood."

Perhaps the most credible Federalist charge concerned Jefferson's philosophical nature and agricultural orientation. The Virginian, it was contended, would be too impractical for the Presidency, and his rural bias would spell hardship for America's struggling commercial and industrial enterprises. Giving no quarter in their struggle for political survival, the Federalists also attacked Jefferson's personal morality. It was alleged that the master of Monticello had defrauded a poor widow of her inheritance and had fathered several children by one of his slaves. The first charge could be dismissed quickly, for Jefferson kept himself in chronic poverty as a result of honoring financial promises made to unlucky acquaintances. As for the illegitimate children, substantial evidence suggests that as a widower in the 1790s Jefferson enjoyed a mutually satisfying intimacy with a black girl named Sally Hemings, who was the half-sister of his deceased wife and who had been with him for part of his stay in France.

The Republican campaign of 1800 was based on the simple promise to return the nation to the path of freedom from which it had strayed under Federalist guidance. Hamilton, Adams, even Washington were accused of undermining the intent of the American Revolution. The strategy proved successful. Not even the forest fires the Federalists lit on election day to preoccupy the country people who were largely Republican could prevent Jefferson and his running mate, Aaron Burr, from sweeping to victory with 73 electoral votes each. The unanticipated tie threw the election into the House of Representatives. The embittered Federalists tried every means to block Jefferson's bid, but after more than 30 inconclusive ballots, he emerged as President.

In later years Jefferson spoke of the outcome of the election as the "revolution of 1800," adding that it was "as real a revolution in the principles of our government as that of 1776 was in form." In one sense, of course, this was incorrect. The election of Thomas Jefferson took place under procedures established by the Constitution. There was no overthrow of the government's principles. No secession or civil war followed the counting of the votes. Neither did the new President revolutionize economic or legal procedures. Jefferson himself interpreted the national mood quite accurately in his inaugural address, when he declared that "every difference of opinion is not a difference of principle. . . . We are all Republicans, we are all Federalists."

Still, a social and intellectual change of such scope that some might call it revolutionary did occur in 1800. The Federalists were an avowed aristocracy. Openly distrusting the masses of common men, they took as their model the privileged upper classes of the Old World.

They insisted that men must keep their place. Those who owned the country ought to govern it, and challenges should be summarily crushed. The Jeffersonians, on the other hand, drew their inspiration from the New World. They had confidence in the reasonableness of mankind and advocated an open, fluid social order. Their elite would be a natural one, the product of talent and diligence. Every man should, they believed, enjoy equality of opportunity and the freedom to exploit his potential to the fullest. Under federalism, in sum, the nation drifted away from democracy. After 1800 the cause of the people was in the ascendancy, at least as an ideal.

President Jefferson surrounded himself with a distinguished group of associates headed by James Madison as secretary of state and Albert Gallatin as secretary of the treasury. Among the first problems facing their administration was one created by a Federalist-dominated national judicial system. John Adams, tired and bitter at the close of his administration, deliberately filled the national courts with Federalist judges. These "midnight" appointments were designed to give the Federalists a measure of influence in Jefferson's administration. Already suspicious of the judiciary because of its distance from popular control (judges had life tenure), the Republicans attacked. At one stroke Congress abolished sixteen circuit courts and their sixteen Federalist judges. The House of Representatives moved on to impeach the highly partisan Supreme Court Justice Samuel Chase, but after a sensational trial, the Senate wisely refused to supply the necessary confirmation.

The real center of judicial power, however, was John Marshall, Chief Justice of the Supreme Court. Marshall was a Virginian and a distant relative of Jefferson, but there was no love lost between the two. A leading Federalist and Adams's secretary of state, Marshall was appointed in the closing weeks of the Adams administration. For the outgoing President's purposes, the choice was brilliant. Marshall, who dominated the Supreme Court for thirty-four years, handed down a series of decisions that institutionalized the Federalist interpretation of the Constitution. His first important ruling, and the foundation of many of the rest, concerned the power to determine the constitutionality of laws passed by Congress. Jefferson believed the authors of the Constitution intended that all three branches of the federal government work together, checking and balancing, to determine the meaning of that document. Marshall took the position that the Constitution was "superior paramount law," unalterable by legislative act or executive order. Hence only the judicial branch could pronounce on the question of constitutionality.

In 1803 Marshall found an opportunity to create a precedent. The case of *Marbury* v. *Madison* involved William Marbury, a Federalist who had received one of Adams's controversial appointments, and the secretary of state, James Madison, who refused to honor his appointment. Marbury went straight to the Supreme Court with the intention of using a section of the Judiciary Act of 1789 to force the executive branch to honor the commitment. Marshall agreed that the law was on Marbury's side, but ruled against him on the grounds that the Judiciary Act gave the Supreme Court an unconstitutional power. The Chief Justice thus decided against both his party and the power of his court, but he established a far more important principle—the right of the judicial branch to decide if an act of Congress was in conformity with the Constitution.

After *Marbury* v. *Madison* Jefferson and his Republican successors to the Presidency could only chafe in frustration as the "crafty chief judge," in Jefferson's words, handed down a series of major decisions. *Martin* v. *Hunter's Lessee* (1816) and *Cohens* v. *Virginia* (1821) resulted in the establishment of the right of the Supreme Court to review, and if necessary to reverse, the decisions of state courts respecting the Constitution. The ruling confirmed the principle of federal supremacy. In *Fletcher* v. *Peck* (1810) and *Dartmouth College* v. *Woodward* (1819), the Marshall Court protected the structure of American business by affirming the obligation of contracts in the face of popular criticism. Hamilton would have been delighted. *McCulloch* v. *Maryland* (1819) set forth the broad or "loose" interpretation of the powers of the federal government under the Constitution. If the purpose was legitimate and constitutional, Marshall ruled, then Congress had the power to take any constitutional action necessary to achieve that purpose. The decision was a direct slap at the Jeffersonians' narrow or "strict" interpretation of constitutional authority.

The Jeffersonians in theory were proponents of weak central government. But relative positions had much to do with this preference. When the Federalists held the national reins, the Jeffersonians opposed a strong central government. Once in control themselves, a powerful nation acquired much greater appeal. In fact, the deposed Federalists soon became the new critics of strong national authority.

The course of events soon substantiated this reversal of roles. In contrast to what many had hoped—or feared—the Republicans did not use their control of Congress and the Presidency to undo major Federalist policies and institutions. The Bank of the United States was left intact, and in 1816 Jefferson's successor, James Madison, created a central bank more than three times the size of Hamilton's prototype. Neither did Jefferson change the Federalist objectives of upholding the national credit, assuming state debts incurred in the Revolutionary War, and encouraging shipping and commerce. In time, the Republicans even instituted and improved upon a Hamiltonian ideal, a protective tariff to encourage manufacturing. The new President did reduce the size of the army as part of his plan for federal economy, yet he took a leading role in establishing the United States Military Academy at West Point, New York. Jefferson also started a sixteen-year plan to abolish the national debt the Federalists had deliberately created for the purpose of securing loyalty to the central government. Secretary of the Treasury Gallatin worked brilliantly at the reduction plan and, for a time, succeeded. But a final accounting showed that Jefferson and Madison were as skillful spenders as the Federalists. After the allotted sixteen years, the indebtedness of the United States had never been higher.

Jefferson's foreign policy also changed with his acquisition of power. Previously sympathetic toward France, he turned hostile when Spain's sale of Louisiana to France became public. Jefferson even contemplated alliance with his old nemesis, Great Britain, to prevent the French takeover on the western border. Napoleon, however, solved the problem. In 1803 France gave up plans for a New World empire and sold all of Louisiana (later carved into thirteen states) to the United States for $15 million. This incredible bargain violated Jefferson's ideals of frugality and constitutionality. And, the Federalists, of all people, accused Jefferson of going beyond the limits of his authority in buying land. In truth, there was nothing in the Constitution sanctioning such action. Jefferson wrestled with the problem for several months, finally rationalized the Louisiana Purchase as an extension of the "empire of liberty," and pushed the required treaty

NORTH AMERICA FOLLOWING THE LOUISIANA PURCHASE

BRITISH POSSESSIONS

ATLANTIC OCEAN

MAINE
VERMONT
NEW HAMPSHIRE
MASSACHUSETTS
R.I.
CONNECTICUT
NEW YORK
NEW JERSEY
PA.
MD.
DEL.
NORTHWEST TERRITORY
VIRGINIA
NORTH CAROLINA
SOUTH CAROLINA
SPANISH FLORIDA
INDIANA TERRITORY
KENTUCKY
TENNESSEE
GEORGIA
MISSISSIPPI TERRITORY

St. Louis

PIKE 1805-1806

Mississippi River

GULF OF MEXICO

400 miles
200
0

LOUISIANA PURCHASE (1803)

Missouri   River

Ft. Mandan

PIKE 1806

Red   River

PIKE 1807

▲ PIKES PEAK

Santa Fe

SPANISH POSSESSIONS

LEWIS 1806

CLARK 1806

Colorado   River

1804-1805

Snake R.

OREGON COUNTRY

LEWIS & CLARK

Columbia R.

Ft. Clatsop

PACIFIC OCEAN

through the Senate as quietly as possible. Even he realized that theory had to give way occasionally to practical considerations.

Planning for the exploration and settlement of the West was considerably more enjoyable for Jefferson. In 1804 he fulfilled a dream by sending an expedition under his private secretary, Meriwether Lewis, and William Clark to the headwaters of the Missouri and thence down the Columbia to the Pacific Ocean. Two years and over 7000 miles later Lewis and Clark returned from the wilderness with a wealth of information. Zebulon Pike brought back additional data from his expeditions to the source of the Mississippi and to the Colorado Rockies. The blank map of the American West was gradually being filled in, and Jefferson was delighted both as a citizen and a scientist. He also took pleasure in the thought that the virgin land to the west would soon support a population of hardy yeoman farmers, those mainstays of the republic. To help them the Jefferson administration altered the land laws to make possible the purchase of small farms at attractive prices. Under the Land Act of 1804 a man could obtain title to 160 acres for as little as $80 (one-fourth the purchase price) down.

As the pressures and conflicts of national politics swirled around him, there were times when Jefferson thought wistfully of Monticello —if not of Lewis and Clark's lonely camps. The strange case of Aaron Burr caused him special pain. A suicidally ambitious man, Vice-President Burr became disenchanted with the Republicans midway through Jefferson's first term. Seeking a fresh ladder, he turned to a group of embittered Federalists who were exploring the possibility of persuading New York and the New England states to secede from the union. In the course of this plot Burr's enormous ego ran afoul of Hamilton's, and a feud quickly developed. The climax was a duel July 11, 1804, on the western bank of the Hudson River. Hamilton reputedly fired first and missed, whereupon Burr coolly delivered a fatal shot. He next appeared in the Mississippi Valley, again investigating the chances for leading a revolt from Jefferson's government. The complex deal, involving both Spain and England, collapsed in 1806, and Jefferson ordered Burr arrested on charges of treason. But Chief Justice Marshall, before whom the case was tried, defined treason so narrowly as to ensure Burr's acquittal.

Jefferson was deeply embarrassed, but the bulk of the American people, those who had swept him to a decisive victory in the election of 1804, stood behind their President. Burr was nearly lynched and was eventually obliged to leave the country. Jefferson and his party stood unchallenged. The citizenry had become fond of the President's understated, effective, and unmistakably American style. They liked his abolition of the weekly "levee," a Federalist holdover from the fashionable world of European courts. They chuckled at his insistence on a round table for state dinners so no guest would have precedence over another. And they roared with glee when the new British ambassador, dress sword and all, was received by Jefferson in bedroom slippers!

It was one thing to slight England at a diplomatic reception, something else again on the high seas. In 1805 Lord Nelson reconfirmed British mastery of the oceans with a smashing victory in the Battle of Trafalgar. But Napoleonic France remained the master of continental Europe, and war between the powers continued. One result was that American ships engaged in international trade were subject to seizure by one or the other of the belligerents. It was not a trifling matter for President Jefferson. Between 1804 and 1807 over 1500 American vessels were seized and searched. The British went further, "impressing" American seamen. Under this ancient practice the captain of a warship could in time of emergency compel service from any of his countrymen. Theoretically, then, only Englishmen could be impressed, but on the high seas such niceties were often ignored. Many American citizens found themselves working for the British navy under circumstances that amounted to slavery.

In June 1807 Jefferson received word that the British frigate *Leopard* had dared to fire upon and search America's *Chesapeake* within sight of the Virginia coast. Three Americans died in the encounter, and four men were impressed. The people were furious. Jefferson noted that "never since the battle of Lexington have I seen this country in such a state of exasperation." There was more than enough support to declare war on England, but Jefferson stood by his opposition to America's "entangling" herself in the affairs of Europe. Instead of taking sides in the Anglo-French conflict, he proposed an embargo on all American trade with Europe. Jefferson hoped that the boycott would force respect for the rights of neutral nations.

Instituted December 22, 1807, the embargo proved a failure. The volume of American trade was too small to cause France or England real economic hardship. Moreover, the United States was not united behind the policy. Shippers and merchants, especially those in New England, regarded the whole idea as a Jeffersonian plot to destroy commerce and punish the Federalists. Many merchants simply resorted to smuggling to move their goods. Still, American exports dropped by 80 percent and bankruptcies rose by an equal amount. Jefferson received a torrent of abuse. "You Infernal Villain," one New Englander wrote, "how much longer are you going to keep this damned Embargo on to starve us poor people."

The election of 1808 reflected this criticism. Jefferson declined renomination, feeling that Washington had set an admirable precedent in limiting his service to two terms. Instead he advanced the candidacy of his secretary of state. Madison won, but New England was solid in its opposition. It appeared to Jefferson that continuation of the embargo would only further divide the country, so he repealed it March 1, 1809, three days before leaving office. Now an observer rather than a participant, Jefferson watched as the final acts of the diplomatic drama were played out to a sad conclusion. Madison tried several modified trade boycotts without success. Impressment continued. Finally, Napoleon maneuvered Madison into believing that France would cooperate in respecting neutral rights. Madison thereupon sided with France and severed diplomatic relations with England. In good time England also repealed its offensive maritime policies, but too late. Before news of the repeal reached America, Madison asked Congress for a declaration of war. In June 1812, for the second time in less than forty years, America was at war with England.

Both Jefferson and Madison were well aware that the explanation for the War of 1812 was more complicated than violation of maritime rights. Many westerners were anxious to remove the British from Canada. There was the danger of English-inspired Indian attacks from this quarter; moreover, there was the prospect of annexing Canada. Henry Clay and the other "War Hawks" in Congress effectively marshaled this sentiment into an argument for war. Another motive was the vague but potent sense of national honor. Regardless of where they lived or how they made their living, Americans resented being treated as if they were still colonists. Perhaps, they reasoned, a second war of independence was needed to convince the world that the new republic meant to be taken seriously.

Gratefully retired to Monticello after four decades of continuous public service, Jefferson eagerly turned to his library, his gardens, his inventions, his science, the founding of the University of Virginia, and a correspondence that amounted to over a thousand handwritten letters a year. There was also a steady stream of visitors paying homage to the Sage of Monticello. As a participant in the beginnings of the controversy, Jefferson took a keen interest in the War of 1812.

Its formal outcome, embodied in the Treaty of Ghent, December 24, 1814, was inconclusive and unsatisfying. But Americans proved adept at finding, or perhaps making, glory. Oliver Hazard Perry was elevated to the rank of national hero after his September 1813 victory over the British fleet on Lake Erie. A year later the invasion of Baltimore was repulsed, and Francis Scott Key created a song that later became the national anthem. But from the standpoint of the national ego, nothing compared to the Battle of New Orleans. Jefferson shared the thrill that rippled through the nation when news arrived that on January 8, 1815, Andrew Jackson and an untrained force of frontier riflemen had crushed the cream of the British army. Two thousand Englishmen died in the encounter and only six Americans—one of the most lopsided victories in military history. Newspapers headlined their accounts of the battle "Almost Incredible Victory!!" and "Rising Glory of the American Republic."

Few could doubt it, and in the aftermath of the War of 1812 a feeling of national unity and well-being prevailed. President Madison and Henry Clay advanced an "American System" under which domestic manufacturing and consumption were encouraged by protective tariffs and improvements in internal transportation. The last vestiges of the Federalists as a national political party withered in the sun of the new nationalism. One indication was the collapse of the plan for revising the Constitution that a group of New England Federalists formulated at Hartford, Connecticut, late in 1814. Representatives of the gathering arrived in Washington at the same time as news of New Orleans, and the Federalists attracted only jeers. This is not to say, however, that the United States entered a political "era of good feelings" after 1814. Jefferson, for one, knew better. Factionalism was inherent in politics. Beneath the veneer of national solidarity were ambitious men eager to crack the hold of Virginia (of the first five Presidents, only John Adams had come from a different state) and the Republicans on the central government.

Sectionalism offered one means of shaking up this political status quo. In his declining years Jefferson observed a sharp intensification of sectional consciousness. The financial panic of 1819 and the subsequent depression set hard-pressed westerners and laborers everywhere against eastern financial interests. Far more serious in Jefferson's estimation was the crisis of 1819 and 1820 occasioned by the application of the territory of Missouri for admission to the union. At issue was the geographical extension of slavery.

As a young man Jefferson, along with most national leaders, entertained the vague hope that slavery would gradually disappear. To this end Jefferson wrote a passage for the Declaration of Independence attacking the international slave trade as a violation of the "sacred rights . . . of a distant people." Although the passage was deleted from the final version of the document, Jefferson continued his campaign. In 1784 he called for the exclusion of slavery from the western territories, and he applauded the action of the Constitutional Convention of 1787, which did provide for cessation of the slave trade after twenty years. But all the while Jefferson struggled with massive uncertainties. If the slave *trade* and the *extension* of slavery were wrong, what about slavery itself? Jefferson the philosopher of liberty and natural rights answered this question one way; Jefferson the southerner and owner of some two hundred slaves answered it another. The latter viewpoint prevailed, but only because Jefferson carefully created and maintained in the face of increasing evidence to the contrary the myth of innate black inferiority. All men were created equal, in other words, but blacks were not fully men. This shabby reasoning was the only way Thomas Jefferson could reconcile his conflicting beliefs.

Contrary to Jefferson's expectations, the passage of time did not bring the weakening of slavery. The advent of large-scale cotton production in the early nineteenth century underlay a dramatic rise in the value of slaves. Moreover, the abolition of the slave trade in 1808 was more than offset by rising birth rates among the black population and smuggling. By 1820 most southern slaveowners regretfully accepted black bondage as an unpleasant necessity, and some had come to see it as a positive good. Considerations of fear as well as economics shaped their point of view. Jefferson and his fellow slaveholders disliked and feared blacks. Even if they had wished to do it, slavery could not have been abolished without creating in the South a large population of free blacks who would, southern whites believed, run rampant over every civilized value and institution. Colonization of freed blacks in Africa

THE MISSOURI COMPROMISE: 1820-1821

ATLANTIC OCEAN

PACIFIC OCEAN

GULF OF MEXICO

BRITISH POSSESSIONS

OREGON COUNTRY
U.S. & GREAT BRITAIN

BRITISH TREATY LINE 1818

MICHIGAN TERRITORY

MAINE
VT. N. H. MASS.
R. I.
CONN.
NEW YORK
N. J.
PA.
MD. DEL.
Washington
VIRGINIA
N. C. • Raleigh
S. C. • Columbia
GEORGIA
• Atlanta
Savannah
St. Augustine
FLA.
CEDED BY SPAIN 1819

Detroit
OHIO
• Columbus
IND.
• Indianapolis
• Frankfort
KY.
TENN.
ALA.
MISS.
LA.
• New Orleans
ILL.
• St. Louis

MISSOURI
MISSOURI TERRITORY
1819-1821

ADAMS-ONÍS TREATY LINE 1819

36° 30' MISSOURI COMPROMISE LINE 1820

ARKANSAS TERRITORY

SPANISH TERRITORY

• San Antonio de Béxar

Free states and territories

Free territory by Missouri Compromise

Slave states and territories

Slave territory by Missouri Compromise

had long been considered a solution to this dilemma, but it had never materialized. White America, it appeared, was stuck with blacks and, because of the supposed need for their social control, with the institution of slavery. "We have the wolf by the ears," Jefferson lamented in 1820, "and we can neither hold him, nor safely let go." Then, in a comment that penetrated to the heart of his personal dilemma, he added: "justice is in one scale, self-preservation in the other."

With a Jefferson one might hope the former would take precedence, but the plain fact is that it did not. During the Missouri controversy he joined the most closed-minded southerners in regarding the whole issue as a Federalist plot and resisting any limitation of slavery. Henry Clay eventually bailed the nation out with a compromise proposal that accepted slavery in Missouri, balanced that state's admission to the union with the inclusion of Maine, and set the latitude 36°30′ as henceforth the northern limit of slave labor in territory acquired in the Louisiana Purchase. Jefferson doubted the compromise would work. He knew that an arbitrary line was no way to settle a difference of moral principle. The Missouri debates, "like a fire bell in the night," filled Jefferson with terror. "In the gloomiest moments of the Revolutionary War," he wrote in 1820, "I never had any apprehensions equal to what I feel from this source." Upon the shoals of the slavery issue, he predicted, the union would founder.

In October 1823 Jefferson, now eighty years old, was flattered to receive a communication from President Monroe soliciting his advice on a delicate question of foreign policy. England, it appeared, was concerned that Spain, with assistance from France, Austria, and Russia, might try to recover her rebellious colonies in South America. The British foreign minister approached the United States with the idea of issuing a joint declaration opposing any further changes in the political geography of the New World. Jefferson thought the proposal had much merit, and advised Monroe to abandon for once the policy of nonentanglement. An alliance with powerful England would be of considerable assistance in keeping the New World independent.

The President tended to Jefferson's position, but Secretary of State John Quincy Adams opposed it on the grounds that the United States should not preclude her *own* territorial expansion by agreeing to preserve the current arrangement. Florida, he argued, had been acquired from Spain in 1821, and there was reason to believe that Cuba, Texas, and perhaps all South America would one day join the union.

Moreover, Adams did not favor riding England's coattails in this matter. Why not, he asked, make a separate statement that the Western Hemisphere was not open to further colonization by any European power? In the end Adams prevailed. The Monroe Doctrine of December 2, 1823, rejected England's proposition, affirmed the principle of New World autonomy, and kept the door open for American expansion.

Late in June 1826 Thomas Jefferson marked the approach of the fiftieth anniversary of American independence by writing a brief statement for the celebration of July 4th. The American Revolution, he reflected, had been a "signal" for oppressed people everywhere to burst their chains and "assume the blessings and security of self-government." Reason and the free exchange of opinion had been substituted for ignorance, superstition, and fear. Because of July 4th, Jefferson continued, "all eyes are opened, or opening, to the rights of man."

John Adams knew that few men had played a more important role in this process than his old friend and sometime opponent, Thomas Jefferson. On July 4, 1826, Adams lay dying at his home in Quincy, Massachusetts, and his mind wandered back to the stirring days of the Revolution. His last words were, "Thomas Jefferson still survives." But just a few hours earlier, also, curiously, on the fiftieth anniversary of the day he had done so much to distinguish, Jefferson too had died.

SELECTED READINGS

The Person

*BOORSTIN, DANIEL J.: *The Lost World of Thomas Jefferson* (1948). Places Jefferson in the context of the American Enlightenment.

BOYD, JULIAN (ed.): *The Papers of Thomas Jefferson* (1950–   ). The authoritative collection, expected to reach fifty volumes.

BRODIE, FAWN: *Thomas Jefferson: An Intimate History* (1974). An essentially critical interpretation of Jefferson as a libertarian aristocrat.

*KOCH, ADRIENNE: *The Philosophy of Thomas Jefferson* (1943). An analysis of the many facets of Jefferson's thought.

* Available in paperback.

KOCH, ADRIENNE, and WILLIAM PEDEN: *The Life and Selected Writings of Thomas Jefferson* (1944). The best one-volume treatment.

MALONE, DUMAS: *Jefferson and His Time* (1948–1977). A definitive multivolume biography.

PETERSON, MERRILL D.: *Jefferson and the New Nation* (1970). The most recent biography.

The Period

*ADAMS, HENRY: *History of the United States during the Administrations of Thomas Jefferson and James Madison* (9 vols., 1889–1891). One of the classics of American historical writing. Adams treats social and intellectual as well as political and economic history in an elegant literary style.

*CUNNINGHAM, NOBLE: *The Jeffersonian Republicans* (2 vols., 1957–1963). The rise to power of a political party.

*DANGERFIELD, GEORGE: *The Era of Good Feelings* (1952). National political developments in Jefferson's declining years.

DAVIS, DAVID BRION: *The Problem of Slavery in the Age of Revolution, 1770–1823* (1975). An exploration of the intellectual dilemmas that slavery created for revolutionaires like Jefferson.

*HORSMAN, REGINALD: *The Causes of the War of 1812* (1962). One interpretation of a much-discussed war.

*JENSEN, MERRILL: *The New Nation* (1950). The achievements of Americans in constructing their first federal organization.

*JORDAN, WINTHROP: *White Over Black* (1974). Broad treatment of the difficulties that slaveholding posed for Jefferson as a natural-rights philosopher.

*MOORE, GLOVER: *The Missouri Controversy, 1819–1821* (1953). An exploration of the beginnings of sectionalism.

NETTELS, CURTIS P.: *The Emergence of a National Economy* (1962). A reliable survey of the nation's early economic history.

*NYE, RUSSEL B.: *The Cultural Life of the New Nation* (1960). Intellectual and social history.

*WOOD, GORDON: *Creation of the American Republic 1776–1787* (1969). Political theory and political institutions.

WRIGHT, LOUIS B.: *The First Gentlemen of Virginia* (1940). Social history of the milieu from which Jefferson emerged.

* Available in paperback.

Tecumseh

It was hard to see in the twilight that filtered to the floor of the Ohio forest. Sensing something wrong, the Shawnee boy, Tecumseh, and his mother paused to look. Then they saw the body. Sprawled beside the trail was Tecumseh's father, mortally wounded but able to murmur "behold the faith of white men!" Puckeshinwa had been accosted on the trail earlier that day by a band of frontiersmen. In violation of 1774 agreements, the white men were in recognized Indian territory. Outraged to see them so near his home, Puckeshinwa refused to be their guide and protested their presence. Their response was a bullet in his chest

Shocked and scared, Tecumseh watched his mother kneel in the quiet forest next to his dying father. He heard her tell him that in time he would avenge his father; he would become a great warrior chief and "scatter desolation and death" among the whites. The impassioned woman saw the day when her son would be "a fire spreading over the hill and the valley, consuming the race of dark souls." Tecumseh later took this charge to mean advocacy of a united stand of all Indians against the expanding white civilization. With his brother, The Prophet, he dreamed of an independent Indian nation strong enough to push the "Long Knives" off the continent altogether. The next best alternative was to coexist with the United States in North America. His fanatical yet skillful pursuit of this ideal was a wonder of the Old Northwest in the early nineteenth century. Even Tecumseh's archenemy, the future President William Henry Harrison, recognized the Shawnee as "one of those uncommon geniuses which spring up occasionally to produce revolutions and overturn the established order of things." A few Americans of Tecumseh's generation may even have recognized that his crusade for native independence paralleled their own recent revolution against Great Britain. But Tecumseh stood in the way of forces too strong for even his abilities to resist. His dream of Indian nationalism sank in the inexorable flood of American expansion. Like his father, Tecumseh also died on the floor of a forest, shot in 1813 by the guns of land-hungry frontiersmen.

Before Tecumseh was born, in 1768, hundreds of centuries of his people's history in the New World had unfolded. The precise time and circumstances of the real beginning of American history swirl imprecisely in the mists of long ago. But there is general support for the following hypotheses: 1) *Homo sapiens* did not evolve in the Western Hemisphere. Every American has been an immigrant. 2) Man first reached the New World in Alaska, and he came from Asia. 3) The date of the first arrival is between ten and forty thousand years ago.

The vast ice fields and glaciers of the late Pleistocene were the most important factors influencing the timing and direction of prehistoric migrations. With massive quantities of frozen water on the land, the sea level dropped by as much as 300 feet. For Tecumseh's distant ancestors, the greatest consequence was the transformation of the 60-mile-wide Bering Strait between Siberia and Alaska into a grass-covered land bridge. Like the Isthmus of Panama, the exposed land provided a highway between continents.

The same glaciation that lowered the sea also determined the pattern of life on land. There is evidence that expanding Siberian glaciers pushed animals and the men who hunted them against the east coast of Asia and eventually funneled them across the Bering bridge. North America had glaciers, too. They spread outward over the Canadian Shield from the area of Hudson Bay. But for thousands of years in the Pleistocene, much of lower-elevation Alaska was free of ice. Given prehistory's long time span, it was possible for successive generations of hunters to filter up the Yukon River along the base of the Brooks Range, down the Mackenzie River Valley, and then south along the unglaciated corridor east of the Canadian and American Rocky Mountains. At the height of Pleistocene glaciation, it is true, the ice probably cut off this route. By this time, the first Americans could have been south of the snow, spreading through the temperate and tropical latitudes.

This image of the first generations of humans exploding into a territory where there was no human competition has inspired some anthropologists to postulate the theory of a very rapid occupancy of the New World. Perhaps in only a thousand years the skilled hunters of the north raced from Alaska to the tip of South America. Physically, this was possible. In the course of his missions to outlying tribes, Tecumseh regularly traveled on foot 2000 miles a year. But the pace of the geographical expansion of his racial stock need not have been so hurried. Hunting and gathering people were not explorers by choice. They certainly were not tourists. They vacated a territory only when forced to do so as a result of a diminishing food supply or when challenged by superior tribes. More determined, fiercer, and better-armed groups pushed weaker ones out of the way. The Navahos and Apaches, for instance, arrived in the Southwest only a century or two before the Spaniards. A powerful people, they annihilated prior occupants of the area or drove them away. So Siberian hunting people moved down the mountainous continental spine to stand at land's end. Beyond Tierra del Fuego was only the Antarctic. Man had extended his range from one ice cap to another. It was one of his greatest achievements. Thus the European colonization of North America was only the most recent act in a drama of human competition as old as man in the New World.

Tecumseh's distant ancestors had many geographical options along the way. There were ecological niches in which a hunter with limited agricultural skills could fit. Wave after wave of migrants crossed the Bering bridge, penetrating to the far corners of the continent. Some braved the Southwest, not yet a desert in the Pleistocene, to reach the California coast. This route eventually helped to people the Pacific Northwest and British Columbia, forming a great arc again pointing northward. Others followed the slope of the land down the rivers of the Great Plains and into the eastern woodlands. Tecumseh's people were among them.

"Shawnee" meant "southerner," but the itinerant language group that went by this name ranged widely in the eastern forests. The constantly shifting stream of time and people that produced Tecumseh ran back some four thousand years to a sophisticated Indian culture that existed in the Ohio Valley and southeast along the Appalachian Mountains to the Gulf of Mexico.

It was one of the supremely arrogant ideas of American history to regard these people as a handful of ragged savages living precariously on the brink of starvation. Although less sophisticated than the Mayas and Aztecs of Mexico (whose civilizations rivaled Europe's and even surpassed them in some areas), many woodland Indians of North America lived in well-organized towns. They constructed elaborate burial mounds and ceremonial centers. Buildings, such as the longhouse of the Iroquois, reached a height of 300 feet. Their Six Nations confederation was a triumph of constitutional government. The eastern Indians farmed expertly, a fact the first English settlers appreciated, and they practiced an effective medicine based on the use of plants and herbs. Mining for the purpose of fashioning art objects was well developed, and the native Americans traded in a loose confederation extending from New York to Kansas. Relying on the tradition of such contact among the dozens of tribes and subtribes, Tecumseh later attempted to build unified resistance to the white presence.

The number of Indians in the New World at the time of first

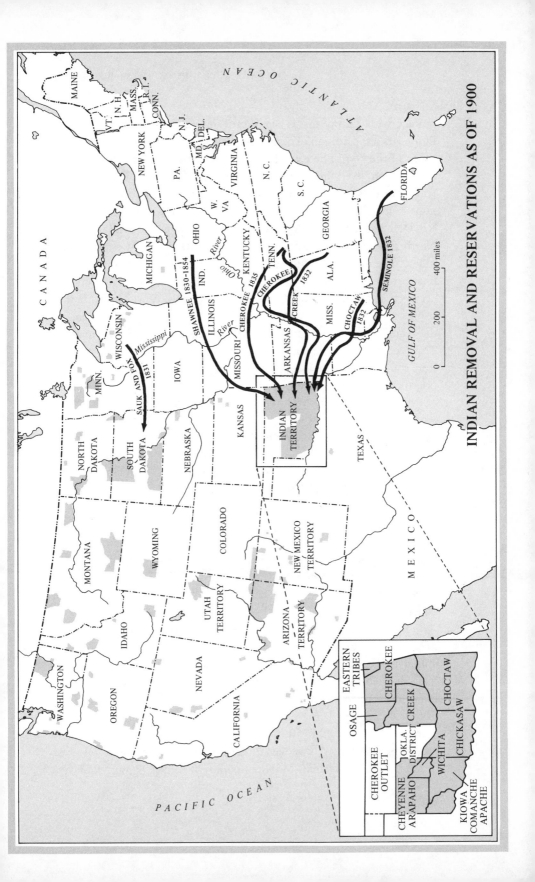

INDIAN REMOVAL AND RESERVATIONS AS OF 1900

ATLANTIC OCEAN

CANADA

MAINE
VT. N.H.
MASS.
CONN. R.I.
NEW YORK
PA.
N.J.
MD. DEL.
W. VA.
VIRGINIA
OHIO
KENTUCKY
N.C.
S.C.
GEORGIA
TENN.
ALA.
MISS.
FLORIDA

MICHIGAN
IND.
ILLINOIS
WISCONSIN
MINN.
IOWA
MISSOURI
ARKANSAS

Ohio River
Mississippi River

SHAWNEE 1830-1854
SAUK AND FOX 1831
CHEROKEE 1835
CHEROKEE 1832
CREEK 1832
CHOCTAW 1832
SEMINOLE 1832

INDIAN TERRITORY
KANSAS
NEBRASKA
NORTH DAKOTA
SOUTH DAKOTA
WYOMING
COLORADO
NEW MEXICO TERRITORY
TEXAS

MONTANA
IDAHO
UTAH TERRITORY
ARIZONA TERRITORY
WASHINGTON
OREGON
NEVADA
CALIFORNIA

PACIFIC OCEAN

GULF OF MEXICO

MEXICO

0   200   400 miles

EASTERN TRIBES
OSAGE
CHEROKEE
CHEROKEE OUTLET
OKLA.
DISTRICT
CREEK
CHEYENNE ARAPAHO
WICHITA
CHICKASAW
CHOCTAW
KIOWA COMANCHE APACHE

contact with Europeans is significant in judging the legitimacy of European dispossession. To suppose that the pre-contact Indian population of the hemisphere totalled about ten million, of which less than one million lived in North America, is, at least in European and American eyes, to justify dispossession. There are, after all, about the same number of Indians living in the United States today. More recent scholarship, however, suggests much higher figures: 9,800,000 for North America and an astounding 90,043,000 for the Western Hemisphere. The total is more than the combined population of the Western European nations at the time of Christopher Columbus. From this perspective, the European occupation of the New World needs radical reassessment. The land was hardly "vacant." European acquisition of the Americas was less discovery and exploration than it was invasion. The white newcomers did not settle a wilderness so much as they stole someone else's home. The knowledge of this fired the determination of patriot chiefs like Tecumseh.

"Tecumseh" was a Europeanized spelling of a term Shawnees would have understood as "panther lying in wait." Events proved the aptness of the name. Tecumseh's birthplace (in March 1768) and the home of his youth was Old Piqua, a village on the Mad River in central Ohio, not far from its confluence with the Miami and the present city of Dayton. The Shawnees were wanderers. Puckeshinwa, whom Tecumseh watched die near Old Piqua about 1775, was born in Florida. The pressure of advancing white settlement had pushed Puckeshinwa's band out of Pennsylvania and into a nomadic existence that led far south. Around the year 1740 his people entered the Creek country in eastern Alabama. There he married Tecumseh's mother, Methoataska. Tecumseh was her fifth child and the first born at Old Piqua.

Shawnees like Tecumseh's family were already refugees when they moved to Ohio, and the problem of resisting American expansion dominated the first discussion the boy remembered. In 1774, when he was six, Methoataske told him that his father and oldest brother had left Old Piqua to contest the hunting grounds called Kentucky, south of the Ohio River. Tension had been building in the region for several decades. As early as 1750 Dr. Thomas Walker and a small party prospecting for land discovered Cumberland Gap, a natural pass through the Appalachian Mountains into "Kaintuck". John Finley, a

Pennsylvania trader, brought back additional reports after a 1752 adventure. Captured by Shawnee warriors as he floated down the Ohio River in a canoe, Finley had been taken to their village in the heart of the bluegrass country. After being released, he returned glowing with news about a lush land abounding in deer, wild turkey, and buffalo, which at that time still existed in the eastern woodlands. Reports like Finley's fueled the fires of westward expansion, but the French and Indian (or Seven Years') War during the 1750s temporarily halted colonial contact with Kentucky.

Then, in the late 1760s, came the backwoodsmen, preeminent among them a man named Daniel Boone. Living in the remote Yadkin Valley of North Carolina, Boone spent the winter of 1768 with John Finley. In the spring the men secured financial backing and supplies from Judge Richard Henderson, a part-time land speculator, and headed through Cumberland Gap. For two years Boone roamed Kentucky. He was alone for months at a time, living off the land in the manner of the Indians whose skills he imitated and perfected. In December 1769, when Tecumseh was a year old, a band of Shawnees captured Boone and Finley and took most of their supplies. The men escaped by diving into a canebrake and eluding the Indians in the dense, 30 foot-high vegetation. Continuing to trap and hunt, Boone began his return to the frontier settlements in the spring of 1771. He had a modest fortune in furs. But near the western entrance to Cumberland Gap, Indians stole his furs, horses, and remaining supplies. A disappointed Boone walked back to his cabin empty-handed after two years.

The reports of white faces in Kentucky which filtered back to Tecumseh's village were profoundly disturbing. The Shawnees were aware that the British had proclaimed, in 1763, that no settlement could take place west of a line drawn down the crest of the Appalachians. But here were the "long hunters," so-called because, like Boone, they made extended hunting trips into the backcountry, in the forbidden territory. In 1773 the first group of land speculators entered what came to be called the "Dark and Bloody Ground." Equipped with land bounties issued to Virginia soldiers during the Seven Years' War, the speculators contended that they were not bound by the Proclamation of 1763. Rejecting this reasoning, the Shawnees organized to resist. They were unable to secure the aid of either the Iroquois Six

Nations or the Cherokees, who were kept on the English side by skilled Indian agents William Johnson and George Croghan, but the Ottawa and Mingo tribes became allies.

War became inevitable in 1774 when Virginia claimed Kentucky under its 1609 charter and sent Dr. John Connolly to Pittsburgh to enforce its title. Connolly, who had an eye for rich land holdings, aroused frontiersmen against the "savages." The Shawnees, under their chief, Cornstalk, called for peace and rational discussion. But in this land dispute the English had little to gain by reasoning with a society that preceded them in the area by several thousand years. From their perspective, the best policy was simply to drive the Indians off the contested land. So the Shawnees' efforts to work with Pennsylvania Quakers, the only colonial group that consistently recognized Indian rights, and to send peace messengers to Connolly at Pittsburgh proved futile. On June 10, 1774, after Shawnees killed thirteen whites to avenge the death of an equal number of their own tribesmen, Lord Dunmore, governor of Virginia, declared a state of war. Daniel Boone walked 800 miles in 60 days to warn the outlying settlements.

In July 1774 Governor Dunmore began his war of territorial conquest by sending 1500 frontiersmen against the Shawnees. Chief Cornstalk responded by gathering 1000 warriors, including Tecumseh's father and brother, crossing the Ohio River, and moving toward an encounter with the Virginia army at the mouth of the Great Kanawha River. The Battle of Point Pleasant began on October 9, 1774. It was a typical behind-the-trees frontier fight, with no clear gains by either side. With the coming of darkness, however, Cornstalk acted on misinformation regarding colonial reinforcements and ordered a retreat. The Shawnees recrossed the Ohio. Seizing the advantage, Dunmore marched on Indian villages in Kentucky with the avowed purpose of slaughtering every man, woman, and child. Terrified, the Shawnee leaders agreed to peace; it was, understandably, on terms dictated by the Virginians. The Treaty of Camp Charlotte obliged the Shawnees to acquiesce to the English occupation of Kentucky, to stop hunting in that region, and to refrain from attacking boats on the Ohio River. For their part, the Virginians agreed not to disturb Old Piqua, where Tecumseh was a boy of six, and the other Shawnee villages north of the Ohio. The betrayal of this assurance explained Puckeshinwa's outrage at finding invaders near Old Piqua shortly after the treaty, and the protest that resulted in his murder.

Despite the fact that Cornstalk emerged the loser from Lord Dunmore's War, Tecumseh idolized the dignified Shawnee chief. In his youthful innocence he may have believed that, at the price of Kentucky, Cornstalk had bought peace and territorial security for the Ohio Shawnees. Events belied this assumption. The settlements south of the Ohio grew rapidly in size and confidence. After a brief fling with Richard Henderson's semifeudal plans for a separate colony of Transylvania, Kentucky was annexed to Virginia in 1777. About the same time, Cornstalk paid a friendly visit to the American fort at Point Pleasant, scene of his retreat three years earlier. Unfortunately, a Kentuckian had recently been killed along the Ohio River. Assuming the murderer to be an Indian, and applying the principles of Old Testament justice so common on the frontier, enraged soldiers broke into Cornstalk's cabin and gunned down the defenseless Shawnee chief. Old enough to feel injustice keenly, Tecumseh must have experienced the same helpless anger that overwhelmed Americans at the assassination of Abraham Lincoln in the 1860s and at the murder of John Fitzgerald Kennedy a century later.

By the late 1770s the fortunes of Tecumseh's Shawnee and other tribes were caught up in the American Revolution. From the very beginning of hostilities, in 1775, it was clear that the Indians would play a vital role in the conflict. Both the English and the rebellious American colonists attempted to secure Indian allies. The British were more persuasive in this endeavor. Their Indian superintendents, John Stuart in the South and John Johnson in the North, were widely respected. The English also had strong frontier posts, notably Detroit and Niagara, a well-organized fur trade, and superior trading goods. The American rebels could offer the Indians little more than rhetoric about liberty and natural rights, which, in view of frontier disregard for Indian claims to ancestral lands, were hardly compelling. In fact, many Ohio Valley tribes such as the Shawnee, Delaware, and Miami, regarded the hostilities surrounding America's attempt at independence as an opportune moment to remove the settlers from their hunting grounds. In general, red men and redcoats fought together in the War for American Independence.

The Shawnees used the murder of Cornstalk to initiate raids against Kentucky settlements. Chief Blackfish, Tecumseh's adopted father, and 300 warriors so terrorized the frontier that by 1777 the pioneers were forced to take refuge in "Kentucky Stations." These rectangular forts, with blockhouses located at each corner, proved effective in withstanding Indian attack. But the beseiged Americans quickly found their supplies dangerously low as Blackfish continued to rampage through their abandoned cabins and fields. In January 1778 Daniel Boone led an expedition from one of the Kentucky forts to obtain a supply of salt from a spring on the Licking River. On February 7, while hunting alone, Boone was surprised by 4 Shawnees; they also captured his 26 companions. The ten-year-old Tecumseh was on hand when the warriors returned in triumph to Blackfish's village, Chillicothe. Boone lived with the Shawnees for five months and proved so impressive a woodsman that Blackfish adopted him into the tribe as his foster son. Through this tie Boone became foster brother to Tecumseh.

Despite the honor of adoption, Boone's assumptions and ambitions remained worlds apart from the Shawnees'. In the late spring of 1778 he learned of Blackfish's intended attack on Boonesborough, in Kentucky. Realizing that he must warn the settlers, Boone lagged behind a group of Shawnees walking on a trail and just "melted away" into the forest. Four days and 160 miles later the legendary frontiersman pounded on the gates of the fort at Boonesborough. By the time a furious Blackfish arrived on the scene, the fort was secured against attack. Before his abortive siege, the Shawnee chief tried to persuade Boone to return as his son, but the white man refused. The significance of the incident was not lost on young Tecumseh, who would later face the same kind of cultural choice involving an American girl whom he loved.

Despite resistance to Blackfish at Boonesborough, the American war effort on the western frontier was not impressive in the early years of the Revolution. In the Ohio Valley Americans cowered in the available forts. In western New York the powerful leader of the confederated Iroquois, Joseph Brant, ravaged outlying settlements almost at will. The British appreciated, and in some instances paid bounties for, scalps and prisoners brought to their posts. American fortunes began to improve in June 1778, when a young Kentucky woodsman, George Rogers Clark, took the offensive. Together with a company of veteran Indian-fighters, Clark marched on the British posts in the Illinois country, capturing Kaskaskia, Cahokia, and Vincennes. French inhabitants of the area were won over to the American side by Clark's announcement of the alliance that the Continental Congress had concluded with France on February 6, 1778. Even the Indians were impressed with Clark's toughness and fighting skills. But the warriors were disillusioned because the undermanned and poorly equipped Armies failed to mount an attack on the key British post at Detroit. Clark agreed that a golden chance had been missed, blaming the unwillingness of frontiersmen to fight outside their immediate neighborhoods as the fundamental cause. By the end of 1780 the Indians were solidly pro-British, and the Americans had lost almost everything Clark had gained in Illinois.

But if Americans lost the war in the west, they won the peace. Taking advantage of animosity between Great Britain, France, and Spain, John Adams and his colleagues at the Paris peace talks secured the Mississippi, rather than the Ohio, River as the western boundary of the new nation. The preliminary accord of November 1782 (ratified September 3, 1783) opened the entire Old Northwest to American expansion. The fact that thousands of Indians also had claims to this territory never occurred to the negotiators in Paris.

Young Tecumseh saw a considerable portion of the Revolutionary War in the west in and around his home in central Ohio. Old Piqua, his birthplace, was burned by the Americans and rebuilt—inevitably farther west—on the Miami River. Chillicothe, where Tecumseh lived with Blackfish, was burned to the ground three times between 1779 and 1782. George Rogers Clark directed the last two raids. In the summer of 1782 Tecumseh furthered his training as a warrior by watching his tribesmen and a British force from Detroit lead overeager Kentuckians into an ambush on the Licking River and thrash them soundly. Later that same summer fourteen-year-old Tecumseh participated in his first battle against white men. It was not an auspicious beginning. When his older brother was wounded, Tecumseh ran in panic from the battlefield. Overcome with personal shame and filled with rage against the invaders of his homeland, he vowed that this moment of cowardice would be the last time he would ever show fear.

The vow may have influenced Tecumseh's decision not to follow the large group of Shawnees, including his mother, who wearied of the strife in Ohio. Hoping to find peace and security, they headed for what in the 1780s was the far west—Missouri. Tecumseh knew better. He was already forming the belief that guided his life: the Indians' only real and permanent security would come from resisting the white invasion and forcing recognition of Indian territorial rights. It was necessary to take a stand; with the newly independent American nation gaining westward momentum every year, the time for effective action was running out.

The end of the American Revolution saw Tecumseh's people living north of the Ohio River, without an ally, in the face of a territorially ambitious United States. The territorial settlement of 1783 (Peace of Paris), which conferred the Northwest Territory to the United States, was synonymous, in most American minds, with possession of the land itself. The Indians had a different idea. The 1780s witnessed increasing hostility on the part of the Shawnees toward the advancing Americans. Tecumseh, by now well over his early qualms about battle, joined with, and soon led, one of the bands attacking boats on the Ohio. By 1786 the new nation, rather than the individual states, was injured in such hostilities. Maryland's 1778 refusal to ratify the Articles of Confederation unless the states claiming western lands ceded them to the central government was the first in a series of rejections of all state claims to the politically unorganized West.

So it was that a commission appointed by Congress and representing the nation as a whole began, in the winter of 1784–1785 to negotiate with Indians regarding the Ohio country. From the Shawnees' perspective, the resulting treaties of Fort Stanwix, Fort McIntosh, and Fort Finney were insults. Valuable land concessions were wrung out of the Indians in exchange for trifling gifts. Even more infuriating was the fact that the American commissioners cajoled the Iroquois into signing away other tribes' interests in lands north of the Ohio. From the American point of view, *any* Indian's agreement sufficed to validate a land treaty. The Shawnees found this incomprehensible and outrageous. By 1788 they had repudiated the treaties and taken steps, with covert British encouragement, to organize a multitribe Indian nation that could resist American acquisition of the Ohio country. Two factors worked against this plan. One was the chronic difficulty of the various tribes to act in a concerted fashion. The other was the fact that, authorized or not, Americans were already dividing the land spoils of the Old Northwest. The Land Ordinance of 1785 created a legal apparatus within which they could operate. Two years later, the Ohio Company organized to promote settlement of a huge plot of rich land in the Muskingum Valley. Conniving with members of the central government who wanted a piece of the action without publicity, the sale of 1.5 million acres was arranged at about eight cents an acre. An additional 5 million acres went to the Scioto Company. From the white man's standpoint, these deals must rank among the best in the history of real-estate transactions.

While the land promoters opened the doors in the East, Tecumseh and his forest guerillas were more directly concerned with the unorganized squatters and frontier ruffians who swarmed across the Ohio into lands still claimed and occupied by Indians at the conclusion of the Revolution. The national government attempted to check this premature and unauthorized surge. Calling the white intruders "banditti whose actions are a disgrace to human nature," Colonel Josiah Harmar tried unsuccessfully to bully them into leaving. Democracy, however, was in vogue following the Revolution, and the pioneers assumed it was their "right" as citizens to settle on the newly acquired public domain.

Unable to intimidate his own countrymen, Colonel Harmar tried his luck with the Indians. In 1790, commandeering 1400 troops, he marched on the Shawnees and the Miamis. Chief Little Turtle of the Miami issued a call for warriors. Tecumseh was now twenty-two, strikingly handsome, and gifted both physically and intellectually. Burning with indignation at the cumulative personal and tribal losses that began with his father's death, Tecumseh responded at once to Little Turtle's appeal. He played a major role in the ambush that cost Harmar 183 men, then turned, in the fall of 1791, to the 3000-man army of Arthur St. Clair. Little Turtle, along with Blue Jacket of the Shawnees and Buckongahelos of the Delaware, were the commanding chiefs who planned the surprise attack on the inept Americans the night of November third. At dawn the next day, the Indians struck. Tecumseh was in the thick of the action. St. Clair finally managed to break through the encircling warriors, but he left over 900 men behind, 630 dead, and the rest wounded. It was one of the worst defeats in the history of Indian warfare in North America.

Emerging from the encounter with St. Clair as a leading warrior of his tribe, Tecumseh led effective raids against settlements in both Ohio and Kentucky. In 1792 he responded to a call from his eldest brother, traveled to Tennessee to help the Cherokees resist white expansion, and, after a particularly fierce encounter, buried his adored brother. Now Tecumseh was recognized as war leader of the Shawnees in the South. Several months of raiding, from Tennessee to Florida, added to his growing reputation. In the summer of 1793 war messages circulated through the eastern woodlands. They told Tecumseh that the United States Army, this time under the command of General Anthony Wayne, was again on the move in the Ohio country. Hurrying north, Tecumseh learned that British spokesmen at Detroit had assured the Indians full support in their campaign against Wayne. To an eager Tecumseh it seemed the opportune moment to drive the Americans back across the Ohio and to proclaim an Indian nation. Supported by 2000 warriors, Tecumseh took up a position near England's Fort Miami, just west of Lake Erie. Deploying themselves among an extensive tangle of wind-felled trees, the Indians waited for the climactic encounter. But when it came to forest fighting, Wayne was no St. Clair. He knew that Indians customarily fasted before battle. Announcing his day of attack as August 17, 1794, Wayne instead waited until the 20th, when many Indians, weak from hunger, sought food at Fort Miami. Then he struck frontally and on the Indians' left flank. Tecumseh raged among the downed logs, inspiring his warriors to battle. But seeing that the promised aid from the British garrison was not forthcoming, the Indians fled. The Battle of Fallen Timbers, a year in preparation, was over in less than two hours. Only 50 Indians died, including another of Tecumseh's brothers, but their cause in the Ohio country received a severe check.

Pressing his advantage, Wayne called the defeated chiefs together in 1795 at Fort Greenville, located in the central Ohio region near Tecumseh's birthplace. The Treaty of Greenville (August 3, 1795) fueled the fires of hatred between Indians and Americans in the Old Northwest for the next two decades. The agreement was essentially Wayne's dictation. The Indians who were present agreed, for a small monetary payment, to surrender most of Ohio, including the Shawnee homeland, to the United States. The Indians also gave up the sites of cities later to be called Chicago, Detroit, Toledo, and Peoria.

Tecumseh did not attend Wayne's council at Greenville. After the council's damaging results became known, he denounced the treaty and the Shawnee negotiator, Blue Jacket. Tecumseh declared that Blue Jacket did not speak for him. He did not regard the fight at Fallen Timbers as decisive, and he would not give up his homeland. Behind Tecumseh's adamant refusal, which won him widespread respect and an extensive following in the late 1790s, was a deeply rooted attitude toward land and its significance in Indian culture.

Tecumseh conceived of land in a way entirely different from Europeans and Americans. In the first place, land could not be bought and sold. The earth, created by the Great Spirit, was the basis of a life community to which the Indian belonged. He used the land, but it was not "his" in the same sense that a buckskin garment or a knife was property. True, a tribe like the Shawnee occupied a region, and families had responsibility for fields of crops and hunting territories. But such occupancy and use did not, in Indian culture, confer the right to sell what had initially been a gift from the Great Spirit. "Sell a country?" Tecumseh incredulously asked William Henry Harrison in 1810. "Why not sell the air, the clouds, and the great sea?"

It is fair to say that many North American Indians misconstrued the whole treaty-making process. The Americans understood a treaty like the one executed at Greenville in 1795 as a sale of land by the Indians. The Indians, with no conception of selling land in their culture, interpreted the treaty as a gift to the whites in the same sense that the Great Spirit initially gave the land to them. In many instances the Indians clearly did not feel that "transferring title" to the land meant anything more than a willingness to share the area with the newcomers. So when the white men appeared, treaty in hand, and told the Indians to leave land that now "belonged" to them, there was disbelief, confusion, and, finally, anger and resistance.

Even if Blue Jacket and the other chiefs at Greenville understood that they were "selling" Ohio, Tecumseh had reason to protest. The use of land, he believed, was an inherent right of the Indian race as a whole. Every member had a right to use the earth. It consequently followed that no single member could surrender the rights of those who did not agree with the transaction. This was the philosophical basis of Tecumseh's conviction that no portion of the Ohio Valley could be sold or ceded to the Americans without the consent of *all* Indians everywhere.

There was also the question in Tecumseh's mind of appropriate ways of using the earth. He shared the Shawnee belief that the land was sacred, literally Mother Earth, and that various life forms had a rightful share in its bounty. Cutting away the forests, "clearing" the land, was wrong, as was the use of metal tools to plough the soil. According to Shawnee tradition, only a pointed stick or a bone hoe should be sunk into the body of Mother Earth. From this viewpoint, the white passion to transform the environment with the most sophisticated technology available was—treaty or no treaty—morally wrong.

Whereas Wayne saw the 1795 Treaty of Greenville as the end of "the Indian problem" in the Ohio country, Tecumseh knew it was only the beginning. After Greenville, Tecumseh became the dominant Indian leader in the Old Northwest. Handsome and powerful, he impressed everyone with whom he came into contact. He was close to six feet in height. A British officer described his eyes as "clear, transparent hazel, with a mild, pleasant expression when in repose . . . but when excited in his orations, or by the enthusiasm of conflict, or when in anger, they appeared like balls of fire." He stood erect, elegantly dressed in tanned buckskin and, according to the Englishman, was "one of the finest looking men I have ever seen." Among his own people, Tecumseh was stern and fiery. When challenged, he would say, "I am Tecumseh" and simply touch the handle of his tomahawk.

Around the charismatic Shawnee, who had moved west to Indiana following Greenville, there gathered independent and disgruntled warriors from several woodland tribes. They watched in despair as the traders' liquor ravished those Indians who remained close to the expanding line of settlements. The once-proud Miamis, who joined Tecumseh's Shawnees in 1791 to defeat St. Clair, became, in the words of one American observer, "a poor, miserable drunken set, diminishing every year." Many became beggars or thieves. Tecumseh refused to drink and opposed unsuccessfully the traders who created and then fed the Indians' habit. He had no more success resisting the succession of land cessions that Governor William Henry Harrison, of the Indiana Territory, engineered after 1802. Hardly disguising his hunger for Indian land, Harrison's standard technique was to call the chiefs together and, when they refused to agree to his demands, inform them that the land in question already belonged to the United States and would eventually be occupied by force. In this position Harrison had the full support of President Thomas Jefferson, who, despite his democratic principles concerning white Americans, informed him on February 27, 1803, that "our strength and their weakness is now so visible that they must see we have only to shut our hand to crush them." The tribes, Jefferson declared, had only two options: incorporation into the United States as citizens or removal beyond the Mississippi. "Should any tribe be foolhardy enough to take up the hatchet at any time, the seizing the whole country of that tribe . . . would be an example to others and a furtherance of our final consolidation." It was a matter, then, of taking what Harrison offered or risking getting nothing at all. Bribes to key chiefs and an ample supply of whiskey were also standard tools of Harrison's trade. By 1805 Indian claims had been "extinguished" from most of Michigan, Indiana, Illinois, and part of Wisconsin.

It was a low point in Tecumseh's life. He must have wondered if resistance could be anything but temporary and symbolic. Then, in 1805, he caught fire. Crucial to the revival of Tecumseh's determination was a remarkable transformation in the life of one of his remaining brothers, Laulewasika. A twin to another of Tecumseh's siblings— and thus, according to Shawnee culture, endowed with magical abilities—Laulewasika displayed no special talents for some years. Much to his brother Tecumseh's disgust, he became a heavy drinker. A handkerchief covering the eye he lost in an accident, Laulewasika, who was also an epileptic, devoted his life to loafing and bragging in the reflected glory of his famous brother. Even his name was appropriate: it meant "the loud mouth."

Then, in 1805, Laulewasika changed his life completely. An epidemic among the Shawnees living in Indiana apparently filled him with fear and brought him face to face with the possibility of death. Emerging from a trance, he reported meeting the Master of Life, an Indian deity, who showed him the evils of drink. At the same time, the religious revivals sweeping frontier settlements influenced the Shawnee. He may have heard of the great camp meeting at Cane Ridge, Bourbon County, Kentucky, in 1801, where twenty thousand people gathered in the hope of conversion and salvation. Laulewasika was certainly familiar with the work of itinerant Shaker preachers, whose strange jerking dances were not too different from the epileptic fits the Indian himself suffered. It was a curious grafting of American and Indian religion that led him to change his name, in 1805, to

Tenskwatawa. It meant "the open door," a reference to Jesus' saying, "I am the door." Within two years Tecumseh's brother was known widely on the frontier to red and white men alike by his famous nickname, The Prophet.

The message of The Prophet, which he claimed to derive directly from the Master of Life or from Jesus, but which Tecumseh's philosophy influenced heavily, included abstinence from alcohol. It went on to advocate the end of intertribal bickering and the adoption of a united Indian front against American civilization. An Indian confederacy, The Prophet believed, could resist the piecemeal erosion of Indian land holdings. Finally, the Shawnee Prophet invoked Indian pride, dignity, and self-respect. He urged his people to cease imitating the ways, and using the materials, of the white man. Only by being true to their own cultural traditions could Indians maintain the strength and the will to resist dispossession.

Tecumseh was overjoyed at the transformation in his brother. Indeed, many of The Prophet's ideas were simply those of the Shawnee war chief stated in a more emotional and mystical manner. The brothers made a formidable team: the prophet who could envisage better times and the warrior who could fulfill the prophecy with the force of arms. In 1806, Tecumseh and The Prophet moved from Indiana back east to Greenville, Ohio, where they built a village at the exact site where Anthony Wayne had wrung land cessions from the tribes a decade earlier. Their following grew daily, swelled by dissatisfied Indians from various woodland tribes.

At this point, in April 1806, Indiana territorial governor William Henry Harrison inadvertently aided the cause of the two Shawnees. In a speech to the Delaware tribe, Harrison issued warnings about following a "pretended prophet" into renewed resistance. Demand proof of this prophet's powers, said Harrison. "If he is really a prophet, ask of him to cause the sun to stand still—the moon to alter its course—the rivers to cease to flow or the dead to rise from their graves." When news of Harrison's challenge reached Tecumseh and The Prophet, they were delighted; they knew from American informants that a total eclipse of the sun would occur on June 16, 1806. Calling a huge assembly of Indians together at Greenville, The Prophet waited for the right moment. At 11:32 A.M. the moon began to move between the sun and the earth. The Prophet commanded night to fall.

It did. Then he commanded the sun to reappear, which, of course, it did. The performance astounded the assembled Indians. Reports of The Prophet's miracle and his message were carried far up the Missouri to the Sioux, Blackfeet, and Arikaras—tribes hardly aware, in 1806, of the enemy presence to the east.

Before the last great eastern Indian resistance movement could progress any further, Tecumseh, its natural leader, had to pass through an intense emotional crisis that led him to question the validity of his entire philosophy. It began innocently enough, in 1798, when Tecumseh returned to the site of his Ohio boyhood home, the traditional Shawnee village of Chillicothe. There he met the family of James Galloway. A participant in the 1782 expedition of George Rogers Clark against Chillicothe, Galloway had returned to the beautiful spot on the Little Miami River to make his home. Tecumseh spoke excellent English, although as part of his antiwhite philosophy he refused to use it in formal situations involving American leaders. But Galloway was just a pioneer farmer, traveling with his family into land opened for settlement by the Treaty of Greenville, and Tecumseh liked his manner. When they parted, Galloway extended an open invitation for the Shawnee to be his guest.

A continuous traveler, Tecumseh had several contacts with the Galloway family over the next decade. He delighted in Galloway's library, which, at three hundred volumes, was probably one of the best in the territory at that time. The many hours that Tecumseh spent with his host opened a whole new dimension to him. He learned that the white man's culture did not mean just rifles, hatred of Indians, and land hunger, but also Homer, Shakespeare, the Bible, and the Declaration of Independence. By 1807 he also knew that white culture meant Rebecca Galloway. Then fifteen, blond, and beautiful, Rebecca spent days reading with Tecumseh and perfecting his command of the English language. The Shawnee, who had been briefly and unhappily married to an older woman in 1796, brought Rebecca gifts, including a small, perfectly made bark canoe to paddle on the Little Miami. In 1808 Tecumseh asked James Galloway for his daughter's hand in marriage. Although marriages between Americans and Indians were not common, Galloway did not reject the idea. He admired the intelligent, dignified Shawnee. But the decision would have to be Rebecca's, and she needed time to think. When Tecumseh returned to the Galloway cabin, she was ready with her answer. She would marry Tecumseh, but only if he gave up the ways of the Indian and became, in effect, an American.

Now it was Tecumseh's turn to think deeply about his whole system of values. On the one hand, there was Rebecca and alliance with a culture Tecumseh discovered to have assets as well as liabilities. Moreover, there was the prospect of joining the side that appeared to be winning the struggle for control of North America rather than fighting a losing battle. But Tecumseh could not bring himself to make the switch, especially at a time when The Prophet's fame was underscoring the need for a leader, Tecumseh could not desert the Indian cause. And his father's death still needed to be avenged. With a heart that must have been heavy beyond description, Tecumseh informed the Galloways of his decision. Then he moved with The Prophet and their followers from Ohio back to Indiana. He never saw Rebecca Galloway again, but he never took another wife.

The new Prophet's Town rose in 1808 at the confluence of the Wabash and Tippecanoe Rivers, on Kickapoo and Potawatomi land in Indiana. From this base, Tecumseh began his crusade to make The Prophet's dream of a great Indian confederacy stretching from Florida to the upper Missouri a reality. In the next three years he traveled from the Seminole tribe in Florida to the Osage in Missouri, and from the Iroquois in New York to the Sauk and Fox in Wisconsin.

At the hundreds of council fires he attended, Tecumseh adopted a standard role. The pacifism and intertribal rivalries of the older chiefs had to be discredited in favor of the fiercer spirit of the younger braves, who realized that the only rivalry that really mattered was that between the red man and the white. From the reports of Americans who occasionally observed Tecumseh in action, we know something of his manner and his message. After the requisite number of ceremonial pipes were passed, Tecumseh began by offering his audience a history lesson. "Where today is the Pequod?" he asked. "Where the Narragansetts, the Mohawks, Pocanokets, and many other once powerful tribes of our race?" Because of the tendency of some of their leaders to believe the promises of the newcomers from Europe, these people had "vanished before the avarice and oppression of the white man, as snow before a summer sun."

As a widely traveled, intertribal diplomat, and a keen observer of the injustices suffered by his race, Tecumseh knew a great deal about the history of Indian-white relations in North America, and he used this historical knowledge effectively in his orations. His reference to the Pequod (or Pequot) Indians was particularly effective. In 1637 the desire of Massachusetts settlers for land south and west of Narragansett Bay launched the Pequot War. In one ruthless campaign the entire tribe—every man, woman, and child—was exterminated. The Narragansett were next in line along the route of white in Connecticut, Rhode Island, and Massachusetts. But under the leadership of a Wampanoag chief the colonists called King Philip, they struck back. Anticipating Tecumseh in his advocacy of an all-Indian alliance against the settlers, Philip succeeded, in 1675 and 1676, in actually pushing back the New England frontier. The Deerfield Massacre was his work. In all, one-sixth of the colonial male population of New England was killed in King Philip's war.

But systematic destruction of Indian grain fields in the Connecticut Valley changed the momentum. The English began the task, as one colonist put it, of "exterminating the rabid animals." Even Roger Williams, who was almost unique in his questioning of the ethics involved in dispossessing Indians, turned against the Pequots and their allies. It was an all-out racial war; barbarism characterized the behavior of both sides. The New Englanders, with their superior weapons, prevailed. Aware that he was at the end of his ability to resist, Philip returned to his homeland, where, on August 12, 1676, he was betrayed by an Indian, cornered in a Massachusetts swamp, and shot. The overjoyed frontiersmen brought Philip's head to Plymouth, where it remained on display for a quarter of a century, stuck on the end of a pole. His severed hand was pickled in a pail of rum and displayed by the Indian betrayer "to such gentlemen as would bestow gratuities upon him."

As an advocate of Indian unity, Tecumseh prized past examples of concerted Indian action. The most notable achievement in this field in North America was the confederacy or "League" of the Iroquois. Its origins antedate the coming of Europeans, and its purpose appears to have been directed at establishing a "Great Peace" among the constantly warring tribes of the eastern woodlands. The legendary Hiawatha was the architect of a federal government remarkable for its constitution of laws and its democratic principles. A tireless traveler,

A pipe, tomahawk, and spear rolled into one. During the eighteenth century, these objects were traded by the English and French to Indians throughout the eastern woodlands. The engraving on this tomahawk is by the Indian owner. It clearly illustrates the dream of Indian power (note the relative size of the figures) to which Tecumseh devoted his life.

This 1790 lithograph shows how Fort Harmar (foreground) and the Ohio Company's village of Marietta looked when Tecumseh was 22 years old. It was at about this time that he adopted the warrior's stance against the expansion of white civilization into the Ohio Valley. Note the almost unbroken forest covering in the background. Today Ohio is largely cleared of trees.

Catherine Reynolds, the teenage daughter of a British officer stationed at Fort Malden, in Canada, painted this watercolor in 1813. It shows Tecumseh a few months before his death. Miss Reynolds has painted Tecumseh in British military trousers and a Shawnee headdress, thereby symbolically underscoring his role as a war leader of both forces.

This elaborate pipe (note the opening of the bowl in the back of the bear) is only three-and-one-half inches high. Painted quills dangle from the bottom. The pipestem was attached to the "log" beneath the seated Indian. The carving, made by a Wyandot Indian about 1800, suggests the close sense of kinship existing between men and animals, a hallmark of non-Christian peoples.

as Tecumseh later proved to be, Hiawatha visited tribes as distant from his New York home as the Sauk in Wisconsin. Only five eastern "Nations" joined the Iroquois League in the sixteenth century; a sixth entered about 1715. But the government was strong enough to last for two centuries and to make the Iroquois the foremost Indian power prior to the American Revolution. The political theory and concepts of social morality which underlay the strength of the Six Nations was the object of extensive, if rather embarrassing, colonial admiration. Even as they were breaking the Iroquois' power, Benjamin Franklin and other architects of colonial and (later) state unity found the Indians' confederation instructive and inspiring. Joseph Brant, a talented Iroquois leader of the 1770s and 1780s, had a direct influence on the maturation of Tecumseh's vision of power through unity.

The Ottawa war chief Pontiac offered Tecumseh the best recent example of aggressive Indian leadership. The conclusion in 1763, of the French and Indian (or Seven Years') War eliminated French holdings on the mainland of North America. It was a major setback for the Indians because French colonial aims centered on fur rather than farms. Hence, France had no reason to dispossess Indians of their hunting grounds. On the contrary, Indian hunters were needed as the first step in the lucrative fur trade. Moreover, with England as the sole dominant force, Indians could no longer play one nation off against another. Without competition, fur traders and land speculators could be even more unscrupulous in their dealings with Indians. But westward expansion remained the dominant problem. Great Britain did nothing to solve it in issuing the Proclamation of 1763, which, in theory, prevented settlement west of the crest of the Appalachians. In practice the matter was rather different. Acquiring land was essential to the colonization of North America, and the colonists were not about to be restrained by such considerations as Parliamentary authority and Indians' rights. There were, to be sure, a few colonists who cared. Sir William Johnson, his assistant George Croghan, and Colonel John Stuart were Indian superintendents, and they took seriously their job of establishing fair-trade relations with the tribes. This was difficult, however, when Lord Jeffrey Amherst, their superior, openly advocated distributing blankets loaded with smallpox germs to the Indians. Driven to the breaking point, in the summer of 1763, Pontiac struck back. His skills as a warrior had been honed against the British in the recently concluded French and Indian War. He was also, in the pattern Tecumseh would follow, a compelling orator, a charismatic leader, and a crusader for unified Indian action. The attacks he led in 1763 featured Shawnee warriors. They staggered Great Britain in the West: eight out of twelve British forts in Indian country were captured and hundreds of settlers were killed. For a moment Pontiac must have believed that his temporary alliance of eighteen tribes would drive the British away. But Pontiac did not understand the terms on which the French and Indian War ended. France was through with North America. The assistance he counted on in his war against Great Britain did not materialize, and in 1764 the English launched an effective counterstrike against the Shawnees and the Delawares. Pontiac's "conspiracy"—as nineteenth-century historian Francis Parkman curiously dubbed this war for native self-determination—had failed. British supremacy in the trans-Appalachian West continued. But Pontiac's example inspired the Shawnee chief Cornstalk, who, in turn, fired Tecumseh's youthful enthusiasm. The cause of Indian resistance would also continue.

Drawing on these and other examples, Tecumseh invariably directed many of his speeches to a consideration of the future. "Will we not soon be driven from our respective countries and the graves of our ancestors?" he asked his audiences, his superb voice rising with emotion. There was even a worse fate in store for those who did not resist encroachments on Indian liberty. Tecumseh was fully aware of the institution of slavery, and he asked his listeners to consider how long it would be before the Americans "tie us to a post and whip us, and make us work for them in their cornfields as they do . . . their black-faces." The only way to prevent such a catastrophe, Tecumseh continued, was to "form one body, one heart, and defend to the last warrior our country, our liberty, and the graves of our fathers." This was not an easy point for the native Americans to grasp. The Indians were not all one tribe. Thousands of years of competition for territory had left a legacy of diversity and enmity. Indians had never acted together as Tecumseh now called on them to do.

Building to a climax at the conclusion of his talk, Tecumseh would demand all-out war: "Back, whence they came, upon a trail of blood, they must be driven . . . Burn their dwellings! Destroy their stock! Slay their wives and children! . . . Dig their very corpses from the grave." Tecumseh's hatred of white men, a tribesman once observed, "was the most bitter of any Indian I ever knew." Tecumseh himself admitted, presumably after his love affair with Rebecca Galloway, that he "could not look upon the face of a white man without feeling the flesh crawl on his bones."

At times as many as five thousand Indians gathered to hear Tecumseh deliver such speeches. He habitually spoke bare-chested, in breechclout and moccasins. He held a tomahawk. Red war paint lined his eyes. Those who heard him and reported their impressions were astonished at his oratorical abilities. His words, said General Sam Dale, a white military officer, "fell in avalanches from his lips . . . His eyes burned with supernatural lustre, and his whole frame trembled with emotion. His voice resounded over the multitude—now sinking in low and musical whispers, now rising to the highest key, hurling out his words like a succession of thunderbolts." The general concluded his report with the observation that he had heard many great orators "but I never saw one with the vocal powers of Tecumseh."

Tecumseh frequently made effective use of The Prophet's alleged connections with the Great Spirit, enlisting that potent Indian deity on the side of his program. As a representative of the Great Spirit, Tecumseh could do wondrous things. In 1811 he told the Creek tribe, on several occasions, that when he returned to Tippecanoe (Prophet's Town), he would stamp his foot and the ground a thousand miles to the south would tremble and houses would collapse. Then, in December 1811, came the great New Madrid earthquake, which altered the course of the Mississippi River and thoroughly shook the trans-Appalachian West. As their houses fell, Indians remembered Tecumseh's words and flocked to his cause. Prizing the red-painted sticks he had given them as a symbol of his wrath, the Creeks launched a major war against the United States in the Old Southwest.

In the summer of 1810 Tecumseh and Governor William Henry Harrison met at Harrison's headquarters in Vincennes, Indiana. It was one of the most dramatic confrontations in the history of Indian-white relations in North America. Harrison had recently concluded another of his land-grabbing treaties with a handful of older and weaker chiefs. In return for $7000 and some liquor, they ceded 3 million

acres of land, much of it not even under their control, to the United
States. Determined to confront him with the injustice of this 1809
Treaty of Fort Wayne, Tecumseh and several hundred brightly
painted warriors accepted Harrison's invitation to come to Vincennes.
They traveled down the Wabash River, sweeping up to a landing a few
miles above Harrison's headquarters in eighty gaudily decorated war
canoes. An American soldier at the scene observed that Tecumseh "is
one of the finest looking men I ever saw—about six feet high, straight,
with fine features, and altogether a daring, bold-looking fellow." On
August 20, 1810, the two men, representing such different cultural
perspectives, met for the first time. Harrison wished to hold the talks
on the porch of his house and offered Tecumseh a chair, saying, "Your
father offers you a seat." The Shawnee bristled at Harrison's patroniz-
ing attitude: "*My* father! *My* father!" he sarcastically aped the governor. "The Sun is my father, and the Earth my mother; she gives me
sustenance, and I will rest on her bosom!" Whereupon Tecumseh
stalked to a nearby grove of trees and sat on the ground "with as lofty
and commanding an air," a bystander reported, "as if the green sward
beneath him had been the throne of the Caesars." Harrison's only choice
was to follow the Indian.

Speaking Shawnee as he always did at such formal occasions,
Tecumseh denounced the Fort Wayne agreement. The land, he said,
had been ceded by a few powerless chiefs whom Tecumseh would kill
if the agreement was not invalidated. Harrison must recognize that,
according to the Indian concept of property, no individual or small
group could sell land. There were no "owners" of Indian land; it
belonged equally to all the natives. In accepting the cession from the
discredited chiefs, the white people proved once again that they could
not be trusted. Mocking Harrison—and drawing on knowledge acquired at the Galloway home in Ohio—Tecumseh noted that "when
Jesus Christ came upon the earth, you killed Him, and nailed Him to
a cross. You thought He was dead, but you were mistaken." Cleverly,
the Shawnee also called Harrison's attention to the fact that Indian
unity was only an application of the example of the various colonies
in forming the United States. "Why," Tecumseh wondered, "should
they censure the Indians for following it?"

Harrison replied the only way he could, upholding his principal
objectives. The treaties were valid. The land in question would be

occupied by force if necessary. The United States had always been fair in its dealings with Indians. "It is false! He lies!" Tecumseh screamed, leaping to his feet. There was a moment of confusion and fear in which swords and tomahawks were drawn. Then Harrison stalked angrily away. Tecumseh waved his warriors back to their camp and later sent apologies to Harrison for losing his temper. In the morning Harrison came to the Shawnees' camp for final talks. Tecumseh used humor to make his point. When the men took seats on a bench, Tecumseh took a position very near Harrison and continually edged him toward one end of the board. The governor readjusted his position several times and, finally, as he was about to be pushed off completely, protested. Tecumseh capitalized at once on the opportunity to draw a moral about American treatment of Indians. If present trends continued, he remarked, the United States would drive the red people "into the Great Lake, where they can't either stand or walk." But Tecumseh made clear that his followers were determined to retreat no longer. Harrison was also adamant, although he wisely withheld his remarks until a few weeks following the conference with Tecumseh. Concerning the remaining Indian land in the Northwest, Harrison asked: "is one of the fairest portions of the globe to remain in a state of nature, the haunt of a few wretched savages, when it seems destined, by the creator, to give support to a large population, and to be the seat of civilization, of science, and true religion?" It was a sentiment typical of the frontier mind and, set against Tecumseh's philosophy, it could only mean renewed war.

Tecumseh and Harrison met again at Vincennes, Indiana, in the summer of 1811. This time the immediate problem was the death of several settlers at the hands of Indians whom Harrison had accused of being followers of The Prophet and Tecumseh. They probably were, but Tecumseh refused to give them up to Harrison's type of justice. Instead, he left Prophet's Town for another long southern journey aimed at recruiting tribes to his cause. Harrison, the crafty soldier, seized on Tecumseh's absence to march on Prophet's Town. At the Battle of Tippecanoe, on November 7, 1811, Harrison scattered the Indians and burned their town. In terms of losses, the engagement was a draw, but it established Harrison's reputation as an Indian-fighter and paved his way to the Presidency of the United States in 1840.

Returning from the southern tribes early in 1812, Tecumseh seethed with anger upon hearing what had happened. First he turned against his brother, The Prophet, berating him for his ineptitude in the Battle of Tippecanoe and driving him from the rebuilt Prophet's Town. Next, Tecumseh launched raids against American outposts throughout the Northwest. Even in the by now densely populated region of Kentucky and Ohio, settlers banded together in fear as they had twenty-five years earlier. But the Shawnee chief remained disturbed at the tendency of warrior bands to act independently of each other and without a clear sense of the long-term objective of an Indian nation.

On June 18, 1812, a new factor entered the already stormy seas of Western affairs: war with Great Britain. The Indian hostilities that Tecumseh had inspired played an important role in causing the War of 1812. Western settlers blamed the British for arousing the Indians against the Americans. In a typical overstatement, William Henry Harrison said, "the whole of the Indians on this frontier have been completely armed and equipped from the British King's stores." To settlers in the West, it seemed that the only answer to the problem was conquest of Canada. The economic pressures that Thomas Jefferson and James Madison's administrations attempted to use against Great Britain as early as 1807 had not been signally successful. It was imperative, insisted war hawks like Henry Clay of Kentucky, to break the British-Indian alliance by eliminating English territorial holdings in North America.

While frontier statesmen like Clay and Harrison tended to see Tecumseh as a puppet of the British, the Shawnee leader had a different perspective. The British were invaders and consequently no better than the Americans, but they could be used. If the white men were divided and at war, Indians might emerge the biggest winners. Tecumseh saw in the War of 1812 a golden opportunity to drive the Americans out of the West—and perhaps even off the continent. At an 1812 council at Fort Wayne, called by the Americans to win Indian support—or at least neutrality—in the war, Tecumseh made his position clear: "Here is a chance," he told the assembly, ". . . yes, a chance such as will never occur again—for us Indians of North America to form ourselves into one great combination and cast our lot with the British in this war." If the British won, Tecumseh reasoned, the woodland tribes could reestablish their claim to the Northwest. The King would welcome a buffer nation confining the recently rebelled colonists. An American victory, on the other hand, would confront the Indians with a monolithic power. Then, he continued, "it will not be many years before our last place of abode and our last hunting ground will be taken from us, and the remnants of the different tribes . . . will all be driven toward the setting sun." It was a prophetic observation. The War of 1812 was indeed the Indians' last real chance to resist the American invasion. For a moment, a free Indian nation hung in the balance. By the time the tribes of the Great Plains waged the last campaigns of Indian resistance, the "chance" Tecumseh spoke of was gone.

At the conclusion of the Fort Wayne council, Tecumseh broke the peace pipe offered him by an American representative. Then, at the head of about 1000 warriors, he marched north to the British garrison at Fort Malden. In late July and early August 1812, Tecumseh and his warriors succeeded in bewildering and defeating the inept American forces under Detroit-based General William Hull. By this time the Shawnee's name was legendary; the very rumor that Tecumseh was in the forest across the line of battle was enough to panic American troops. On August 13, with Tecumseh holding Hull at bay in Detroit, General Isaac Brock arrived at Fort Malden with British reinforcements. His relationship with Tecumseh was one of mutual admiration; together they almost realized the Indian's dreams. At the time of their initial meeting, the dignified talented Brock clearly acknowledged Tecumseh's skills by expressing his desire to "take lessons from you and your warriors, that we may learn how to make war in these great forests." Brock then assured Tecumseh that "their great father beyond the great salt lake" would protect the interest of "his red children" against the Americans. Sizing up Brock, who was well over six feet tall and powerfully built, Tecumseh simply turned to his followers, stretched out his hand, and exclaimed, "Hoo-e: This is a man!"

Immediately thereafter, Brock and Tecumseh planned the capture of Detroit. Overruling the opinion of his own staff, Brock took the advice of the Indian and launched an immediate attack. He also allowed one of his couriers to be captured by the Americans. The courier carried false news that 5000 Chippewa were on their way

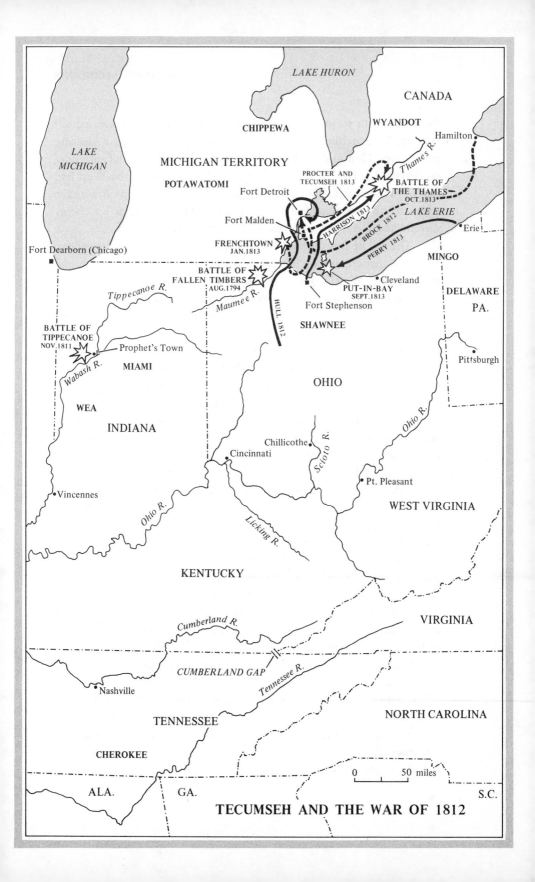

LAKE HURON

CANADA

LAKE MICHIGAN

CHIPPEWA

WYANDOT

Hamilton

MICHIGAN TERRITORY

POTAWATOMI

Fort Detroit

PROCTER AND
TECUMSEH 1813

Thames R.

BATTLE OF
THE THAMES
OCT.1813

Fort Malden

FRENCHTOWN
JAN.1813

HARRISON 1813

BROCK 1812

LAKE ERIE

Fort Dearborn (Chicago)

BATTLE OF
FALLEN TIMBERS
AUG.1794

PERRY 1813

Erie

MINGO

Cleveland

PUT-IN-BAY
SEPT.1813

DELAWARE

Tippecanoe R.

Maumee R.

HULL 1812

Fort Stephenson

SHAWNEE

PA.

BATTLE OF
TIPPECANOE
NOV.1811

Prophet's Town

Wabash R.

MIAMI

OHIO

Pittsburgh

WEA

INDIANA

Chillicothe

Cincinnati

Scioto R.

Ohio R.

Vincennes

Pt. Pleasant

WEST VIRGINIA

Ohio R.

Licking R.

KENTUCKY

Cumberland R.

VIRGINIA

CUMBERLAND GAP

Tennessee R.

Nashville

TENNESSEE

NORTH CAROLINA

CHEROKEE

0   50 miles

ALA.

GA.

S.C.

TECUMSEH AND THE WAR OF 1812

from the north to join Tecumseh. For his part, Tecumseh carried out the ruse by marching 1000 warriors in single file through a clearing three times. Thoroughly shaken, Hull raised the white flag of surrender on August 16, 1812. The most important border post in the West had fallen. Tecumseh's humane treatment of the captured Americans added to his growing legend. Brock noted that as soon as an enemy surrendered, his life was sacred in the eyes of Tecumseh.

The fall of Detroit fired Tecumseh with hope for his independent, all-Indian nation, and he left in the winter of 1812 for another round of recruiting councils among the southern tribes. The content of his message was the same, only more impassioned: "Let the white race perish. They seize your land, they corrupt your women, they trample on the ashes of your dead! Back whence they came, upon a trail of blood, they must be driven." Then Tecumseh added his standard plea: "Unless every tribe unanimously combines to give a check to the ambition and avarice of the whites, they will soon conquer us apart and disunited, and we will be driven away from our native country and scattered as autumnal leaves before the wind." He returned in April 1813 and was greeted with the news that his friend Brock had been killed in action against the Americans near Fort Niagara. Although he could not have realized it at the time, the loss of Brock tipped the scales of history against Tecumseh and his dreams.

The chief must have sensed trouble when he met Brock's replacement as the military leader in the West. Colonel Henry Proctor was a weak, unimaginative man who despised "savages" whether they fought on his side or not. Although Proctor and an Indian force had scored a major victory, on January 22, 1813, against an American army at the River Raisin, near Detroit, in the aftermath of the battle Proctor exercised no control over the Indians. Without a Tecumseh to provide leadership, butchery of the defenseless American captives took place. Such behavior had no place in Tecumseh's code of conduct as a warrior. In April 1813, after leading a brilliant victory (480 Americans killed, 150 captured) against William Henry Harrison's reinforcements, near Fort Meigs, Tecumseh learned that Proctor was once again permitting the murder of captives on their way to the British camp. Riding full speed into the midst of the slaughter, Tecumseh screamed, "Are there no men here?" The killing and scalping stopped abruptly. Next Tecumseh confronted Proctor, demanding to know why he permitted such behavior. The Englishman had no answer. "You are unfit to command," Tecumseh told him. "Go and put on petticoats."

In the ensuing months, British-Indian relations deteriorated rapidly. Over Tecumseh's heated objections, the vacillating Proctor abandoned the siege of Harrison and Fort Meigs. The time for decisive action against the Americans in the West was running out. The balance of power was shifting. Then, in the early fall of 1813, the end came with stunning suddenness. The first setback for the British and the Indian cause was signaled by American Commodore Oliver Hazard Perry's victory at Put-in-Bay, in Lake Erie. Aggressive British policy, such as Brock would have favored, could have destroyed the American ships while they were still under construction on the lake shore at Erie, Pennsylvania. But Proctor delayed repeatedly. Finally, in a single day (September 10, 1813), Perry's newly built vessels completely destroyed British naval power and supply routes on the Great Lakes. His famous message to William Henry Harrison was written on the back of an old envelope the following day: "We have met the enemy and they are ours." So, it turned out, was the Indian.

With his source of supply cut off, the timed Proctor began preparations for a British retreat along the north shore of Lake Erie. Harrison moved his forces against the British. Tecumseh pleaded with Proctor to stand firm, and when his pleas failed, he shouted: "Listen, Father! You have the arms and ammunition which our great father sent for his red children. If you have an idea of going away, give them to us, and you may go and welcome. Our lives are in the hands of the Great Spirit. He gave to our ancestors the lands which we possess. We are determined to defend them, and if it is His will, our bones shall whiten on them, but we will never give them up." Failing to persuade the badly frightened Englishman, Tecumseh ended by calling him "a miserable old squaw" to his face.

Knowledgeable in military strategy, Tecumseh knew the British retreat was the beginning of the end. "We are going to follow the British," he notified his warriors, "and I feel certain that we shall never return." On the night of October 4, his pessimism was directed more at himself: "Brother warriors," Tecumseh told the men who had followed his cause for a decade, "we are about to enter an engagement from which I shall not return."

The Battle of the Thames began on October 5, 1813. Proctor's spirit was totally broken; he fled eastward in a special carriage after the first clash with Harrison's advancing soldiers. Tecumseh became the commander-in-chief of the combined British and Indian forces. Raging through the forest like one possessed, he urged the men to hold firm, at the same time throwing his own formidable strength into the heaviest fighting. Toward dusk, Tecumseh was shot and killed at close range by Harrison's troops. The fact that his body was not recovered, or at least not clearly identified, gave rise to years of wild speculation that the great Shawnee still lived. Even the memory of Tecumseh was enough to make the nocturnal forests of the Northwest Territory a terrifying place for the new American owners.

It was better, in many respects, that Tecumseh did not live to see the final curtain of the drama in which he had starred. At the conclusion of the War of 1812 the Americans mounted a massive assault against the woodland Indians. With no leader to take Tecumseh's place, Indian resistance vanished. The Creek, whom Tecumseh had inspired by his visits in 1811 and 1812, fought bravely but were overwhelmed by forces under the leadership of General Andrew Jackson at the Battle of Horseshoe Bend (March 27, 1814) in Alabama. Forced land cessions followed the Indian defeat, and in 1827 even those Creek who adopted a peaceful agricultural existence were "removed" (for their own good, according to the James Monroe administration) across the Mississippi River. The once-proud Cherokees followed a decade later, prodded at bayonet point along the "Trail of Tears" to "Indian Territory" established by federal legislation on May 28, 1830. But even that sorry excuse for Tecumseh's ideal of an independent Indian homeland was not left undisturbed. On April 22, 1889, after a decade of intense pressure by the last of the frontiersmen, the United States opened a large portion of the Indian Territory to settlement. "Boomers" rushed in, and by 1907 Oklahoma was recognized as a state. The Indians had lost again.

To the north, the final acts of eastern Indian resistance were led by another Tecumseh-inspired chief, Black Hawk of the Sauk and Fox tribes. However, the Black Hawk War ended in 1832, like all the others, with the Indians being driven across the Mississippi. As for Tecumseh's own tribe, the pathetic remnants of the Shawnee tribe were pushed west again and again by advancing white settlers. They finally were allowed to settle in Oklahoma on marginal lands whites regarded as good for nothing else.

Even more crushing to Tecumseh's ideals than the removal of Indians from their homeland was the *cultural* dispossession United States policy had instituted. According to the Dawes Severalty Act of February 8, 1887, Indians would become Americans politically, economically, and socially. The act provided for the division of the remaining tribal lands or "reservations" into individual holdings. The head of each family would receive 160 acres which he was supposed to farm or ranch just like a homesteader. The Indian landholder would also become a citizen of the United States. Henry L. Dawes, the Massachusetts senator who sponsored the 1887 act, was a genuine friend of the Indians, but his proposal completed the destruction of the independent tribal existence Tecumseh, for one, had tried so hard to defend. Under the Dawes Severalty Act, the Indian "way of life," even if it was pursued on a reservation, was considered illegal.

Conversion of the Indians to the white life style remained United States policy for half a century. But in 1934, at the height of the misery Indians were experiencing during the Great Depression, the Commissioner of Indian Affairs, John Collier, drafted and saw passed the Indian Reorganization Act. Based on the philosophy that Indians were, after all, Indians, and that Indian culture was worthy of preservation, the act revived the concepts of the self-governing tribe and common holding of land. Native languages, arts, ceremonies, and religion, which earlier policy had attempted to suppress, were, after 1934, permitted and encouraged. It would be incorrect to say that Indians of the 1930s universally rejoiced in the Collier program. Time had dimmed the old tribal identities. Many Indians adopted and liked "white" values. But others saw the Indian Reorganization Act as a means of reviving their racial roots and traditions and, most importantly, their pride as Indians.

In the 1960s and 1970s Indian author-intellectuals like Vine Deloria, a Sioux, and N. Scott Momaday, a member of the Kiowas, called the rich heritage of Indian culture to national attention. The few older Indians who still recalled their cultural heritage began to instruct younger tribesmen in rituals like the Sun Dance and the Corn Dance. In 1973, the radical American Indian Movement even led a revival of the Ghost Dance at Wounded Knee, South Dakota. Inspired by a vision of the miraculous disappearance of the white man from North America, Sioux ghost dancers had staged the last major resistance to United States authority on the same ground, at Wounded Knee, in 1890. In the 1970s the end of American domination is, of course, even less realistic than it had been in the 1890s. But the desire of American Indians for an independent cultural identity receives increasing support. In this cause, the spirit of Tecumseh finds its clearest contemporary expression.

SELECTED READINGS

The Person

DRAKE, BENJAMIN: *The Life of Tecumseh and His Brother the Prophet* (1841). The first biography.

ECKERT, ALLAN W.: *The Frontiersmen: A Narrative* (1967). Although fictionalized, the book is based on fact and features Tecumseh.

JOSEPHY, ALVIN M., JR.: "Tecumseh, The Greatest Indian," in Josephy, *The Patriot Chiefs: A Chronicle of American Indian Resistance* (1958), pp. 131–173. The best short biography, with a sensitive understanding of the historical forces that shaped Tecumseh's life.

KLINCK, CARL F.: *Tecumseh: Fact and Fiction in Early Records* (1961). Edited documents about and by Tecumseh, including his important speeches.

OSKINSON, JOHN M.: *Tecumseh and His Times* (1938).

TUCKER, GLENN: *Tecumseh: Vision of Glory* (1956). The best, complete biography.

The Period

ARNOW, HARRIETTE S.: *Seedtime on the Cumberland* (1960). A history of the trans-Appalachian white frontier.

BAKELESS, JOHN: *Daniel Boone* (1938). A biography of a man Tecumseh opposed but also admired.

BILLINGTON, RAY ALLEN: *Westward Expansion: A History of the American Frontier* (2nd. ed., 1960). The best single volume on a subject that involves Indians at almost every juncture.

BRANDON, WILLIAM: *The Last Americans: The Indian in American Culture* (1974). A monumental cultural history of the whole Indian experience.

CARTER, SAMUEL, III: *Cherokee Sunset: A Nation Betrayed* (1976). The expulsion of the Cherokees was even more brutal than that of the Shawnees.

CLEAVES, FREEMAN: *Old Tippecanoe: William Henry Harrison and His Time* (1939). The white perspective on the Indian wars of the Old Northwest.

HAGEN, WILLIAM T.: *American Indians* (1961). A brief, fast-paced history of the entire Indian experience.

JACOBS, WILBUR R.: *Dispossessing the American Indian: Indians and Whites on the Colonial Frontier* (1972). Valuable interpretations of the woodland Indians and the effect of their contact with white civilization.

JENNINGS, FRANCIS: *The Invasion of America: Indians, Colonialism, and the Century of Conquest* (1975). A revisionist interpretation of the settlement of North America, particularly the Northeast, that stresses the injustices of the white dispossession of the Indian.

JOSEPHY, ALVIN M., JR.: *The Patriot Chiefs: A Chronicle of American Indian Resistance* (1958). Essays on Indian leaders, from Hiawatha to Chief Joseph, which illuminate the entire course of Indian-white relations.

UNDERHILL, RUTH MURRAY: *Red Man's America* (rev. ed., 1971). An ethnologist's interpretation of Indian history.

*WASHBURN, WILCOMB E.: *The Indian in America* (1975). Inclusive chapters dealing with Indian personality, social structure, and religion are blended with a chronological history.

WASHBURN, WILCOMB E. (ed.): *The Indian and the White Man* (1964). A collection of documents.

* Available in paperback.

CHAPTER SIX

Jim Bridger

Booming southwest through the narrowing Cache Valley, the Bear River gathered speed. Jim Bridger also quickened his step. Tall and spare, with long hair protruding beneath a beaver hat, he rounded one last bend and overlooked a great plain extending as far as he could see. In the center, also fading into the horizon, lay an enormous body of water. Bridger's pulse leaped at the discovery. Breaking into a jog, he wove through the sagebrush to the water's edge. Kneeling, he drank, then spat in disgust. Salt!

But in a second Bridger's disappointment turned to awe.
Hurriedly returning to his trapping companions, who were camped
that fall of 1824 in the upper Cache Valley, Bridger reported that
he had found an arm of the Pacific Ocean! Only later did
further exploration reveal what Bridger's "ocean" really was: Utah's
Great Salt Lake.

In 1804, the year of Bridger's birth, the American frontier
began at St. Louis, and Lewis and Clark were making plans to
explore the great unknown to the west. When Bridger died
seventy-seven years later, his nation had spanned the continent, and
the frontier was rapidly becoming history. Bridger figured
prominently in this process of discovery, exploration, settlement, and
development. He neither read nor wrote, but in his time and
circumstance it mattered little. Like Christopher Columbus, Jim
Bridger had the good fortune of living in an age of expanding
horizons.

On March 17, 1804, in a small room over a roadside inn near Richmond, Virginia, Chloe Tyler Bridger, a distant relative of the tenth President of the United States, John Tyler, gave birth to her first son, James. The family owned the inn, but business was poor. Travelers using the James River as a highway into the interior generally carried their own food and saved money by sleeping in their wagons. The Bridgers existed largely on the trade of "locals" who purchased occasional shots of whiskey and mugs of beer. Young Jim and two other children helped with the chores (school was out of the question), but the family slipped steadily further into poverty. Jim's father tried to make ends meet by working a small farm near Fredericksburg, but a century and a half of continuous tobacco production had exhausted the soil. Surveying, which the elder Bridger also tried, proved little better in an old community where boundaries were long established. The cheap, fertile land that underlay the Jeffersons' wealth had vanished east of the Appalachians. Finally, the hard times that accompanied the economic boycotts preceding the War of 1812 added further burdens.

In this dark picture there was one bright spot—the West. People like the Bridgers talked about it as a dreamland of opportunity. As the New World once attracted Europe's dissatisfied, so the land beyond the Appalachians beckoned failures in the seaboard states. The urge to move was a compound of pushing and pulling forces. Adversity in the East pushed pioneers westward, while visions of success across the mountains drew them like a magnet. In 1812 the Bridger family succumbed to the dual force, packed its belongings into a red Conestoga wagon, and sought a new start in the West.

As they left Virginia, families such as the Bridgers took advantage of several policies of the United States. Two of these were the systems of land sale and territorial government established in the 1780s and now functioning with great success. Low minimum acreage requirements, cheap prices, and liberal credit allowances permitted men of modest means to get a start on the public domain. Granted that extreme poverty, such as that of some immigrants and factory laborers, precluded pioneer farming, it was possible for people like the Bridgers, who could sell eastern property, to raise the requisite capital. As for government, stories such as that of the growth of Ohio to independent statehood impressed everyone. A wilderness in 1790, the territory claimed 60,000 settlers in 1803, enough for statehood under the terms of the Northwest Ordinance. By 1810 the population of Ohio stood at 231,000.

A major factor in this growth was the improvement of overland transportation to the Ohio Valley. Graded, paved all-weather roads facilitated the movement of people and produce. Many of these were privately built "turnpikes" that charged tolls, but the condition of the trail-like alternatives made the private roads cheap at almost any price. In 1806 Congress authorized government financing for a road from western Maryland across the Appalachians to Wheeling on the Ohio River. Although delayed by the War of 1812, the National Road soon became the primary artery of east-west travel.

The gradual establishment of the authority of the United States in trans-Appalachia was another precondition to migrations such as that of the Bridgers. French western intrigue ended in the mid-1790s when George Washington and Thomas Jefferson blocked the efforts of Citizen Edmund Genêt to recruit a private army in support of the French Revolution. Spanish claims were weakened in 1796 with the approval of the Treaty of San Lorenzo (the Pinckney Treaty). The new states of Kentucky (1792) and Tennessee (1796) were now safe from Spanish intrigue and the possibility of secession. Also, by this treaty the United States obtained a promise of free navigation on the Mississippi River and the right to deposit goods for transshipment at New Orleans, a port essential to the western economy. Spain's sale of Louisiana to France in 1800 and the resale of it to the United States three years later substantially ended the claims of both foreign powers to trans-Appalachia. Spain did retain possession of East Florida, and claimed a strip of land along the Gulf of Mexico (West Florida), until the invasion by General Andrew Jackson in 1818 and the negotiation of the Adams-Onís Treaty the following year. As for England, she was slow to evacuate her frontier posts following the American Revolution and, with a foothold in Canada, retained an active interest in the Ohio Valley until the conclusion of the War of 1812.

The Bridgers' route west in 1812 took them across the Appalachians and along the route of the National Road to the Ohio River. There they sold the red Conestoga and procured passage on a flatboat. The peacefulness of floating down the big river toward its confluence with the Mississippi belied the tension along its banks. For over a generation, the Ohio Valley had been the object of a bitter conflict between its original Indian occupants and white newcomers, like the family of Jim Bridger. Many flatboats similar to their own had been stopped by warriors and their occupants slaughtered. In 1812 the name "Tecumseh" was never absent for long from conversations along the Ohio. The brilliant Shawnee war chief (see Chapter 5), in collaboration with General Isaac Brock of Great Britain, captured the key American post at Detroit in the opening action of the War of 1812. The fall of Detroit, on August 16, spread fear throughout the Old Northwest that Tecumseh and his three thousand warriors would soon be ravaging white settlements on the Indians' ancestral homeland. Around Ohio Valley campfires frightened minds turned shadows into Indians. In fact, as the Bridgers floated down the Ohio River in the fall of 1812, they ran the possibility of an encounter with the southward-moving Tecumseh, who was engaged in his final effort to recruit southern tribes for his Indian confederation. Eight-year-old Jim was too young to stand guard, but he had his first experience in coping with the problem of hostile Indians—an experience that would never be absent for long in his later life.

The moving carpet of water carried the Bridgers swiftly to the confluence of the Ohio and Mississipi. Progress upstream was more difficult, but at last the family arrived at St. Louis. Located near the strategic junction of the Missouri and Mississippi rivers, St. Louis already claimed several thousand inhabitants and a settled hinterland extending up and down the Mississippi for 40 miles. The Bridgers bought a small farm at the northern edge of the settlement. Although subject to seasonal flooding, the soil was rich, and the future of this new enterprise seemed bright. James Bridger, Sr., found steady employment as a surveyor, and young Jim toiled at the farm chores. Just breaking the tough prairie sod was a monumental task. For women, frontier farming was particularly demanding, and Chloe Bridger died in 1816, when Jim was twelve. An aunt arrived from Virginia to help raise the children, but by Christmas 1817 Jim's father and younger brother were buried near his mother.

Although Jim Bridger matured quickly on the farm, he was now placed in the position of fending entirely for himself. At first he obtained a canoe and ran a muskrat and mink line in the Mississippi bottomlands. However, by 1817 thirty to fifty wagons filled with immigrants were crossing the Mississippi at St. Louis daily, and Jim saw profit to be made in their service. Ferrying people and their belongings across the river became his principal occupation in the summer months. In winter Jim labored in a blacksmith shop, building heavy muscles and a knowledge of both horses and men. There was considerable talk around the shop and in St. Louis generally about the Far West. Lewis and Clark, of course, were legendary names in the city, and there were later explorers and trappers, dressed in the buckskins of the mountainman, who spoke of a wilderness of snow-capped peaks and roaring rivers. As he repaired their traps and rifles at his forge, Jim Bridger, like Ben Franklin in the printing shop, developed the ambitions that shaped his life.

Fur was the principal product of St. Louis in Bridger's time. After the return of Lewis and Clark, numerous expeditions pushed northwest on the trail of the beaver. Every spring they left the city, poling and pulling keelboats laden with trade goods and traps. One of the first to organize the business was Manuel Lisa, a man whose Spanish heritage did not preclude a Yankee eye for the dollar. In 1807, just a year after the return of Lewis and Clark, Lisa followed the Missouri and the Yellowstone to the mouth of the Bighorn River in present-day Montana. There Lisa built a fort, which he modestly named Fort Manuel. He then sent John Colter, a veteran of the Lewis and Clark expedition, up the Bighorn and into the Yellowstone country. Traveling alone in midwinter with only a 30-pound pack, Colter covered 500 miles and returned with stories of geysers and boiling springs that men found hard to believe. But the unbelievable was always part of the New World's fascination, and when Colter's report reached St. Louis, it only increased the determination of the adventurous to go west.

Jim Bridger's opportunity came in 1822, when an advertisement appeared in the *Missouri Republican*. William H. Ashley, the lieutenant-governor of the new state, was seeking "one hundred young men to ascend the Missouri River to its source, there to be employed for one, two or three years." Excitedly, Bridger sought out Ashley's associate in the trapping venture, Major Andrew Henry, and signed on. The departure date was only a month away, in April. From Pittsburgh, Ashley had acquired two 65-foot keelboats with a loading capacity of 25 tons, equivalent to an entire wagon train. Bridger was assigned to help maneuver the heavy boats upstream against the power of the Missouri. As one man kept the boat in the water with the use of a sweep-rudder, the others trudged along on shore pulling long ropes attached to its bow. It was an exhausting business requiring the men to stumble over rocks and fallen logs, wade side streams, and climb steep embankments. Occasionally an upriver wind and a crude sail would offer some relief, but otherwise it was blisters and sweat.

On May 1, 1822, the Ashley-Henry party reached Fort Atkinson near Council Bluffs and the Platte River. The garrison at the fort had warnings of Indian hostility, and some of the men in the party chose to return to St. Louis. Jim Bridger, however, was just warming up. With the remainder of the Ashley-Henry group he continued up the Missouri and into the Dakotas, where the Mandan Indians made their home. Among these friendly tribes Bridger began to gain the knowledge of native tongues and customs that played a major role in his later success as a scout and guide. Pushing on to the mouth of the Yellowstone, the Ashley-Henry men constructed shelters and ran trap lines. Before winter there was a rich harvest of pelts to send back to St. Louis.

There were also Indian problems. Outraged at the white man's invasion of their traditional hunting grounds, the Arikaras and Blackfeet struck back. In one surprise attack the Indians killed fourteen Ashley trappers. Bridger managed to survive, and joined a force of trappers, Sioux Indians, and federal soldiers under Colonel Henry Leavenworth in the destruction of the Arikara village. Nevertheless, Ashley decided to move his operations from the northern to the central Rocky Mountains, where Indian opposition was less intense. In the winter of 1823–1824 he dispatched Bridger, Thomas Fitzpatrick, Jedediah Smith, and several others to probe the country west of Wyoming's Wind River Mountains.

Hiking along the eastern face of the towering Wind River range and up the Sweetwater River, Bridger and his companions discovered South Pass, a low and level route across the Continental Divide and the key to the opening of the West. Its significance was not lost on the trappers. Here, they realized, was a route by which loaded wagons could reach the Columbia River watershed and the Pacific Northwest. Later, South Pass became the gateway to the Oregon Trail and an important factor in Bridger's career as a provisioner and guide. But in 1823 it led only to the headwaters of the Green River and to beaver country of a richness beyond Bridger's wildest dreams. So enthusiastic was his report that Ashley determined to send scores of trappers into the area the following season. Reluctant to build Indian-provoking forts, he hit upon an ingenious plan for exploiting the fur resources. Under the rendezvous system trappers like Bridger were dispatched in small groups to work widely scattered waterways. In the early summer they gathered at a prearranged spot in the mountains for several weeks of trading, gambling, boasting, drinking, and sex. The wagons that had brought trade goods from St. Louis were ready to return loaded with beaver pelts. The first rendezvous, held in July 1825 at Henry's Fork on the Green River, attracted over a hundred trappers and Indians. Bridger was there and became a center of attention with his tale of Great Salt Lake. In subsequent years the annual rendezvous grew larger and more profitable. After the 1826 season Ashley retired, a wealthy man, to St. Louis and a political career. Jedediah Smith, David Jackson, and William Sublette assumed direction of his Rocky Mountain Fur Company.

Even more than at other times America seemed to be on the move
in the early nineteenth century, and the direction of travel was invariably
west. This is the Fairview Inn on the National (or Cumberland) Road
near Baltimore. The high-wheeled Conestoga (or "covered") wagons
(right) are similar to the one the Bridger family used to travel over this
route from Virginia to the Ohio River in 1812.

In 1837 a young Scottish-born painter, Albert J. Miller, accompanied
the Scottish nobleman William Drummond Stewart to the fur traders'
annual rendezvous. Among the participants that year was Jim
Bridger (left foreground), dressed, in Miller's sketch, in the suit of
armor Stewart presented him.

J. Goldsborough Bruff was one of the thousands who responded to the news of the discovery of gold in California. A genuine "forty-niner" (he went west in 1849), Bruff's sketch shows how the travelers "circled up" for the night as a precaution against Indian attack. There is a sense of vastness in the sketch, a feeling for the bigness of the sky and the insignificance of the pioneers.

The construction of this fort on a tributary of the Green River in 1843 marked Jim Bridger's transformation from trapper to trader. Located just west of the continental divide, Fort Bridger became a popular way station for travelers on the Oregon and California trails.

The decade after 1825 marked the high point of the fur trade and the mountain man. Jim Bridger rose with the tide. He was fearless, tough, and wise in the ways of a wilderness that usually permitted a man only one mistake. He had a knack for geography, an innate sense of direction, and after a decade in the West probably had in his mind the best single map of that region. When asked specifically about a certain area, Bridger would squat on his haunches and sketch in the dirt a remarkably accurate description of the country in question. He put the same talent to work on his own travels. For example, in 1825, when Bridger became the second man after Colter to explore the Yellowstone country, he confirmed his belief that the Missouri, Green, and Snake rivers rose within a few miles of each other on this continental rooftop. At the next rendezvous this information became common property.

Conversely, Bridger learned from his colleagues. In 1826, Jedediah Smith left the rendezvous in Cache Valley, Utah, with fifteen men, a Bible, and plenty of rifles to explore the Southwest. Skirting west of the Wasatch Range and the high plateaus of central Utah, Smith reached the Virgin River and then the Colorado. The next leg of the journey carried him across the Mojave Desert, through Cajon Pass, and into the Los Angeles basin. The Mexicans were surprised, to say the least, at the appearance of the first Americans to make the overland crossing to California, and they requested Smith to leave *pronto* by the same route he had entered their territory. Blithely disregarding the orders, Smith led his men up California's Central Valley and then, in an incredible feat, over the main crest of the Sierra Nevada and across Nevada's arid Great Basin, where they nearly died of thirst, to the 1827 rendezvous at Bear Lake in southern Idaho. A few days swapping adventures with Bridger and others, and the remarkable wanderer set out again. This time Smith traveled from southern California to the Columbia River, sold his furs to the Hudson's Bay Company, and threaded his way through the mountains and canyons of Idaho to the rendezvous at Pierre's Hole.

Hostile Indians were part of the life of the trapper. Bridger fought them doggedly for years. Once he and the black trapper, Jim Beckwourth, led two hundred of their fellows in pursuit of a band of Bannock and Snake Indians accused of stealing pelts to an island in the Green River, where they collected an alleged 488 scalps. But sometimes the tables were turned. At the 1835 rendezvous Dr. Marcus Whitman, the Oregon missionary pioneer, extracted a 3-inch Blackfoot arrowhead that had been embedded in Bridger's back for three years. Others were not as lucky. After he had "retired" to the supposed safety of the Santa Fe trade, Jedediah Smith was slain by Comanches at a water hole on the Great Plains. And every rendezvous produced stories of trappers whose hair had been "lifted." Indeed, Jim Bridger was an exception among the trappers in that he died of old age. Yet in the final analysis the mountain man had much in common with the Indian. Jim Beckwourth actually joined the Crow tribe. Bridger lived happily with three Indian wives and was devoted to his several "half-breed" children.

It is easy and has long been the custom to style mountain men like Jim Bridger carefree primitivists, and the fur trade a romantic adventure. The western trapper seemingly had cut the ties with civilization and, by virtue of his leap into the wilderness of the Far West, stood apart from the mainstream of American life. Actually, the mountain men and the residents of the eastern states had a great deal in common. The trapper was a highly skilled professional, motivated by the same considerations of monetary gain that moved his eastern countrymen in the era of Andrew Jackson. And the fur trade was a sophisticated industry, in the forefront of the evolution of American economic life toward patterns at once larger and more integrated. Fur was among the first American businesses to function on a nationwide scale. The values and institutions known as Jacksonianism, in short, extended across the wide Missouri to both shape and reflect the aspirations of Jim Bridger and his colleagues.[1]

In 1828 and again in 1832 Andrew Jackson—Tennesseean, Indian-fighter, hero of the Battle of New Orleans—was elected President of the United States. Especially in comparison to the previous occupant of that office, the staid New Englander John Quincy Adams, Jackson appeared to be the man of the people, a champion of democracy. What Jackson really championed was equality of opportunity. He and his followers believed in loosening the hold of an

---

[1] For the meaning of Jacksonianism for Mark Twain, see Chapter 7.

entrenched, privileged, and usually wealthy elite on American political and economic life. When he attacked the most glaring special interest of the time—the Bank of the United States—in 1832, Jackson himself declared that he opposed those "artificial distinctions" whereby the "rich and powerful" came to dominate and suppress the ambitions of the "humble members of society." Jacksonians did not mean to imply by this that they opposed all privilege or that they rejected the concept of failure. Rather, they felt that privilege and prosperity should be the result of ability and ability alone. Failure should result from inability. Distinctions between men, in other words, were to be natural.

The Jacksonian philosophy was an extension of the Jeffersonian concept of a natural aristocracy, and it was therefore essential that everyone (and Jackson defined this term more liberally than Jefferson) have a chance at success. Its pursuit, furthermore, was to be regulated by rules that ensured the triumph of the talented. Jacksonianism did not pit the poor against the rich; it was the attempt of the poor to *become* rich. The liberation, not the destruction, of capitalism and its rewards were the objectives of the Jacksonian democrat. Typically, he was an ambitious entrepreneur. Hardly a revolutionary or anarchist, he wanted to tear down privilege and interfere with private property only when he believed they blocked his own pursuit of these goals. Jacksonianism, in sum, defined human rights as the free opportunity to get rich. It was the perfect philosophy for an acquisitive society such as Jim Bridger's.

To examine the evolution of the fur trade and the lives of the mountain men is to see excellent examples of Jacksonianism in practice. The West in the early nineteenth century meant equal opportunity. Special interests, family, and background counted for little. Performance—what a man could *do*—mattered. The wilderness played no favorites, and only the talented succeeded and survived. It was the ideal Jacksonian situation. Consider Bridger. The advertisement that induced him to go into the mountains was headed "To Enterprising Young Men!!!" and the young men who responded were economically on the make. Contrary to romantic legend, they did not go west to escape from civilization, but rather to extend it and rise within it. Beaver pelts were not an excuse for a wilderness outing to Bridger but, in his jargon, "hairy bank notes," cold cash. Risks were great, but so were returns. A few boat- or wagonloads of pelts in St. Louis meant affluence.

In this environment the capitalistic entrepreneur, so crucial a part of the age of Jackson, flourished. Manuel Lisa is an example. He was the first trader to recognize that only large, well-organized, and well-heeled companies would succeed in exploiting the fur potential of the Rockies. Another economic visionary was John Jacob Astor, who in 1808 organized the American Fur Company. Astor planned to construct a chain of forts from the Great Lakes to the Pacific Northwest and compete with the Hudson's Bay Company. He sent a land and a sea expedition to the Columbia River and founded Astoria at its mouth. But the War of 1812 ruined Astor's plans, and Indian hostility frustrated Lisa. Still, these entrepreneurs were portents of the new economic order that began to flower during Jackson's presidency.

A sure sign of the presence of Jacksonian aspirations among the mountain men was the fact that few of them passed up the opportunity of entrepreneurial leadership. The pull of power and position almost always overcame the call of the wild. Jim Bridger was no exception. Beginning as a hired hand with Ashley and Henry, he moved up quickly to the leadership of one of their brigades. In this capacity he directed the operations of a group of trappers and earned the nickname "Old Gabe" from Jedediah Smith, who knew that the angel Gabriel was the communicator of God's will to his subordinates. In modern terminology, Bridger was a good "organization man."

In 1830 Bridger *became* the organization. Smith and his associates transferred their interests in the Rocky Mountain Fur Company to Bridger and several others. Now in command of six hundred trappers, Bridger combed over the last untouched beaver country. But he soon learned an axiom of capitalism: where there were profits, there would be competition. It came first in the form of smaller companies whose agents began to appear at the annual rendezvous and bid for the trappers' harvests. After 1832 the American Fur Company offered stiffer competition. With the large and diversified Astor assets behind it, American Fur was in a position to outbid and outlast Bridger and Rocky Mountain Fur. Its advantage increased when its steamboat, *Yellowstone,* reached the confluence of that river and the Missouri in June 1832. Not the smallest dividend of the unprecedented voyage was the awe that the "Fire Boat That Walked on the Waters" produced among the Indians, who now confined their trade to American Fur agents.

After several more years of fierce competition, Bridger saw that he was losing ground. In 1834 he sold out to and became an employee of his larger rival. But the climax of the economic war over fur came with the entrance of the venerable Hudson's Bay Company into the Rocky Mountain arena. Beaver were disappearing in the Pacific Northwest, and the Bay's men moved farther and farther up the Snake River. A race began. Frantically, American trappers pursued the remaining beaver, to the detriment and near destruction of the resource on which they depended. By the late 1830s the end was in sight for those who could bring themselves to look. The 1840 rendezvous was the last. The trappers became disgruntled, and with easy profits gone, few elected to live the free wilderness life that legend has them loving for its own sake. Instead, these Jacksonians pursued opportunities in ranching, farming, shopkeeping, politics, banking, and even opera house management. They developed the West.

While Jacksonianism was influencing the frontier, the frontier style was shaping national politics. Jackson was the first President from a nonseaboard state and the first to step out of the gentlemanly tradition of the Virginia dynasty (Washington, Jefferson, Madison, Monroe) and the Harvard line (John Adams, John Quincy Adams). Hardly embarrassed at this fact, Jackson based his 1828 campaign on his experience as a man of action, a warrior-hero, and a supreme individualist who blended nature and civilization into a new, allegedly superior, and distinctively American character. The fact that in the winter of 1814–1815 he defeated both the powerful Creek tribe (at the Battle of Horeshoe Bend) and the best of England's army (at the Battle of New Orleans) lent substance to this claim. In the person of Jackson, the frontiersman acquired the status of a superman.

Next to Old Hickory, as Jackson was called, the hero of the 1830s was unquestionably Davy Crockett, king of the wild frontier. Crockett deliberately turned down an honorary degree from Harvard and cultivated a demagogic, bombastic, and often fraudulent political style in his congressional campaign. But at a time when the spread of universal white male suffrage was transforming the guiding values of politics from gentlemanly idealism to win-at-any-price, Crockett succeeded in spectacular fashion. Jackson's momentum carried his Vice-President, Martin Van Buren, to the Presidency in 1836. By this time opponents of Jackson and the Democrats had organized the Whig party around Henry Clay, Daniel Webster, and John C. Calhoun, none of whom gained the highest prize in American politics. That was reserved, in 1840, for the old Indian-fighter and hero of the Battle of Tippecanoe: William Henry Harrison. Discarding gentlemanly politics, the Whigs elected Harrison with a grass-roots, frontier-style approach. Their campaign of 1840 featured log cabins (Harrison was born in one) and the frontier wine—hard cider. Harrison's running mate, John Tyler, was reputedly a distant relative of Jim Bridger's mother. Four years later the Jacksonian faction regained the White House with James K. Polk of Tennessee, an enthusiastic exponent of the expanding American frontier.

Jim Bridger was among the last of the mountain men to accept as fact the demise of trapping. For several years after dissolving the Rocky Mountain Fur Company, he struggled against decreasing beaver and increasing competition. Seeking financial backing for his trapping ventures, Bridger floated down the Missouri to St. Louis in 1839. For seventeen years he had been in the wilderness. Now he could scarcely recognize his former home. Its population had grown to 384,000. The river bottoms where a teen-aged Bridger set traps and paddled his canoe now teemed with steamboats at the wharves. The explorer wandered, lost, through the wilderness of city streets, but he succeeded in finding financial backing for another trapping venture on the upper Green River. The past and the future intersected one day on the Green, when Bridger and his trappers met an old colleague, Tom Fitzpatrick, leading a group of emigrants to Oregon. The year was 1840, and this was the first true emigrant train—a long string of dusty, white-topped wagons filled with men, women, and children. The sight must have reminded Bridger of his own family's westward trek a quarter-century ago and 2000 miles to the east. Fitzpatrick told Bridger the settlers were desperate for equipment and provisions and pointed out that the future lay in providing these wants rather than in fur.

At first Bridger scoffed at Fitzpatrick's suggestion. But in 1842 he again met his old partner on the trail near Fort Laramie with an even larger emigrant train. Soon afterward he encountered another mountain man, Kit Carson, guiding a group of United States Engineers under Lieutenant John C. Frémont. These soldier-explorers were scientifically mapping the West and laying the official basis for its settlement. Frémont was called the Pathfinder, but men like Carson and Bridger knew the territory. Jim began to see a new field for his abilities. But the summer of 1843 again found Bridger plying the trapper's trade. This year, however, he built a fort on Blacks Fork on the Green River, to the west of South Pass and on the best route to Great Salt Lake, Oregon, and California. When he returned to the fort in the early fall, Bridger learned that over a thousand emigrants had passed by, as well as another contingent of army engineers. In December 1843 Bridger made his decision. He would turn Fort Bridger into a permanent establishment with a store and a blacksmith shop and cater to the needs of travelers on the Oregon Trail. For Bridger it was the end of one era and the beginning of another. The day of the mountain man was over.

As he settled into his new vocation, Jim Bridger became the beneficiary of several concepts prevalent in the United States of the 1840s. One was the agrarian myth. The roots of this complex of emotions, values, and hopes lay in the mystique surrounding the New World and drew sustenance from both the Spanish mirage of El Dorado and the romantic notion of the noble savage. But the major sources of the agrarian myth were the dreams of everyday Americans and the promises of those who wished to lure them west. The myth held the American West to be a pastoral paradise in which self-sufficient yeoman farmers lived wholesome, happy lives in a beautiful environment close to nature. It was a rose-colored view of the frontier, laced with Jeffersonian republicanism, that ignored the realities of both the West and of human nature. Still, around the kitchen table or living-room fireplace of dissatisfied easterners or Europeans, the myth was hard to resist. Even if they did not move west themselves, people liked to think that the idyllic life really existed in the direction of the setting sun. For Americans, it was a basis for national pride.

Obviously, land speculators and western developers benefited from promoting the agrarian myth. The innumerable emigrant guide-

TRAILS AND TRANSPORTATION WEST IN THE MID-NINETEENTH CENTURY: 1850

books that appeared in the nineteenth century sounded a chorus of praise for life on the frontier. In most of the descriptions Eden itself paled by comparison. Of course, there was the counterimage of a Great American Desert filled with bloodthirsty savages and wracked by fierce storms and searing droughts. Bountiful harvests did not always spring up at the sower's bidding, and log cabins could be intellectual and moral vacuums. But most Americans chose to believe the contrary, and the belief was a prerequisite to undertaking the major dislocations that emigration entailed. Jim Bridger, of course, knew the difference between the myth and the reality. The emigrants who reached his fort were beginning to understand, but some of the fire still burned in the eyes of those who continued westward.

The second complex of ideas that moved the nation west was Manifest Destiny. The term was coined two years after the founding of Fort Bridger by John L. O'Sullivan, a Jacksonian journalist. It drew heavily on the old idea of American mission and the belief that the nation had a right, indeed a duty and God-appointed destiny, to expand across the continent to the Pacific Ocean. Proponents of Manifest Destiny argued that because America had a mission to lead mankind to a better life, the expansion of American civilization was unquestionably good. Freedom and democracy as well as heavenly purposes would be served. There was, to be sure, the problem caused by previous occupants of the land. But expansionists using the Manifest Destiny doctrine blithely dismissed the claims of the Indians, the Mexicans, and the English with the argument that although American civilization might not be immediately appreciated, it would eventually benefit those to whom it was given. Skeptics contended that Manifest Destiny was merely a rationale for American land hunger, intellectual oil to assuage guilty consciences and smooth the way west, but most of Bridgers' contemporaries did not question the legitimacy of such a convenient idea.

The expansion of the United States, which opened a new career for Jim Bridger, inevitably pressed at the territory of Mexico, its neighbor to the south and west. That nation won its independence from Spain in 1821 and at first welcomed American settlers to the northeastern part of the state of Coahuila, which was called Texas. Moses Austin and his son Stephen took advantage of the opportunity and in the early 1820s led the first Americans into Mexico. By 1825 about two thousand Americans, a quarter of whom were slaves, lived south of the border. Cotton production flourished, but the settlers, predictably, chafed under Mexican rule, and compared their situation to that of the American colonists before 1776. After 1830 the Mexican government, aware of a problem, tried to discourage American immigration, but it was too late. The combination of an authoritarian Mexican ruler, Santa Anna, and the inclination to autonomy charac- teristic of frontiersmen proved too much for the tenuous relationship.

On March 2, 1836, the American-Mexicans declared their inde- pendence. In the ensuing war, Santa Anna killed every one of the 200 Texans defending the Alamo mission, including frontier heroes Davy Crockett and Jim Bowie, but at a cost of 1544 Mexican lives. Crying "Remember the Alamo!" aroused Americans organized under Sam Houston, and on April 21, 1836, crushed Santa Anna at the Battle of San Jacinto. Mexico still did not officially recognize Texan inde- pendence, but on the frontier possession and strength counted heavily. The Americans had both, and in the fall of 1836 they created the Republic of Texas with Houston as president. A movement for joining the United States began at once, but antislavery interests opposed the addition of another slave state and the consequent disruption of the delicate sectional balance. As a result, Texas existed under its own Lone Star flag until 1845, when a joint resolution of Congress ap- proved annexation.

"Make way, I say, for the young American Buffalo," an eastern politician shouted during the heyday of Manifest Destiny, "he has not yet got land enough." Ironic as the remark sounds in the light of the near extermination of the buffalo by Bridger and his kind, it is true that the annexation of Texas seemed only to whet the nation's appetite for expansion. One logical outlet for these energies was the Southwest. Santa Fe, located on the upper Rio Grande at the eastern edge of the Rocky Mountains, was a focus of interest. Spain had not permitted economic intercourse with the United States, but with the advent of Mexican control, restrictions were relaxed and the Santa Fe trade begun. Every spring a long wagon train assembled at Independence, Missouri, for the journey over the plains. Many of Jim Bridger's fellow trappers found employment on the Santa Fe Trail. Indian attacks, such as the one that claimed the life of Jedediah Smith, were a chronic problem, but the traders learned to draw their wagons into a tight circle when protection was required. Santa Fe, and the community of Taos to the north, were also known to the mountain men as sources of provisions, equipment, and recreation hundreds of miles closer to the trapping grounds than St. Louis.

The other object of American interest in Mexican territory was California. Ecstatic reports of this lotus land beyond the mountains had filtered back east as a result of early commercial contacts involving sea otters, whales, and cattle. A few gentleman-adventurers added embellishments, most notably Richard Henry Dana in *Two Years before the Mast,* which described an 1835–1836 journey. "In the hands of an enterprising people," Dana exulted, "what a country this might be!" The Mexicans, in his estimation, were charming but ill-equipped to spearhead progress. After the pathbreaking overland journeys of Jedediah Smith (1826), James Ohio Pattie (1828), and Joseph Reddeford Walker (1833), the number of Americans living in California gradually increased. Remembering Texas, the Mexican government exhibited a marked coolness toward them, but the immigration persisted. In 1841 John Bidwell led the first emigrant party over the Sierra and into the promised land. Luck, rather than geographic knowledge or wilderness skill, explained Bidwell's successful migration, but after 1843 California emigrants had the benefit of Jim Bridger's fort and advice to help them over the last thousand-mile leg of the journey.

Advice of a different quality came from one Lansford W. Hastings. Hastings made the California trek in 1843, after which he wrote *The Emigrant's Guide to Oregon and California* and set himself up as the resident expert at Fort Bridger, dispensing advice at $10 per person. The gist of it consisted of a recommendation to abandon the accepted California Trail, which ran north from Fort Bridger to the Hudson's Bay Company's Fort Hall and then followed the Humboldt and Truckee rivers to the Sierra Nevada. Hastings instead advocated a cut off through the rugged Wasatch Mountains, south of Great Salt Lake, and across the most arid part of the Great Basin. This was the route that had almost killed Jedediah Smith on his return from California in 1827, and Bridger knew it to be virtually suicidal for slow-moving emigrant parties. Still, the promise of cutting hundreds of miles off the California trip appealed to trail-weary travelers.

Among those who took Hastings's suggestion was a group from Illinois under the leadership of George and Jacob Donner. Leaving Fort Bridger very late in the summer of 1846, the Donner party wasted precious time struggling through the Wasatch range, only to spend six waterless days on the desert west of the Great Salt Lake. The ordeal broke the emigrants' spirit and discipline. They quarreled incessantly and refused to share precious supplies. By now fall was well advanced and the Sierra still blocked the way to California. Tragedy was in the making. A heavy snow trapped the Donner party in the mountains, and the death toll mounted. Of the eighty-nine who started from Fort Bridger, forty-five survived, and some of these only by cannibalism. Blame for the Donner tragedy was subsequently laid at Bridger's door, but he maintained it was Hastings who had urged the ill-fated detour. Certainly Jim had too much respect for geography to deliberately tempt the fates in the manner of the Donners.

By the time the remnants of the Donner party straggled down from their nightmare in the Sierra, the California question was entwined with the larger issue of the war with Mexico. James K. Polk's election to the Presidency in 1844 was pivotal, since the only question in his mind was *how* to get New Mexico and California. First he tried negotiation; John Slidell was sent to Mexico City in 1845 with a cash offer and other concessions. But the Mexicans, already incensed at the annexation of Texas, were not about to cooperate. Enraged at what he considered a snub, Polk began to make ready for war. A skirmish between American and Mexican troops on disputed land facilitated his job. On May 13, 1846, the United States declared war on Mexico. Even at this height of Manifest Destiny many Americans were ashamed of the bullying tactics and the undisguised land greed of the Polk Administration. Only the Vietnam conflict has approached the Mexican War in domestic unpopularity. The Massachusetts legislature, for instance, solemnly proclaimed it "hateful in its objects . . . wanton, unjust, and unconstitutional," and New England refused to provide dollars and troops for what it regarded as a fight to extend slavery. Henry David Thoreau, the mild-mannered Transcendentalist, went to jail rather than pay taxes in support of the Mexican War. But the South and the West were generally for the war, and their support enabled Polk's Army of the West under Stephen W. Kearny to capture Santa Fe and march on California.

Before reaching it, however, Kearny encountered Kit Carson and a band of mountain men heading east. They reported that the weak Mexican government in California had already fallen to the United States Navy and to resident Americans who had organized the Bear Flag Revolt with the assistance of the explorer John C. Frémont and these same mountain men. Delighted, Kearny pushed on to claim California for the United States and the governorship for himself. Official confirmation of the conquest, however, awaited the fall of Mexico City to General Winfield Scott on September 14, 1847, and the signing of the Treaty of Guadalupe Hidalgo on February 2, 1848. According to the agreement, the United States, for $15 million, received California, the sprawling New Mexico territory, and the Rio Grande as the southwest border to Texas. All of Mexico might have been annexed had not Polk's repudiated agent, Nicholas Trist, defied recall and negotiated a treaty without proper authorization.

While stepping with seven-league boots into the Southwest, Americans were also preparing to annex the Oregon country. Jim Bridger was well aware of these developments. He had been at the Pierre's Hole rendezvous in 1832 when the Cambridge, Massachusetts, merchant Nathaniel J. Wyeth rode in with a few dozen followers bound for Oregon. Wyeth's expedition was a response to the frantic promotional efforts of Congressman John Floyd of Virginia and Hall J. Kelley, a Massachusetts schoolteacher obsessed with the idea of transplanting an entire New England town to the Pacific Northwest. Both Floyd and Kelley, along with Wyeth, were convinced that if Americans did not settle this region, Great Britain would. They also knew that the flag followed the fireplace. But the wilderness journey took a toll of the Wyeth party's idealism. At Pierre's Hole Bridger listened, amused, as the group bickered and finally split over the question of continuing. At last Wyeth and ten companions reached Fort Vancouver on the Columbia, only to learn that the ship that carried their heavy goods had been lost attempting to round South America. Crushed, Wyeth returned overland to Boston, but in 1834 he was

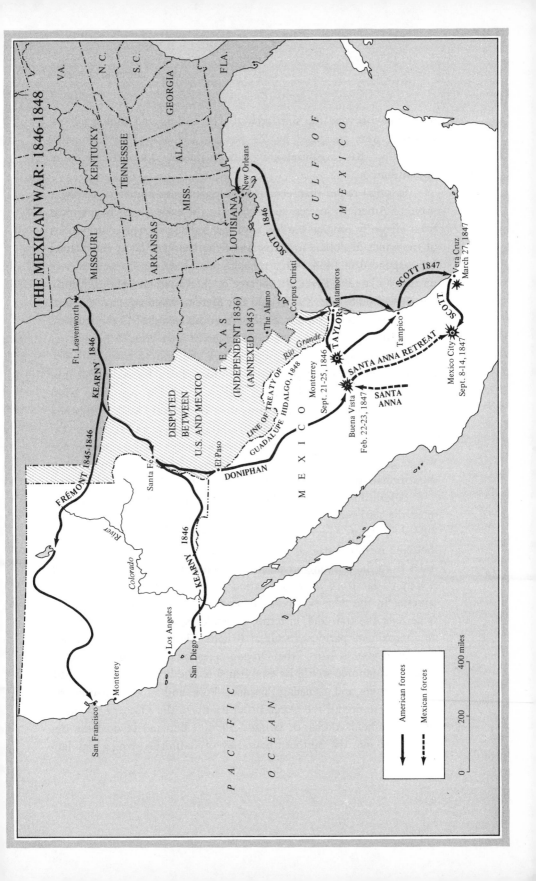

THE MEXICAN WAR: 1846-1848

VA.
N.C.
S.C.
GEORGIA
FLA.
KENTUCKY
TENNESSEE
ALA.
MISS.
ARKANSAS
MISSOURI
LOUISIANA
New Orleans

Ft. Leavenworth

GULF OF MEXICO

SCOTT 1846

KEARNY 1846

FRÉMONT 1845-1846

San Francisco
Monterey
Los Angeles
San Diego

KEARNY 1846

Colorado River

Santa Fe
El Paso
DONIPHAN

TEXAS
(INDEPENDENT 1836)
(ANNEXED 1845)

DISPUTED
BETWEEN
U.S. AND MEXICO

The Alamo
Corpus Christi

LINE OF TREATY OF GUADALUPE HIDALGO, 1848
Rio Grande

Matamoros
TAYLOR
Monterrey
Sept. 21-25, 1846

Buena Vista
Feb. 22-23, 1847

SANTA
ANNA

M E X I C O

Tampico

SCOTT 1847

SANTA ANNA RETREAT

Vera Cruz
March 27, 1847

SCOTT

Mexico City
Sept. 8-14, 1847

PACIFIC OCEAN

American forces
Mexican forces

0   200   400 miles

back, and this time the ship arrived. His trading and fishing efforts, however, were frustrated by the powerful Hudson's Bay Company. Eventually that organization's wily manager, John McLoughlin, bought him out.

Spiritual rather than economic considerations motivated the next wave of American interest in Oregon. In the early 1830s bogus pleas from allegedly religion-starved Flathead Indians elicited contributions of thousands of dollars to Christianize the heathen. Jason and Daniel Lee responded in 1834 with a mission, school, and temperance society on the Willamette River, a tributary of the Columbia. The following year Reverend Samuel Parker and Dr. Marcus Whitman took the trail for Oregon with the support of the American Board of Commissioners for Foreign Missions. At the rendezvous of that year, Whitman removed the arrowhead from Bridger's back and won his friendship. The following spring Whitman, who had returned east for additional support, again met Bridger in the mountains. With him was Mrs. Whitman, the first white woman to cross the Continental Divide. Impressed with his first sight of such a creature in a dozen years, Bridger promised the Whitmans to send his daughter to their school in Oregon. He was as good as his word, too, but Mary Ann Bridger died in 1848 in the aftermath of the massacre of the Whitmans by Cayuse Indians.

Before this unhappy ending Whitman had done his best to promote the settlement of the Pacific Northwest. In 1843 he personally guided a long emigrant train over the Oregon Trail. Its one thousand members paused gratefully at Fort Bridger, which was 1070 miles from the jumping-off place, Independence, Missouri, and almost exactly as far from their destination, Fort Vancouver and the Willamette. In the next two years about four thousand more emigrants came over the trail and, in terms of residents, gave the United States an approximate parity with Great Britain. The growth also increased the urgency of solving "the Oregon question." The key was what parallel of latitude would be established as the boundary between the United States and Canada. President Polk and other expansionists wanted to secure all the Oregon country up to the southern boundary of Russian-held Alaska, or latitude 54°40′. England favored the opposite extreme; the northern boundary of California, which was latitude 42°. The settlement of 1846, designating 49°, was a reasonable compromise, since it extended the eastern Canadian-American boundary to the Pacific.

From the standpoint of the Oregon pioneers, the boundary settlement did not rank in importance with the details of local government. Contrary to their reputation in song and story and on television, frontiersmen were not a lawless lot. On the contrary, for every outlaw with smoking six-shooter, there were a dozen families and businessmen determined to put local affairs on an orderly basis. The extreme individualism of Jim Bridger's generation of mountain men typified only the first wave of pioneers—men who lived a nomadic, wilderness existence and, because they were few, could literally be a law unto themselves. But when settlers arrived they quickly erected a legal framework and enforced it, when necessary, with informal but effective vigilante justice—posses and hangmen's nooses. In Oregon the need to dispose of the estate of a man who died without leaving a will occasioned the first steps toward political organization. In true social compact tradition, the neighbors of the deceased convened to decide the issue. Someone vaguely recalled the New York law dealing with unbequeathed property, so that statute became the Oregon guideline. In 1843 a First Organic Law was pieced together from the fragmentary legal knowledge of the community. Two years later a more complete set of laws regularized such matters as marriage, landholding, and criminal procedures. Taxation was voluntary, but with the understanding that those who did not pay had no vote and no recourse to the law for any purpose. Under such conditions, few refused. The machinery of government was therefore well established by 1848, when Oregon finally became a territory of the United States.

Another example of the orderly extension of civilization occurred in the Great Basin west of Fort Bridger. This time religion provided cohesion and order. The Church of Jesus Christ of Latter-Day Saints had begun in the "burned-over" district of western New York, a region frequently marked by the "fire" of reformers and religious zealots who bore the intellectual legacy of New England Calvinism. The sect had its origins in 1830 in the mind of Joseph Smith, who claimed mystical intimacy with the word of God. Transcribing the Book of Mormon from golden plates he alone had seen, Smith attracted 15,000 followers and moved them successively to Ohio, Missouri, and Illinois. But Smith's advocacy of polygamy and his acceptance of dictatorial authority to the extent of defying federal law subjected the Mormons, as outsiders termed them, to fierce criticism and, ultimately, violence.

In 1844 a mob murdered Smith and sent the Mormons, in the manner of the Puritans, searching for a sanctuary where they could live according to their beliefs. The trans-Mississippi West was an obvious candidate, and in Brigham Young the Mormons had a leader with the brilliance and tenacity to effect the migration. Like John Winthrop over two centuries before, Young was prepared to stake everything on the American wilderness. Midsummer 1847 found him and a well-organized pioneer band at Fort Bridger conversing with the proprietor about the prospects of settling thousands of people in the Salt Lake Valley. Bridger scoffed at the idea. The country was too arid, its discoverer explained, and to dramatize his point he allegedly offered Young $1,000 for the first ear of corn it produced. Bridger suggested the Mormons try Oregon's rich Willamette Valley, but the saints were not easily swayed. Their primary requirement was isolation, and Salt Lake had that in abundance.

The Mormons counted on Jim Bridger's personal guidance through the mountains, but the plans did not materialize. Trusting instead to their God, the emigrants missed the easier routes and struggled through the tortuous Emigrant Canyon to their haven. Once installed in Salt Lake Valley, however, they made few mistakes. Hard work, a genius for irrigation, and the assistance of a timely invasion of insect-devouring sea gulls solved the agricultural problem, and the relieved settlers joked about Bridger's $1,000 ear of corn. In 1848 the main body of migrating Mormons filed past Fort Bridger in a caravan that one observer described as being "six hundred miles and forty days long." Brigham Young proved a skillful administrator, able to subordinate individual desires to the welfare of the community. The result was rapid and efficient Mormon colonization of the Great Basin from Idaho to southern California. When the United States acquired this territory at the end of the Mexican War, the worried Mormons proposed the creation of a gigantic State of Deseret including all of present-day Utah, all of Arizona, most of Nevada, and parts of Idaho, Wyoming, Colorado, and California, with an

Salt Lake City, Utah, shown here in 1853, was something of a miracle. Less than a decade before, only lizards and jackrabbits had occupied the arid sagebrush benchland between Great Salt Lake and the Wasatch Mountains. The growth of the town was a tribute to the perseverance of the Mormons—one of the most effective groups of pioneers in American history.

The meeting of the rails of the Union Pacific and Central Pacific railroads at Promontory, Utah, north of Great Salt Lake, on May 10, 1869 was an unmistakable sign that the American frontier was vanishing. Americans at the time celebrated the event with as much enthusiasm as later generations displayed in the aftermath of Neil Armstrong's walk on the moon.

ocean port at San Diego. Congress disapproved, but in 1850 President Millard Fillmore did make Brigham Young governor of the more modest Territory of Utah.

As Brigham Young became more powerful in the Great Basin, his initial dislike of Jim Bridger grew into active hostility. The men had little in common. In the eyes of the easy-going, hard-living mountain man, Young seemed stiff, self-assured and incredibly "green" in the ways of the West. The saint, on his part, regarded Bridger as an unregenerate libertine little better than the animals he hunted and trapped. In time Young openly accused Bridger of arousing the Ute Indians against his people. Young was jealous of Bridger's position of authority in territory he was coming to regard as a Mormon empire. There was also an economic factor in the antipathy. Instead of trading at Fort Bridger, the migrating Mormons relied on relief caravans sent east by their brothers at Salt Lake. Mormon traders also endeavored to intercept non-Mormon emigrant parties before they reached Bridger's post. In 1849 the economic war was sharpened as some 40,000 Americans streamed west in quest of the gold that had been discovered the previous year on the property of John A. Sutter near Sacramento, California. As a rule, the Forty-Niners were abysmally prepared for the transcontinental journey and sorely in need of food, equipment, and draft animals when they reached the Green River–Salt Lake frontier. Moreover, the travelers frequently had furniture, machinery, and manufactured goods which they had to unload and would sell at any price before crossing the desert and mountains to California. For the Mormons, the result was affluence; for California, with 100,000 residents by 1850, it was statehood.

As a territorial governor Brigham Young felt it within his power in 1853 to order Jim Bridger arrested on the grounds of instigating Indian attacks. In August a posse of Young's "destroying angels" arrived at Fort Bridger, but found that Jim had headed for the hills. Frustrated, they burned most of the fort to the ground. Jim subsequently returned and sadly kicked through the ashes as he contemplated the perils of property ownership. In the old days such an insult would have been met with immediate retaliation. But the Mormons were too strong. Just as the Indians found themselves crowded into the unwanted corners of their lands, so Jim Bridger was made to yield to a variety of progress he did not fully understand.

In 1857 Bridger had a measure of revenge when he received an appointment as a guide and Indian interpreter in the United States Army. His mission was to lead 2500 troops under Colonel Albert Sidney Johnston against the Mormons, who enjoyed an uncontested theocracy. The soldiers stood firm against a series of Mormon guerrilla attacks and then made winter camp near the ruins of Jim Bridger's old fort. While waiting for spring to open the passes and—it seemed inevitable—a full-scale war, news came of the massacre of 120 emigrants by Mormons in southern Utah. But instead of precipitating bloodshed, the Mountain Meadow Massacre convinced a cool-headed Buchanan Administration, preoccupied, it must be said, by the impending sectional conflict, that civil war in the West had to be avoided. Mediation hurriedly took place in the winter of 1857–1858. Much to Bridger's amazement and disgust, Brigham Young was pardoned and in practice allowed to rule Utah. What Bridger did not understand was that the principle of federal authority had been unequivocally asserted and reluctantly accepted.

After the "Mormon War" Jim Bridger turned to guiding as his principal vocation. A full 6 feet in height, lean and rawboned, with greying hair and a detailed knowledge of the Rocky Mountains, Bridger was a wilderness veteran who commanded respect in any company. A large proportion of his clients were in the transport business. Western developers and proponents of Manifest Destiny had always recognized the need for reliable overland transportation. The frontier, almost by definition, receded as the transportation network advanced. First to appear were the road builders and the organizers of stagecoach lines and express companies. Bridger helped them find key routes, and in the process left his name on western maps. The Bridger Trail ran north from the North Platte River and the Oregon Trail to the Yellowstone River and Bozeman, Montana. Bridger's Ferry took the Oregon Trail across the North Platte. As an all-weather alternative to that famous pathway, Bridger blazed a route from western Nebraska to northern Utah over Bridger's Pass. In 1861, along with Captain E. L. Berthoud and the Central Overland, California, and Pike's Peak Express Company, he laid out the Bridger-Berthoud Road west from Denver. And the South Pass–Green River–Salt Lake corridor that Bridger discovered in the early 1820s became the major east-west transcontinental route.

By 1860, thanks to generous federal subsidies, people and light produce were moving along these roads on a more or less regular basis. The glamour company was the Butterfield Overland Mail, whose horse-drawn coaches in 1858 raced from Missouri to California in twenty-four days. "I congratulate you on the result," a proud President Buchanan wired Butterfield, "it is a glorious triumph for civilization and the Union." But even this achievement paled in comparison to that of the Pony Express, whose team of daredevil horsemen carried the mail across the same distance in just ten days in 1860. A year later the time was cut to seconds when wires were joined on the first transcontinental telegraph.

The efficient transport of items heavier than paper and people awaited the railroads. The two decades before the Civil War saw track mileage in the United States leap from 3,000 to 30,000. These years also witnessed the birth of a plan for a transcontinental railroad, but it foundered on the rocks of sectional competition and uncertain financing. When the Civil War eliminated the first problem and federal subsidies the second, the plans revived. In the mid-1860s the Central Pacific began its push east from California. Generous grants of the public domain, which made the railroads the largest landowners in the West, and federal loans on a per-mile basis encouraged construction. In 1867 the Central Pacific's tracks extended across the Sierra. Meanwhile, the Union Pacific was advancing west from Omaha, Nebraska. Its route, through South Pass, was the one Jim Bridger had showed General Grenville M. Dodge and Union Pacific officials a few years before. The competition between the Central and Union crews resulted in rapid, if careless, construction which over favorable terrain reached the rate of 10 miles per day. The lines met on May 10, 1869, at Promontory, Utah. Only forty-five years before, Jim Bridger had stood at almost the same place, the first white man to see Great Salt Lake.

Even as the golden spike was driven at Promontory, other railroads were being lengthened westward to provide the transportation network on which settlement depended. To the north of the Central Pacific–Union Pacific axis, the Northern Pacific and James J. Hill's Great Northern opened the Dakotas and Montana. In the south the Santa Fe Railroad followed the route of the old Santa Fe Trail, and the Southern Pacific claimed the Texas-California traffic. A Bridger-

MAJOR RAILROAD LINES ABOUT 1885

discovered route from Denver to Salt Lake City became the main line of the Denver and Rio Grande Railroad.

The advent of rapid, dependable, and relatively inexpensive transportation of heavy, bulky items helped make possible a series of economic bonanzas in the West. Like the fur trade, which began the process, each bonanza brought a wave of civilization surging westward across the Great Plains or eastward from California and Oregon. When the exploitable resource was depleted the wave receded, but not without leaving a residue of permanent settlement. Second only to the trappers were the miners. After the great California gold rush of 1849, there were similar mineral booms in Nevada, Colorado, Arizona, Idaho, Montana, and Wyoming. Denver developed from gold strikes that attracted frontiersmen like bees to honey, and so did Helena, Montana, and Boise, Idaho. The richest concentration of gold and silver was struck on the eastern slope of the Sierra—the fabulous Comstock Lode. Thanks to the miners who flooded in, Nevada became a state in 1864. Thanks to Mark Twain, the state, and especially Virginia City, became an American legend. Life in all the mining camps was rough and tumble, with the usual frontier assortment of gamblers, whores, and outlaws, but the need for a framework of law and order to protect the gains of the fortunate quickly spawned simple democracy, vigilante justice, and—in time—territorial status and statehood.

By 1875 the easy pickings were over. The early arrivals had skimmed the cream off the West's mineral riches, just as they had its furs. The next bonanza involved production, rather than mere gathering, and was concentrated on cattle. Southern Texas was the seedbed of the business. For two decades after the Civil War cowboys drove huge herds north along the Chisholm and other trails to the railhead towns of Abilene and Dodge City, Kansas. But the increase of settlers with their barbed wire fences spelled the end of the open range and the cattle bonanza.

Wheat, corn, and hay figured in the next economic era. Making farming possible were technological improvements such as the windmill pump, the Oliver deep plow, and large-capacity planters and threshers. The development of both irrigation and dry-farming techniques also proved vital. But farmers were necessary too, and the

Homestead Act of 1862, with its promise of virtually free land to anyone who would reside on and improve it, helped draw them from the eastern states and Europe. For unsurveyed land the Preemption Act of 1841 recognized land titles on a first-come basis. Of course these acts, and others like the notorious Desert Land Act (1877) and the Timber and Stone Act (1878), did not prevent choice western lands from falling into the hands of speculators and quick-profit exploiters. The West, with its apparently unlimited and certainly unclaimed abundance, seemed to encourage such behavior. Bridger and the mountain men showed the way with their trap-out-and-get-out methods of operation.

Along with the entrepreneurs of western transportation and resource exploitation, the other major client for Jim Bridger's guiding skills was the United States Army. To the soldiers fell the major responsibility for what was called Indian "removal." Less friendly observers of the process might have called it "extermination" of a culture, if not an entire race. The task began, of course, with the first permanent white settlement of North America. It continued through the uprooting of the eastern woodland Indians, like Tecumseh's Shawnees, to locations west of the Mississippi. This was obviously not a solution. The "permanent Indian frontier" lasted only until white men were ready to cross it. Jim Bridger and the early trappers proved that.

For several decades Bridger and the mountain men fought western tribes like the Crow and the Blackfeet on roughly equal numerical terms. Time brought increasing advantage to the white man. By the 1860s the pressure of miners and railroad builders on the western Indians was such as to precipitate a series of bloody clashes. The first occurred in Colorado in November 1864, when Colonel J. M. Chivington butchered a Cheyenne village. The army followed this Sand Creek Massacre with a campaign against the Sioux in northern Wyoming and southern Montana—the Powder River country. Jim Bridger knew this region like the back of his hand; he also had a knack for understanding the Indian way of warfare. Pressed into service by the Army, he led several successful marches against Chief Red Cloud's Sioux. When Bridger's advice was disregarded, as it was in 1866 by Captain William J. Fetterman, eighty-one soldiers were surprised and

CANADA

ATLANTIC OCEAN

PACIFIC OCEAN

GULF OF MEXICO

MEXICO

LAKE SUPERIOR
LAKE HURON
LAKE ONTARIO
LAKE ERIE
LAKE MICHIGAN

VT.
N. H.
MASS.
CONN.
NEW YORK
N.J.
PA.
MD.
DEL.
Richmond • VIRGINIA
W. VA.
OHIO
N. C.
S. C.
GEORGIA
FLORIDA

WISCONSIN
MICHIGAN
MINN.
IOWA
ILLINOIS
IND.
KENTUCKY
TENN.
ALA.
MISS.
LOUISIANA

Mississippi R.
Ohio R.
Mississippi R.

Council Bluffs •
St. Louis •
Independence •
MISSOURI
ARKANSAS
KANSAS
INDIAN TERRITORY
Red R.
TEXAS

NORTH DAKOTA
SOUTH DAKOTA
BATTLE OF WOUNDED KNEE 1890 ✳
NEBRASKA
Platte R.
OREGON TRAIL
SAND CREEK MASSACRE 1864 ✳

CUSTER MASSACRE 1876 ✳
MONTANA
YELLOWSTONE NATIONAL PARK
WYOMING
Denver •
COLORADO
Santa Fe •
Taos •
NEW MEXICO TERRITORY

Missouri River
ROCKY
SOUTH PASS
Fort Bridger •
JACKSON HOLE
Promontory
WASATCH MTS.
Salt Lake City •
GREAT SALT LAKE
UTAH TERRITORY
MOUNTAINS
Colorado R.
ARIZONA TERRITORY

IDAHO
Snake R.
GREAT BASIN
NEVADA
MOJAVE DESERT

WASHINGTON
OREGON
Columbia R.
Sacramento R.
SIERRA NEVADA
CALIFORNIA
Los Angeles •

Astoria •

400 miles
200
0

JIM BRIDGER'S AMERICA

killed. General warfare continued on the western plains throughout the next decade. The climax came in June 1876 when Chiefs Sitting Bull and Crazy Horse killed Colonel George A. Custer and all his 265 men in the Battle of the Little Big Horn.

The Indian victory over Custer only delayed the inevitable. Four months later General Alfred H. Terry forced the surrender of the bulk of the Sioux nation. This broke the back of serious Indian resistance on the Great Plains. The year 1877 saw the extraordinary running fight of Chief Joseph, of the Oregon Nez Perce tribe, end in defeat only a few miles from the sanctuary in Canada. Joseph was the last great patriot chief, a man Bridger would have respected for his knowledge of the land and how it might be put to a militarily advantageous use. Thereafter, it was a mop-up operation. Indians occasionally left their reservations on raids, but these were short-lived. It was not just that the army herded them back. The environmental basis that had made their culture possible was gone. The buffalo, for instance, was almost exterminated in the 1800s. Less than a thousand animals remained of the millions that once ranged from Kentucky to the Rockies.

For Jim Bridger, too, it was the end of the game. His way of life, like that of the Indians, depended on a quantity of wilderness that was incompatible with an expanding American civilization. Bridger's achievements were, in fact, ironic. The very success of men like him destroyed forever the chance to live a mountain man's existence in the American West. Long celebrated as classic American heroes, the Boones and Bridgers might well be reconsidered in the light of their role in dispossessing the Indian and ruthlessly assaulting wildlife and forests.

After guiding in the Indian wars, Bridger returned to his Missouri farm. The last decade of his life was spent quietly at home with his innumerable stories and a cluster of children fascinated with tales of a life they could never lead. Friends who knew of Bridger's contact with the region may have told him that in 1872 the federal government set aside 3000 square miles in northwestern Wyoming as Yellowstone National Park. This need for protection of a region that only John Colter, Jim Bridger, and a handful of others had seen before the 1870s was a sure sign that the frontier was vanishing.

In 1875 Bridger went totally blind. Weather permitting, he spent his remaining six years on the porch of his farmhouse, leaning forward in a chair, chin resting on a cane. His visitors reported that he always faced the west.

SELECTED READINGS

The Person

ALTER, J. CECIL: *Jim Bridger* (rev. ed., 1962). A reissue, with illustrative material and maps, of the first biography.

CAESAR, GENE: *King of the Mountain Men: The Life of Jim Bridger* (1961). The most recent biography.

ISMERT, CORNELIUS M.: "Jim Bridger," in LeRoy R. Hofen (ed.): *The Mountain Men and the Fur Trade of the Far West* (8 vols., 1965–1971). Vol. VI, pp. 85–104. A good short biography.

*VESTAL, STANLEY: *Jim Bridger, Mountain Man* (1946). A rather romanticized account.

The Period

BILLINGTON, RAY A.: *Westward Expansion* (rev. ed., 1967). The best general treatment of America's frontiers.

CHITTENDEN, HIRAM M.: *The American Fur Trade of the Far West* (2 vols., 1935). An old but thorough account.

*DE VOTO, BERNARD: *Across the Wide Missouri* (1947). The early history of the Far West. De Voto's *The Year of Decision, 1846* (1943) examines a pivotal point in the nation's history.

*GATES, PAUL W.: *The Farmer's Age* (1960). Agricultural history before the Civil War.

*MERK, FREDERICK: *Manifest Destiny and Mission in American History* (1963). Examines two concepts of great import for the West.

SLOTKIN, RICHARD: *Regeneration Through Violence: The Mythology of the American Frontier, 1600–1860* (1973). An imaginative interpretation of the forces affecting Bridger's time and place.

* Available in paperback.

*SMITH, HENRY NASH: *Virgin Land: The American West as Symbol and Myth* (1950). Explores the idea, as distinct from the reality, of the West as held by Americans in the eighteenth and nineteenth centuries.

*TAYLOR, GEORGE R.: *The Transportation Revolution, 1815–1860* (1951). An examination of the most important factor in the opening of the West.

* Available in paperback.

Engraved by J.C. Buttre.

Frederick Douglass

The tall teen-aged slave had one foot on the stable loft ladder when he felt a hand close about his ankle. A quick pull brought him crashing to the floor. From a prone position Frederick Douglass looked up at the grinning face of Edward Covey, professional slavebreaker. The white man began to slip a noose over Douglass's legs in preparation for yet another session of the torture that had made the first six months of 1834 a nightmare of pain. Only two days before Douglass had lain half-dead in the woods near Covey's.

It was the low point of his life. "I would have exchanged my manhood," he later recalled, "for the brutehood of an ox." Now, lying on the stable floor, Douglass was seized by a blinding anger. Springing away from the noose, he grappled with the surprised Covey. For the better part of an hour the men struggled desperately. Finally Covey staggered away. Douglass, by his own admission, was a changed man. The act of resistance "recalled to life my crushed self-respect and my self-confidence, and inspired me with a renewed determination to be a free man." *Four years later he escaped to freedom. Four decades later he stood as the foremost spokesman of black America.*

"Genealogical trees," Frederick Douglass wryly observed, "did not flourish among slaves." Few knew their ancestry or even their age. Douglass was no exception. He believed he was born in 1817. His mother was black and a slave. He saw her only a few times. He supposed his father was white, and he was told that Indian blood ran in his veins.

For his first seven years Frederick Douglass lived a relatively comfortable life with his grandmother on a plantation in Maryland's Talbot County, east of Chesapeake Bay. Fishing and watching squirrels and playing on the dirt floor of his grandmother's cabin, he did not understand what it meant to be a slave. Gradually, however, his child's mind learned there was someone called "Old Master." This vague figure, he found out, owned not only the land and the cabin, but his grandmother, his playmates, and his own self. It seemed inconceivable. The older slaves tried hard to shield Douglass from the full implications of his condition. Still, it was impossible to miss the involuntary shudder that invariably accompanied any discussion of Old Master. "Thus early," Douglass remembered, "did clouds and shadows begin to fall upon my path."

At about the age of seven Douglass began a more intensive course of instruction in the meaning of slavery. On what he clearly remembered as a beautiful summer morning, he was taken from his grandmother's cabin to Old Master's plantation. The master in this case was Captain Aaron Anthony, who owned several farms and some thirty slaves. But Anthony, in turn, reported to an even bigger master, Colonel Edward Lloyd. A power in eastern Maryland, Lloyd held twenty-five farms and over a thousand slaves. And as it happened, Lloyd made his personal residence on Anthony's plantation, and Douglass received a memorable impression of the Old South at its zenith.

The grandeur of the place astonished the boy. Like most large Southern plantations of the 1820s, Lloyd's gardens and pastures, mills and craft shops constituted a nearly self-sufficient economic unit. Old Master lived in "the great house," which was built of white-painted wood. Three spacious wings branched out from a broad front porch with its row of white columns. Leading from the porch to the gate a quarter-mile distant was a graveled driveway and a lush lawn planted with trees and flowers. In imitation of English nobles, Lloyd released rabbits, deer, and other game to roam the estate. To the rear of the great house another lawn ran down to the Wye River, Lloyd's chief artery of communication and trade. From his landing the tobacco that sustained the plantation was shipped to market. A pleasure sloop, the *Sally Lloyd,* swung at its mooring, a rowboat trailing behind.

Taking all this in, Douglass could not suppress a thrill at the "elaborate exhibition of wealth, power, and beauty." For him and his fellows, however, home meant one of the miserable slave huts scattered, half-hidden, about the plantation. And Douglass quickly learned that beneath the genteel surface lay a tangled skein of brutality, passion, and blood. Shortly after his arrival at Lloyd's, a young black woman who worked on another farm had been savagely beaten by an overseer. The girl knew she belonged to Lloyd, and with blood streaming down her face and back, dragged herself 12 miles to seek his protection. Douglass was there when she arrived. Lloyd refused to acknowledge her presence, and turned the problem over to the chief overseer, Anthony. Up to this time Douglass had entertained a favorable image of Anthony, who sometimes led him by the hand and patted his head in a paternal fashion. Now he saw the other side of the man. Cursing the bleeding girl, Anthony declared that " 'she deserved every bit of [the beating], and if she did not go home instantly he would himself take the remaining skin from her neck and back.' ".

Douglass realized that the girl had no alternative but to return the 12 miles to still more floggings. Absolute repression, he saw, was the keystone of the slave system.

In the next few years Douglass's perspective on slavery expanded considerably. He saw mothers tied to trees and whipped to unconsciousness in front of their crying children. He learned that when his beloved grandmother became too old to work, she was left in a hut in the middle of a forest to die of starvation. He watched an enraged overseer shoot and kill a slave who dared to run from a threatened flogging. Maryland justice did not regard this deed as a crime. Douglass never knew a slave murderer to receive the slightest punishment. Rape of black women (sometimes for the purpose of breeding) was common and also outside the law. But Douglass noted that the offspring of such unions caused Old Master some embarrassment. Although the children were black, they were usually exempt from the punishment dealt other slaves. Problems invariably followed. Lloyd was finally obliged to slip one of his troublesome black sons enough money to buy his freedom.

Douglass noticed that Lloyd's house servants always received preferential treatment on the plantation. In contrast to the field hands, these favored slaves rendered personal service in the great house. Many deliberately copied Old Master in dress, speech, and mannerisms and hardly deigned to associate with their brothers in the fields. But the house servants' social superiority was entirely self-assumed. The master race was blind to anything but color.

The potential for atrocities, Douglass believed, made the slaveholder as well as the slave a victim of the system. There was no chance on either side for character development. "Reason," he wrote, "is imprisoned here, and passions run wild." The slave experience, he concluded, made livestock of human beings. Indeed, the slaves had a worse fate. Old Master's "horses and dogs," Douglass maintained, "fared better than his men."

The slave system in which Frederick Douglass found himself mired in the 1820s had its American origins in 1619, when the captain of a Dutch ship sold twenty bewildered Africans to the tobacco planters of Jamestown, Virginia. The slave trade was already well established. Portuguese and Spanish traders carried human cargoes from West Africa's Gold Coast to Europe as early as the fifteenth century.

Native black kings along the African coast made the trade possible by selling their own slaves or procuring them from the interior. Without exonerating whites for their role in slavery, we cannot ignore evidence that the profit motive which fed the trade existed irrespective of color.

The settlement of the New World opened new opportunities for slavery. Initial hopes centered on easy wealth from a paradisiacal land. Slaves had no role in this economy. But the dreams faded quickly under the impact of the New World reality: men would have to *work* for a living. However, the gentlemen-adventurers who composed the first waves of settlers in the Caribbean and in England's southern colonies were not inclined to perform the hard field labor that the production of sugar, tobacco, and later cotton demanded. Moreover, it was difficult to convince immigrants from their own countries to be employees. In America everyone wanted to be an employer. Slaves filled the resulting labor vacuum.

About 10 million blacks came to the Americas in the three centuries of slave trade. The typical commercial pattern began with the shipment of liquor and manufactured goods from England or her American colonies to Africa. The next leg, the middle passage, took slaves to the markets in the Americas. Hundreds of thousands of blacks died in the foul holds of crowded ships on the journey, but the profits in the business sustained it even if only half the cargo survived. Completing the economic triangle, sugar, tobacco, and cotton were then shipped in the slavers to commercial centers of Europe and the northern colonies. Frederick Douglass's ancestors reached America as a result of these exchanges.

The social status of the first black Americans was not immediately clear. There is some evidence that the African immigrants were regarded by their seventeenth-century contemporaries as indentured servants rather than slaves. In other words, the blacks, like white servants, owed a certain amount of labor to the person who paid their way to America, but they were not his property. They possessed the rights and immunities of human beings. In time, they could expect to earn their freedom. Their children, in any case, were free.

On the other hand, there is also evidence that all seventeenth-century servants were not equal. The black ones had fewer rights from the beginning. In a very short time, their inferior status jelled into hereditary lifetime service. They became property. The reason for this

Twenty Dollars Reward.

RAN away from the subscribers, living at New Rochelle, on Sunday evening, the 9th instant; two indented GERMAN SERVANTS: John Jacob Wittmer, belonging to Mr. Lispenard, about five feet five inches high, well set, has a remarkable large head, short neck and broad face; halts as he walks, his right leg being much shorter than the left; had on, or took with him when he went off, a blue broad cloth coat, with brass buttons, short white waistcoat, with red embroidered flowers; corduroy breeches; light coloured worsted stockings; new shoes, and new round hat, with a band and buckle. Mr. Williams's servant is a tall slim fellow, five feet eleven inches high; somewhat freckled; long hair, tyed behind; had on a mixed blue and white coat; black breeches; and took with him a pair of clouded overalls, red, blue and white, which he may probably wear. Whoever apprehends the above servants, and will bring them to their masters, at this place, shall receive the above reward, or ten dollars for either of them, with an allowance for all reasonable charges.

LEONARD LISPENARD, jun.
DANIEL WILLIAMS.

New Rochelle, October 13, 1785.   33-6

Essentially, slavery was a form of livestock business, with institutions comparable to those associated with the management of cattle or horses. There were auctions (opposite, top), in which the merchandise was freely examined and sold to the top bidder. An advertisement for such an event (opposite, bottom) underscores the close association in the white South's mind of horses and slaves. Both kinds of livestock occasionally ran away, but the human fugitives proved much harder to catch. Despite newspaper notices and rewards (above), many escaped slaves were never recovered. One reason was the existence of the "underground railroad" (below). This was actually a loose organization of Northerners who assisted fugitives in their flight to freedom.

LIBERTY LINE.
NEW ARRANGEMENT---NIGHT AND DAY.

The improved and splendid Locomotives, Clarkson and Lundy, with their trains fitted up in the best style of accommodation for passengers, will run their regular trips during the present season, between the borders of the Patriarchal Dominion and Libertyville, Upper Canada. Gentlemen and Ladies, who may wish to improve their health or circumstances, by a northern tour, are respectfully invited to give us their patronage.

SEATS FREE, *irrespective of color.*

Necessary Clothing furnished gratuitously to such as have "*fallen among thieves.*"

"Hide the outcasts—let the oppressed go free."—*Bible.*

☞For seats apply at any of the trap doors, or to the conductor of the train.

J. CROSS, *Proprietor.*

N. B. For the special benefit of Pro-Slavery Police Officers, an extra heavy wagon for Texas, will be furnished, whenever it may be necessary, in which they will be forwarded as dead freight, to the "Valley of Rascals," always at the risk of the owners.

☞Extra Overcoats provided for such of them as are afflicted with protracted *chilly-phobia.*

rapid hardening seems to be a deeply rooted bias in the Anglo-American mind against black men. Part of it stemmed from their color itself. In the eyes of whites, a black man was at once shocking, inexplicable, and frightening—associated because of his color with the powers of darkness. Given this bias, slavery seemed a way for white society to live with the disturbing strangers in its midst. Also significant in stamping slavery on the African was his social visibility. A white servant at least looked like everyone else. Taken from his place of servitude, he blended into society. He could thus reap the benefits of the fluid social and economic structure of a growing country. But the black was a marked man. His color constantly testified to his menial origins. It was easy to pin on him the label "slave." In any event, by 1700 it was clearly understood throughout the American colonies that slavery concerned blacks only. The slave, as Frederick Douglass learned at a very tender age, had lost his manhood.

But the young Douglass also learned that there were varieties of slavery, some more pleasant than others. While still a boy he was sent from the Lloyd plantation to Baltimore and the home of Hugh Auld. Specifically, Douglass was a gift to the Aulds' young son, Tommy. In this capacity he lived a better life than he had thought possible. He had clean clothes, regular food, a bed, and a mistress who at first treated him more as a stepson than a slave. Mrs. Auld even began to teach Douglass to read. She made the mistake, however, of informing her husband of the boy's rapid progress. Auld became enraged and forbade the lessons. "Learning," he declared in Douglass's presence, "will spoil the best nigger in the world." If the boy learned to read the Bible, Auld continued, "it will forever unfit him to be a slave." Education, Auld concluded, could only make slaves "disconsolate and unhappy."

Frederick Douglass, however, chose this path. He sensed that the reason slaveholders opposed educating blacks was a fear it would promote a desire for freedom. Douglass agreed and redoubled his efforts to read and write. His teachers were the street society of Baltimore and a battered copy of Noah Webster's famous spelling book that he somehow acquired and carefully hid. Instruction in writing came from copying the letters on the sides of shipping crates on Baltimore's docks. When he was thirteen, Douglass earned his first money blackening boots and used it, in the manner of Benjamin Franklin, to buy a book: *The Columbian Orator.* The volume contained stirring speeches advocating natural rights, and some of the orations even concerned the abolition of slavery. Exposure to them heightened Douglass's desire for freedom. No matter how kind his treatment, he knew he was someone's property, and the thought incensed him. Precisely as Auld predicted, education and slavery were poor partners.

About the time he learned to read and write Douglass left the Auld household to work in the shipyards of Baltimore. He thereby joined the ranks of a select group—the city slaves. These blacks constituted a substantial percentage of the slave labor force. They worked in the cities and towns of the South, but under conditions different from those of the plantation slaves. Normally the city slave had his own quarters and the liberty to come and go in the town as he pleased. His labor was frequently "hired out" to businessmen in the community, the wages accruing to the master. But occasionally a slave would be permitted to work part of the time for himself and in this way accumulate the funds to buy his freedom. Such self-freed blacks were not common in the South, but their presence constitutes evidence against the interpretation of American slavery as a completely closed, spirit-breaking system.

For a time in Baltimore Douglass entertained hopes of being permitted to earn the money to buy himself from his master. His growing skill as a caulker of ships lent substance to this dream. But in 1833 Douglass's luck took a turn for the worse. His master died, and the resulting adjustments sent him back to a farm. Having tasted the liberal variety of slavery in Baltimore, resubmission to the harsher rural pattern was doubly hard. Douglass tried to maintain his dignity. He organized a Sunday school class for black children on the plantation, but saw it disbanded by an angry mob of pious leaders of the local church. Moreover, Douglass's new master warned him in no uncertain terms that such behavior would bring him to the same fate as Nat Turner.

Nat Turner was not just a name in the South in 1833, but the foremost symbol of the greatest horror a southern white could imagine: slave revolt. Try as he might, the southerner could not deny the possibility of black insurrection. Slaves, after all, were not like other livestock. They could think, plan, organize, kill, rape, and plunder. And the slave system was not the benign, paternalistic welfare institution its apologists maintained. Behind the façade of moonlight, magnolias, and happy darkies singing for a beloved Old Master was force and fear. To understand the white viewpoint, it is necessary only to note that in many parts of the South blacks outnumbered whites. Indeed, in the tidewater region where Douglass lived and in the Mississippi Valley, the ratio rose to as much as 9 to 1. If the blacks in these areas had rebelled, they could have easily crushed the white establishment. Whites knew this far better than blacks, and they exerted every effort to keep the South a white man's country. American slavery was as much a means of social control as it was a method of economic exploitation. Any sign of slave resistance, especially organized group resistance, met with hysterical repression.

The pattern became clear as early as 1739, when one Cato led a group of South Carolina slaves on a rampage of killing and destruction. Reacting immediately, the white community crushed the revolt and slaughtered every black even remotely associated with the disturbance. In the 1790s a full-scale racial war swept over the island of Hispaniola in the Caribbean. The leader of the blacks, Toussaint L'Ouverture, eventually established political control. Frightened American slaveowners took pains to keep news of the conflict out of southern newspapers and even out of southern conversation for fear of inspiring local blacks. But the American tradition of slave rebellion was extended by Gabriel's Revolt in 1801, the Denmark Vesey Conspiracy in 1822, and particularly by the Nat Turner Insurrection of 1831. It was the last that touched the life of Frederick Douglass.

Turner was a slave in Virginia. He knew how to read, studied the Bible, and found in it a justification for slaves turning against tyrannical masters. Turner was also a preacher with a considerable following in the black community of his region. In August 1831 he struck. A force of slaves descended on a series of plantations, knives in hand. In a short while fifty-seven whites, mostly women and children, lay dead. Turner hoped his example would provoke a general slave revolt, but the whites retaliated with a crushing show of force. For a time, any black in the vicinity of the insurrection was shot on sight. Throughout the South terrified slaveowners searched for the slightest indication of insubordination and met it with whips, guns, and rigid codes defining acceptable behavior. Nat Turner brought the fear latent in the slave system into the open.

Frederick Douglass

The Turner revolt coincided with and contributed to a gradual hardening of southern attitudes toward slavery. To be sure, the "positive good" argument was well established in 1820 at the time of the Missouri Compromise. But up to the 1830s many Southern whites were at least willing to weigh the advantages and liabilities of the system and to contemplate its eventual elimination. Indeed, before 1830 the American abolitionist movement centered in the South. Of 130 early antislavery societies in the country, 100 were Southern. But after Nat Turner, Southern criticism of slavery gradually stilled. Like Thomas Jefferson, many Southern whites reached the conclusion that slavery might not be desirable, but it was necessary. Others went still further, defending slavery as a positive good.

Economics, particularly the cotton boom, figured in this shift of attitude. So did the multifaceted proslavery argument that drew on sources as diverse as Scripture and physiology. Slaves, it was argued, had the minds of children and needed the protective guidance of masters. The upshot was the collapse of the colonization movement and with it the hope of sending freed slaves back to Africa. This, in turn, killed Southern abolitionism, the whole point of which had been to get blacks out of the South. Also influential in the closing of the Southern mind regarding slavery was the marked increase of Northern criticism of the institution. Self-criticism, they discovered, was one thing; outside denunciation of their life style something quite different and quite intolerable. Furiously, Southerners pointed out that William Lloyd Garrison began publication of his rabidly antislavery newspaper *The Liberator* a few months before the Nat Turner Insurrection. The effect of such external criticism was to silence the internal kind. By the time Frederick Douglass was a teenager, slavery was untouchable, a topic on which objective discussion was impossible in the South. The need for keeping a feared race permanently subordinated transcended all other considerations.

With the specter of Nat Turner seared into the Southern mind, the emergence of Frederick Douglass as a literate, outspoken black with a taste for religion and a talent for leadership aroused instant suspicion. The consequence was a term at Edward Covey's slave-breaking establishment. But in this instance it was Covey who broke, and Douglass left his farm determined to be free. His first attempt to run away, however, proved a dismal and almost disastrous failure. In

1836 Douglass and five fellow slaves laid plans to escape to the North by boat up the Chesapeake Bay. But one of the blacks disclosed the plans to his master. Douglass landed in jail with every expectation of being sold "down the river" to the cotton plantations of the Deep South. But, almost miraculously, he received a reprieve from the Aulds, who recognized that slavery would be considerably safer *without* men of Douglass's spirit and intelligence. Auld arranged for Douglass to return to Baltimore and accumulate money as a hired-out laborer. He would be set free, Auld promised, at the age of twenty-five.

In Baltimore again Douglass's life became entangled in the relationships of Southern whites. The central fact here was that although slaveholders comprised a very small percentage (about 10 percent) of all white southerners, these same slaveholders were an elite which dominated the power structure of the section. They maintained their favored position only by resisting the challenge of the nonslaveholders. Sometimes the clash was direct, as in Virginia where in early 1832 the legislature debated a resolution abolishing slavery in that state. The tidewater planters lined up solidly against the proposal, but the nonslaveholding upcountry farmers were just as solidly for it. The latter believed, with good reason, that their opportunities would be increased by the elimination of the slave oligarchy.

The Virginia vote was surprisingly close, 73 to 58, and slaveowners throughout the South took steps to protect their status. One involved convincing the nonslaveholders that the perpetuation of slavery served their interests too. The technique was to argue, according to Douglass, that "slavery was the only power that could prevent the laboring white man from falling to the level of the slave's poverty and degradation." In other words, without slavery there would be several million blacks competing with whites for jobs and for status in the South. With slavery, even the lowliest Southern white had a social cushion securely beneath him. The planters also made it clear that if a black insurrection came, it would engulf all whites, not just slaveholders. The Southern way of life was at stake, alleged the slaveholders, and they represented themselves as its champions and defenders. These arguments proved effective. By 1836 in Baltimore the hatred of nonslaveholding whites for blacks, both slave and free, had been honed to a fine edge. When Douglass began work in the city's shipyards, he was met by a team of white workers who beat him unmercifully as fifty of their fellows cheered.

The experience in the shipyards discouraged Douglass about the chances of earning freedom in the South, and once again his thoughts turned to escape. In addition, he had met a free black woman, Anna Murray, whom he wished to marry as a free man. On September 3, 1838, Douglass made his move. From a free black sailor of his acquaintance he borrowed a suit of clothes and a set of "protection" or "free" papers. Thus equipped, he boarded a train for Philadelphia and New York. In the course of the trip he encountered several white men who knew him, but he remained unrecognized. His closest call came just south of the Mason-Dixon line separating Maryland from Pennsylvania and slavery from freedom. In making a routine check, a conductor asked Douglass for his free papers. Comparison of the description of the rightful owner with Douglass's appearance would have revealed the subterfuge immediately, but the conductor only glanced, nodded, and moved on up the car. Frederick Douglass was a free man.

The North to which Frederick Douglass immigrated in 1838 was already fully aware of, and uneasy about, the South he left. The tension generated by the Missouri crisis eighteen years before still lingered. Indeed, the intervening years sharpened sectional consciousness. The election of 1824 found no less than five candidates, each with strong sectional ties, in the running. John C. Calhoun and William H. Crawford represented the South in their distrust of strong central government, high protective tariffs, and manufacturing. Henry Clay and Andrew Jackson drew the largest part of their support from the West and the more commercial Middle Atlantic states. The Northeast backed John Quincy Adams, who ultimately won the election after a widely criticized bargain that made Clay secretary of state.

During Adams's administration, the tariff continued to be a focus of sectional dispute. An analysis of congressional votes shows the South solidly against high tariffs, the Middle Atlantic states just as solidly for them, and New England mixed but shifting toward a protariff stand as its stake in manufacturing increased. The climax came in 1828, when Congress enacted the highest tariff yet in American history. Southerners immediately branded it the Tariff of Abominations. Led by Vice-President Calhoun of South Carolina, they argued that the levy on foreign goods was, in effect, a tax on southern planters for the benefit of northern manufacturers. A high tariff had the effect of raising the price of foreign goods southerners consumed. Many also believed that by reducing the income of European textile manufacturers, the tariff prevented their buying more southern cotton. Moreover, the South saw Congress's power over the tariff as a bad omen for the future of other southern interests, particularly slavery. The extent of the South's displeasure became clear in Calhoun's 1828 essay, "The South Carolina Exposition and Protest." In it he argued that a state which judged the federal government to have exceeded the powers granted under the Constitution of 1787 might nullify a federal act. This was the ultimate in states rights, a political posture that became increasingly important to the South as its consciousness of its minority status in the nation increased.

The first chance to test the doctrine of nullification came in 1832, when Congress passed a new tariff bill unacceptable to the South. Led by Calhoun and Senator Robert Y. Hayne, famous for his debates with Daniel Webster over the nature of the federal union, the South Carolina legislature nullified the law, and Calhoun resigned as Vice-President. In a rage, President Andrew Jackson threatened to hang Calhoun, dispatched a fleet of warships to Charleston, and declared it his intention to lead an overland force against the rebels. For a few anxious months at the beginning of 1833, the fate of the union hung in the balance. But South Carolina's position was weakened by the fact that no other southern state came to its support, and on March 15 the legislature accepted a compromise engineered by Henry Clay. Fortunately, the tariff was an issue susceptible to compromise; one could easily find the middle ground between a duty of 50 percent and one of 30 percent. But there were other issues coming to the fore for which such compromises were impossible. As Frederick Douglass knew so well, a man was either slave or free.

The exhilaration Frederick Douglass initially experienced on reaching New York quickly gave way to frustration and despair. In terms of the position of the black, he found the city in many ways an extension of the South. Slavecatchers, eager to return runaways to their masters, were everywhere. No one could be trusted. For a few dollars some blacks would even betray their brothers. Moreover, the country was in the throes of financial depression following the Panic of 1837, and jobs were scarce. For blacks it was worse. Just as in Baltimore, white laborers made sure that black ones were the last to be hired and the first to be fired. Douglass walked the streets for a few days until his money ran out. Then, in desperation, he turned to David Ruggles, a local black leader. Ruggles sheltered Douglass and arranged for his marriage to Anna Murray, who had arrived from Maryland. He also advised the newlyweds to leave New York for a safer location farther north.

Following Ruggles's suggestion, the Douglasses pushed on to New Bedford, Massachusetts. In this maritime center, the capital of the American whaling industry, Douglass hoped to find a chance to exercise his trade as a skilled caulker of ships. But on applying for a job, he learned that all the white workers in the yards would quit if a black one were hired. Douglass had to eke out a living sawing wood, shoveling coal, and sweeping chimneys. Anna served as a domestic when she was not caring for her two babies. Besides the economic struggle, there were other disturbing facts of northern life. Most of the churches refused to accept blacks as members of the congregation. Public transportation was also segregated. Douglass learned that even if he purchased a first-class train ticket he was obliged to sit in the uncomfortable segregated car, reserved for blacks only. He concluded that northern society, lacking slavery, had been adept at finding alternate means to express its prejudice.

Still, there were reasons to take heart. A passion for reforming man and his institutions flourished in the North at the time Douglass arrived. "In the history of the world," Ralph Waldo Emerson wrote in 1841, "the doctrine of Reform had never such scope as at the present hour." What Emerson had in mind was a series of interrelated ideas centered on the possibility of human betterment. The reformer of the 1830s and 1840s believed that every man was basically good. Strip away handicaps such as ignorance or lack of opportunity, and the innate goodness would shine through. No one was hopeless, no one beyond help. Each individual contained what Emerson and his fellow Transcendentalists termed a "spark of divinity." It followed that the poor, the drunk, the insane, and the black were all susceptible to improvement—perhaps, the most enthusiastic reformers believed, even to perfection. Reform philosophy exuded a confidence stemming at once from the Enlightenment, Romanticism, and the American sense of mission. As a celebration of individual potential, it was entirely consistent with American circumstances and ideals.

The abolition of slavery had a place of special importance in the galaxy of American reform crusades. In the abolitionist mind both the slaveholder and the slave were ripe for improvement. Slavery, they believed, was a sin. Moreover, it was a blot on the American record of championing individual rights and freedoms, an embarrassing anomaly in a nation dedicated to liberty. By denying a person control over his own destiny, slavery went against the grain of the entire New World experience.

Abolitionism as an organized reform movement began among the Quakers in the eighteenth century. At the time of the American Revolution they did not hesitate to point out the contradictions between slavery and the ideals motivating American independence. There was some response: most Northern states declared slavery illegal before 1800. Some went further, and agitated for national emancipation. Pennsylvania's antislavery society had Benjamin Franklin as its president in 1787. In the South, however, abolitionism was considerably less successful. Even blacks did not support it because of the plan for colonizing freed slaves in Africa that was invariably part of southern abolition. Douglass, for instance, declared: "we are *American* citizens, born with natural, inherent and just rights; and . . . the . . . intolerable scheme of the American Colonization Society shall never entice or drive *us* away from our native soil." The more radical white reformers, believing that colonization was a poor substitute for full freedom for all men in the United States, shared this opinion.

The debate over colonization came to a head in Baltimore at the very time Frederick Douglass was enslaved there. He did not know it, but Benjamin Lundy, a New Jersey Quaker, edited an antislavery newspaper entitled *The Genius of Universal Emancipation* in that city. Lundy believed in gradual, compensated emancipation of slaves and their subsequent colonization in Africa. His co-editor, however, disagreed violently. Indeed, violent disagreement was characteristic of William Lloyd Garrison. In sharp contrast to Lundy, he defended immediate, total, and uncompensated emancipation; rejected colonization; and denounced the United States Constitution, which he regarded as proslavery, as "a covenant with death and an agreement with hell." Aggressive to the point of belligerence, convinced he was morally right, and driven by an obsession with becoming famous, Garrison broke with Lundy and went North to enter the abolition business on his own.

In 1831 Garrison launched a weekly antislavery newspaper, *The Liberator*, in Boston. Totally committed, he gave no quarter and asked none. "I *will*," he thundered in the first issue, "be as harsh as truth, and as uncompromising as justice. On this subject, I do not wish to think, or speak, or write with moderation. . . . I am in earnest—I will not equivocate—I will not excuse—I will not retreat a single inch— AND I WILL BE HEARD." Shortly after starting the newspaper, Garrison organized the New England Antislavery Society. Its agents fanned out and organized enthusiastically. They drew encouragement from the news that in 1833 the British abolition movement had borne fruit with the emancipation of slaves in the British West Indies. By the time Douglass came to New England in 1838, about two thousand local societies with a membership of nearly 200,000 existed in the North.

Garrison and Wendell Phillips dominated the movement in New England, Gerritt Smith and the wealthy Tappan family in New York, and Theodore Dwight Weld in the Ohio Valley. Yet abolitionism was not universally popular in the North. Quite probably a majority of northerners saw Garrison and his colleagues as irresponsible fanatics —revolutionaries who would tear the fabric of American political, social, and economic life in their intemperate zeal to end slavery. In 1835 Garrison was mobbed and beaten by his critics. He escaped lightly, however, compared with Elijah Lovejoy, who was killed in an encounter in Illinois two years later.

Frederick Douglass's first contact with abolitionism occurred early in 1839, a few months after his escape, when a copy of *The Liberator* fell into his hands. He had not known about Garrison before, but the position of the newspaper moved him so deeply that despite his poverty he became a regular subscriber. "The paper became my meat and drink," Douglass later wrote. "Its sympathy for my brethren in bonds—its scathing denunciations of slaveholders . . . sent a thrill of joy through my soul." Douglass also joined the local abolition society in New Bedford and, in his words, "took right hold of the cause." By March 1839 he was addressing meetings of New Bedford blacks on the disadvantages of colonization. He also used these occasions to commend Garrison as a man "deserving of our support and confidence."

The first meeting between Douglass and Garrison occurred on August 9, 1841, when the abolitionist leader came to speak in New Bedford. "No face or form," Douglass acknowledged, "ever impressed me with such sentiments." Two days later both men were again together at an antislavery convention on the island of Nantucket. Friends persuaded Douglass to address the gathering, and at last he came forward, hesitant, embarrassed, and so nervous he could hardly stand. As Garrison remembered, Douglass's first words were apologetic. "Slavery," he said, "was a poor school for the human intellect." Then, drawing himself up to his full height of over 6 feet, he began to narrate his experiences as a slave. The audience was transfixed by the simple presentation. At its conclusion, Garrison himself arose to declare that "Patrick Henry . . . never made a speech more eloquent in the cause of liberty, than the one we . . . just listened to from the lips of a hunted fugitive." Capitalizing on the drama of the situation, Garrison next asked the assembly: "Have we been listening to a thing, a piece of property, or to a man?" A thousand voices responded, "A man! A man!" Would the audience allow Douglass to be taken back into slavery? "No!" came the roaring response.

In the evening session of the convention Douglass spoke again. By this time Garrison and the other officers of the Massachusetts Antislavery Society were convinced that the young black with the deep voice might be one of the most potent weapons in their arsenal of persuasion. They offered Douglass a job as a lecturer on the antislavery circuit at a salary of $450 a year. But the astonished Douglass accepted only a three-month appointment, convinced that he would be of limited value. As it turned out, he greatly underrated himself. The opportunity opened at Nantucket launched Frederick Douglass on a lifelong career as a liberator of his people.

The life of an antislavery lecturer, particularly a black one, was hardly dull. Many of the audiences Douglass faced were openly hostile and came armed with eggs and rotten vegetables. In 1843 Douglass and his colleagues were occasionally run off the stage and even beaten. It was during this sustained tour that people began to doubt Douglass's assertion that he was really an escaped slave. Sensing this reaction, his fellow abolitionists tried to persuade him to use more of the speech and mannerisms of the plantation. Douglass, they bluntly declared, was supposed to be an exhibit to accompany the presentations of the white speakers. But Douglass refused to hide his talents. In answer, he wrote his autobiographical *Narrative of the Life of Frederick Douglass: An American Slave.* Wendell Phillips advised him to burn the manuscript, since it could well lead to his capture and return to slavery. Douglass, however, published his book in 1845 and watched with pleasure as sales quickly mounted to 30,000 copies. He did heed Phillips's advice to the extent of seeking temporary sanctuary in England, where for two years he enjoyed a huge success as a lecturer on a variety of reform subjects. Douglass returned to his family and country in 1847 with enough money to purchase his freedom. This was duly accomplished with the transmission of $710.96 to the Auld family in Baltimore. For the first time in almost a decade, Douglass emerged from the shadow of reenslavement.

Ambitious and determined after his sojourn abroad, Douglass decided to set his own course within the abolition movement. Late in 1847 he moved to Rochester, New York, and began publication of his own newspaper, *The North Star.* Many white abolitionists objected, but Douglass defended his venture as providing evidence of the black man's capability. Only by such independent participation in American life could blacks foster a sense of pride and self-reliance. His goal, he made clear, was not just freeing slaves, but permitting a life of dignity for all black people throughout the nation. The newspaper, and plans for the education of free blacks whom Douglass sponsored, contributed to this end. *The North Star* also aided Douglass in formulating and expressing his own reform philosophy.

For a decade, he was a Garrisonian. By the late 1840s, however, he had developed doubts about Garrison's rejection of political action as an abolitionist weapon. Garrison burned the Constitution, but in Douglass's opinion that document could be construed as a guarantee of freedom to all Americans regardless of color. The problem was to allow everyone to share the liberties it defined. For this reason Douglass felt political action was needed along with moral persuasion. Garrison stood on the principle of "no union with slaveholders." Douglass felt that southern institutions could be changed through the political process by pressure from the majority of Americans. It was essential, therefore, to extend the vote to all adults.

When Douglass called for extension of the vote, he had women in mind as well as blacks. In his eyes these two social groups occupied a similar relationship to the white, male establishment. They also constituted the majority of the population. Douglass believed that there was strength in unity, and he pressed for civil rights on both fronts. In fact, *The North Star* carried on its masthead the slogan "Right is of no sex—Truth is of no color." In 1848 Douglass proved the sincerity of his belief: he was the only man to take an active part in the Seneca Falls Convention that launched the women's rights movement in the United States.

While Frederick Douglass labored in Rochester on the broad front of reform, the course of national politics once again brought sectional competition into prominence. The catalyst of the renewed tension was westward expansion. Both North and South knew that western resources, commerce, and votes were vital to achieving national dominance. At first, the South had enjoyed a major geographical advantage. The Appalachian Mountains, slanting northeast-southwest across the eastern United States, posed a major barrier to communication and trade between the North and the West. Southerners, on the other hand, were connected to the West by the Mississippi River. Places as widely separated as western Pennsylvania and northern Wisconsin could ship their products down the Mississippi to the port of New Orleans. But in the early nineteenth century the Mississippi was a one-way street. Rivermen took their wooden flatboats down with the current, sold them for lumber, and walked back north along trails such as the Natchez Trace. In 1811, however, the first steamboat on the Mississippi enabled goods to move upstream. Commerce between West and South was possible, and political alliance seemed sure to follow.

The South's early success in the competition for the western trade and vote stirred the North to action. In 1825 New York completed the Erie Canal between Albany on the Hudson River and Buffalo on Lake Erie. This easy route west facilitated communication with the whole Great Lakes watershed. Moreover, the Erie Canal led to an excellent market and manufacturing center—New York City. New Orleans lacked these characteristics. In addition, the South and the West, both producers of raw materials, were not economically compatible. This became increasingly apparent after the opening of the Erie Canal. In

1838, the year Douglass came north, receipts at Buffalo exceeded those at New Orleans for the first time. It was a poor omen for the South. By this time, too, Pennsylvania's Main Line of canals and roads from Philadelphia to Pittsburgh was open for business. But the outcome of the North-South struggle for the West awaited the trans-Appalachian railroads in the 1850s. The systems developed by the New York Central, Pennsylvania, and Baltimore and Ohio Railroads made it impractical to use the Mississippi except for passenger traffic and local trade. A revolution in technology and transportation left the South economically and politically isolated.

Nervous about this situation, Southerners reacted angrily in 1846 when David Wilmot of Pennsylvania rose in the House of Representatives to propose that slavery be prohibited in any part of the territory to be acquired from the Mexican War. President James Polk attempted to soothe the South by suggesting that the land in question was unsuited to slavery for reasons of climate and soil. Cotton, tobacco, and slavery, he argued, had reached the natural limits of their expansion. Southerners were not so sure. In the first place, slave-owners saw no reason why slaves could not be used for tasks other than picking cotton. Black bondsmen like Frederick Douglass had long worked effectively in cities, and their potential as miners, lumberjacks, and ranchers in the West was apparent. It was conceivable, John C. Calhoun argued, that slavery could become the normal institution for managing all labor in the United States. Furthermore, there was the question of property rights. Calhoun again led the way, a year after Wilmot's suggestion, in arguing that Congress had no authority to limit slavery and thus deprive a citizen of his right to move where he pleased and take his property, slaves included, along. In effect, Calhoun was saying that the Missouri Compromise of 1820 (which prohibited slaves north of 36°30′) was unconstitutional.

The issue of slavery expansion became pressing in 1849, when California applied for admission to the union as a free (nonslave) state. The South objected strenuously, and threatened secession. For a few anxious months at the beginning of 1850, the Union teetered on the brink of dissolution. But Henry Clay, Daniel Webster, and Stephen A. Douglas engineered a compromise in the Unted States Senate. As signed by President Millard Fillmore in September 1850, the series of acts admitted California as a free state, organized the remaining terri-

Frederick Douglass helped raise black soldiers like these for the Union cause in the Civil War. Although the victims of blatant discrimination on the part of their white colleagues, the black regiments distinguished themselves on numerous occasions. By 1865 blacks comprised almost a fifth of all Union troops.

During the Civil War era photography became a major source of historical documentation. This excellent print shows President Abraham Lincoln at the headquarters of the Army of the Potomac, October 4, 1862. Notice how the lanky Lincoln, even without his top hat, towers over his companions.

The enormous physical, social, and intellectual task called "reconstruction" is dramatized in this photograph of Charleston, South Carolina after its surrender on February 18, 1865. The end of the Civil War was less than two months away, but the problem of rebuilding American society was just beginning.

Here former slaves are registering to vote in Macon, Georgia under the supervision of the Union Army. The date is September 1867. Two years later Congress proposed the Fifteenth Amendment (ratified 1870) with the intent of guaranteeing black suffrage. But left to Southern whites, rather than the army, black voting rights quickly became a travesty.

tory acquired from Mexico without restrictions on slavery, abolished the slave trade (but not slavery) in the District of Columbia, and strengthened the procedure for returning fugitive slaves to their masters.

For Frederick Douglass, the most important part of the Compromise of 1850 was the Fugitive Slave Law. Deliberately favorable to the slaveowner, the measure was intended as a sweetener for an otherwise pro-North compromise. It was aimed at stopping the operation of the underground railroad. This shadowy volunteer organization assisted blacks fleeing slavery by passing them from hand to friendly hand until they were safe. In 1838 Frederick Douglass received help of this kind in New York City from David Ruggles. Not really a railroad, the enterprise supposedly received its name from the complaint of a frustrated slaveowner whose failure to trace his fugitives prompted him to remark that once in the free states, slaves vanished as if they had boarded a subterranean train. But the hunters often captured their quarry, and there were countless narrow escapes. A "conductor" on the underground railroad might awaken in the middle of the night to find a frightened fugitive in his yard and the owner's forces in hot pursuit. He then had to hide the slave in an attic or secret stairwell. The following night the slave might be buried under a wagonload of hay and carried to the next "station."

In southern minds such assistance to fugitive slaves was outright stealing—a violation of the natural law respecting the sanctity of property. The Fugitive Slave Law of 1850 reflected this viewpoint. Recapturing escaped slaves became a national rather than a state process. This policy bypassed the personal liberty laws with which many northern states blocked the operation of earlier fugitive slave legislation. The new measure created commissioners who could issue warrants for the arrest of fugitives, and who also served as judges in cases involving runaways. But there was no jury, and the testimony of blacks was not admitted as evidence. Finally, the Fugitive Slave Law provided that any white who aided a fugitive (even by looking the other way as he passed by) was subject to fine and imprisonment, and forced to reimburse the slaveowner for the full value of his lost property.

Attitudes toward the Fugitive Slave Law differed sharply. Southerners and Northern moderates regarded its successful operation as vital to the effectiveness of the Compromise of 1850 and consequently to the existence of peace and union. Extremists spoke openly of secession if the law was not obeyed. "Before God and man," a Raleigh, North Carolina, editorial warned, ". . . if you fail in this simple act of justice, THE BONDS WILL BE DISSOLVED." In antislavery circles, on the other hand, opposition to the law was equally intense. "This filthy enactment," declared the normally mild-mannered Ralph Waldo Emerson, "was made in the nineteenth century, by people who could read and write. I will not obey it, by God!" Frederick Douglass was quick to point out the effect of "this atrocious and shameless law" on free blacks. It subjected them to kidnapping. "The oaths of any two villains," Douglass observed, "were sufficient to consign a free man to slavery for life." Indeed, for several weeks following the passage of the Fugitive Slave Law, Douglass feared for his own safety. Friends posted guard around his house in Rochester. There was no trouble, but nearer to the South a virtual border war ensued.

This tense atmosphere formed the backdrop for the most spectacular of the fugitive slave cases occurring after the Compromise of 1850. On September 11, 1851, a Maryland planter named Edward Gorsuch came to the tiny hamlet of Christiana in southern Pennsylvania where, he heard, several of his fugitive slaves were harbored. The runaways were indeed there, but so were a group of blacks and some white sympathizers determined to prevent their recapture. The inevitable confrontation came at the house of William Parker, the black leader. As the slaves cowered upstairs, Parker met Gorsuch at the door. "My property is in this house. I've come for it," the slaveowner declared. Indignantly, Parker suggested that Gorsuch "go in the room . . . and see if there is anything there belonging to you. There are beds and a bureau, chairs and other things. Then go out to the barn; there you will find a cow and some hogs. See if any of them are yours." It was a case of right versus right; neither side would compromise principles each considered sacred.

At last a mob of blacks charged Gorsuch, knocking him down. When he struggled to his feet, he received a shot in the chest and slumped in the dust—dead. Never before had an owner been a victim in the fugitive slave business, and Parker and his colleagues were suddenly struck by the sure consequences of their action. Before nightfall on September 11 they were enroute to Canada via Frederick

Douglass's house in Rochester. Douglass received the men warmly. "I could not look upon them as murderers," he wrote, "to me, they were heroic defenders of the just rights of man against manstealers and murderers." Acting swiftly before news of the Christiana Riot reached Rochester, Douglass hurried the blacks on a steamboat bound for Toronto. Not until the gangplank lifted did he return home, carrying as a memento from Parker the pistol of Edward Gorsuch.

Although such resistance to the Fugitive Slave Law delighted Douglass, it caused despair among moderates in the North and South alike. They had hoped, desperately, that the Compromise of 1850 would be a final settlement of the sectional differences. But it seemed that the old belligerence had not died. Indeed sectional polarization continued with renewed vigor in the 1850s. Indicative was the reception accorded *Uncle Tom's Cabin,* which appeared in 1852. A searing indictment of the slave system by Harriet Beecher Stowe of Andover, Massachusetts, the novel sold over 1 million copies the first year. Southerners attacked *Uncle Tom's Cabin* as a gross distortion—the product of an oversentimental woman who had no first-hand knowledge of her subject. Many in the North, however, were deeply moved. Frederick Douglass, whose own life testified to the truth of much of what Mrs. Stowe wrote, called her account "a work of marvelous depth and power."

After *Uncle Tom's Cabin* opinion on both sides of the Mason-Dixon line hardened rapidly. Americans were increasingly less willing to discuss their differences, more inclined to fight to uphold their respective conceptions of "right." Once again the question of westward expansion brought the competing moralities into direct confrontation. This time the issue was over the status of slavery in the unorganized territory beyond Missouri. Stephen A. Douglas, a dynamic Senator from Illinois, triggered the controversy in January 1854 when he introduced a bill that made the fate of slavery in the territories of Kansas and Nebraska subject to local self-determination. Douglas's formula, known as popular sovereignty or squatter sovereignty, provided that the majority of residents of a territory, acting through their legislature, could vote slavery in or out before statehood. The Kansas-Nebraska Act, then, repealed the Missouri Compromise and its idea of a demarcation line between slavery and free soil. It made slavery at least a possibility in every part of the unorganized

West. Frederick Douglass called Stephen A. Douglas's plan "perfidious," and many in the North agreed. As Horace Greeley put it, Douglas and President Franklin Pierce "made more abolitionists in a month than Garrison and Phillips had made in a lifetime."

In Kansas itself, the result of popular sovereignty was civil war. Proslavery and antislavery partisans surged into previously uninhabited Kansas, each side set on becoming the determining majority. For two years they fought with ballots, but in 1856 they began to use bullets. Raiding parties from the slave state of Missouri attacked free soil communities in Kansas. The free soilers retaliated with "Beecher's Bibles," rifles collected by New England abolitionists at the suggestion of the Reverend Henry Ward Beecher, the brother of Harriet Beecher Stowe.

At this point the enigmatic figure of John Brown strode onto the Kansas prairie. Frederick Douglass had met him a decade earlier and been immensely impressed. "He was lean, strong, and sinewy," Douglass wrote, "of the best New England mould, built for times of trouble, fitted to grapple with the flintiest hardships." Brown hated slavery with the intensity of a fanatic. He told Douglass that the end of slavery justified any means. What Brown meant became apparent in Kansas. In May 1856, in the company of his sons (he had twenty children, but ten died in their infancy) and a few friends, Brown swooped down on the proslave settlements along Pottawatomie Creek. Arousing five settlers from their sleep, Brown proceeded to run them through with a sword in the name of the Lord. Afterward, he mutilated the corpses. Even Douglass called the act "a terrible remedy."

The shock waves emanating from "bleeding" Kansas were felt throughout the nation. Emotion took over, and both factions turned away from democracy in efforts to press their claims. Douglass noted "the display of pistols, bludgeons, and plantation manners in the Congress of the nation." In May 1856 Congressman Preston Brooks of South Carolina entered the Senate chamber and beat Massachusetts Senator Charles Sumner unconscious with a cane. Clearly, the cohesive forces holding the union together were weakening. The process was both reflected in and encouraged by the realignment of national politics. The Whig party succumbed to the slavery issue, and the Democrats split over it. In 1854 a new political coalition based on the principle of resistance to the expansion of slavery entered the lists under the name of the Republican party. By 1856, when Republican Presidential nominee John Frémont ran a strong second to Democrat James Buchanan, it was evident that Republicans and northerners were increasingly one and the same. Slavery expansion had come to symbolize sectional economic and political dominance. But in the final analysis it was the moral dimension of the issue that split the nation. As a rising Republican politician named Abraham Lincoln expressed it in a letter to a Georgian: "You think slavery is right and ought to be extended, while we think it is *wrong* and ought to be restricted. That I suppose is the rub."

The most disturbing event of the 1850s for Frederick Douglass was the Dred Scott decision of 1857. Scott was a slave whose master had taken him into the free soil state of Illinois. Anxious to construct a test case, Scott and his supporters sued for his freedom. When the case reached the Supreme Court, the justices decided to press the case to its ultimate implications for slavery in the United States. By a vote of 6 to 3 the Court sided with Chief Justice Roger Taney of Maryland in holding that as a slave Scott was property and must remain so no matter where his master decided to live. In effect this meant that Congress could not close a territory to slavery. The Missouri Compromise, already repealed by the Kansas-Nebraska Act, was now declared unconstitutional. The Taney Court went on to declare that slaves were not entitled to federal citizenship. Moreover, even free blacks—with the exception of those descended from people who were citizens before 1787—lacked the rights of citizenship.

Taney's majority opinion maintained that Americans had always regarded blacks as "being of an inferior order" with "no rights which any white man was bound to respect." Frederick Douglass, who was barred from citizenship under the Dred Scott decision, was astounded. Taney had cut the bottom out of his campaign to win blacks constitutional rights. On second thought, Douglass realized that the Supreme Court was "not the only power in the world. It is very great, but the Supreme Court of the Almighty is greater. Judge Taney . . . cannot change the essential nature of things—making evil good, and good, evil." Believing that the majority of Americans agreed with him rather than with Taney, Douglass took heart that the Dred Scott verdict might backfire by its very severity. He also knew that after the Taney decision, "the portentous shadow of a stupendous civil war became more and more visible."

In 1858 the trails of John Brown and Frederick Douglass crossed again. With his work in Kansas completed (Kansans rejected the pro-slavery Lecompton Constitution in 1858), Brown came east bent on new assaults against slavery. For several weeks he lived under Douglass's roof in Rochester, and the men discussed Brown's plan for attracting fugitive slaves to forts in the mountains of Virginia and Maryland. Overlooking Brown's record of dishonesty and crime, and a long history of insanity in his family, Douglass approved the idea. But when Brown abandoned guerrilla tactics in favor of capturing the federal arsenal at Harpers Ferry, Virginia, and starting a general slave insurrection, Douglass objected. The plan, he felt, was suicide. Undaunted, Brown persisted. On October 16, 1859, he struck at Harpers Ferry and succeeded in capturing the arsenal. But as Douglass predicted, he was quickly hemmed in by state and federal forces. John Brown's Raid ended October 17, when a force under United States Army Lieutenant-Colonel Robert E. Lee stormed the arsenal. Brown was captured, tried for treason, convicted, and sentenced to death by hanging. Northern pleas for leniency were rejected by a terrified and outraged South, which saw in the raid a threat to the whole fabric of Southern life. According to Virginia's governor, the slave insurrection Brown desired struck at "life, law, property, and civil liberty itself." Such things were sacred. Those who challenged them deserved to die.

In antislavery circles, on the contrary, John Brown became a hero and a martyr. Many Northerners thrilled to his last speech, in which he termed his raid "not wrong, but right" and welcomed the opportunity of mingling his blood with that shed by millions of slaves. Soon after the execution a song appeared to commemorate the event. The second verse of "John Brown's Body" suggested that many in the North associated their cause with God's: "He's gone to be a soldier in the army of the Lord! His soul is marching on." Ralph Waldo Emerson simply said that Brown's gallows had become a cross. Douglass called Brown a "noble old hero" and made no apologies for his violence against slaveholders who "voluntarily placed themselves beyond the laws of justice and honor." He had not joined the raiders, he explained, only because he disagreed with their means.

Just before John Brown's execution the governor of Virginia summed up the cause for the furor, and, incidentally, for the Civil War, in seven words. In speaking of the impossibility of pardoning Brown and of the radical divergence of opinion respecting him, the governor declared: "There is no middle ground of mitigation." The absence of such middle ground greatly increased the probability of war. The nation, in other words, had lost the consensus on fundamental definitions and values that holds a society together.

Soon after the capture of John Brown, Douglass learned that despite his disavowal of the raid, his name was implicated. Knowing he could expect no sympathy from the Buchanan Administration, Douglass hurriedly packed and, once more a fugitive, left for Canada and later for England. On returning in the summer of 1860 he found a tense Presidential campaign underway. The Democrats convened in April in Charleston, South Carolina, but their party was fatally torn. Stephen A. Douglas had the support of northern Democrats with his popular sovereignty formula for settling disputes over slavery. Southern Democrats believed that any restriction of the institution was illegal and the first step toward its abolition. The climax occurred when radical southerner William L. Yancey called on the convention to endorse a plank in the party platform stating that "slavery was right." The reply came from an Ohioan: "Gentlemen of the South, you mistake us—*we will not do it.*" Whereupon Yancey led the southern faction out of the convention hall. They later nominated John C. Breckinridge of Kentucky. Meanwhile, the northern Democrats chose Stephen A. Douglas. The schism virtually assured election of the Republican candidate, Abraham Lincoln.

Frederick Douglass was not happy with the Republican slogan for the 1860 campaign. He wished it read "Death to Slavery" rather than "No More Slave States." But as the election approached, Douglass gave up his efforts on behalf of Gerritt Smith, the candidate of the Radical Abolition party, and took the stump for Lincoln. His victory in November, with no electoral and very few popular votes from the South, Douglass termed a "glorious assertion of freedom and independence on the part of the North." The South was also prepared to assert its independence. South Carolina led the way on December 20, 1860, when a state convention unanimously approved an ordinance proclaiming the dissolution of the union between it and the other states. Within six weeks, five other states in the Deep South also

THE ELECTION OF 1860

MAINE 8

VT. 5

N.H. 5

MASS. 13

R.I. 4

CONN. 6

N.J. 7

DEL. 3

MD. 8

N.Y. 35

PA. 27

OHIO 23

MICH. 6

WIS. 5

MINN. 4

IOWA 4

ILL. 11

IND. 13

MO. 9

KY. 12

VA. 15

N.C. 10

S.C. 8

GA. 10

FLA. 3

TENN. 12

ALA. 9

MISS. 7

ARK. 4

LA. 6

TEXAS 4

OREG. 3

CALIF. 4

UNORGANIZED TERRITORY

	ELECTORAL	POPULAR (in thousands)
Lincoln (Rep.)	180	1,866
Douglas (Dem., No.)	12	1,383
Breckinridge (Dem., So.)	72	848
Bell (Con. U.)	39	593

seceded, and in February 1861 they formed a new nation: the Confederate States of America.

The lame-duck Buchanan Administration struggled to repair the crumbling nation. Senator John J. Crittenden of Kentucky advanced the idea of a compromise along the lines of the old Missouri and popular sovereignty formulas. Douglass regarded these proposals as evasions, but many in both camps favored them. Eight slave states, after all, had not seceded. Moderate southerners pointed out that President-elect Lincoln had promised not to interfere with slavery where it already existed even if he did oppose its extension to the territories. And in the North there was a widespread feeling that although slavery was bad, the breakup of the union was worse. A wave of anger rose against the abolitionists. Douglass personally experienced mob action. "The talk," he observed, "was that the blood of some abolitionist must be shed to . . . restore peaceful relations between the two sections of the country."

Many Americans in the winter of 1860–1861 simply could not conceive of civil war as a serious possibility. Someone would engineer a solution short of the battlefield, they thought. But there were many in both North and South who nodded in agreement when Lincoln applied to the United States the biblical warning that " 'a house divided against itself cannot stand.' " "I believe," Lincoln added, "this government cannot endure permanently half slave and half free." The issue, in other words, was not the extension of slavery, but slavery itself. And slavery, or more precisely the ethical conflict that the system engendered, was social dynamite. Men do not compromise their fundamental values; they fight to preserve them.

Indicative of the presence of these deeper layers of conflict was the fact that the minor matter of provisioning federally owned Fort Sumter in Charleston harbor touched off the Civil War in early April 1861. "Thank God," Douglass sighed, grateful at last to have the issue come to a head. But the initial stages of the war were disappointing. On the field of battle the disorganized Union forces suffered a humiliating defeat in the first major encounter of the war—the Battle of Bull Run in July 1861. A little over a year later, the Second Battle of Bull Run produced a similar outcome. Confederate commander Robert E. Lee proved vastly superior to any of the several generals with whom Lincoln experimented. The North fared better in its blockade of the Southern coast and in the Mississippi River theater of operations, but by 1863 the Union had not achieved military advantage in keeping with its marked superiority in numbers, wealth, and industrial capacity.

For people of Frederick Douglass's persuasion, the early stages of the Civil War were also frustrating on ideological grounds. President Lincoln steadfastly refused to define the conflict in terms of slavery. "My paramount object in this struggle," he wrote to *New York Tribune* editor Horace Greeley in 1862, "*is* to save the Union, and is *not* either to save or destroy Slavery." Douglass read these widely publicized words with a sense of profound discouragement. It was reinforced by Lincoln's initial refusal to accept black volunteers for the Union Army and his revival of the old African colonization scheme. The fact was, and Douglass knew it well, that much as Abraham Lincoln disliked slavery, he held no brief for blacks. The product of a self-made yeoman farming background, Lincoln resented the competition free blacks posed. And his prejudice ran deeper. In 1857 Lincoln spoke of the "natural disgust" which "indiscriminate amalgamation of the white and black races" produced in the minds of "nearly all white people." A year later he rejected the idea of political and social equality of the races on the grounds of a "physical difference." Lincoln candidly added that inasmuch as discrimination was necessary, "I am in favor of the race to which I belong having the superior position."

It was to Douglass's credit that he could overlook such expressions of prejudice in an attempt to understand and work with the President. Looking retrospectively at Lincoln's wartime record, Douglass remarked that in the first year of conflict the faith of black Americans in the federal government "was taxed and strained to the uttermost." On "genuine abolition grounds" Lincoln seemed to Douglass to be "tardy, cold, dull, and indifferent." Yet measuring his conduct in terms of the sentiment of the country as a whole, Lincoln appeared "swift, zealous, radical, and determined." The President, Douglass came to see, acted as a barometer, carefully gauging and expressing the public mind. Lincoln knew that to move too quickly against slavery would be to lose support vital to the prosecution of the war. The question of border states like Maryland and Tennessee was particularly delicate. Union, then, provided safer grounds than slavery on which to launch an attack on involuntary black servitude.

Lincoln was a master of practical politics, and his strategy became clearer on September 22, 1862, when he issued a preliminary draft of the Emancipation Proclamation. Carefully timed in the light of the progress of the war, Northern public opinion, and British relations to the Confederacy, the document stated Lincoln's intention on January 1, 1863, to free the slaves in all areas *not* under control of the Union. Douglass realized that this policy did not really free any slaves, but it nonetheless gave freedom higher priority as a war goal.

The Emancipation Proclamation restored Douglass's confidence in Lincoln's and the North's ultimate purposes. "The first of January 1863," he remarked, "was a memorable day in the progress of American liberty and civilization. It was the turning-point in the conflict between freedom and slavery." Shortly thereafter the War Department announced that it would accept black volunteers. Overjoyed, Douglass responded with a whirlwind of activity. Too old to fight personally, he traveled thousands of miles pleading with Northern blacks to enlist. The 54th and 55th Massachusetts regiments, which included two of Douglass's sons, were the result.

But it soon became clear that prejudice extended into the military. Not only were black regiments discriminated against in pay, equipment, and courts martial, they were regularly given preference over white troops for suicidal missions. Word came to Douglass in July 1863, for instance, that the Massachusetts 54th, exhausted from eight days of front-line service and forced marching, was ordered to storm a Confederate stronghold. Although the 54th fought bravely, 42 percent of its men were killed. Furious, Douglass stopped recruiting black soldiers and requested an interview with the President. Lincoln, who knew of Douglass's work, received him warmly, listened to his complaints, and responded, Douglass felt, honestly. Just the existence of black soldiers, Lincoln pointed out, was a gain. The remaining inequities would take time to eradicate. Disappointed as he was at such procrastination when blacks were paying the ultimate tribute to their nation on the field of battle, Douglass still campaigned in Lincoln's successful bid for reelection in 1864.

By this time the tide of war had swung toward the North. The turning point, many felt, came in early July 1863. On the third of that month at Gettysburg, Pennsylvania, an invading Confederate force under Robert E. Lee was repulsed, after furious fighting, by the army of George G. Meade. The next day, a thousand miles away, Ulysses S. Grant captured Vicksburg, Mississippi, and with it 30,000 Confed-

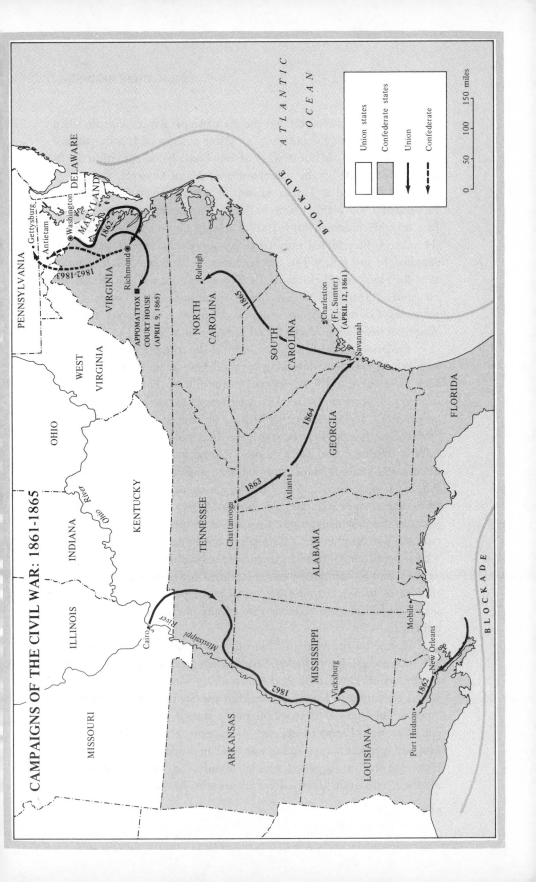

CAMPAIGNS OF THE CIVIL WAR: 1861–1865

Union states
Confederate states
Union
Confederate

0   50   100   150 miles

ATLANTIC OCEAN

BLOCKADE

BLOCKADE

PENNSYLVANIA

DELAWARE

MARYLAND

Gettysburg
Antietam
Washington
1862

VIRGINIA

Richmond

1862-1863

APPOMATTOX
COURT HOUSE
(APRIL 9, 1865)

WEST VIRGINIA

OHIO

INDIANA

ILLINOIS

MISSOURI

KENTUCKY

Ohio River

NORTH CAROLINA

Raleigh

1865

SOUTH CAROLINA

Charleston
(Ft. Sumter)
(APRIL 12, 1861)

Savannah

TENNESSEE

Chattanooga

1863

Atlanta

1864

GEORGIA

ALABAMA

FLORIDA

Mobile

New Orleans

Cairo

Mississippi River

1862

Vicksburg

MISSISSIPPI

ARKANSAS

LOUISIANA

Port Hudson

1862

erate soldiers and control of the Mississippi River. Lincoln then brought Grant east to confront Lee. After a series of bloody encounters, Grant settled in for a siege of the Confederate capital at Richmond. Meanwhile, in the western theater Major General William T. Sherman followed a Union victory at Chattanooga, Tennessee, in November 1863 with a march to the sea that isolated the Deep South. Late in 1864 Sherman turned north toward Grant's force. Caught in the pincers, Lee offered inspired resistance. Outnumbered and undersupplied, he still inflicted staggering losses on the dogged Grant. But in time the physical superiority of the North began to tell. Richmond fell on April 2, 1865. Seven days later Lee surrendered to Grant at Appomattox Court House in Virginia. Four years and over 600,000 American lives had been consumed in the Civil War.

Frederick Douglass received news of the collapse of the rebellion with mixed emotions. Speaking at a celebration in Boston's Faneuil Hall on April 4, 1865, he rejoiced in the fall of the slave power but questioned whether his countrymen, North as well as South, were prepared to accept blacks as citizens in the reconstructed United States. Douglass at first believed the best policy was to let the 4 million freedmen (ex-slaves) alone. "Do nothing with them," he advised white society, "mind your business and let them mind theirs." All black men needed was "simple justice, and an equal chance." Obtaining it, however, was not simple. While the war was still in progress, Lincoln had proposed a plan of reconstruction that restored citizenship to Southerners who pledged loyalty to the Constitution and who supported a Thirteenth Amendment abolishing slavery. When 10 percent of the voters in a state met this requirement, it would be readmitted to the Union. Douglass opposed the plan. Nothing in it guaranteed blacks the right to vote or any of the other privileges of citizenship.

Debate on the merits of Lincoln's plan ended abruptly on April 14, 1865, when John Wilkes Booth, a Southern fanatic, assassinated the President. Douglass hoped the resulting wave of Northern anger would encourage a harder line toward the South, but Vice-President Andrew Johnson's reconstruction policy was, if anything, more lenient. The new President refused to support black suffrage on the grounds it would cause racial war, and in response to demands for black equality, he suggested African colonization. By the end of 1865 all the Confederate states except Texas were ready to be readmitted under Johnson's plan. Former slaveholders had regained political dominance. Black Codes had been adopted that made it a crime for a black to be unemployed. The ex-slaves, of course, had no work. Once arrested, they were hired to their former masters to pay off their fines. Douglass, who had had personal experience with such a hiring-out arrangement, loudly protested it as thinly disguised slavery. Freedom, it appeared, would make little difference to the Southern black. Abandoning plans to retire at the age of fifty, Douglass resumed his crusade for black dignity.

The attitude of Northern whites was crucial to the success of Douglass's effort. Some, like William Lloyd Garrison, ended their efforts on behalf of blacks when the Thirteenth Amendment was adopted in December 1865. As an abolitionist, Garrison maintained, his work was done. Douglass insisted it was just beginning. Fortunately for Douglass, his viewpoint was shared by the Radical Republicans. These Northern congressmen, led by Thaddeus Stevens of Pennsylvania and Charles Sumner of Massachusetts, favored harsher treatment of the defeated South. Their motives stemmed from political and economic ambitions for their party and section as well as from a humanitarian concern for blacks. They believed, moreover, that Congress, not the President, should control the reconstruction process.

By 1866 a civil war existed in the government. Presidential vetoes and congressional overrides were the weapons. Douglass, by now a national figure, took to the lecture circuit to denounce Johnson as "a traitor to the cause of freedom." The congressional elections of 1866 suggested that many Americans agreed. Emboldened, the Radical Republicans pushed their own plan of reconstruction over Johnson's veto. It rejected all existing state governments in the South and divided the section into five military districts. A guarantee of black citizenship and suffrage (subsequently embodied in the Fourteenth and Fifteenth Amendments) was set as a precondition for readmission to the Union.

Douglass applauded this toughened federal policy toward the South, but he also realized the importance of economic assistance at the grass-roots level. Without the much-discussed "forty acres and a mule," freedmen were destined to descend into the quasi-slavery of tenant farming and sharecropping. In the summer of 1867 Douglass had a chance to help when President Johnson offered him a position as head of the Freedman's Bureau. Although tempted by the power of this federal welfare agency, Douglass did not accept a post that he correctly interpreted as an insincere gesture to ward off political criticism. Praise for Douglass was widespread and lavish. "The greatest black man in the nation," wrote one editor, "did not become a tool of the meanest white." Douglass looked even better when a few months after his refusal a movement to impeach the President came within a single Senate vote of success. But the impeachment trial was only symbolic. Ulysses S. Grant had already won the election of 1868 with the crucial assistance of a half-million black voters. The Republicans' desire for black suffrage was not entirely altruistic.

Radical Reconstruction proved less advantageous for the freedmen than Douglass had hoped. Changing Southern laws was one thing; changing behavior quite another. The military protection was largely on paper. In practice the ex-slaves were victims of systematic repression and terror. Southern whites found ways to minimize the black vote by keeping the site of the polls secret or falsely arresting hundreds of blacks on election day. Plantation owners joined in a resolution not to sell land to any black. When a freedman managed to establish himself as an independent farmer, he was subjected to raids and vandalism. White terrorist groups such as the Pale Faces, the Knights of the White Camellia, and the Ku Klux Klan appeared throughout the South. Nominally these were rifle clubs, but Douglass well knew the nature of their favorite target. Other club activities consisted of burning the schools, churches, and homes of blacks who did not keep their white-defined place. But in truth there was surprisingly little desire among the ex-slaves to challenge the traditional social order. Many of them continued voluntarily in the old ruts of servility. Slavery, it appeared, had left scars on the black personality that were not quickly or easily erased.

By the 1870s Douglass sensed that the nation was tiring of the black problem. For half a century it had been wracked with controversy over race and section. Men of all parties yearned for peace and the chance to settle down to the business of business. Northern investors had a special desire for a final settlement of the sectional animosity. Despite its agricultural past, the South possessed the potential for an urban, industrial economy. If the tense, unsettled atmosphere of military Reconstruction could end, Northern money might combine with Southern managerial talent to build a "New South" of mines, mills, railroads, and cities.

This line of reasoning argued for returning control over Southern affairs to Southern whites. The gradual withdrawal of troops from the South in the early 1870s marked the beginning of this process. It ended in 1877 when the last troops departed after an informal agreement among sectional politicians: Rutherford B. Hayes, the Republican, would be awarded the Presidency in the disputed election of 1876; he in turn would terminate Reconstruction. The treatment of Southern blacks was tacitly understood to be a regional problem rather than a national one. In effect, this meant the end of all black rights except freedom from slavery.

For Frederick Douglass, now old in the service of his people, the postwar abandonment of the black was a bitter pill. The Fourteenth and Fifteenth Amendments still stood, but in practice black Americans were second-class citizens. When the Supreme Court declared the Civil Rights Act of 1875 unconstitutional, Douglass realized the full extent to which the federal government had turned its back on blacks. Now a black man could not even sit as an equal with whites on public conveyances or dine with them at public inns. The era of "Jim Crow" laws began. Douglass angrily attacked the decision as "a further illustration" of a "malignant, vulgar, and pitiless prejudice" in the United States.

Douglass devoted the closing years of his life to the problem of how such prejudice could be overcome. Resuming his old vocation as editor, he launched *The New Era.* Its motto was "Free men, free soil, free speech, a free press, everywhere in the land. The ballot for all, education for all, fair wages for all." Education was especially important in Douglass's eyes despite the fact that he had achieved his personal successes (climaxed by his appointment as minister to Haiti in 1891) without a single day of formal schooling. Reviving a plan he had discussed in the 1850s with Harriet Beecher Stowe, Douglass called for an "industrial college" for blacks. Remarkably well conceived, his plan rested on his conviction that black Americans were not sufficiently prepared to benefit from regular high schools and colleges. Anticipating the philosophy of Booker T. Washington and his Tuskegee Institute (founded in 1881), Douglass declared that his people "needed more to learn how to make a good living than to learn Latin and Greek." On the other hand, Douglass was not prepared to accept vocational education alone. A compromise was possible: blacks should be taught "to use their hands as well as their heads."

The most powerful weapon in Douglass's possession during the 1880s was persistent agitation of the American conscience. The man who had delivered thousands of lectures summoned the energy to give hundreds more. His last talk, at a women's rights meeting, took place just a few hours before his death on February 20, 1895. He also led by example, by simply refusing to accept discrimination when he encountered it in his personal life. On many occasions Douglass deliberately challenged Jim Crow laws and then patiently explained his viewpoint to irate whites. Sometimes he convinced them. On one occasion when he did not, he held on to his seat so tightly that when he was finally ejected, the chair went with him.

In 1884, eighteen months after the death of Anna, Douglass quietly married his secretary, Helen Pitts, a middle-aged, college-trained woman. The fact that she was white raised eyebrows and voices in both the white and black communities. Helen answered them by simply saying, "I was not afraid to marry the man I loved because of his color." Douglass, more philosophical, pointed out that the marriage was in keeping with his teachings of a lifetime. Color, he had always insisted, was an artificial issue raised to degrade and repress blacks. As for intermixing races, Douglass saw nothing unusual about what had been a fact of American life for two and a half centuries. Glancing with a smile at his own bronze skin, he liked to squelch his critics with the observation that his first wife "was the color of my mother, and the second, the color of my father."

SELECTED READINGS

The Person

*DOUGLASS, FREDERICK: *Life and Times of Frederick Douglass.* Originally published in 1892 and subsequently rewritten several times. The most convenient edition is that edited in 1962 by Rayford W. Logan.

*FONER, PHILIP: *Frederick Douglass* (1963). A recent biographical interpretation.

*FONER, PHILIP (ed.): *The Life and Writings of Frederick Douglass* (4 vols., 1950–1955). The most extensive collection.

* Available in paperback.

*QUARLES, BENJAMIN: *Frederick Douglass* (1948). A frequently laudatory early life.

*QUARLES, BENJAMIN (ed.): *Frederick Douglass* (1968). A sampling of Douglass's writings, along with opinions of him by representative figures of his time and today.

The Period

DAVIS, DAVID BRION: *The Problem of Slavery in Western Culture* (1966). The definitive study of slavery in the American context.

*ELKINS, STANLEY: *Slavery* 3rd ed., 1976. An imaginative but controversial interpretation that Douglass's life does not support.

ENGERMAN, STANLEY L.: *The Reinterpretation of American Economic History* (1971). New light on the economics of slavery. See, also Engerman's collaborative work with Robert Fogel, *Time on the Cross: The Economics of American Negro Slavery* (1974).

*GENOVESE, EUGENE D.: *The Political Economy of Slavery* (1965). A recent Marxist interpretation. See, also, Genovese's *Roll, Jordan, Roll: The World the Slaves Made* (1974).

GUTMAN, HERBERT G.: *The Black Family in Slavery and Freedom, 1750–1925* (1976). The best social history of the slave experience.

JORDAN, WINTHROP: *White Over Black* (1974). The symbolic and emotional components of the bias Douglass spent his life resisting.

*MCPHERSON, JAMES M.: *The Struggle for Equality: Abolitionists and the Negro in the Civil War and Reconstruction* (1964). Social as well as political history.

*MEIER, AUGUST: *Negro Thought in America, 1880–1915* (1963). An exploration of a forgotten corner of American intellectual history.

*PHILLIPS, ULRICH B.: *American Negro Slavery* (1918). A controversial early portrayal of the institution in a relatively favorable light.

RANDALL, J. G., and DAVID DONALD: *The Civil War and Reconstruction* (2nd ed., 1961). The best one-volume account.

*STAMPP, KENNETH M.: *The Peculiar Institution* (1956). The most balanced history of slavery in the United States.

*WOODWARD, C. VANN: *Origins of the New South, 1877–1913* (1951). The story of the South's recovery from the Civil War.

Mark Twain

*The young reporter with the slow Missouri drawl stamped the cold
of the high Nevada desert out of his feet as he entered the offices
of the Virginia City* Territorial Enterprise. *It was early in 1863. The
newspaper's editor, Joseph T. Goodman, looked puzzled at seeing
his Carson City correspondent in the home office, but Sam Clemens
came right to the point. "Joe, I want to sign my articles. I want
to be identified to a wider audience." The editor, already impressed
with his colleague of six months, readily agreed. Then came the*

question of a pen name, since few aspiring writers of the time used their legal names. Clemens had something in mind: "I want to sign them 'Mark Twain,' " he declared. "It is an old river term, a leads-man's call, signifying two fathoms—twelve feet. It has a richness about it; it was always a pleasant sound for a pilot to hear on a dark night; it meant safe water."

For Mark Twain, the whole experience of growing up on the Mississippi River had "a richness about it." The flavor of that experience pervaded his best writing and happiest memories. But more and more, Twain wrote about a myth. The river, the nation, and Twain himself changed radically during his lifetime, and much of the old magic rubbed off. One factor was their passage through the searing fire of civil war into an often sordid and ugly Gilded Age of industrialization and urbanization. There was also an experiment with imperialism. By that time the frontier, which had been close to Twain's Missouri boyhood in the 1830s, had retreated to the far corners of the continent. In many ways Mark Twain and America grew up together—and neither aged gracefully. Gradually the sunny humor left Twain's writing; he died in 1910, bitter and pessimistic about his country and his countrymen.

Mark Twain was fond of tracing his ancestry to one Flavius Clemens, a literary character noted for his "want of energy." In reality, his roots ran back to a Gregory Clemens whose excessive energy on behalf of Oliver Cromwell in the English uprisings of the 1640s earned his severed head a place on a pole atop London's Westminster Hall. Gregory's family, however, escaped to the American colonies. Twain's grandfather owned property in Virginia, but his father, in characteristic American fashion, sought fresher fields over the mountains in Kentucky and Tennessee. Wealthy enough to own a few slaves and study law, John Clemens steadfastly pursued the material success that was the surest definition of status in the new society. In 1823 he married Jane Lampton. Twain's mother was descended from a long line of Kentucky pioneers, some of whom followed Daniel Boone through the Cumberland Gap in 1767 and remained to contest the ownership of the rich bluegrass country with bears and Indians.

For twelve years John and Jane Clemens followed a typical frontier pattern. There were children, frequent moves from one small town to another, and always the gnawing hunger for fame and fortune that Jacksonian America easily aroused but only grudgingly satisfied. For a time John Clemens pursued the law. But the mountain people frequently turned to more direct methods of settling their differences, so Clemens added storekeeping to his professions. And, like almost all frontiersmen, Clemens dabbled in land—75,000 acres of it, in fact, which he bought in eastern Tennessee about 1826 for an incredible $400. Even this price was high for the struggling Clemenses, but they fully expected the investment to yield millions. Mark Twain's first memories were of stories of the magical Tennessee land. By virtue of possessing so much land, John Clemens entered the social aristocracy of the Appalachian frontier. He bore the title "Squire" with a relish that seems surprising only to those who would make Jacksonians more democratic than in fact they were. Provided there was equality of opportunity, most Americans had no reservations about accepting the trappings of Old World social differentiation.

Despite their intensity, the hopes of Mark Twain's family for status and wealth were short-lived. In 1834 John and Jane Clemens became victims of the fierce and tangled financial wars of the early nineteenth century. The roots of the nation's financial difficulties ran back to the Panic of 1819, the first great financial dislocation in American history. As in most subsequent economic crises, a combination of optimism and greed that blinded people to the realities of the marketplace was the underlying problem. In this case three years of surging cotton-based prosperity following the conclusion of the War of 1812 pushed the price of prime land up to the unheard-of level of $100 per acre. But even at this figure there was no shortage of buyers, because the Bank of the United States issued credit freely. In fact, the amount loaned exceeded by ten times the amount of hard cash in the Bank's possession.

The various state banks were even more irresponsible in their issuance of paper money, and the nation eagerly moved further and further out on the economic limb. It began to crack late in 1818 when a slackening demand for cotton coincided with a major banking failure in England. Inexorably the chain of credit, which extended across the Atlantic, began to tighten. First the Bank of the United States and then the smaller banks began to call in their loans. The paper money on which the boom had fed became virtually worthless scrap. Foreclosures multiplied, and panic gripped the public. There were even soup stations on the streets of major American cities. The depression, which lasted until 1822, was especially severe in the trans-Appalachian West where the Clemenses struggled for success.

Bewildered, afraid, and unwilling to blame their own excessive optimism, Americans turned savagely on banks in general, and particularly on the Bank of the United States. In popular parlance it became "the Monster," a mysterious and sinister presence that dwelled in the East and preyed on the common man of the South and West. Seeking to slay the dragon of paper money and offset the unfair advantage it allegedly gave the rich, political leaders like Thomas Hart "Old Bullion" Benton of Missouri fired the first shots in "the Bank War."

Andrew Jackson, from the Clemenses home state of Tennessee, was in the forefront of the assault. In his unsuccessful 1824 presidential campaign and in his successful 1828 and 1832 campaigns, Jackson made the Bank of the United States a primary issue. He had personally been burned by bankers, and as an old soldier he spared no quarter in his hatred. Jackson particularly distrusted Nicholas Biddle, the suave, wealthy Philadelphian who since 1823 had directed the Bank of the United States.

In point of fact, Biddle was a talented administrator who used the Bank to give some semblance of order to the growing nation's economy. But Jackson and his supporters saw in Biddle only a haughty aristocrat using "the Monster" to suppress men on the make. "The Bank," Jackson declared with typical frontier directness, "is trying to kill me, but I will kill it." An opportunity to do so arose in 1832, when Biddle applied to Congress for an extension of the Bank's charter. Congress approved but Jackson, confident of reelection in the fall, vetoed the bill with unconcealed relish on July 10, 1832. The President followed this act by withdrawing federal funds from the presumably moribund institution and distributing them to numerous state or "pet" banks.

Now it was Biddle's turn to fight. "The worthy President," he acidly remarked, "thinks that because he has scalped Indians, . . . he is to have his way with the Bank. He is mistaken." Choosing his weapons carefully, Biddle called in loans, and just as in 1819 unemployment and business failure swept the nation. Among the hopeful entrepreneurs destroyed in the "Biddle panic" of 1833–1834 was John Clemens. "In that storm," Mark Twain later wrote, "my Father's fortunes were wrecked." Jackson, however, held firm. Centralized banking was not restored, and, by the terms of the Specie Circular (1836), paper money was rejected as a means of payment for public lands.

A casualty of the Bank War, John Clemens looked for a new place to pursue his dreams. His choice meant that Mark Twain would come in contact with the Mississippi. The Clemenses' decision to go west—men seeking to improve their position in this period hardly ever considered going east—was made in the spring of 1835. Their destination was Florida, Missouri, a frontier town at the fork of the Salt River. Some of Jane Clemens's relatives had settled the town a few years previously, and in the best booster tradition urged everyone to come and share a glorious future. Realism suggested that such confidence was badly misplaced. Florida, Missouri, was in the middle of nowhere and, in Mark Twain's words, "nearly invisible." It consisted, in fact, of seventeen log and four frame houses, a long church that doubled as a school, two stores, and about three hundred people. But 50 miles down the Salt River lay the Mississippi, an established highway of empire and potentially one of commerce as well. The first article of faith in Florida was that the town's proximity to the great river was a guarantee of prosperity. Dams and locks would make the stream navigable by steamboat. This meant direct water communication with commercial centers like St. Louis, Cincinnati, and New Orleans. Beyond that entrepôt lay the world, and from the dirt streets of Florida men's dreams spiraled upward and outward.

It was the same throughout the trans-Appalachian West. Every village fully expected that the magic of internal improvements would make it a major city. Navigational aids and canals figured in the first wave of hope. Florida, Missouri, for example, anticipated transforming the shallow Salt River into an all-season, deep-water highway. Twain's father headed a navigation company that obtained incorporation papers from the Missouri legislature. It built a dock and a small boat—which never sailed. Missouri provided no help in building the costly locks, and Andrew Jackson, in his 1830 veto of federal aid to

Kentucky's Maysville Road, closed the federal treasury to local improvement projects. But it was a revolutionary new form of transportation, railroads, that struck the final blow at Florida's dreams. Trains could run almost anywhere, at any season, and were less expensive than a canal-lock-dam system. Between 1830 and 1860 railroads came to dominate American transportation, and tiny Florida did not become part of the network of rails.

Jane Clemens was pregnant with Mark Twain when she arrived in Florida. He was born November 30, 1835. With five children now dependent on him, John Clemens struggled to make ends meet. He tried storekeeping and practiced law, but economic survival was a battle. One reason was the Specie Circular, which punctured the paper-money prosperity that followed the demise of the Bank of the United States. In 1837 tightening credit and a drop in land sales produced a panic that led to one of the worst depressions in American history. Not until the mid-1840s did the economy turn upward again.

The Clemenses responded to the renewal of hard times by moving once again. This time they went to Hannibal, Missouri, the town identified with Mark Twain's youth, his fondest memories, and his best writing. Hannibal had one distinct advantage over Florida and the Tennessee hamlets. It was directly on the Mississippi, 100 miles north of St. Louis. Mark Twain always remembered it as "a heavenly place for a boy," a "white town drowsing in the sunshine of a summer's morning; . . . the great Mississippi, the majestic, the magnificent Mississippi, rolling its mile-wide tide along, shining in the sun; the dense forest away on the other side." There were unlimited places to roam— woods and field and, if one dared, caves—and there was the river. After several narrow escapes from drowning, Twain mastered swimming. Thereafter there was no containing him. In company with a gang of contemporaries, many of whom made their way directly into *The Adventures of Tom Sawyer* and *The Adventures of Huckleberry Finn,* Twain turned the Mississippi into a giant playground. His days consisted of fishing, swimming, exploring islands, sneaking a ride on a raft or steamboat. School was only a temporary and distasteful interruption.

There was, to be sure, the seamier side of frontier life. The young Mark Twain saw an old man shot down on Hannibal's main street at high noon. He was present when a drunk stabbed an immigrant with a bowie knife and remarked on the way the blood spurted from the wound in powerful jets. Cowering in the bushes, he watched a widow mow down a local ruffian who had designs on her daughter. Fights and whippings were standard fare on the frontier, and Twain never seemed to be far from the center of action. On numerous occasions he stumbled over corpses in his rambles along the river. And there was the fact of slavery.

The Clemenses had owned a few slaves in Tennessee and, as a result of the Compromise of 1820, were able to take them to their new home in Missouri. Like the family's fancy two-horse carriage, slaves were both practical and an indication of status. A black house girl permitted Jane Clemens to at least approach the Southern ideal of ladyhood. A field hand allowed "Squire" Clemens to regard himself as something more than a storekeeper or farmer. Slaveholding, in sum, linked the Clemenses to the great planters whose several hundred slaves actually permitted the life of genteel ease that was the intellectual and emotional lifeblood of the antebellum South. To be sure, these big planters constituted only a small fragment of Southern society. Over half the slaveowners had less than five blacks, which was about the number John Clemens owned in good times. To own more than twenty slaves was exceptional and a mark of high standing. And the really large slaveholders, whose holdings in human property ran to one hundred or more, could have met together in a single hall. Yet it was this elite that dominated the South's economic and political life and set the social standards to which humbler men aspired. Significantly, of the South's total white population on the eve of the Civil War of 8,000,000, less than 400,000 owned slaves. But such was the hold of the planter ideal on the mind and institutions of the South that the tail wagged the dog. A civil war in defense of an institution that only a minority enjoyed was one result.

In time Mark Twain came to understand and despise slavery, but in his youth slaves were an accepted part of life. Jennie, the Clemens house girl, was a second mother to Twain, and the slave children were his playmates. On winter evenings the whole family, black and white, would gather in front of an open fire to hear Uncle Ned, a slave, tell weird and wonderful stories about ghosts, spells, charms, and other manifestations of the supernatural. On at least one occasion a slave saved Mark from drowning. Such human relationships with blacks were the source of Twain's tender account of Huckleberry Finn and the runaway slave Jim on their Mississippi raft. There is little doubt that Huck and, by implication, Mark Twain found more genuine affection and fatherly guidance in black men than he ever did in whites. The busy, cold John Clemens, in particular, was never close to his children. He died when Mark was twelve.

Still, Twain came to appreciate at an early age the significance of the color line. The boy learned that blacks, unlike other people, could be bought and sold. They were property in a frighteningly absolute sense. For instance, during a trip in 1842 John Clemens wrote the family an account of the difficulties he was experiencing in selling one "Charlie." "The highest price I had offered for him in New Orleans was $50, in Vicksburg $40. After performing the journey to Tennessee, I expect to sell him for whatever he will bring." It was just a livestock transaction.

On another occasion the house girl snatched a whip from the upraised hand of Jane Clemens. This challenge to authority produced an immediate and violent response. John Clemens tied Jennie's wrists and lashed her shoulders with rawhide. Confused and afraid, Mark Twain watched in silence. He also saw a runaway slave cornered and beaten by six whites. He saw a slave killed with a rock for a trifling offense. He was present when a Hannibal mob attacked and almost lynched an abolitionist. The man was spared only through the efforts of a minister who convinced the mob that the intended victim was insane rather than serious. As for slave auctions, the raw nerve end of the institution, Twain's boyhood recollection is hazy. But he did "vividly remember," he later wrote, "seeing a dozen black men and women chained together lying in a group on the pavement, waiting shipment to a Southern slave-market. They had the saddest faces I ever saw."

After his father's death in 1847, Twain abandoned forever his career as a reluctant schoolboy and apprenticed himself to a Hannibal printer. The pay was in the usual form of board and clothes—"more board than clothes, and not much of either," Twain recollected. But the printing job opened Twain's eyes, as it had Benjamin Franklin's, to the larger world. In time Twain wanted to see it for himself. Again like Franklin, he left the printing shop to try his fortune in New York and Philadelphia. The two lives crossed briefly in 1853 when an unknown Twain stood before the grave of the famous Philadelphian. The young man recorded the event, without comment, in a letter home. He was more impressed with the size and pace of urban life. In awed tones the country boy described New York's Crystal Palace Fair, which had 6,000 visitors—double Hannibal's entire population—every day. New York itself contained an incredible 400,000 people and hummed with commercial activity.

It was during his year and a half in the East that Twain first became aware that the slaves who had been an accepted part of his Missouri boyhood were the subject of a national controversy of growing intensity. The newspaper offices in which he worked fairly buzzed with discussion of the Compromise of 1850, especially its Fugitive Slave Law. The efforts of the Free Soil party, organized in 1848, to exclude slaves from the western territories was highly controversial. For the first time Twain encountered widespread, vigorous abolitionism. Harriet Beecher Stowe's *Uncle Tom's Cabin* was the best-selling novel of the day, and the Missourian must have discussed it frequently. In Twain's small-farming upper South, the pictures Stowe painted of huge plantations and brutal overseers did not ring true. But her charges were undoubtedly the basis of a certain amount of harassment of Twain by his northern colleagues in the newspaper offices. On November 28, 1853, for example, Twain wrote to his brother Orion: "How do you like 'free soil'?—I would like amazingly to see a good old-fashioned negro." But the problem refused to disappear. Abolitionists like Stowe and blacks who refused to be "old-fashioned" like Frederick Douglass gave Twain's and the nation's conscience little rest.

Late in 1854, having proved his independence and obtained a not-altogether-pleasing taste of the outside world, Twain returned to his beloved Mississippi Valley. But the slavery controversy followed him West. By the fall of 1854 it was gnawing at the western edge of his home state. Missourians, in fact, played a major role in escalating the Kansas-Nebraska issue into a preview of the Civil War. Intensely proslave "border ruffians" from Twain's state swarmed into neighboring Kansas to vote and, after 1855, to fight the advocates of free soil.

On the great river to the east of "bleeding Kansas," however, the pace of life was still measured. Mark Twain pursued his calling as a printer in several locations and found time to dream of going to South

Western Steamboat, with full cargo.

Engineer on duty : two feet water on lower deck.

A Hot Boat.—Ten 56lbs. weights on safety-valve.

Pittsburgh on a clear morning.

Running on a Bank.

Going over Falls of Ohio.—[Not exaggerated.]

Harper's Monthly, *a leading American magazine, printed these impressions of travel on the Ohio and Mississippi rivers in its issue of December 1858. Mark Twain was piloting steamboats at this time and undoubtedly witnessed most of the scenes. The "hot boat" resulted from a captain's desire for maximum speed. The inoperative safety valve sometimes produced colossal explosions such as that which killed Twain's brother.*

America and making a fortune on the upper Amazon. But in the spring of 1857 he turned to an even older dream—steamboating. Twain's chance came when a veteran river pilot, Horace Bixby, agreed to take him on as an apprentice or "cub." The next step was to "learn the river" upstream and down, day and night, high water and low. After eighteen months Twain qualified as a pilot. The next two years were unquestionably the happiest of his life. He reveled in the glamour and excitement that came with being a star performer in the golden age of American steamboating. In peak periods there was a solid mile of the big black-stacked, triple-decked boats tied to the wharves of Cincinnati or St. Louis or New Orleans. Piles of produce lined the docks, and the waterfronts seethed with activity. There was power and growth in these scenes, and at least in the 1850s Twain was proud to be a part of them. He also loved the quiet moments when, high in his glass-walled pilothouse, the beauty of the river was overwhelming. He poured the magic of these moments into the best descriptive passages of *Huckleberry Finn*.

For the United States as well as for Mark Twain, the decades immediately preceding the Civil War were, on the whole, a time of confidence. To be sure, the rumblings of the sectional controversy were disturbing, but few before 1860 interpreted them as harbingers of real war. The nation's future appeared bright. The anxious, uncertain years after independence were well behind. The continuing growth of capitalism, combined with the natural abundance of the continent, promised unceasing prosperity. God, nature, and the course of history were on America's side. Reformers would take care of any problems that rapid growth might bring; progress, it appeared, was inevitable. Walt Whitman sensed this at his editor's desk in Brooklyn when he boasted in 1846 that "thirty years from this date, America will be confessed the first nation on earth." And Henry Adams, in his measured manner, recalled that as a young man in Massachusetts he too subscribed to the faith that held the world to be simple, moral, well-ordered, and secure. Mark Twain agreed. His pilot's view of the world bred confidence. Within a quarter of a century all three men would come to hold radically different opinions, but in the halcyon antebellum years there was little reason to question man's goodness or the nation's greatness.

Mark Twain had his first doubts about this idyllic world in June

1858. At the time Twain belonged to the crew of the sleek new *Pennsylvania,* a steamboat sufficiently fast to make the round trip between St. Louis and New Orleans in thirty-five days. Through his connections Mark obtained a clerkship on the *Pennsylvania* for his younger brother, Henry. Then disaster struck. While taking on wood from a flatboat 60 miles below Memphis, the *Pennsylvania,* for no apparent reason, exploded. The entire forward half of the boat blew out and scalding clouds of steam from the ship's boilers enveloped the trapped passengers and crew. By a quirk of fate Mark Twain was not among them. A quarrel with another pilot on the *Pennsylvania* had caused him to hire on a different boat and miss the ill-fated run. But Henry was present and horribly injured. Mark rushed to his bedside only to watch him die.

The personal loss was paramount for Mark Twain, but as he reflected on the explosion of the *Pennsylvania,* he perceived a level of tragedy at once broader and deeper. Technology, which the steamboat symbolized and which constituted so vital a part of the nineteenth-century American idea of progress, had betrayed its worshippers. For a horrible moment the machine had turned on its maker. The lesson was there for those who dared read it: the best condition for man might well be the unmechanized past and not the technological future. Of course, neither Twain nor America gave up on mechanization as a result of incidents like the *Pennsylvania* explosion. They could always be thought of as aberrations, temporary problems that a higher technology would surely solve. On the other hand, there were seeds of a later and deeper disillusionment in Twain's discovery of tragedy on the shining Mississippi.

The second shock to Twain's confidence in his nation was, of course, the Civil War. Few Americans who lived through that cataclysm were unaffected. In the first place, there was the spectacle of the vaunted democratic process shattering completely on the rocks of the slavery controversy. The Compromise of 1850, which many expected to be a final settlement of the sectional differences, proved only a temporary check. Westward expansion kept the old wounds open. Only three years after the compromise, Twain found "free soil" as burning an issue as ever. He also found American statesmen helpless. Franklin Pierce, a Democrat elected President in 1852, displayed an extraordinary lack of leadership during the Kansas-Nebraska controversy. His successor, James Buchanan, also proved adept at side-stepping the main issues. The best politician of the era, Senator Stephen A. Douglas of Illinois, could only devise a formula (popular sovereignty) that shifted the battlefield from the federal to the state and local level. By 1860, when the Republican Abraham Lincoln swept to victory without a single electoral vote from a slave state, it was clear that the national government was more a bone of contention than an agent of cohesion. Yet, in fairness to the politicians of the time, they faced a difficult—perhaps an impossible—problem of governing a house divided.

Mark Twain supported John Bell of Tennessee and his Constitutional Union party in the four-man election of 1860. It was the best of a poor slate for old-line Whigs like the Clemenses. But Bell, with his condemnation of sectional parties and loyalty to the Constitution and the Union, carried only three states, all in the upper South. Missouri, thoroughly divided, gave its nine electoral votes to the Northern Democrat Stephen A. Douglas. After the election Twain watched, only half-believing, as the secession process began. Along with most of his contemporaries, he fully expected that the nation would come to its senses long before it came to blows. Yet another compromiser would appear. But the firing on Fort Sumter, South Carolina, on April 12, 1861, and its surrender two days later ended all illusions. On the Mississippi River men began to take sides. Twain's instructor in piloting, Horace Bixby, went with the North and eventually rose to chief of the Union River Service. Mark Twain cast his lot with the Confederacy. But Twain and his associates were not radical; for a time, they saw validity in both positions. Moreover, the rivermen were in a sense men without a section. Their business was intersectional, and they thought in terms of long-distance trade and communication.

Gradually, however, attitudes hardened. On his last run up the Mississippi in April 1861, Twain heard plenty of war talk and saw men seriously preparing to fight. At Memphis he and a companion were in the pilothouse when a cannon roared on the shore. Ignorant of its meaning, they steamed on. A second blast, this time no warning, sent a ball screaming into the deck immediately in front of the pilots. "Good Lord Almighty!" Twain's friend gasped, "what do they mean by that?" Slowing and turning toward shore, Twain drawled, "I guess they want us to wait a minute." He was correct. After examination, the boat was allowed to pass. But it was the last steamboat to make the journey from New Orleans to St. Louis, for war severed the natural artery of the river. It also ended Twain's career as a riverman.

Undecided about his next step in a society crumbling before his eyes, Twain went home to Hannibal. In this border state the claims of the North and the South hung in the balance for most of the war. Governor Claiborne F. Jackson tried to lead Missouri out of the Union in March 1861, but failed to command the necessary legislative support. Neither was Missouri prepared to side with the Union. When Lincoln asked the state for troops for the Union Army, he was bluntly refused. As a result of this ambivalence, the state began to experience its own civil war as neighbors took up arms against one another. Still, in the beginning it was all very amusing and terribly romantic. Twain recalled how companies of soldiers formed in and around Hannibal without the slightest idea of the nature of their cause or the identity of their enemy. It was a gay military lark, with the bonus of kissing one's girlfriend goodbye before marching off to war. Twain himself went through this ritual after deciding, like Robert E. Lee, that he would defend his state from the Northern invaders. His older brother Orion, however, became a Union sympathizer, Lincoln Republican, and abolitionist.

As a Confederate soldier Mark Twain joined 30,000 other Missourians, but 109,000 men in that state eventually fought for the Union. Missouri as a whole never chose sides, remaining, along with Kentucky, Maryland, and Delaware, a slave state that did not join the Confederacy. Lincoln obviously wanted to preserve this indecision on the part of the border states and took every step, including some clearly illegal ones, to ensure the continuance of their neutrality. His success was a major factor in the outcome of the war.

For the first few weeks Mark Twain's military endeavors were only slightly more sophisticated than the games of war he had played as a child. The major armies had the same experience. Men dashed off to the First Battle of Bull Run, Virginia, in July 1861 in a holiday mood. No one expected the fighting to last more than a few months, but gradually the full meaning of civil war became apparent to Twain and to the nation. First of all there was the hard work of warfare. After the exciting farewells, Twain's band of fifteen self-styled Marion Rangers settled into an uncomfortable camp life from which all traces of grandeur quickly vanished. There were ludicrous blunders—a Ranger shot his horse as it approached him in the dark—and there was the genuine fear of actually encountering the enemy. But what finally soured Twain on the war was his recognition that its essence was organized killing.

He expressed his feelings in a short story centering on the panic murder by the Rangers of an unarmed stranger who innocently rode through their camp one night. The incident was fictitious, but unquestionably Twain felt it was possible, and the thought made him sick. Also distressing were the accounts of warfare in the East. At Bull Run troops only slightly better trained than the Marion Rangers engaged in a wild medley of mistakes that would have been funny if the costs were not calculated in lives. And the slaughter had just begun. Twain, however, had seen enough. He had no personal stake in slavery and did not sympathize with the political and social philosophies he allegedly defended. It was therefore with little regret that Second Lieutenant Twain allowed a sprained ankle to force him out of the war.

Quitting the war with a curse for both belligerents, Twain traveled to Iowa to join Orion Clemens. The disillusioned soldier found his brother in a frenzy of excitement. A friend in the Lincoln Administration had just secured for him an appointment as secretary of the territorial governor of Nevada. Orion, in turn, needed an assistant, and Mark did not hesitate to offer his services. Disgusted with the war that had transformed the happy valley of his youth into a nightmare, Twain was fully prepared to exercise the option he later extended to Huckleberry Finn and "light out for the Territory ahead of the rest." At the same time he intended to catch up to the rapidly retreating American frontier that had been such an important component of antebellum Hannibal's appeal.

On July 26, 1861, the Clemens brothers boarded a sixteen-horse stagecoach of the recently formed Butterfield Overland Mail Company at St. Joseph, Missouri. Nineteen days and 1700 miles later they arrived in Carson City, Nevada. It was a glorious trip, really an escape, for Mark Twain. There were just enough outlaws and Indians to lend excitement without creating serious danger. Twain described his feelings a decade later in *Roughing It*: "even at this day it thrills me through and through to think of the life, the gladness, and the wild sense of freedom that used to make the blood dance in my face on those fine Overland mornings." The stage followed the South Pass route Jim Bridger pioneered a quarter-century earlier and rumbled past Fort Bridger, which the old mountain man still operated. Twain enjoyed a few days of rest in Salt Lake City and later delighted in poking fun at the Mormon residents of that city. But Nevada was his goal, and soon the rejuvenated horses were racing across the Great Basin to the territorial capital on the eastern flanks of the Sierra.

When Mark Twain descended from the hot, dusty stagecoach in August 1861, he entered an extraordinary world. Only two years before Henry T. P. Comstock and several colleagues struck rich veins of gold and silver directly across the Sierra from the California strikes of 1849 that had launched the mining boom. By the time Twain arrived, the frantic heart of the bonanza had shifted from California and Colorado to Nevada. One of the richest single deposits ever found, the Comstock Lode yielded $350 million between 1859 and 1879. To harvest the wealth cities appeared in the wilderness almost overnight. They were raw and violent. Virginia City's first twenty-six graves were those of murdered men. Mark Twain was impressed with the entire spectacle. "The country is fabulously rich," he wrote back home, "in gold, silver, copper, lead . . . thieves, murderers, desperadoes, ladies . . . lawyers, Christians, Indians, Chinamen, Spaniards, gamblers, sharpers, coyotes . . . poets, preachers, and jackass rabbits." The desert environment, of course, was new and shocking for the man from well-watered Missouri. "The birds that fly over the land carry their provisions with them," he remarked with a flash of the wit that was to make him famous.

Twain originally intended to stay in the West a few months; he remained five and a half years. The principal reason was his enchantment with the region. It is apparent in his account of his first visit to Lake Tahoe. With another uprooted middle westerner, Twain hiked from Carson City to the lake soon after his arrival in Nevada. Deep blue and fully 20 miles long, Tahoe sits on the Sierra slope at 6300 feet. The surrounding snow-capped peaks rise several thousand feet higher. Twain was stunned by his first view: "as it lay there with the shadows of the mountains brilliantly photographed upon its surface I thought it must surely be the fairest picture the whole world affords." Twain and his friend had utilitarian reasons for coming to Tahoe. They intended to stake claims to several hundred acres of yellow pine forest on the lake shore. But the beauty and peacefulness of the location sapped their acquisitiveness. Drifting in a borrowed rowboat, much as Twain had drifted on the Mississippi, they joked, and smoked, and counted the massive trout plainly visible in a hundred feet of crystal water. Twain had indeed recaptured the magic of his Missouri boyhood. His happiness was nearly perfect. "Three months of camp life on Lake Tahoe," he wrote in *Roughing It*, "would restore an Egyptian mummy to his pristine vigor, and give him an appetite like an alligator." The only discordant note was a forest fire Twain's campfire ignited, but "conservation" was not yet in the American vocabulary, and the sight of bright flames licking up the hillsides struck Twain as a spectacle worthy of Tahoe's beauty.

While one part of Mark Twain's mind responded to the solitude and natural beauty of Tahoe, another part was infected by the get-rich-quick frenzy that seized western Nevada. In this ambivalence he was representative of American society in the middle decades of the nineteenth century. Here, too, was the frequently contradictory attraction to an older, simpler pastoralism and a future that was complex and increasingly urban. For Twain the call of the civilized sounded with a vengeance just after his return from Tahoe. By early 1862 he was fully engrossed in the silver fever. Racing from strike to strike, frantically laying out claims and abandoning them just as impulsively, he became part of a money-crazed society. Taking it for granted that he would become a millionaire before the year was out, Twain's fertile imagination dwelled on the life style such affluence would permit: "San Francisco . . . , Brown stone front—French plate glass—billiard-room off the dining-room—statuary and paintings—shrubbery and two-acre grass plot—greenhouse—iron dog on the front stoop—gray horses—landau, and a coachman with a bug on his hat!" It was a far cry from Hannibal or Tahoe, and Twain was also capable of bitterly attacking such materialism. But in this indecisiveness he expressed quite accurately the American dilemma about progress.

For Mark Twain as for so many other actors in the drama of bonanza mining, success always remained just out of reach. But after several rounds of near-misses, Twain gave up on precious metals and turned to the pursuit of his real bonanza—writing. This quest took him first, in August 1862, to the *Territorial Enterprise* of Virginia City, Nevada, in the heart of the Comstock Lode. The printer-riverman-secretary-miner with the most successful pen name in literary history fitted perfectly into the staff of the newspaper. All the reporters relied on a brand of irreverent humor that Mark Twain soon made his forte. In Virginia City, where he wrote until 1864, and then in San Francisco, the California mining camps, and, briefly, the Hawaiian Islands, Twain perfected his art. He learned much in these years from contact with Artemus Ward, the dean of American humorists, and Bret Harte, an aspiring local-color writer. In 1865 Twain took a giant step toward literary recognition with the publication of "The Celebrated Jumping Frog of Calaveras County." Short, funny, and somewhat sadistic (the story concerned a live frog filled so completely with lead pellets that it could not jump), the tale was carefully constructed and used dialect adroitly. Widely circulated in the East, it put Twain's name before a national audience as a fresh, new talent.

By December 1866 Twain felt his literary apprenticeship was over. He was anxious to return to the "states" and claim the rewards of growing fame. An important factor in his decision to head East was the fact that the Civil War was over at last. Twain's side had lost, an outcome that had seemed improbable at the beginning. The South had had the advantage of being on the defensive. In order to win the Confederacy did not have to invade and defeat the North, but only protect its newly proclaimed sovereignty. On the Union fell the burden of aggression and the necessity of invasion. Like England in 1776, the North faced the task of forcing the rebels back into the fold. This involved fighting on the enemy's home ground and a dangerous extension of lines of communication and supply. (The English effort ultimately foundered on such rocks.) Moreover, the Southerners had the advantage of brilliant military leadership. Most of the officers in the United States Army on the eve of the Civil War were from the South, where traditions of militarism and gentlemanly bearing were closely entwined. Ironically, the federal military academy at West Point, New York, was the training ground for most Confederate officers, among them the talented Robert E. Lee. Also advantageous to the South was its dominance of world cotton production. Most observers initially felt this fact would bring textile producers like England and France hurrying to the aid of their principal supplier.

Beneath this optimistic surface, however, there were problems. "Cotton diplomacy" did not succeed in securing European assistance.

Not only did alternate sources of raw cotton appear, but England in particular was loath to support a society that condoned slavery. Without foreign aid, the South's advantage was gradually eliminated by the North's superiority in money, population, industry, and transportation. An agricultural society simply could not muster the munitions necessary to wage a prolonged war. But an important factor in the Union victory was the internal weakness of the Confederacy itself, which centered on the South's deification of the states rights philosophy, its abhorrence of centralized control. The problem existed on all levels. Confederate President Jefferson Davis, Vice-President Alexander Stephens, the Cabinet, and the Congress attacked each other with a vindictiveness unheard of in most nations, particularly in time of national emergency. This put a premium on the states, which was entirely consistent with Confederate political theory. But the various governors invariably put their own interests ahead of those of the Confederacy. Governor Joseph Brown of Georgia, for example, refused to allow Georgia troops to fight outside the state. Brown also dealt diplomatically with European nations as if Georgia were a sovereign entity. This was a case, it must be understood, of being too loyal, rather than disloyal, to Confederate ideals. The point is that they were poor ideals with which to prosecute a war.

In his brief tenure as second lieutenant of the Marion Rangers, Mark Twain had had ample confirmation that even at the lowest level no Southerner took orders easily. Everyone regarded himself as an officer. Twain's "The Private History of a Campaign That Failed" records the inevitable consequences. The ill-starred regiment's officers begged rather than ordered their soldiers to fight. A majority decision frequently obliged them to change their plans. Such methods of operation did not win many battles. Then, too, there was the question of slavery. For nonslaveholders like most of the Marion Rangers and most Confederate soldiers, the Civil War gradually came to make little sense. Why sacrifice to perpetuate an institution that benefited the planter elite? The war brought the social tension latent in the white South for decades boiling to the surface.

For Mark Twain full recognition of his "de-Southernizing," as a friend described it, came in Virginia City. His early writings for the *Territorial Enterprise* were intensely pro-South. Still associating himself with the old cavalier ideals, he was, in his own words, "the most conceited ass in the Territory." On one occasion he disparaged a dance staged in Carson City as a benefit for the Sanitary Commission (a kind of Red Cross organized by the Union), calling it a scheme to promote miscegenation. Several outraged readers of Twain's column immediately challenged him to duels. Ordinarily a Southern gentleman would have debated only the choice of weapons, but the challenges caused Twain to debate in his own mind the whole rationale of the southern way of life. Always frank, he concluded there wasn't much in it worth dueling about. The easiest way out of his predicament was to run away, and this he did, leaving Nevada for California in 1864. It was not that he was afraid; he simply was no longer committed to the Southern cause. This same lack of commitment among Twain's contemporaries back in the theater of war sapped the vigor of the Southern military effort. Without denying the valor of many Confederate troops in the heat of battle, it is plausible to think that the North did not win the war so much as the South lost it. Mark Twain would certainly have agreed with that analysis.

Whether in Nevada or California, the Civil War had an element of unreality for Twain. A fortnight away from even news dispatches, it was almost as if the battles took place in another country. The First Battle of Bull Run in Virginia, the encounter that shocked Americans into awareness that the war was real, took place in July 1861 when Twain was riding a stagecoach west. In April the following year 23,000 Americans lost their lives in the two-day Battle of Shiloh in Tennessee. It was the most deadly military engagement to that time in North America, but Twain's feverish pursuit of silver left him little time even to notice the event. In September 1862 over 20,000 men died in a single day of fighting along Antietam Creek in western Maryland. Technically Antietam was a draw, but in effect the encounter broke the back of Lee's northern advance and marked a decisive turning point in the general conflict. Twain, meanwhile, was beginning his career with the *Territorial Enterprise*. At Gettysburg, Pennsylvania, in July 1863 a do-or-die Confederate effort resulted in an incredible total loss of 50,000 men, more than a quarter of those participating. For Twain, however, it was a time to write witty newspaper essays such as "All About the Fashions" and "How to Cure a Cold." The war, obviously, was lightly regarded and easily dismissed by the one-time second lieutenant.

When Mark Twain returned to the East early in 1867, he sensed at once that the western sojourn which had spared him a confrontation with the full meaning of the Civil War made him an exception. The bulk of his countrymen knew that the war set them apart from earlier generations. A new mood prevailed. People had been forced to understand that for all America's pretensions to being a model society, a new Eden, the nation was not to be exempt from tragedy and suffering. The optimistic, innocent expectations of progress, even of perfection, that characterized the prewar decades seemed a mockery after four bloody years. Also mocked in the war-caused deaths of 600,000 Americans was the vaunted democratic process. Where was substance for the belief that majority rule was the key to the millennium? The war and the shocking assassination of Abraham Lincoln in its aftermath (April 15, 1865) left men with little choice but to accept the fact that force superseded reason and morality as a prime mover in human affairs. Perhaps, as the English biologist Charles Darwin argued in his 1859 *Origin of Species,* life on earth was best understood in terms of a struggle for existence in which only the fittest survived. Perhaps man was merely a pawn in the hands of forces beyond his control and even beyond his comprehension. Some said the nation grew up in the Civil War years; others felt it began to die. But no one disputed that it became sadder, wiser, and less certain about the future.

Twain could read the new mood in the faces he encountered after his return from California. He also found it in the awkward silence that followed his inquiry about old friends along the Mississippi. "The eight years in America from 1860 to 1868," Twain concluded, "uprooted institutions that were centuries old, changed the politics of a people, transformed the social life of half the country, and wrought so profoundly upon the entire national character that the influence cannot be measured short of two or three generations."

Twain's shock at discovering the Civil War after his lark on the frontier was certainly a factor in his acceptance of an opportunity to leave America once again—this time on one of the first organized pleasure cruises in maritime history. The *Quaker City* left New York June 8, 1867, for the Mediterranean. Twain sailed as a correspondent for the San Francisco *Alta California,* and his reaction to the Old World was thoroughly western. Confident in himself and in his country, Twain scoffed irreverently at the cultural treasures of Europe. Gone from his attitude was the embarrassed provincialism that caused earlier generations of Americans to disparage their native culture and slavishly imitate European social and esthetic taste. Poking fun at the cult of Michelangelo he encountered in Italy, Twain remarked that "the Creator made Italy from designs by Michelangelo." And his impressions on seeing the Czar of Russia were straight from the American frontier; this great personage was merely a man, and "if I chose I could knock him down."

Twain's patriotism is on display constantly in *Innocents Abroad*, the book that appeared in 1869 and described his tour. On one occasion in the Straits of Gibraltar, the *Quaker City* crossed the path of a strange sailing vessel. "She was one towering mass of bellying sail," Twain exulted, but when the ship displayed the American flag, his excitement knew no bounds. "She was beautiful before—she was radiant now." Then Twain philosophized on the meaning of the flag in a foreign locale: "to see it is to see a vision of home itself and its idols, and feel a thrill that would stir a very river of sluggish blood."

As Mark Twain gradually discovered after his return to New York in November 1867, it was easier to love America at a distance than up close. An era Twain later named "the Gilded Age" was already in full swing. As the Missourian began to fathom its ends and means, his disenchantment increased sharply. The vantage point for his initial investigations could not have been better. Before the *Quaker City* landed, Twain accepted a position as private secretary to Senator William M. Stewart of Nevada in Washington. The job was a complete sinecure and allowed Twain plenty of time to explore the quality of national politics and politicians. His notebooks recorded his findings. "Whiskey is taken into the committee rooms in demijohns," Twain reported, "and carried out in demagogues." Government, he discovered, was a business. Everyone was out to enrich himself, and corruption was the standard means. The openness with which bribery, graft, and influence peddling occurred shocked Twain. There seemed no checks on immorality. As Senator Roscoe Conkling of New York put it, "nothing counts except to win." And winning was defined in strictly material terms. Watching the near-impeachment of President Andrew Johnson play its ludicrous course, Twain lost respect for the whole political process. When he wrote "there are some pitiful intellects in this Congress," he likely understated his feelings.

Twain left Washington in disgust in 1868 to pursue a literary life, but the spoilsmen were just warming up. Under Ulysses S. Grant, who was elected President in 1868 and again in 1872, corrupt government flourished. The Civil War hero was not personally involved, but he was one of the most unqualified men ever to hold the office. Totally lacking in judgment in civilian situations, he let his administration become the tool of smarter but less principled men. For Twain, who met Grant early in 1868 and greatly admired him as a soldier, it was particularly painful to see the way the President allowed unscrupulous financial manipulators like Jim Fisk and Jay Gould to enjoy the protection of his friendship. Following close on the heels of Fisk's and Gould's attempts to corner the gold and the stock market in 1869 were scandals involving railroad contractors, whiskey distillers, and Indian traders. The threads of guilt in these cases ran through the House and Senate to the Cabinet and even as far as the Vice-Presidency. Still, in Twain's mind, Grant was untouchable, a rock of integrity in a sea of spoils. Henry Adams, who also observed Washington in the late 1860s, was not as charitable. The succession of Presidents from his great-grandfather to Grant, he thought, was evidence enough to destroy Darwin's argument for evolution. Grant, in Adam's opinion, was a Stone-Age President.

Although the Washington scandals were disturbing, the greatest moral explosion of the postwar decade for Mark Twain and many contemporaries involved a religious rather than a political figure. Henry Ward Beecher was the foremost clergyman of his time. Before the Civil War he had led a host of reform crusades, most prominently that of antislavery. In fact, the guns shipped to Kansas in the 1850s to defend free soil principles were popularly known as "Beecher's Bibles." The minister's sister was none other than the author of *Uncle Tom's Cabin*, Harriet Beecher Stowe. Striking in appearance and a master of eloquent expression, Beecher seemed to be the embodiment of morality and idealism. His writings, sermons, and lectures inspired millions of Americans with confidence that man could transcend base urges and, in the words of Ralph Waldo Emerson, hitch his wagon to a star.

Mark Twain had known and admired Henry Ward Beecher since

Travel in Mark Twain's day could be just as dangerous as on today's freeways. The cause of this 1856 accident was probably a front wheel catching on the logs of the bridge and snapping off. Twain went to Nevada in 1861 in a larger coach pulled by sixteen horses.

In 1859 Henry Comstock (left) staked the first claim on one of the world's most concentrated deposits of gold and silver ore. It soon acquired the name Comstock Lode. At this time wild game (foreground) was still plentiful, but by 1861, when Twain arrived, miners were obliged to pay grossly inflated prices for provisions.

Virginia City, perched on the sides of a mountain in western Nevada, was Mark Twain's home from 1862 to 1864. The town literally rested on some of the world's richest gold and silver deposits.

On the afternoon of February 15, 1898, one of the United States mightiest battleships, the Maine, floated in the harbor of Havana, Cuba. The following morning it looked like this. An explosion that was never fully explained had sunk the ship and claimed 260 lives. Public furor, goaded by hysterial press coverage, led directly to war with Spain.

1867, when the celebrated clergyman had played a leading role in organizing the *Quaker City* tour. At the last minute Beecher found it impossible to join the cruise, but many members of his congregation did, and at its conclusion he entertained Twain at a dinner party. A brother of Henry Ward Beecher married Twain to Olivia Langdon early in 1870. When the couple settled in the fashionable Nook Farm area near Hartford, Connecticut, they became neighbors and friends of still more Beechers. Then the bomb dropped. In 1871 stories began to circulate in New York linking the Reverend Beecher to Mrs. Elizabeth Tilton in an adulterous relationship. Twain was outraged at what he considered a cruel slander of the magnificent Beecher. But the stories continued and, through the efforts of the militant feminist Victoria Woodhull, even appeared in print.

Twain denounced them. Beecher was vitally important to him and to his time as a bastion of order and decency, an assurance that the nation had not lost its moral compass in a wilderness of materialism. Gradually, however, Twain's eyes were forced open. Beecher's own sister declared that he was guilty of adultery. And Mrs. Tilton, who with her husband was a member of Beecher's congregation, quietly admitted being a party to the illicit relationship. Beecher even wrote a letter of apology to Mr. Tilton. Unsatisfied, Tilton in 1874 brought an alienation of affections suit against Beecher. The subsequent trial made headlines throughout the nation. Twain was, in the words of a friend, "tremendoulsy worked up" by the Beecher-Tilton affair and even attended a few of the court sessions. The ultimate inability or unwillingness of the jury to pin blame on Beecher was not really a relief. The whole business left a bad taste in Twain's mouth. Had considerations of right and wrong become so obscured or irrelevant that even the nation's foremost religious leader could ignore them? Was force—in this case, lust—more powerful than reason and morality? For Twain, the Beecher-Tilton affair, like the explosion of the *Pennsylvania* and the Civil War, was a shock that cast shadows of doubt over America's future. Antebellum expectations, at any rate, were made to appear innocent, naive, and unfounded.

Early in 1873 Mark Twain struck back at what he called the "moral ulcers" of his age with the best weapon he could muster—a book. The idea for *The Gilded Age* began at a dinner party at which Twain and his guest Charles Dudley Warner accepted a challenge from their wives to write a better novel than the current crop of best-sellers. The coauthors also intended to write a truer novel. The resulting manuscript, completed in three months of intense work, was a searing indictment of the social, economic, and political fabric of American life following the Civil War. Many of its characters and incidents came directly from the lives of Warner and Twain. There were the vote-buying congressman, the pretentious but hollow society ladies, the attractive younger ladies who parlayed their sexual favors into wealth and prominence, and a succession of various confidence men, frauds, and crooks. The protagonist of *The Gilded Age*, Harry Brierly, is a young idealist with plans for internal improvements in a middle western town strongly reminiscent of Twain's native Florida, Missouri. In the course of the novel Brierly learns the price of obtaining an appropriation from Congress. A series of bribes distributed to secure the grant finally leaves no funds to be used for the intended purposes. When he discovers this in the plush office of the bogus Columbia River Slackwater Navigation Company, Brierly's disillusionment and disgust are intense.

While satire like *The Gilded Age* was one outlet for Twain's feelings about the 1870s, the resurrection of earlier and allegedly better times was another. In the years after the Civil War, Twain found his thoughts straying back more and more to antebellum Hannibal and his boyhood on the river. In part this was a form of escape, just as the trip to Nevada had been. Old times on the Mississippi was a pleasant subject to contemplate compared with the "moral ulcers" of postbellum America. Moreover, in Twain's hands, nostalgia produced good literature. *The Adventures of Tom Sawyer*, which appeared in 1876, was the result of happy summer hours recollecting happy summer hours thirty years before. The book was, in large part, pure evocative writing, a thinly disguised autobiography. But just beneath the surface Twain snaps and snarls at the business-minded society in which he lived. *Tom Sawyer* is a paean to irresponsibility. The Franklinesque virtues of discipline, hard work, and material success are deliberately juxtaposed with the happy idleness and nonsense of boyhood on the river. At the root of this juxtaposition are disturbing questions about traditional American definitions of prosperity and progress.

Twain continued his oblique attack on the established national creed in a series of clever essays. In "Advice to Youth" he appeared to agree with Franklin in advising aspiring boys to get up with the birds, provided the birds slept until half-past nine. In "Autobiography of a Damned Fool" Twain parodies Franklin's famous autobiography by showing how the recommended cold swim every morning resulted in stolen clothing and death by exposure. Twain made his point explicit in two essays written about 1875. "The Story of the Bad Little Boy" and "The Story of the Good Little Boy" show that in terms of success, at least, wrong is right. The essays raised questions about ethical criteria as well as about success, and they presaged Huckleberry Finn's "wrong" decision with regard to his black rafting companion, Jim.[1] But at the same time Twain was challenging the validity of American values, most of his countrymen were cheering them. Horatio Alger's 119 books, beginning in 1868 with *Ragged Dick*, almost all dwelt on the theme of rising from rags to riches by dint of hard work, ability, and good luck. Expressing the heart of the American dream, Alger's books sold by the millions. Indeed, by the end of the century he was the only American writer with the same level of public recognition as Mark Twain.

While Twain might question Alger's easy acceptance of Franklinesque virtues, he could not deny that it was the Benjamin Franklins, not the Tom Sawyers, who dominated the nation in the Gilded Age. Awakened in the 1830s by the Jacksonian policy of liberating capitalism, the national economy survived the depressions that dashed John Clemens's hopes and, after 1843, entered a period of extraordinary expansion. The Civil War certainly slowed the economic growth rate, but the war also created opportunities. Moreover, Union victory placed the federal government in the hands of those who believed that the business of America was business. Industrial expansion became a major objective of wartime and postwar politics. With the South eliminated as a factor in national decision-making, there were few obstacles on the way to wealth.

The results of an accelerating economy boggled the mind of a small-town boy like Mark Twain. Between 1860 and 1900 the United States grew from a second-rate industrial power to the world's leader. In fact, the value of American manufactured goods almost equaled the total production of the three former leaders combined. New England

[1] See pages 32–34.

alone produced more goods per capita than any country in the world. The most intense economic surge occurred between 1877 and 1893, when a depression temporarily checked growth. In these sixteen years the national output of copper increased 7 times, crude oil 4 times, and manufacturing as a whole $2\frac{1}{2}$ times. The electric power industry, which did not even exist in 1877, was a 23-million-dollar business by 1893. By that date the United States had no equal in the timber, steel, oil, meatpacking, coal, iron, and telephone industries. American locomotives and American pianos were the best in the world.

The men who made this industrial bonanza possible were systems builders. They possessed the ability and accumulated the resources to order and integrate huge sectors of the American economy. Pragmatic, efficient, and extremely ambitious, they became the winners in the intense, wide-open competition that characterized the heyday of American capitalism. Consider Andrew Carnegie, a man Mark Twain knew and always regarded as the epitome of the self-made captain of industry. "Saint Andrew," Twain called the steel king and, naturally, received the appellation "Saint Mark" in return. Carnegie, like Twain, was born in 1835 in a small village, but the country was Scotland. When he was thirteen Carnegie came to America, settled with his impoverished parents in Pennsylvania, and began work as a bobbin boy in a cotton factory at a salary of $1.20 a *week*. Instead of being discouraged, Carnegie was thrilled at the prospect of being on the capitalistic ladder. In the next ten years he climbed it with astonishing speed. First railroads, then bridges, and finally steel occupied his attention. The huge Homestead steel plant on the Monongahela River near Pittsburgh, Pennsylvania, was started in 1872. By the end of the century the Carnegie Steel Company had emerged the victor in a struggle for existence that initially involved hundreds of competitors. In the course of the battle Carnegie became one of the richest men in America. In 1900 the one-time bobbin boy enjoyed an *income* of $25 million. The following year Carnegie sold his interests to the financier J. P. Morgan, the architect of an even larger conglomerate called United States Steel. The purchase price of the Carnegie Steel Company was nearly half a billion dollars.

Controversial figures in their own time, the verdict is still not in on Andrew Carnegie and his colleagues in industrial empire-building. Mark Twain, for example, could not suppress a sense of awe in the presence of Carnegie and his accomplishments. In an acquisitive age, Carnegie was a god. But Twain could also turn bitterly against acquisition. Once, according to Twain, Americans "desired money"; now they "fall down and worship it." The new gospel, he added, was: "get money. Get it quickly. Get it in abundance. Get it in prodigious abundance. Get it dishonestly if you can, honestly if you must." One of the problems Twain and his contemporaries encountered in evaluating industrialization as personified by a man like Carnegie was that the process involved new techniques of organization that seemed wrong only because they were strange. Early in his rise to prominence, for example, Carnegie discarded the old idea of small-unit competition— the free-for-all that characterized the Jacksonian economic ideal. The need for ordering giant, nationwide industries, Carnegie realized, simply could not be met by small companies. Their size did not permit the economies of scale that were the key to large-scale production. Nor could the small units possibly command sufficient capital to undertake such tasks as building a transcontinental railroad or moving a mountain of iron ore from northern Minnesota to Pittsburgh's refineries.

The new economic units Carnegie envisioned and developed were built around the principles of either vertical or horizontal ordering. In the former, the firm controlled all the steps in producing and marketing its product. Thus the Carnegie Steel Company did everything from mining the ore to producing finished steel. John D. Rockefeller's Standard Oil Company owned not only the wells, but the ships, refineries, distributorships, and even the barrel manufacturing companies necessary to market oil products. Horizontal ordering, on the other hand, meant controlling all the production at a particular stage in the industrial process—all barrel manufacturing in the nation, for instance. Two techniques existed. The *pool* preserved scattered ownership, but instituted corporate management; the *trust* (pioneered by Standard Oil in 1879) actually absorbed the participating units in a supercompany. Both these arrangements, as well as the holding companies that used stock control to accomplish their ends, worked to limit competition in the interest of efficiency and profits.

Many in Mark Twain's generation suspected the new economic combinations of foul play. After 1882, when a vocal critic of Standard Oil named Henry Demarest Lloyd coined it, the label "robber barons" was frequently attached to men like Carnegie, Rockefeller, and Cornelius Vanderbilt. These men undeniably mowed down competitors with ruthless precision, but they also made possible remarkable industrial progress from which the nation as a whole benefited. "Did Vanderbilt keep any of you down," Edward Atkinson asked a group of disgruntled citizens in 1886, "by saving you $2.75 on a barrel of flour, while he was making 14 cents?" Implicit in the statement was the idea that the large capitalists' achievement of greater efficiency should be a cause for national celebration. The defenders of the so-called industrial statesmen also pointed out that only the old, inefficient forms of competition had died. Newer and higher forms still held capitalism together. The market system still worked to punish errors in production and pricing. And competition still existed between *ways* of doing the same thing. The struggle between oil and electricity as a source of energy is a case in point. Mark Twain would learn to his sorrow that real competition also existed between alternative approaches to the mechanization of typesetting in the printing industry. The man who built a better mousetrap still had an advantage.

Although on occasion Twain could be highly critical of the modernization of America by machines and millionaires, a complete understanding of the man as well as his time demands recognition of a concurrent zeal for money and mechanization. In a period of rapid change such as the late nineteenth century it was natural to find aspirations split between the future and the past. Twain demonstrated such ambivalence when he alternated between awe at Lake Tahoe's wild beauty and delight at the prospect of striking it rich on the Comstock Lode. After his entrance into the national literary limelight in the late 1860s, Twain continued shifting back and forth. While idealizing Tom Sawyer's barefoot days on the Mississippi, he maintained and delighted in a grandiose standard of living. Twain's expenditures for the single year 1881 amounted to more than $100,000. The money came from his writing and from lecturing, as well as from his wife's substantial estate. But Twain remained unsatisfied, and his pursuit of success led him into a series of unfortunate investments. Indeed, Twain was so fascinated with the new technology that he became known as an easy mark for inventors interested in raising capital. In the early 1880s he poured thousands of dollars into a steam generator, a steam pulley, a new kind of watch, a device for marine telegraphy, and a new engraving process. There were lesser projects too, such as a hinged pants button, a self-pasting scrapbook, and a mechanical organ.

But Twain's most revealing and most disastrous speculation began innocuously enough when a Hartford jeweler cornered him in his billiard room and peddled $2000 worth of stock in a typesetting machine invented by James W. Paige. Twain paid the money sight unseen. A former printer, he knew the value of a device that could perform the most laborious task in the business. On seeing the type-setter in action, he immediately subscribed an additional $3000. The machine seemed almost human to Twain, a triumph of applied tech-nology. Of Paige he wrote: "he is the Shakespeare of mechanical invention. In all the ages he has no peer." Paige came to Twain for more money, and the writer obliged first with $30,000, then $80,000, and ultimately a total of almost $200,000. Of course Twain expected to realize millions. He envisaged himself a Carnegie of typesetting, a new star in the national industrial constellation. But as with the Nevada mines, success always remained just beyond his grasp. Paige was a perfectionist who tended to overrefine his inventions beyond the point of practicality. While he tinkered and spent Twain's money, simpler devices like the linotype, which Twain spurned when offered an inter-est, captured the market. Finally, in 1894 the Paige machine was pronounced a failure and abandoned. Twain never realized a penny on his investments; in fact, the machine dragged him into an ignominious bankruptcy that filled his later years with bitterness. Ruefully, he re-called a conversation with Carnegie in 1893. Twain tried to interest the multimillionaire in the Paige typesetter, citing the old maxim about not putting all one's eggs in the same basket. Carnegie regarded him for a moment with his eyes half-closed; then he offered his own maxim: "put all your eggs in one basket—and watch that basket."

In the 1880s, while the Paige debacle was in the making, Mark Twain wrote two of his most important books. Each contained an unfavorable commentary on progress and a critical assessment of modern America. Twain began *The Adventures of Huckleberry Finn* as a sequel to *The Adventures of Tom Sawyer*. When he started it in 1876, the pages flowed easily from his pen as they usually did when he wrote about his happy boyhood. Brilliantly employing the vernacular style of an untutored boy, Twain described Huck's relationship to St. Petersburg (Hannibal) and introduced him to the runaway slave Jim.

In the next block of chapters Huck and Jim begin drifting down the Mississippi. "You feel mighty free and easy and comfortable on a raft," Huck declares, and the picture Twain describes is indeed idyllic. But then, in Chapter 16, the raft drifts by the mouth of the Ohio River in a fog. The Ohio was to have been Jim's escape route to the North and freedom, but now the Mississippi was carrying him further and further into the heart of the South. At this point in the narrative Huck and Mark Twain faced a dilemma. Jim was a fugitive from justice; Huck, in effect, was stealing him. To continue to protect him on the raft demanded that Huck reject society and its institutions. As a white boy Huck felt the tug of duty, but as an individual he also felt strong affection for Jim, a surrogate father. What should he do? Twain's dilemma was somewhat larger. To have Huck support society and betray Jim involved a judgment on the merits of that society which Twain was not prepared to make. He therefore stopped writing. Before he could make Huck's decision, he had to make his own.

For six years Twain avoided the *Huckleberry Finn* manuscript except for the addition of a few chapters that did not bear on he dominant question of what to do about Jim. He even considered burning the entire manuscript. He continued, however, to gather impressions about his society pertinent to his impending judgment. Then, in 1882, he returned to the river, and took a steamboat over the route he used to pilot. The changes astonished and depressed him. Civilization had caught up to the Mississippi. Fields had replaced the forest Twain knew in his youth; factories dotted the river banks; towns that barely existed in Twain's day now boasted 50,000 people. And money dominated. Even steamboating had deteriorated from a romantic adventure to a crass business. "The world I knew in its blossoming youth," Twain wrote in his account of the 1882 trip, "is old and bowed and melancholy . . . the fire is gone out of its eyes. . . . In Hannibal the steamboatman is no longer a god." Part of the reason for Twain's disappointing reunion with the river was the fact that by 1882 he was no longer young. But neither was his country. Both had passed through a brothers' war and into an age of industrialization. The society he found, at any rate, seemed a far cry from that which he remembered and wrote about in the first half of *Huckleberry Finn*. Instead of the peacefulness and innate decency he associated with the earlier time, he found petty materialism, depravity, and callous in-humanity.

Returning to his studio in Hartford, Twain was ready to make his judgment and complete his novel. The last half of *Huckleberry Finn* is a series of exposures of a squalid civilization. Huck and Jim witness families engaged in bloody, pointless feuds; they see townsmen cheer-ing as a drunk dies in the street; they watch as confidence men brazenly dupe a public which itself is gullible, cowardly, and hypocritical. Huck's verdict is also Twain's: "it was enough to make a body ashamed of the human race . . . I never seen anything so disgusting." Now it was easy to decide what to do about Jim. Huck would not betray him; America wasn't worthy of that decision. In a further ges-ture of rebellion, Huck heads west to the territories just as Twain had done in 1861. But for Twain in 1884, the year of *Huckleberry Finn's* publication, there was little territory left as an escape avenue. Con-siderations of debt and family further restricted him. Obliged, as a consequence, to remain and further contemplate the maladies of American civilization, Twain became increasingly bitter in his social criticism.

In *A Connecticut Yankee in King Arthur's Court*, published in 1889, Twain continued his scrutiny of modern America. When he wrote this novel he considered it his literary farewell. Twain opens the tale by transporting a nineteenth-century Yankee from Connecticut, Hank Morgan, back to the sixth-century England of King Arthur. With Yankee ingenuity, Hank proceeds to transform Arthurian England (a place strikingly similar to antebellum Hannibal) into a replica of America in the 1880s, complete with democracy, universal education, and a sophisticated technology. For a while the book con-ceals its purpose; Twain seems proud of the shining machines and towering edifices that Hank's leadership makes possible. Perhaps progress is beneficent, mankind innately good. But there are hints of a darker perspective. "There are times," Hank admits, "when one would like to hang the whole human race and finish the farce." Yet Hank himself is a large part of the problem. His technological knowhow not only makes schools, mines, factories, and labor-saving devices, but also revolvers, rifles, cannons, and huge bombs. Moreover, Hank's presence splits King Arthur's court into warring factions: the Yankees versus the knights. In the ensuing civil war the new order wins, slavery is abolished, and, Hank feels, society is firmly directed toward progress and prosperity.

Ended at this juncture, *A Connecticut Yankee in King Arthur's Court* might have taken its place among optimistic utopian novels of the time such as Edward Bellamy's *Looking Backward: 2000–1887*. Bellamy confidently predicted an America lifted to unprecedented heights by applied technology. His message captured the enthusiasm of millions of worried Americans. But Mark Twain was writing primarily for himself, and at the very time he wrote his book he was beginning to appreciate how misplaced was his confidence in James Paige (a technological genius comparable to Hank Morgan). So Twain prepared to give his own interpretation of the pursuit of progress. A new war breaks out in Arthurian England. Swarms of human "sheep" attack Hank and his elite corps of fifty-two boys armed with the latest weapons, including dynamite, Gatling guns, and electric fences. Their success in repelling the attack proves ironic. The stench from 25,000 rotting corpses pollutes Hank's stronghold and kills all the victors. Technology has turned against its creators; science is out of control; man's essential baseness has prevailed. In Mark Twain's opinion this was the way the world would end, and nineteenth-century America was on the right track, going full speed ahead.

Twain's involvement in national politics after the Civil War offers another way of tracing his growing disillusion and pessimism. In 1868 and again in 1872 Twain supported Ulysses S. Grant in his successful bids for the Presidency under the Republican banner. He knew Grant personally (later his publishing company produced Grant's memoirs), and he felt the Union hero would be good insurance against the possibility of the South rising again. On the other hand, Twain found much to like in the candidate of the Liberal Republicans and Democrats, *New York Tribune* editor Horace Greeley. Greeley's emphasis on reform, particularly his preference for civil service over patronage as a means of political appointment, appealed to Twain. But although Grant's scandal-marred administrations were hard to swallow, the cult of the General was strong. In 1876, however, Twain was released from his commitment to Grant and free to follow his inclinations to liberalism. This meant an aversion to political bosses, probusiness politics, and mob-supported demagogues.

The election of 1876 pitted Democrat Samuel J. Tilden against

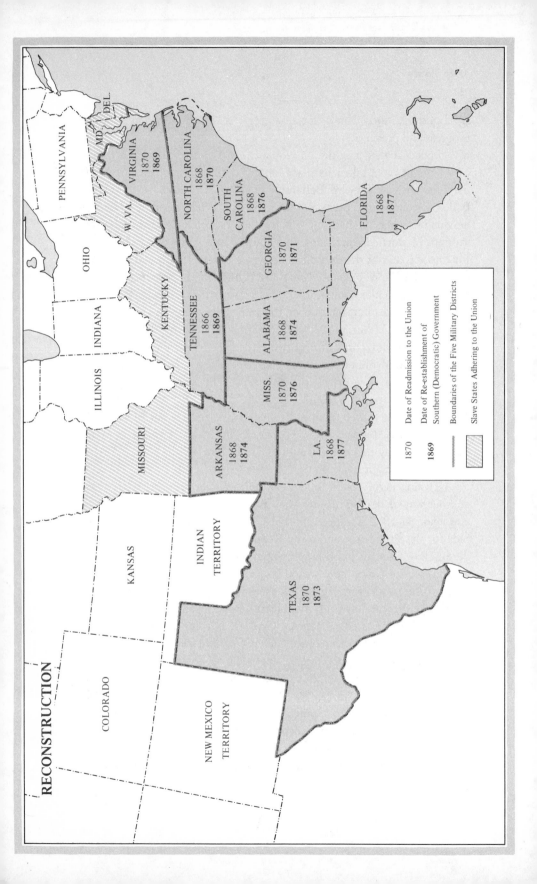

RECONSTRUCTION

PENNSYLVANIA

MD.

DEL.

VIRGINIA
1870
1869

W. VA.

OHIO

NORTH CAROLINA
1868
1870

SOUTH
CAROLINA
1868
1876

FLORIDA
1868
1877

GEORGIA
1870
1871

KENTUCKY

TENNESSEE
1866
1869

ALABAMA
1868
1874

INDIANA

ILLINOIS

MISS.
1870
1876

MISSOURI

ARKANSAS
1868
1874

LA.
1868
1877

INDIAN
TERRITORY

KANSAS

TEXAS
1870
1873

COLORADO

NEW MEXICO
TERRITORY

1870	Date of Readmission to the Union
1869	Date of Re-establishment of Southern (Democratic) Government
	Boundaries of the Five Military Districts
	Slave States Adhering to the Union

Republican Rutherford B. Hayes. As governor of New York Tilden had won Twain's admiration by smashing the infamous Tweed Ring of corrupt party hacks. On the financial front, Tilden was a "hard money" man, opposed to the expansion of currency (and consequent inflation) that the issuance of "soft" or paper money encouraged. Hayes, the Republican, was a comparatively unknown Ohio governor, but he enjoyed a reputation for clean politics, and the famous novelist threw his considerable weight behind the Republican ticket.

In the election itself, one of the most extraordinary in American political history, Tilden, in the opinion of most observers then and now, was elected—but Hayes went to the White House. This curious phenomenon came about as the result of Republican tampering with 20 disputed votes in the electoral college. Nineteen of these were from Southern states, where military Reconstruction still ensured Republican control. Accusing the Democrats of intimidating black voters at the polls, Republican negotiators awarded all the votes and the election to Hayes. But the Democratic South exacted its price for allowing "His Fraudulency" to win. By the unwritten Compromise of 1877 Reconstruction ended, and control of the South returned to white Southern Democrats.

Mark Twain's enthusiasm for Hayes did not last long. The Republican party, he discovered, stubbornly resisted permanent reform. Moreover, the Hayes Administration did little about the strikes and unemployment that were byproducts of industrialization. The human misery occasioned by this process troubled Twain deeply. To the consternation of his wealthy, conservative friends, he began openly sympathizing with the more militant labor organizations such as the Knights of Labor and the Greenback Labor party. Twain also worried about the continuing influence in Republican circles of James G. Blaine, "the filthy Blaine" Twain called him, and Roscoe Conkling. Yet in the election of 1880 Twain supported Republican James G. Garfield over Winfield S. Hancock, the Democrat. His decision reflected less admiration for Garfield and more fear that a now solidly Democratic South might revive the old sectional partisanship. Twain joined Republican orators whose evocation of Civil War atrocities to unify the North behind their party was known as "waving the bloody shirt." By stooping so low and even trotting out General Grant for a speaking tour in which Mark Twain also participated, Republican

THE ELECTION OF 1876

MAINE 7

VT. 5 | N. H. 5

MASS. 13
R. I. 4
CONN. 6
N. J. 9
DEL. 3
MD. 8

N. Y. 35

PA. 29

W. VA. 5

VA. 11

N. C. 10

S. C. 7

FLA. 4

OHIO 22

KY. 12

TENN. 12

GA. 11

ALA. 10

MICH. 11

IND. 15

ILL. 21

MISS. 8

MO. 15

ARK. 6

LA. 8

WIS. 10

IOWA 11

MINN. 5

NEBR. 3

KANS. 5

TEXAS 8

COLO. 3

UNORGANIZED

TERRITORY

OREG. 2

NEV. 3

CALIF. 6

1

	ELECTORAL	POPULAR (in thousands)
Hayes (Rep.)	165	4,037
Disputed*	20*	
Tilden (Dem.)	184	4,284

*Assigned to Hayes by Congressional commission.

leaders revealed their anxiety. In truth their long hold on the Presidency was nearing its end. Garfield, however, squeezed by Hancock, and the Republicans had four more years in which to prove themselves.

The beginning of the Garfield Administration was not auspicious from Twain's point of view. To his dismay, James G. Blaine became secretary of state. Then Garfield was assassinated on July 2, 1881, and succeeded by Vice-President Chester A. Arthur, a former colleague of Conkling in the domination of New York politics. But there were some encouraging signs. In 1881 the federal government succeeded in breaking Conkling's hold in New York and forcing his resignation from the Senate. Two years later the Pendleton Act created a bipartisan Civil Service Commission and instituted competitive exams for many government jobs. The act initially affected only one-tenth of the total federal work force, but it marked a watershed in the philosophy of government service.

The election of 1884 threw Mark Twain into a quandary, for the Republican nominee was his old nemesis Blaine. Deeply troubled, Twain and his fellow Connecticut intellectuals debated the question of party loyalty. Many bowed to the judgment of the smoke-filled rooms, but Twain remained true to his conscience. Throughout the fall of 1884 he tried to persuade Republicans to rise above orthodoxy and support the Democrat, Grover Cleveland. In this cause, which acquired the label "Mugwump," Twain joined such well-known reformers as George William Curtis, E. L. Godkin, Carl Schurz, and Charles Francis Adams.

The Blaine-Cleveland campaign was one of the bitterest ever seen in the United States, with the political smear reaching a new level of sophistication. Blaine's transgressions over the past decade received a full airing, and the Republicans countered with charges that the Democrats were the party of "Rum, Romanism, and Rebellion," a ploy that backfired in many quarters of American society. But the major issue in the campaign involved the Republican charge that Cleveland had fathered an illegitimate child. When the Democratic nominee humbly acknowledged that as a young bachelor he and a consenting widow had indeed had an offspring but added that he had cared for the mother and child ever since, public sympathy swung to his side.

Mark Twain was disgusted at the self-righteousness of Cleveland's detractors. They knew full well, Twain pointed out, "what the bachelor's other alternative was and . . . seem to prefer that to the widow." Then, in a statement suggestive of his growing misanthropy, Twain philosophized: *"isn't* human nature the most consummate sham and lie that was ever invented? Isn't man a creature to be ashamed of in pretty much all his aspects? Is he really fit for anything but to be stood up on a street corner as a convenience for dogs?"

Having campaigned hard for Cleveland, Twain watched his ensuing administration with great interest. Increasingly bitter at the hold of big business on American life, he applauded the passage in 1887 of the Interstate Commerce Act, which prohibited unreasonable, secret, and discriminatory railroad rates and practices. The act also created the Interstate Commerce Commission, the first federal agency authorized to regulate American private enterprise. But intention was one matter, practice quite another. As Twain watched in disgust, America's railroad magnates, aided by a sympathetic Supreme Court and a lukewarm President, systematically evaded the spirit and the letter of the Interstate Commerce Act.

A similar fate befell the Sherman Antitrust Act, passed in 1890 under President Benjamin Harrison, a Republican who spoiled Cleveland's bid for reelection. The Sherman Act grew out of the fear that trusts and other business conglomerates were conspiring to restrict competition and fleece the public. But once again a conservative judiciary was unwilling to apply what few teeth the act possessed. In fact, in a classic distortion of purpose, the antitrust legislation was turned against the emerging labor unions as a consequence of the Supreme Court decision in *United States* v. *Debs* (1894). Like the Interstate Commerce Act, the Sherman Act proved effective mainly as a deterrent to really meaningful reform.

From Mark Twain's perspective, the United States in the 1890s was a nation run by and for a wealthy, conservative elite. Benjamin Harrison's administration regularly favored the rich and powerful at the expense of farmers, laborers, small businessmen, and intellectuals like Twain. Monetary policy was a case in point. The Sherman Silver Purchase Act of 1890 did little to improve on the Bland-Allison Act passed twelve years previously. Neither really increased the amount of circulating currency or promoted inflation as critics of business had hoped. But when it came to the tariff, Congress and the President were quick to pass the highly protectionist (probusiness) McKinley Tariff of 1890.

Grover Cleveland was a personal friend of Mark Twain and entertained him frequently in the White House during his first administration. When Cleveland was elected to another term in 1892, Twain was pleased. He could not help noticing, however, that Cleveland's political and economic philosophy was strongly conservative and really differed little from that of the Republicans. Both camps were friendly to propertied interests and largely deaf to the demands of working people in the nation's farms and factories. Supporting Cleveland in this stance was a complex body of ideas about the nature of success in American history. In the first place, it was defined almost exclusively in material terms. The rich were generally conceded to be the top rung in American society. Second, success was believed possible for anyone possessing the requisite talent and determination. As Horatio Alger and Andrew Carnegie demonstrated in their separate ways, humble origin was not a handicap. This meant, in theory, that anyone could climb the magic ladder. But Mark Twain knew the facts. Even the most talented and energetic were often suppressed by the system. Yet insofar as Twain's contemporaries *believed* in the success myth, they proved willing to accept the prevailing social and economic framework. Rather than reform or abolish the free enterprise system, they hoped to become its beneficiary by trying a little harder. The elegant mansion of a Vanderbilt or a Morgan was an object of envy and aspiration rather than a hated symbol of injustice and oppression. The bona fide rags-to-riches success of a few, like Franklin or Carnegie, proved a narcotic for millions.

The rich in Mark Twain's America resisted reform by parading the philosophy of Social Darwinism and its conception of progress as something that stemmed from competition in which the unfit were weeded from the fit. A corollary of this was the idea that the government and the courts should let free enterprise alone. Only in this way could the scythe of competition do its beneficial work. To aid the unfit, according to this perspective, was to impede evolution—to sustain dinosaurs and other losers in the natural selection sweepstakes. But the major bulwark of the propertied elite was the old Protestant idea that worldly success was both a sign of God's favor and a way of glorifying God. It followed that the rich man could claim to be the beneficiary of divine selection too. As John D. Rockefeller said, "the good Lord gave me my money." Twain's old acquaintance Henry Ward Beecher added, "God has intended the great to be great and the little to be little." But the Reverend William Lawrence put it best when he wrote in 1901: "godliness is in league with riches." Implied was the idea that men with superior character were rewarded with success; poverty was the product of sinfulness, a kind of punishment meted out by an angry God. Russell Conwell, one of the few rivals to Mark Twain as a lecturer in the late nineteenth century, argued in his stock speech, "Acres of Diamonds," that "ninety-eight out of one hundred of the rich men of America are honest. That is why they are rich."

Twain was not fully convinced. The entire gospel of wealth, including the argument that through his philanthropy a rich man performed his obligation to society, seemed to him much like the confidence games he wrote about in the second half of *Huckleberry Finn*. In company with Henry George, whose *Progress and Poverty* appeared in 1879, Twain understood that a self-made man was as improbable as a self-laid egg. The success of individuals was the product of the growth of the whole American economy. Moreover, Twain recognized that while big business was applauding itself, the nation's morality and institutions were becoming so threadbare that they were unable "to protect the body from winter, disease, and death." A partial reckoning would come in the Progressive years, but like Huck Finn, Mark Twain had seen enough. The failure of the Paige typesetter and Twain's consequent backruptcy in 1894 were the last straws in his disenchantment with the cult of success.

Another shadow over Twain's last years was his country's entrance into the contest for international power and prestige called imperialism. Before the 1890s the nation had not been active in this endeavor. Mexico, to be sure, had been pushed out of the path of westward expansion in the 1840s, and in 1867 the United States made one of the best real estate deals in history by purchasing Alaska from Russia. But for the most part the development of the West and the economic colonization of the defeated South kept the imperialist urge in check. By the 1890s, however, a growing nation was pushing at its geographic boundaries. The frontier had vanished, and American appetites, whetted by 250 years of expansion, sought new morsels across the seas. For those requiring philosophic justification there was Josiah Strong's *Our Country* (1885), with its vindication of a "divinely-commissioned" America assuming the role of its "brother's keeper." Strong also employed Social Darwinism, arguing that in the worldwide competition of races it was either eat or be eaten. Naval power advocate Alfred T. Mahan agreed completely.

One of the first opportunities for American expansion was the Hawaiian Islands. Since Twain had visited the area in 1865, a surge of sugar production had made Hawaii a primary target of American business and American empire-building. In 1893, under heavy pressure from President Harrison and Secretary of State Blaine, Queen Liliuokalani capitulated. Republicans hoped for quick annexation of the islands, but Cleveland's return to the White House delayed it for five years. The Democrats, however, displayed their own brand of imperialism in 1895, when Secretary of State Richard Olney revived the Monroe Doctrine of 1823 to assert America's virtual sovereignty in Latin America. The immediate target of Olney's warning was Great Britain, and many restless Americans hoped for a chance to back the secretary's words with bullets. Theodore Roosevelt, then president of the New York police commissioners, confessed: "I rather hope that the fight will come soon. . . . This country needs a war."

Roosevelt got his wish in 1898. Mark Twain was on a round-the-world debt-paying lecture tour when the fever of the new Manifest Destiny infected the nation and produced a war with Spain. The immediate cause was American disapproval of Spain's conduct in a war with its colony, Cuba. Dispassionate analysis indicates that atrocities occurred on both sides, but sensation-hungry American newspapers cast Spain in the villain's role. When the United States battleship *Maine* blew up in the harbor of Havana, Cuba, on February 15, 1898, with the loss of 260 lives, a declaration of war was only a matter of time. It came on April 25, and in four months the most popular war in American history was over. First Commodore George Dewey captured the Philippine Islands and broke Spain's naval power in the Pacific. Then a badly disorganized American force, which included Theodore Roosevelt and his Rough Rider colleagues, managed to defeat an even more mismanaged Spanish army defending Cuba. But the imperialists saw only stars and stripes. As Secretary of State John Hay said, it was "a splendid little war." Roosevelt simply called it "bully." Only 379

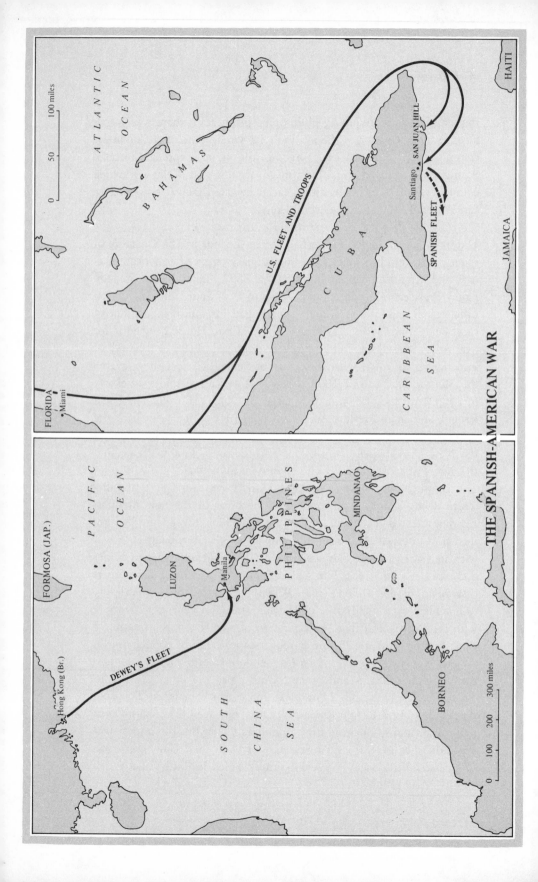

THE SPANISH-AMERICAN WAR

Americans died in combat, although disease, chiefly malaria, claimed more than 5000. Still is seemed a small price for assuaging the anxieties that accompanied America's entrance into national middle age.

By the terms of the Teller Amendment to the declaration of war with Spain, the United States forswore annexation of Cuba. But Guam, Puerto Rico, and the Philippines, all formerly Spanish, were a different matter. American hunger for empire led President William McKinley to support outright acquisition of these islands. The Philippines became the center of attention. Business interests, desirous of Pacific trade, and religious leaders trumpeting an "imperialism of righteousness" backed the administration. With money and God both on his side, McKinley rationalized that "duty determines destiny" and moved to annex the archipelago. The task proved considerably more difficult than defeating the Spanish. Philippine native leaders like Emilio Aguinaldo, whom the United States had supported in a mutual effort against Spain, resisted strenuously. They expected the United States to grant freedom and independence to the islands at the conclusion of the war. When it appeared that McKinley intended to substitute one foreign regime for another, the natives grew restless. For most of 1899 fighting raged on the islands. Thereafter Aguinaldo took his remaining forces to the hills in guerrilla resistance. Mop-up operations by American forces continued until 1902, when the Philippines were declared pacified.

Back in the United States, meanwhile, a groundswell of opposition rose against imperialism and particularly against McKinley's policy in the Philippines. A substantial portion of the American people wanted no part of a colonial empire on both idealistic and practical grounds. Even before the peace treaty with Spain was signed in December 1898, an Anti-Imperialism League was organized and attracted such diverse figures of national importance as Grover Cleveland, Andrew Carnegie, labor leader Samuel Gompers, Charles Eliot, the president of Harvard, and Mark Twain. Twain disliked imperialism from the beginning because he saw through the hypocrisy of its pious pretensions to the underlying considerations of power, profit, and the national ego. His views were contained in a letter written late in 1899. According to Twain, the departing nineteenth century might be seen as bequeathing to the approaching twentieth a Christian civilization "bedraggled, besmirched, and dishonored from pirate raids" throughout the world. "Her soul," Twain bitterly continued, is "full of meanness, her pockets full of boodle, and her mouth full of pious hypocrisies. Give her soap and towel, but hide the looking-glass."

It was soon apparent that Mark Twain was just sharpening his satirical guns against imperialism. His essay "To the Person Sitting in Darkness" in the *North American Review* for February 1901 was a devastating critique of the American foreign missions that carried civilization and the Gospel to allegedly backward peoples. The missions did their job, Twain explained, at the point of a bayonet. Those who really needed enlightenment, he continued, were the missionaries themselves. In another essay Twain reviewed the whole history of American involvement in the Philippines. Of the $20 million given Spain for the islands by the treaty ending the war, he observed, "we bought some islands from a party which did not own them." Of Aguinaldo he wrote, "we went back on an honored guest of the Stars and Stripes when we had no further use for him and chased him to the mountains." Then the nation which began the era of colonial revolutions systematically crushed the natives by destroying their villages, burning their fields, and exiling their leaders. The remaining 10 million were subjugated, according to Twain, by "Benevolent Assimilation, which is the pious new name of the musket."

Twain's essays on imperialism elicited a storm of public opinion. While some of his countrymen praised him for his frankness, others called him a traitor and worse. For these people, questioning imperialism was, in effect, doubting the whole value of America and its progress over the past century. Yet this was precisely Mark Twain's purpose.

By 1900 few could deny that America was greatly changed from what it was at the time of Mark Twain's birth sixty-five years before. Of course, human history is not static; change is the only constant. But the latter part of the nineteenth century brought a rate and scope of change unprecedented in the American experience. Any one of a number of indexes is revealing. Population, for instance, zoomed from about 15 million in 1835 to 75 million at the end of the century. Steel, which was not even produced in the United States until Twain was twenty, was being manufactured at the rate of 26 million tons annually by 1900. Coal surged from a production of 14 million tons when Twain was twenty-five to 257 million when he was sixty-five. Railroad mileage jumped from 30,000 miles on the eve of the Civil War to 193,000 at the century's end.

It is possible to find a spectrum of responses to the changes these figures suggest. At one extreme is the school of thought that applauded the differences. Growth, according to this perspective, was good, and America's progress unquestioned. Those problems that were acknowledged at all were attributed to un-American influences like the immigrants. As for America itself, the cheerleading philosophy could find nothing wrong with God's chosen people. The second broad category of response to a changing America was a free admission that progress had brought some serious problems. Unlike the cheerleaders, holders of this viewpoint did not hesitate to place responsibility on Americans themselves instead of on a scapegoat like the immigrant. But they did not despair in their criticism. Optimistically, they sought means whereby the nation could enjoy the blessings of growth without the blight. With the proper controls and reforms, the high promises of American life could be realized. This school of opinion was constructively critical and forward-looking in its reform endeavors.

On the pessimistic side of the turn-of-the-century spectrum of opinion were destructive critics or backward-looking reformers. Their point of view was that life had been better in the good old days before urbanization and industrialization. Growth brought only problems. Indeed, true progress consisted of restoring the values and institutions of the past. America could still reform, but only if it renounced the technological future toward which it appeared to be heading. Finally, directly opposite the affirming cheerleaders were those who rejected America completely. Reform, either of the forward- or backward-looking variety, was hopeless. The nation was moribund. Total collapse was only a matter of time and would be a blessing.

In his lifetime Mark Twain ranged the full gamut of these attitudes. As a young writer in Europe he cheered the American flag with the zeal of the most ardent imperialist. He devoted a large share of time and energy to the pursuit of material success. He was captivated by machines and their potential for progress. But Twain could also idealize the simple, pastoral America of his own boyhood and viciously attack the Gilded Age. By 1894, when he published *Pudd'nhead Wilson*, Twain was prepared to take the final step into despair.

"Whoever has lived long enough to find out what life is," Twain wrote in a *Pudd'nhead Wilson* chapter heading, "knows what a deep debt of gratitude we owe to Adam, the first great benefactor of our race. He brought death into the world." Most of the book is in a similar vein. In commenting on the anniversary of Columbus's discovery of America, Twain declared: "it was wonderful to find America but it would have been more wonderful to miss it." Only twenty-seven years before, Twain had stood with the crowd at the rail of the *Quaker City* and cheered wildly as a passing ship displayed the American flag. The mood of the two passages could not be more disparate nor the destruction of the American dream more complete. But Twain's misanthropy transcended the United States. In his later years he toyed with the prospect of shutting off the earth's oxygen supply for two minutes and enjoyed contemplating the course of history if Noah had missed the Ark.

It remained for *The Mysterious Stranger* (written about 1905 and published posthumously in 1916) to summarize the matured and final version of Twain's desperation. The setting is once again a town beside a river, but now the locale is Austria, the time the sixteenth century. In the course of the novel a mysterious stranger conducts a young boy (the Austrian equivalent of Tom Sawyer or Huck Finn) on a tour of the chamber of horrors that was and is human civilization. The revelations of cruelty, sadism, and suffering leave the boy with nothing but shame and contempt for his race. He realizes that the ideals of his childhood are naive dreams and that the only hope for men is early death or insanity. Civilization, Christianity, and material progress have left depravity and desolation in their wake. Progress is a myth. The future is revealed to be only a continuation of the errors of the past, but now multiplied by technology. The torture rack and wheel are replaced by bombs that kill thousands. Man's life is as meaningless, Twain decided, as that of the miniature race the mysterious stranger eliminated with the comment that "man is a museum of diseases, a home of impurities; he comes to-day and is gone to-morrow; he begins as dirt and departs as stench." Finally, at the end of *The Mysterious Stranger* the boy is told: "There is no God, no universe, no human race, no earthly life, no heaven, no hell. It is all a dream—a grotesque dream. Nothing exists but you. And you are but a *thought*—a vagrant thought, a useless thought, a homeless thought, wandering forlorn among the empty eternities!"

The dead, Twain concluded, were lucky. In 1910 he joined their ranks. He would no doubt have been astonished at the eulogies written in his honor, essays in which he was portrayed as America's happy humorist and an important source of national pride. The popular image of him is still that of a Tom Sawyer or a cracker-barrel story-teller. Yet perhaps Twain would not have been surprised at all at this distortion of the truth; for him it would have been just one more instance of the gullibility of what he called "the damned human race."

SELECTED READINGS

The Person

BENSON, IVAN: *Mark Twain's Western Years* (1966). The best history of Twain between 1861 and 1866.

*BROOKS, VAN WYCK: *The Ordeal of Mark Twain* (1920). The dark, pessimistic side of Twain's later life.

*DE VOTO, BERNARD: *Mark Twain's America* (1932). A rebuttal of the Brooks interpretation (see above).

LYNN, KENNETH S.: *Mark Twain and Southwestern Humor* (1959). Valuable for its insights into the relationship between Twain's life and his writings.

PAINE, ALBERT BIGELOW: *Mark Twain: A Biography* (4 vols., 1912). A detailed but laudatory account.

*SMITH, HENRY NASH: *Mark Twain: The Development of a Writer* (1962). A study of Twain's literary craftsmanship.

TWAIN, MARK: *Mark Twain's Autobiography* (2 vols., 1924). Part of *The Complete Works of Mark Twain*, the autobiography is neither complete nor entirely accurate.

The Period

*CALLOW, ALEXANDER B., JR.: *The Tweed Ring* (1966). An examination of the classic political machine of the Gilded Age in its New York City setting.

*CASH, W. J.: *The Mind of the South* (1941). Important for its insights into the Southern character and tradition.

*LAFEBER, WALTER: *The New Empire: An Interpretation of American Expansion, 1860–1898* (1963). The background to the controversy over American imperialism.

MCKELVEY, BLAKE: *The Urbanization of America, 1860–1915* (1963). A discussion of one of the main forces of change in Twain's America.

* Available in paperback.

MORGAN, H. WAYNE: *The Gilded Age: A Reappraisal* (1963). A revisionist assessment that makes the late nineteenth century seem more constructive than it did to Twain. See, also, Morgan (ed.), *The Gilded Age* (1970).

*PAUL, RODMAN W.: *Mining Frontiers of the Far West, 1848–1880* (1963). The authoritative account of bonanza mining.

*PRATT, JULIUS: *Expansionists of 1898* (1964). An interpretation of the Spanish-American War.

SPROAT, JOHN: *The Best Men: Liberal Reformers of the Gilded Age* (1968). Unlike Twain, some Americans tried to reform what they did not like about America after the Civil War.

* Available in paperback.

Index

NOTE: Page numbers in *italic* refer to illustrations.

Abolitionists, 242–245, 247, 252, 263, 277, 282
Adams, Henry, 279, 291
Adams, John, 96, 104, 111–112, 125, 127–128, 131, 133–137, 148, 161
Adams, John Quincy, 147, 239
Adams, Samuel, 90, 92, 109
Africa, 5–6, 10–11, 18, 231, 237, 242
Agrarianism, 204
Aguinaldo, Emilio, 313–314
Alamo, the, 207
Alarcón, Hernando de, 21
Alaska, 152–153, 212
Albany Congress, the, 81–82, 85
Alien and Sedition Acts, 133–134
American Philosophical Society, 77
American Revolution, 93–96, 107–110, 120–121, 123, 126, 148, 159, 161
  major campaigns of, map, 98
Americas, the, 4, 17, 19, 22
Amherst, Lord Jeffrey, 174
Andros, Sir Edmund, 65
Anglicanism, 28, 32, 48, 62, 86, 107, 117
Anthony, Captain Aaron, 228–229
Anti-Imperialism League, 313
Antinomianism, 51
Antislavery societies, 237
Arbella, the, 25, 36–37
Arnold, Benedict, 120
Arthur, Chester A., 307
Articles of Confederation, 122–123, 126–128, 162
Ashley, William H., 194–195
Asia, 2, 4, 11, 15–16, 18, 152–153
Astor, John Jacob, 201
Astrolabe, 5, 9
Atkinson, Edward, 299

Atlantic, the, 10
Auld, Hugh, 234, 238
Austin, Moses, 206
Azores, the, 5

Bacon's Rebellion, 108
Balboa, Vasco Nuñez de, 19
Baltimore, 115, 234–235, 238, 244
Banks, 271–274
Bartram, John, 77
Bear-man pipe, *172*
Beckwourth, Jim, 198–199
Beecher, Henry Ward, 253, 291, 294, 310
Bell, John, 281
Bellamy, Edward, 303
Benton, Thomas Hart, 272
Biddle, Nicholas, 272–273
Bidwell, John, 208
Bill of Rights, 128–129
Bixby, Horace, 279, 281
Blackhawk War, 184
Blackstone, William, 37
Blaine, James G., 305, 307, 311
Blue laws, 55
Body of Liberties, the, 43–44
Boone, Daniel, 157–158, 160
Booth, John Wilkes, 262
Boston, 38, 49, 51, 56, 62–66, 76, 94
Boston Massacre, 90
Boston tea party, 92, 109
Bowie, Jim, 207
Bradford, William, 31, 36–37
Brant, Joseph, 160, 174
Breckinridge, John C., 255
Brewster, William, 30
Bridger, Jim, *188,* 189–224
  America as known by, map, 222
Brock, General Isaac, 180, 182, 192
Brooks, Preston, 253
Brown, John, 253, 255–256

Brown, Joseph, 287
Bruff, J. Goldsborough, sketch by, *197*
Buchanan, James, 218, 254, 281
Bull Run, Battle of, 282–283, 288
Bunker Hill, Battle of, 94
Burr, Aaron, 136, 141–142
Butterfield Overland Mail, 218, 283

Cabot, John, 19
Cabrillo, Juan Rodriguez, 21
Calhoun, John C., 203, 239–240, 247
California, 197–198, 208–210, 216, 218, 220, 247, 288–289
Calvert, Sir George, 47
Calvin, John, 27, 29, 52
Canada, 97, 143, 212, 251, 256
Canary Islands, 12
Capitalism, 5, 297–298
Caravels, *8,* 12
Caribbean, the, 14, 16–17
Carnegie, Andrew, 297–298, 309, 313
Carson, Kit, 204, 210
Cartier, Jacques, 19
Catholic Church, 27–28, 30
Cato, slave rebellion by, 236
Cattle, 220
Charles I, 30, 32, 38
Charles II, 66
Charleston, South Carolina, *249*
Chase, Samuel, 137
Chesapeake Bay, 47
Child, Robert, 47
China, 2, 10
Chivingtom, Colonel J. M., 221
Christianity, 4, 7–8, 16, 72
Civil Service Commission, 307
Civil War, 256, 258–260, 262–263, 277, 279–283, 286–289
  black soldiers in, *248,* 260
  campaigns of, map, *261*
  casualties in, 262, 288–289
Clark, George Rogers, 161
Clark, William, 141, 193
Clay, Henry, 143–144, 146, 179, 203, 239–240, 247
Clemens, Samuel. *See* Twain, Mark
Cleveland, Grover, 307–309, 313
Clinton, General Henry, 120
Collier, John, 185
Collinson, Peter, 78
Colorado, 221
Colter, John, 194
Columbus, Christopher, 1–22
  four voyages of, map, *13*
Common Sense, 95, 111, 113
Comstock, Henry P. T., 284
Comstock Lode, 220, 284

Confederate States of America, 258, 260, 262
Conkling, Roscoe, 290, 305
Connolly, John, 158
Constitution, the, 127–129, 136–137, 144, 242, 245
  Fifteenth Amendment to, 263, 265
  Fourteenth Amendment to, 263, 265
  Thirteenth Amendment to, 262–263
Constitutional Convention of 1787, 97, 128, 145
Continental Congress, 93, 110
  First, 93, 110
  Second, 94–96, 111–112, 116, 121–122
Conwell, Russell, 310
Cornwallis, General Charles, 96, 120
Coronado, Francisco Vásquez de, 21
Cortéz, Hernán, 21
Cotton, 247
Cotton, John, 51
Covey, Edward, 227–228, 237
Cowboys, 220
Crawford, William H., 239
Crittenden, John J., 258
Crockett, Davy, 202–203, 207
Croghan, George, 158, 174
Crusades, the, 2
Cuba, 15, 311, 313
Custer, Colonel George A., 223

Dana, Richard Henry, 208
Darwin, Charles, 289
Davis, Jefferson, 287
Dawes Severalty Act, 185
Declaration of Independence, 112–113, *114,* 116–118, 126, 145
Declaratory Act, 90
Democracy, 119
Democrats, 203, 253, 255, 303, 305, 307, 311
Denmark Vesey Conspiracy, 236
Denver, 220
de Soto, Hernando, 21
Detroit, 161, 180, 182, 192
Dewey, Commodore George, 311
Dickinson, John, 222
District of Columbia, 250
Dodge, General Grenville, 218
Donner, George and Jacob, 209
Douglas, Stephen A., 247, 252–253, 255, 281
Douglass, Frederick, *226,* 227–266
Drake, Francis, 26
Dred Scott decision, 254
Dudley, Thomas, 42–43

Earth, the, size and shape of, 6–7
East India Company, 91

Edwards, Jonathan, 73
Elections
    of 1860, map, *257*
    of 1876, map, *306*
Electricity, 77–79
Elizabeth, Queen, 26, 28
Emancipation Proclamation, 260
Embargo, 142–143
Emerson, Ralph Waldo, 241, 251, 255
Endicott, John, 37
England, 4–5, 11, 19, 26–28, 55, 82–
    88, 90–97, 113, 132–133, 141–
    142, 147, 174–175, 179–180, 192,
    210, 212
Erie Canal, 246
Essays to Do Good, 74–75
Europe and Europeans, 2, 4, 6–7, 11,
    16–17, 125, 289–290. *See also* in-
    dividual names of countries
Exploration, 2, 19, 21, 141

Farming, 220–221. *See also* Agrarianism
Federalists, 133–139, 141–142, 144, 147
Ferdinand and Isabella, 11–12, 16, 18
Fetterman, Captain William J., 221
Fillmore, Millard, 216, 247
Finley, John, 156–157
Fisk, Jim, 291
Fitzpatrick, Thomas, 195, 203
Florida, 192
Florida, Missouri, 273–274
Folger, Peter, 64
Foreign missions, 314
Foreign policy, 132
Fort Bridger, *197,* 204, 206, 208–209,
    212, 214, 216
Fort Harmar, *173*
Fort Wayne, Treaty of, 177
Fort Wayne council, 179–180
Forty-niners, 197
France, 11–12, 19, 81, 85, 96, 125, 132–
    135, 139, 142, 174–175, 191
Franklin, Benjamin, *61,* 62–99, 105,
    111, 125, 174, 242, 296
    autobiography of, 68, *70–71*
    at Paris reception, *89*
    pseudonym of, 61–62, 65, 67
Franklin, James, 63, 65
Franklin, Josiah, 62–63
Franklin stove, *89*
Freemen, 42
Frémont, Lieutenant John C., 204, 210
French and Indian War, 85, 88, 157,
    174–175
French Revolution, 125, 135
Freneau, Philip, 116, 131
Frontiersmen, 54–55, 86, 151, 202, 271

Fugitive Slave Law, 250–252, 277
Fur trade, 194–195, 198–203

Gabriel's Revolt, 236
Gage, General Thomas, 92–94
Gallatin, Albert, 137, 139
Galloway, James, 169
Galloway, Joseph, 93
Galloway, Rebecca; 169–170, 176
Gama, Vasco da, 19
Garfield, James G., 305, 307
Garrison, William Lloyd, 237, 242–
    245, 263
Gems, 2, 7
Genêt, Edmund, 191
Genoa, 2, 4
Geography, 6–7
George, Henry, 310
George III, 91–92, 107–108, 110, 112–
    113
Gettysburg, 260, 288
Godfrey, Thomas, 77
Gold, 2, 7, 8, 21, 197
Gold rush, 220
Gorsuch, Edward, 251–252
Gould, Jay, 291
Grant, Ulysses S., 260, 262, 264, 291,
    303
Great Britain. *See* England
Great Salt Lake, 190, 208–209, 218
Greeley, Horace, 253, 259, 303
Green River, 203
Greenville, Treaty of, 164–166, 169
Groton, 27–29, 30, 32

Hamilton, Alexander, 129–134, 141
Hancock, Winfield S., 305, 307
Hannibal, Missouri, 274, 301
Harmar, Colonel Josiah, 163
Harpers Ferry, 255
Harrison, Benjamin, 308, 311
Harrison, William Henry, 165–168,
    176–179, 182–183, 203
Harte, Bret, 286
Hartford, Connecticut, 294, 302
Harvard College, *41,* 56
Hastings, Lansford W., 208–209
Hawaii, 311
Hawkins, John, 26
Hay, John, 371
Hayes, Rutherford B., 265, 305
Hayne, Robert Y., 240
Henderson, Richard, 157, 159
Henry, Major Andrew, 194
Henry, Patrick, 107–109, 129
Henry VIII, 27
Henry the Navigator, Prince, 6, 11

Hiawatha, 171, 174
Hill, James J., 218
Hingham, Massachusetts, 44–45
Hispaniola, 15–18
Holland, 31
Holy Land, the, 2
Homestead Act of 1862, 221
Hudson's Bay Company, 201–202, 212
Hull, General William, 180
Hutchinson, Anne, 50–54, 64
Hutchinson, Thomas, 84, 93
Hutchinson, William, 50

Iceland, 5–6
Illinois, 161
Imago Mundi, 6, 10
Imperialism, 310, 313–314
Indian culture, 185–186
Indian Reorganization Act, 185
Indian reservations, map, *155*
Indian village, *8*
Indiana, 166, 170, 176, 178
Indians, 8, 15, 17–18, 22, 34, 36, 82,
    86, 132, 143, 151, 192, 194–195,
    198–199, 201, 212, 216–217, 221–
    223
Individualism, 4, 53–54
Interstate Commerce Commission, 308
Intolerable Acts, 93
Irish, the, 7, 10
Iroquois League, 174

Jackson, General Andrew, 184, 199–
    203, 239–240, 272–273
Jackson, Claiborne F., 282
Jacksonianism, 199–203, 296, 298
James I, 30, 33
James II, 84
James River flats, *41*
Jamestown, 34–35
Japan, 2, 7, *9*, 10, 15
Jay, John, 133
Jefferson, Peter, 104–105
Jefferson, Thomas, 95, 97, *103*, 104–
    148
    writings of, 110, 121, 166–167
Jim Crow laws, 265–266
John II, King, 10
Johnson, Andrew, 262–264, 290
Johnson, William, 158, 174
Johnston, Colonel Albert Sidney, 217
Junta club, 75, 77

Kansas, 253, 255, 277
Kansas-Nebraska Act, 252, 254
Kearny, Stephen W., 210
Keayne, Robert, 52–54
Keimer, Samuel, 67

Kentucky, 157–160, 164, 167, 179,
    192, 270
Key, Francis Scott, 115, 144

Land Act of 1804, 141
Land Ordinance of 1785, 124, 163
Land speculators, 204, 221
Lawrence, the Reverend William, 310
Leavenworth, Colonel Henry, 195
Lee, Francis L., 109
Lee, Jason and Daniel, 212
Lee, Richard Henry, 96, 109, 111, 129
Lee, Robert E., 255, 258, 260, 262, 286
Lewis, Meriwether, 141, 193
Liberator, The, 243
Lincoln, Abraham, *248*, 254–255, 258–
    260, 262, 281–282, 289
Lisa, Manuel, 193–194, 201
Lloyd, Colonel Edward, 229
Lloyd, Henry Demarest, 298
Locke, John, 84, 108, 112–113
London Company, 35
Louisiana Purchase, 139, 147, 192
L'Ouverture, Toussaint, 236
Lovejoy, Elijah, 243
Lundy, Benjamin, 242–243
Luther, Martin, 27
Lyon, Matthew, 134

McKinley, William, 313
Madeira, 6
Madison, James, 119, 128–129, 137,
    139, 143–144
Maine, 36–37, 147
Maine, the, *293*, 311
Man, 152–153
    pride in, 4
Manifest Destiny, 206–207, 209, 217
Manufacture, 296–297, 314
Marietta, *173*
Marion Rangers, 282–283
Marshall, John, 137–138, 141
Maryland, 47, 162, 229–230, 259
Mason, George, 109, 112
Massachusetts, 42, 45, 50–52, 54–56,
    92–94, 109, 126, 129, 171, 209–
    210, 241
Massachusetts Antislavery Society, 244
Massachusetts Bay, 38–39, 42–43, 45,
    47–49, 51, 64–65, 92
    survey of, *41*
Massachusetts Bay Company, 32–34, 39,
    42
Mather, Cotton, 74–75
Maverick, Samuel, 37
Mayflower, the, 31, 36
Meade, George C., 260
Mercantilism, 87, 113

Mexican War, 209–210
  map of, *211*
Mexico, 206–210
Miller, Albert J., *196*
Mississippi, the, 141, 184, 192–193,
  246–247, 258, 262, 270, 273–274,
  279, *280,* 281, 301
Missouri, 145, 147, 162, 218, 252–253,
  273, 282
Missouri Compromise, 237, 247, 250–
  252, 254, 275, 277, 280
  map of, *146*
Molasses Act, 83
Monetary policy, 308
Money, 74–75, 298, 310. *See also* Rich,
  the
Monroe, James, 147–148
Monroe Doctrine, 148, 311
Montana, 194
Monticello, 104, *115,* 120–121, 126,
  143–144
Morgan, J. P., 297
Mormons, 213–214, 216–217, 284
Murray, Anna, 239, 241

National Road, the, 191–192, *196*
Naváez, Pánfilo de, 21
Navigation, science of, 5, 16
Navigation Acts, 83, 85–86
Nevada, 220, 284–285
New Bedford, 241, 243–244
New England, 28, 31–33, 37, 42–43,
  47–48, 53–56, 62, 64, 83, 141–
  142, 209, 296–297
New England Antislavery Society, 243
New England Company, 32
New England Courant, 61–62, 65
New Mexico, 209–210
New Orleans, 192, 246–247
New World, the, 2, 5, 14, 17, 19, 21,
  25, 27, 32–36, 39, 45, 49, 53, 56,
  76, 137, 147, 152–154
  European exploration of in sixteenth
  century, map, *20*
New York City, 66, 130, 239–241, 246,
  250, 276–277
New York State, 123, 141, 246
Newfoundland, 19
Newton, Sir Isaac, 76–77
Nina, the, 12, 16
North, the, 238–239, 242–243, 246–
  247, 252–253, 255, 258, 260, 262–
  263, 286–287
North America, 7, 22, 26–27, 83, 85,
  174
  extension of settlements in, map, *80*
  Indians of, 152–156
  after Louisiana Purchase, map, *140*

North American Colonies in 1650, map,
  46
North Star, The, 245–246
Northwest Ordinance, 124, 191
Northwest Territory, 162

Ohio, 156, 158–165, 168–169, 179, 191
Ohio River, travel on, *280*
Oklahoma, 184–185
Old Northwest, 161, 163, 166
Olney, Richard, 311
Oregon, 210, 212–213
Oregon Trail, the, 195, 204, 212, 217
O'Sullivan, John L., 206

Pacific Northwest, 195, 201, 210, 212
Paige, James W., 300, 303
Paine, Thomas, 95, 111, 113
Palos, 12
Panic of 1819, 271
Parker, the Reverend Samuel, 212
Parker, William, 251–252
Parson's Cause, the, 107
Pattie, James Ohio, 208
Penn, William, 66–67
Pennsylvania, 66–67, 84–86, 131, 246–
  247, 297
  University of, 75
Pennsylvania Assembly, 81–82
Pequot War, 171
Perry, Oliver Hazard, 144, 183
Philadelphia, 66–68, 74–75, 77, 79, 93,
  127–128, 239, 247, 276
Philip, King, 171
Philippines, the, 311, 313–314
Phillips, Wendell, 243, 245
Pierce, Franklin, 253, 280
Pike, Zebulon, 141
Pilgrims, the, 31, 36, 49
Pinta, the, 2, 12, 16
Plantations, 228–230
Plymouth, 37, 49
Politics, 64, 84, 303, 305, 307–309
Polk, James K., 203, 209, 247
Polo, Marco, 2
Ponce de León, Juan, 21
Poor Richard's Almanac, 67, 74–75
Portugal and the Portuguese, 4–5, 7, 11,
  19
Proctor, Colonel Henry, 182–184
Protestant ethic, the, 53, 74, 76
Protestantism, 54, 56
Protestants, 27–28, 31
Providence, Rhode Island, 50
Puritanism, 29–30, 51, 56, 64–65, 69,
  74
Puritans, 25–26, 28–30, 32–39, 43, 47–
  56, 76

Quakers, 66–67, 242
Quartering Act of 1765, 90
Quebec Act, 92

Radical Abolition party, 256
Railroads, *215,* 218, 247, 274, 315
    major, about 1885, map, *219*
Randolph, Edward, 64
Raleigh, Sir Walter, 19, 34
Reconstruction, *249,* 264–265, 305
    map of, *304*
Reformation, the, 26–28, 30–31, 34, 43,
    49
Reformers, 307
Religion, 47–53, 72–73, 86, 117–119,
    167–168
Republicans, 132–139, 141, 254, 282,
    303, 305, 307–308
    Radical, 263
Revere, Paul, 94
Reynolds, Catherine, 173
Rhode Island, 50, 52
Rich, the, 308–310. *See also* Money
Robinson, John, 31, 108–109
Rochester, New York, 243–246
Rockefeller, John D., 298, 310
Roosevelt, Theodore, 311
Royal Society, the, 76–79
Ruggles, David, 241, 250

St. Louis, 193–195, 203
Salem, 37–38, 49
Salt Lake City, *215,* 220, 284
San Francisco, 285–286
San Salvador, 14–15
Santa Anna, 207
Santa Fe Trail, 207, 218
Santa Maria, the, 1, 12, 16
Saratoga, Battle of, 96
Science, 75–79
Scott, General Winfield, 210
Seneca Falls Convention, 246
Separatism, 54
Separatists, 31
Seven Years' War. *See* French and In-
    dian War
Shawnees, 151–186
Shay's Rebellion, 126–127
Sherman, Major General William T.,
    262
Sherman Antitrust Act, 308
Shiloh, Battle of, 288
Silver, 220
Slavery, 145, 230–231, *232–233,* 234,
    242–244, 247, 250, 253–255, 258–
    259, 277

Slaves, 18, 106, 147, 228–231, *232–
    233,* 234, 240–244, 254, 258–260,
    275–277
    former, voting by, *249*
    fugitive, 40, 250–252, 255, 276–277
Slave trade, 5, 145, 230–231, 250
Slidell, John, 209
Smith, Gerritt, 243, 255
Smith, Jedediah, 195, 198–199, 201,
    208
Smith, John, 35
Smith, Joseph, 213–214
Social Darwinism, 309, 311
South, the, 229, 235–240, 246–247,
    252, 255, 258, 260, 262–265, 277,
    286–288, 305
South America, 18, 147
South Carolina, 240, 256
Southwest, the, 198–199, 207–210
Spain and the Spaniards, 11–12, 19,
    21–22, 26, 31, 97, 133, 147, 191–
    192, 207, 311
Spanish-American War, 311, 313
    map of, *312*
Spectator, The, 63
Speculation, 300. *See also* Land specu-
    lators
Spice Islands, 2, *9*
Spotswood, Alexander, 104
Stamp Act, 86–88, 107–109
Stamp Act rebellion, *71*
Star Spangled Banner, 115
Steamboating, 279, *280,* 281, 301
Stevens, Thaddeus, 263
Stewart, William M., 290
Stowe, Harriet Beecher, 252, 265, 277,
    291
Stuart, John, 174
Sugar Act, 86
Sumner, Charles, 253, 263

Tahoe, Lake, 284–285
Taney, Roger, 254
Tappan family, 243
Tariff, 239–240, 308–309
Tea Act of 1773, 91
Tecumseh, *150,* 151–171, *173,* 174–
    186, 192
    and War of 1812, map, *181*
Telegraph, first transcontinental, 218
Tennessee, 192, 259, 270–272
Terry, General Alfred H., 223
Texas, 206–209, 220, 262
Thoreau, Henry David, 209
Tilden, Samuel J., 303, 305
Tilton, Mrs. Elizabeth, 204
Tippecanoe, Battle of, 178–179

Tobacco, 83, 247
Tomahawk pipe, *172*
Toscanelli, Paul 7, 9
Townships, *124*
Trade routes with the East, map, *3*
Transcendentalists, 209, 241
Transportation, 217–218, *292. See also*
    Railroads
    of mid-nineteenth century West, map,
    205
Trappers, 194–195, 198–199, 202–204
Turks, 2, 4
Turner, Nat, 235–237
Twain, Mark, 220, *268,* 269–317
    writings of, 274, 279, 283, 285–287,
    294–296, 300–303, 310, 314, 316
Tyler, John, 190, 203
Tyndal, Margaret, 32, 34, 38, 56

Uncle Tom's Cabin, 252, 277, 291
Union Pacific and Central Pacific, join-
    ing of, *215*
United States, 97, 178, 185, 204, 212,
    218, 296–297, 314–315
    expansion of, 125, 191, 206–207, 311
United States Army, 221
United States Congress, 137–139, 191,
    207, 239–240, 291
United States House of Representatives,
    137
United States Military Academy, 139
United States State Department, 130,
    132
United States Supreme Court, 137–138,
    254, 265, 308
Utah, 190, 215–217

Vaca, Cabeza de, 21
Van Buren, Martin, 203
Vanderbilt, Cornelius, 298–299
Verrazano, Giovanni, 19
Vespucci, Americus, 18
Vikings, the, 7, 14, 16
Virginia, 35, 47, 56, 83, 103–112, 116–
    123, 129, 144, 190–191
    University of, 120, 144, 236, 238
Virginia City, Nevada, 284–287, *293*

Virginia Company, 31, 33–34, 40–41,
    45
    broadside for, *40*

Waldseemüller, Martin, 18–19
Walker, Joseph Reddeford, 208
Walker, Thomas, 156
Wampum, *172*
War of 1812, 143–144, 179–180, 182–
    184, 191–192, 201
    Tecumseh and, map, *181*
Ward, Artemus, 286
Ward, Nathaniel, 43
Warner, Charles Dudley, 294
Washington, 290
    burning of, *115*
Washington, Booker T., 265
Washington, George, 85, 94, 96–97,
    104–105, 109, 120, 122, 127, 129–
    133, 135
Wayne, General Anthony, 164, 168
Webster, Daniel, 203, 240, 247
Weld, Theodore Dwight, 243
West, the, 86, 141, 190–191, 199–200,
    202, 204, 210, 218, 220–221, 246–
    247
    trails and transportation to, 1850,
    map, *205*
West Indies, 14, 83
Wheelwright, John, 51
Whig party, 203, 253
Whitefield, George, 73
Whitman, Marcus, 199, 212
Whitman, Walt, 279
Williams, Roger, 48–50, 171
Wilmot, David, 247
Winthrop, John, *24,* 25–57, 62–64, 69,
    72, 76, 99
Women's rights movement, 246
Woodhull, Victoria, 294
Wool, 2, 4, 27
Wyeth, Nathaniel J., 210
Wyoming, 195, 223
Wythe, George, 106

Yancey, William L., 255
Yellowstone, the, 194, 198
Yellowstone National Park, 223
Young, Brigham, 214, 216–217

78 79 80 9 8 7 6 5 4 3 2 1